THE ISLAMIC STATE IN KHORASAN

ANTONIO GIUSTOZZI

The Islamic State in Khorasan

*Afghanistan, Pakistan and the
New Central Asian Jihad*

(SECOND EDITION)

HURST & COMPANY, LONDON

First published in the United Kingdom in 2018 by
C. Hurst & Co. (Publishers) Ltd.
This second edition first published in 2022 by
C. Hurst & Co. (Publishers) Ltd.,
New Wing, Somerset House, Strand, London, WC2R 1LA
© Antonio Giustozzi, 2022
All rights reserved.

Distributed in the United States, Canada and Latin America by
Oxford University Press, 198 Madison Avenue, New York, NY 10016,
United States of America.

A Cataloguing-in-Publication data record for this book
is available from the British Library.

ISBN: 9781787386266

This book is printed using paper from registered sustainable
and managed sources.

www.hurstpublishers.com

Printed in Great Britain by Bell and Bain Ltd, Glasgow

CONTENTS

GLOSSARY

Amir	Arabic for 'commander'.
Ba'athist	former member of the Ba'ath party, which ruled Iraq under Saddam Hussein until 2003.
Huis	Chinese Muslims of Han ethnicity.
Khorasan	historical region encompassing Afghanistan, parts of Pakistan, Iran, parts of Central Asia and parts of India.
Pashtunwali	the tribal code of the Pashtuns.
Salafism	Islamic reform movement which aimed to return to the traditions of the origins of Islam.
Shari'a	Islamic Law.
Ushr	Islamic land levy (tax) on agricultural produce.
Wilayah/Wilayat	Arabic for 'province'. The word is also used in Persian (wilayat).
Zakat	Islamic tax on savings.

LIST OF ACRONYMS

AQ	Al-Qaida.
ETIM	East Turkistan Islamic Movement.
IJRPT	Islamic Jihad Renaissance Party of Tajikistan.
IMT	Islamic Movement of Turkmenistan.
IMU	Islamic Movement of Uzbekistan (see List of Groups below).
ISIL	Islamic State in Iraq and the Levant (see List of Groups below).
IS	Islamic State (see List of Groups below).
ISI	Inter-Services Directorate, one of the intelligence services of the Pakistani state.
ISIS	alternative spelling of ISIL, where 'Levant' is substituted with 'Syria'. ISIL is more correct as 'Sham', in the original Arabic, means more than Syria (Levant).
IS-Central	acronym used in this book to identify the central leadership and command structure of IS, based in Iraq and Syria.
IS-I	Islamic state in Iraq (*ad-Dawlah al-ʿIrāq al-Islāmiyah*), denomination used by the organization which developed into the IS between 2006 and 2013.
IS-K	Islamic State in Khorasan (*ad-Dawlah al-Islāmiyah fi Khorasan*), the branch of IS in Khorasan, inclusive of Wilayat Khorasan, of TKK's political structure and of the groups merging into IS.
JuD/LeT	Jamaat-ud-Dawa/Lashkar-e Taiba.
NDS	National Directorate of Security (Afghanistan).
RS	Resolute Support.
TIP	Turkestan Islamic Party.
TKK	Tehrik-e Khilafat Khorasan.

LIST OF ACRONYMS

TKP	Tehrik-e Khilafat Pakistan.
TTP	Tehrik-e Taliban Pakistan.
Wilayat	province (Arabic).

LIST OF GROUPS AND INDIVIDUALS

Al-Nusra: shorthand for *Jabha Al-Nusra* (The Victory Front), an AQ-affiliated insurgent group in the Syrian civil war (2011–). Renamed *Fatah as-Sham* in 2016 and merged into *Tahrir as-Sham* in 2017.

Al-Qaida (AQ): 'The Base', the group founded by Osama Bin Laden to launch his global jihad.

Ansar ul Khilafat Wal Jihad: 'Partisans of the Caliphate and of Jihad', a small jihadist group in Pakistan, which joined the TKP (see below).

Atiqullah Mahaz: a Taliban front linked to the Peshawar Shura and operating mainly in eastern Afghanistan.

Azizullah Haqqani Group: formed by sympathizers of IS in Waziristan, then became one of the component groups of IS-K. Evolved into Defenders of Haqqania (*Modafe'yin Haqqania*).

Bukhari Osmani group: a faction of Central Asian members of IS-K.

Dadullah Mahaz: a Taliban front linked to the Quetta Shura and operating mainly in southern Afghanistan.

Dost Mohammad Mahaz: a Taliban front linked to the Peshawar Shura and operating mainly in eastern Afghanistan.

Fatah as-Sham: 'Conquest of the Levant', see Al-Nusra.

Gansu Hui Group: created within IS to gather Chinese Muslims in a single group. Mostly present in Afghanistan and Syria/Iraq, with perhaps some presence in China as well.

Haji Atiqullah's Salafi Group: an Afghan Salafi group operating in Kunar and not militarily active, which ended up supporting IS-K.

Haqqani network: one of the main Taliban networks, de facto coinciding with the Miran Shah Shura. Led by Serajuddin Haqqani.

Harakat-e Ansar-e Iran: 'Movement of the Partisans of Iran', a Baluchi jihadist insurgent organization in Iran.

Harakat Islami Sistan: 'Islamic Movement of Sistan', a Baluchi jihadist insurgent organization in Iran.

Harakat Khilafat Baluch: 'Baluchi Movement for the Caliphate', a Baluchi jihadist insurgent organization in Iran and Pakistan, with a distinct branch for each country.

Hassan Khan Baluch group: an armed group of smugglers operating across the Iranian–Pakistani border.

Hizb-i Islami: 'Islamic Party', one of the main branches of the Muslim Brotherhood in Afghanistan. Led by Gulbuddin Hekmatyar.

Hizb-ut Tahrir: 'Liberation Party', radical Islamic group advocating the re-establishment of the Caliphate, usually non-violent.

Islamic Movement of Tajikistan: *Harakati Islamii Tajikistan*, a splinter of Jamaat Ansarullah.

Islamic Movement of Gulmorad Halimov: *Harakati Islamii Gulmorad Halimov*, the original IS group in Tajikistan.

Islamic Movement of Turkmenistan (IMT): *Turkmenistan Islamyi Hereket*, jihadist group linked to the IMU and gathering Turkmen militants.

Islamic Movement of Uzbekistan (IMU): *Ozbekiston Islamyi Harakati*, jihadist group established in 1998, gathering mostly Uzbek militants, and linked originally to AQ and the Taliban.

Islamic Organization of Great Afghanistan: a small pro-IS group which briefly appeared in 2014 before disappearing again.

Islamic Jihad Renaissance Party of Tajikistan (IJPRT): *Jihod Hizbi Nahzati Islamii*, a splinter of the once legally registered Islamic Renaissance Party of Tajikistan, dedicated to launch armed resistance inside Tajikistan.

Islamic State (IS): *Al-Dawlah al-Islamiya*, the denomination adopted by ISIL in June 2014.

Islamic State in Iraq and the Levant (ISIL): *Al-Dawlah al-Islamiya fi Iraq wa as-Sham*, how the Islamic State called itself in April 2013–June 2014.

Jamaat Ansarullah: 'Society of Allah's Soldiers', a Tajik jihadist organization linked to IS.

Jamaat al Bukhari: The Bukhara Society, a 2013 split of the IMU, which remained loyal to AQ.

Jamaat-ud-Dawa/Lashkar-e Taiba (JuD/LeT): Pakistani militant organization once mostly militarily active in Kashmir and nowadays active militarily mostly in Afghanistan. Widely alleged to be linked to the Pakistani security establishment.

Jami'at Islah: 'Reform Society', one of the main branches of the Muslim Brotherhood in Afghanistan, influenced by Salafism. It is registered as a civil society organization and not as a party, as it rejects participation in official politics.

Jami'at Islami: 'Islamic Society', one of the main branches of the Muslim Brotherhood in Afghanistan, currently participating in the National Unity Government.

Jaysh ul-Islam: 'Army of Islam', a small Pakistani jihadist organization which joined IS-K and became one of its component groups.

Jaysh ul-Adl: 'Army of Justice', a Baluchi jihadist insurgent organization in Iran.

Jundullah: 'Army of Allah', a Baluchi jihadist insurgent organization in Iran and Pakistan. Emerged from the 2016 merger of two separate but identically named organizations, based respectively in Pakistan and Iran.

Khilafat Afghan: 'Afghan Caliphate', group formed in 2014 by sympathizers of IS in Afghanistan and later incorporated in IS-K as one of the component groups.

Lashkar-e Islam: 'Army of Islam', a Pakistani jihadist group which merged with TTP in 2015, but maintained a separate identity.

Lashkar-e Jhangvi: 'Army of Jhangvi', a Pakistani jihadist group with a strong sectarian (anti-Shi'a) agenda.

Mashhad Office: originally a Taliban liaison office in Iran, became autonomous with support from the Iranian Corps of the Revolutionary Guards in 2014. It gradually became one of the new centres of Taliban power.

Mawlavi Nasrat Salafi Group: an Afghan Salafi group operating in Kunar and not militarily active, which ended up supporting IS-K.

Miran Shah Shura: one of the main centres of Taliban power, operating mainly in the south-east of Afghanistan from Pakistani Waziristan. In practice almost synonymous with the Haqqani network.

Modafe'yin Haqqania (Defenders of Haqqania): evolution of the Azizullah Haqqani group, incorporating members linked to the Haqqani Network.

Mullah Bakhthwar Group: splinter of TTP which joined IS-K in 2016, became one of the component groups and disbanded in late 2016 as leader Mullah Bakhtwar was killed.

Muslim Dost Group: splinter of Khilafat Afghan which seceded over leadership issues, was recognized as another component group of IS-K.

National Directorate of Security: *Riasat-e Amniyat-e Milli*, the intelligence agency of the Afghan government.

Omar Ghazi Group: splinter of the IMU, became one of the component groups of IS-K in 2015.

Peshawar Shura: one of the main centres of Taliban power in 2009–16, when it was autonomous from the Quetta Shura, operating mainly in the east, north-east, north and in the Kabul region. It suspended operations in August 2016 and resumed in November 2016 under a different leadership, having lost its autonomy from Quetta.

Qari Afzal Khan's Salafi group: an Afghan Salafi group operating in Kunar and not militarily active, which ended up supporting IS-K.

Quetta Shura: the main centre of Taliban power, also claiming leadership of the Taliban as a whole. It has been divided by internal factionalism from 2010 onwards.

Resolute Support (RS): the NATO mission to Afghanistan, which started in 2015 and provides training and advice to the Afghan security forces. It also features a combat component, deployed in emergency situations.

Sabir Kuchi Mahaz: Taliban front linked to the Peshawar Shura and operating in eastern Afghanistan.

Samarqandi group: a faction of Central Asian members of IS-K.

Saut-ul Ummah: 'Voice of the Ummah [the community of the faithful]', a small splinter group of Hizb-ut Tahrir in Pakistan.

Shamali Khilafat: 'The Caliphate of the North', one of the component groups of IS-K, linked to the Omar Ghazi Group.

Taliban: shorthand for Islamic Emirate of Afghanistan (*Da Afghanistan Islami Emarat*).

Tehrik-e Khilafat Khorasan (TKK): 'Movement for the Caliphate in Khorasan', initially formed by a group of IS sympathizers in eastern Afghanistan, which then turned into a component group of IS-K.

Tehrik-e Khilafat Pakistan (TKP): 'Movement for the Caliphate in Pakistan', initially formed by a group of IS sympathizers in Pakistan and then turning into a component group of IS-K.

Tehrik-e Taliban Pakistan (TTP): 'Movement of the Taliban in Pakistan', a jihadist organization created from a merger of various groups of those sympathetic with the Afghan Taliban, with links to AQ.

Tora Bora Mahaz: autonomous Taliban front, active in eastern Afghanistan.

Turkestan Islamic Party/East Turkestan Islamic Movement: *Partisy Islam Turkistan*, the main Uyghur independentist organization in China.

Wilayat Khorasan: Khorasan province.

List and description of most important individuals cited in the text

Abdul Bahar Mehsud: ex-TTP commander in Waziristan, appointed head of TKP in late 2014.

Abdul Khadim Rauf: founder and head of Khilafat Afghan, also one of the leading figures in IS-K, until his death in February 2015.

Abdul Manan: Taliban shadow governor of Helmand province in 2015–16.

Abdul Qayum Zakir: former head of the Taliban's Central Military Commission and also head of his own front as of 2016–17.

Abdul Rahim Muslim Dost: founder and head of the Muslim Dost Group, and also one of the leading figures in IS-K.

Abu Abdul Hamza Al Turkistani: founder, or one of the founders, of the Gansu Hui Group.

Abu Bakr: former TTP commander and later one of the founders of TKP.

Abu Bakr al-Baghdadi: founder and leader of IS.

Abu Hafs al Baluchi: leader of Hakarak Khilafat Baluch.

Abu Hamza Al Khorasani: nom de guerre of the special envoy sent by Al-Baghdadi to IS-K, arriving January 2017.

Abu Muhammed al-Adnani: spokesperson of IS until his death in August 2016.

Abu Musab al-Zarqawi: founder of *al-Tawhid wal-Jihad*, precursor organization to IS.

Abu Muslim Turkmani: nom de guerre of Fadel Ahmed Abdullah al-Hiyali, al-Baghdadi's deputy for Iraq, until his death in 2015.

Abu Omar al Shishani: military leader of IS forces until his death in July 2016.

Abu Yasir al-Afghani: nom de guerre of Qari Abdul Yasir, second special envoy of al-Baghdadi in Khorasan from November 2015 to December 2016.

Akhtar Mohammad Mansur: Supreme Leader of the Taliban from July 2015 until May 2016, when he was killed in a US drone strike.

Al-Baghdadi: See Abu Bakr al-Baghdadi.

Al-Zarqawi: see Abu Musab al-Zarqawi.

Azizullah Haqqani: a senior member of the Miran Shah Shura, he formed the Azizullah Haqqani Group in 2014 with other sympathizers of IS. He wore the double hat of being a member of both Miran Shah Shura and IS until November 2016, when he was expelled from the Miran Shah Shura.

Bakhtiar: former Taliban district governor in Nangarhar who quit Taliban in 2015 to become a leading IS-K figure in Nangarhar.

Bakhtwar: known as Mullah Bakhtwar, leader of the Mullah Bakhtwar group until his death in autumn 2016.

Faruq Safi: former district military leader of the Peshawar Shura, was sacked in 2013. Became one of the main leaders of TKK. He is said to be a favourite of al-Baghdadi.

Fazlullah: nom de guerre of Fazal Hayat, the current leader of the TTP since November 2013.

Gul Zaman Fateh: ex-TTP commander in Khyber Agency, became one of the prominent Pakistanis in IS-K.

Gulmorad Halimov: former officer of Tajikistan's special police forces, joined IS in 2015 and became head of the military commission.

Hafiz Dawlat Khan: ex-TTP commander in Kurram, and later one of the senior leaders of TKP.

Hafiz Saeed Khan: former TTP commander in Orakzai and one of the first TTP members to link up with ISIL, became governor of Wilayat Khorasan in January 2015. Killed in a US drone strike in August 2016.

Haji Zahir: the main powerbroker in Nangarhar province, Afghanistan, controlling a large militia.

Hassan Swati: former TTP commander, became one of the leading figures in TKP.

Ibn Taymiyyah: see Taqi ad-Din Ahmad ibn Taymiyyah.

Khalid Mansur: former TTP commander who took refuge in Nangarhar before switching to IS-K and played an important role in the subsequent fighting in Nangarhar.

Mangal Bagh: leader of Lashkar-e Islam.

Mansur Dadullah: leader of Dadullah Mahaz in 2007 and again in 2013–15. Was killed by rival Taliban loyal to Mohammad Akhtar Mansur in 2015.

Mawlavi Haibatullah Akhund: Supreme Leader of the Taliban, appointed in May 2016 to replace Akhtar Mohammad Mansur.

Naeem: known as Mullah Naeem, one of the leading figures among the Iran-based Taliban of the Mashhad Office.

Nasratullah Popalzai: former Talib and one of the leading figures in IS-K.

Obeidullah Peshawari: former TTP commander and later head of IS-K in Peshawar.

Omar: known as Mullah Omar, Supreme Leader of the Taliban until his death in about 2013. His death was only made public in 2015.

Omar Ghazi: former IMU commander, who formed the Omar Ghazi Group in 2015.

Omar Khorasani: one of the leading figures in TKK.

Omar Mansur: former TTP commander and later TKP chief for the Lal Masjid area.

Osman Ghazi: leader of the IMU until he was killed by Taliban in November 2015.

Sa'ad Al Emarati: former Taliban commander expelled in 2012 for unauthorized activities, became a leading figure in IS-K and Amir of Logar.

Sadullah Urgeni: former IMU commander and one of the founders of the Omar Ghazi Group.

Saifullah Kakar 'Al Khorasani': IS-K amir of Zakul province in 2016.

Salam: known as Mullah Salam, Taliban shadow governor and previously military leader for Kunduz province. Died in February 2017 following a suicide attack.

Serajuddin Haqqani: leader of the Haqqani network and of the Miran Shah Shura and from 2015 deputy head of the Quetta Shura of the Taliban.

Shehab al-Muhajir (a.k.a. Abu Hesham Al Muhajir): governor of Khorasan from June 2020.

Shireen: known as Mullah Shireen, head of Quetta Shura's intelligence in 2016.

Wali Rahman: first special envoy of Al-Baghdadi to Khorasan from April 2014 to June 2015.

Shahidullah Shahid: ex-spokesperson of TTP, became one of the leading figures in TKP until his death in July 2015.

Sheikh Mohsin: one of the first TTP members to travel to Syria, later became Amir of Kunar.

Taqi ad-Din Ahmad ibn Taymiyyah: medieval theologian and one of the intellectual sources of Salafism.

Wahidullah Wahid: nephew of Abdul Rauf Khadim and his successor at the head of Khilafat Afghan.

INTRODUCTION

The 'fall' of northern Iraq to what was then called Islamic State of Iraq and the Levant (ISIL), the dramatic gains of the group in Syria and the proclamation of the 'Caliphate' were among the main media events of 2014. The impact of the emergence of the Islamic State reached well beyond the Middle East to Muslim communities across the world, but it had a particular significance for Central and South Asia, for reasons that this book will try to make clear.[1]

There is no question that the modern mass media helped the establishment of the Islamic State resonate widely. Had it only been a matter of media exposure, however, the impact would have been of relatively limited consequence, and rapidly forgotten. Small extremist groups of Muslims would have raised the Islamic State (IS) flag, maybe carried out a few symbolic actions, and little more. Instead, what happened after the Caliphate was proclaimed on 29 June 2014, if not earlier, is that the Islamic State (as it called itself from then onwards) moved quickly to capitalize on the wave of interest and sympathy generated by its rapid expansion. Agents were sent around the world, establishing contact with radical Islamist and Islamic fundamentalist groups of various descriptions, but mostly previously linked to Al-Qaida. Financial support was offered. Finally, relying in part on pre-existing personal and group relations dating back to the beginning of the century, a more sophisticated organizational network was set up in different regions to strengthen the connection, as well as in some cases to co-opt existing groups into the Islamic State or directly recruit individuals into it.

In the summer of 2014, rumours of IS spreading to Afghanistan and Pakistan started circulating. The first 'hard evidence' of IS presence or at least influence in the region were leaflets titled *Fatah* (Conquer), and written in Dari and Pashto, distributed among Afghan refugees in Pakistan.[1]

1

Perhaps unsurprisingly, while the media impact was easily visible, including through social media, the underground organizational expansion of the Islamic State was not.

The impossible mission

Even once it started becoming visible through first reports of propaganda activities and recruitment, and later violent attacks, the predominant attitude among media, policymakers and even analysts was denial and/or incredulity. How could it be, it was argued, that the Islamic State, embattled as it was in Syria and Iraq, could afford to send cash and cadres around the world to launch ostensibly implausible jihads in its every corner? And how could an organization so rooted in the Iraqi context establish roots anywhere else?

The formal announcement by IS-Central of the establishment of a branch of the Islamic State in 'Khorasan' only came in January 2015. 'Khorasan' was meant to include Afghanistan, Pakistan, Iran, all of Central Asia and parts of India and Russia.[2]

The term Islamic State in Khorasan (IS-K) refers in IS parlance, and in this volume as well, to the whole of:

- Wilayat Khorasan, the administrative structure which is part of Al-Baghdadi's 'Caliphate';
- Tehrik-e Khilafat Khorasan (TKK), the political structure set up to absorb the different groups declaring their affiliation to IS (see Chapter 4);
- the groups which declared their affiliation to IS.

At least in the official statements, policymakers were slow in acknowledging the increasingly obvious reality that IS had established a beachhead in Khorasan. Still, in early 2016 it was not uncommon to see some of the authorities of the region issue denials that IS had an organized presence. Pakistani interior minister Nisar Ali Khan, for example, said on 16 February 2016 that 'certain banned groups in the country were using IS's name although no such network existed in Pakistan'. This despite the fact that the Pakistani authorities had felt the need to ban IS on 15 July 2015.[3] The Taliban were no less dismissive of the IS-K threat initially, even denying any presence inside Afghanistan, or dismissing those claiming to be linked to IS as impostors. That of course was only possible until the establishment of Wilayat Khorasan in January 2015. After January, the Taliban stopped dismissing the existence of IS in Afghanistan, although sympathizers on social media were scornful of IS's claim to a monopoly.[4]

Initially the Afghan authorities too were deeming 'alleged activities of Daesh to be nothing more than a cunning public relations scheme', as 'for renegade Taliban factions, the idea of joining Daesh is very alluring, as the media coverage catapults them into the headlines and saves them from insignificance'.[5] Soon, however, that changed, and Afghan authorities ended up trying to attract the attention of the Obama administration in order to convince it to keep its forces in Afghanistan. In this case, there was an obvious tendency to inflate the threat, as when it was reported that 600 IS fighters had appeared in Jowzjan, north-western Afghanistan, in February 2015.[6]

Inflated claims from the Afghan authorities were for several more months met, at least officially, by scepticism among the US military, which in public statements dismissed these claims as scaremongering. Rather, the US military argued, what was going on was just 'superficial rebranding' of existing groups. Department of Defense spokesman Col. Steve Warren argued on one occasion, 'We don't necessarily believe that... the conditions in Afghanistan are such that ISIL would be welcome'.[7] It is not clear whether US military intelligence, weakened by the withdrawal of most assets, really struggled to get confirmation of most Afghan reports of IS activities in 'Khorasan', or whether it was only trying to present the situation in a more positive light. For sure, as discussed below, it soon started tracking and targeting IS-K leaders, at least in the Helmand area.

The picture was undoubtedly made foggier by the variety of small groups that offered their services to the IS, hoping to receive funds, without actually managing to attract any interest in Mosul. One such example was the 'Islamic Organization of Great Afghanistan', which appeared in September 2014; the only incident attributed to a member of the group, spokesperson Wahidi, was the kidnapping of a government official in 2014.[8]

The emergence of IS in Afghanistan was a surprise to many, even in the communities affected by it. An elder in Kajaki recounted:

> I think that it should be me who saw for first time Daesh in our district. It was around nine months ago, I was working on my land and saw one group of around six or seven armed men with black mask and black dress and some of them had military uniforms. I thought that this group might be a special force of Taliban. In the afternoon when I came together with other elders for talking, I mentioned about this group to other elders, they also didn't hear about that kind of group. Around one month later we heard that a new group by the name of Daesh started work in Kajaki district and was based in the Loy Naicha area. Then I understood that the group that I saw belonged to Daesh. Next time when I saw a similar group in our bazaar, they had a loudspeaker and announced that

they belonged to Daesh of Al Baghdadi. They also mentioned the name of Mullah Abdul Rauf Khadim as their leader.[9]

As awareness of the reality of IS in Khorasan started emerging, assessments of its impact varied. Quite a few believed that IS-K would split the insurgency, generate internecine conflict and therefore weaken it. It appeared, in a sense, more a strategic asset to the counter-insurgency effort than a threat. The summer of 2015 represented a first peak for IS-K in the media; its successes in Nangarhar seemed to announce a pattern of rapid advances similar to that seen in Iraq and Syria in the previous year. It was no longer possible to deny that IS-K was a reality. Among the affected population, there was instead already a feeling spreading that its rise could not be contained; suddenly IS-K started looking like an invincible force. Then the unusual convergence of Afghan security forces, American airstrikes, local militias and Taliban pushed IS-K back. The myth of invincibility was rapidly broken. Soon the media, policymakers and observers were downplaying IS-K again, presenting it as a failed organization already in decline.

Why the Islamic State in Khorasan is important

As of the end of 2016, IS-K had undoubtedly not met the expectations of a rapid breakthrough that some of its donors and members had entertained. Without venturing into forecasts now (we leave that to the Conclusion below), even if these assessments were correct, it would still be worth studying IS-K as an experiment in exporting an insurgency. In fact, from an analytical perspective, an 'exported revolution' lacking social roots allows the analyst to identify non-endogenous factors that make the export possible (or not possible). This 'experiment' is all the more valuable in 'Khorasan' because a variety of indigenous insurgent movements were operating there before IS-K appeared, and were thus in competition with it for the loyalty of grassroots members. It is therefore possible to draw comparisons between these movements.

There is another reason why IS-K is important: it serves as a benchmark of regional rivalries and conflicts, and of the shape they are increasingly taking—that is, proxy wars. While IS-K might well never achieve its own original aims, it is much more likely to continue playing a role in the region as a proxy of regional powers in these wars.

In a sense, the original hype that surrounded the emergence and expansion of IS gave us the chance to take an in-depth look at an insurgent movement in the early stages of establishing itself. This is a rare opportunity because usually insurgencies do not get detected, or are not taken seriously, until they expand their operations to a level where they represent a serious threat. By that point, carrying out a study of the insurgency's origins, uncontaminated by the political re-processing of the memories of the participants, becomes very difficult.

Outline

This book is primarily a book about the transplant of the IS model to 'Khorasan', judged virtually impossible by several observers,[10] and what it tells us about the dynamics of social and political organizations and insurgent groups. Chapter 1 describes the origins of the Islamic State in 'Khorasan', in particular looking at the linkages established through Al-Qaida's import of volunteers from Afghanistan, Pakistan and Central Asia in Syria and Iraq. The chapter concludes by tracking the early activities of the veterans of Syria and Iraq, returning initially to Pakistan for the most part, until they came together into a single organizational entity. It also discusses the relationship between the Khorasan IS and the original IS. This relationship has been the subject of much debate. Even after the existence of IS-K started being accepted as a fact, the group was often described as a bunch of opportunists who raised the IS flag in order to secure funding or exploit the media waves. Others have described IS-K as no more than a franchise of the original IS, whereas IS-Central would acknowledge it mainly for the purpose of generating press.[11]

Chapter 1 then also assesses the geopolitics behind the rise of IS-K.

Chapter 2 looks at another essential dimension of IS-K, its aims and strategy: where it would like to get and how it thinks it will get there. The complexity of IS-K's aims and strategy tells us much about the organization's nature, its origins and raison d'être.

Chapter 3 describes in detail the tools that IS-Central has been using to turn IS-K into something more than a conglomerate of sympathizers and imitators. As the reader shall see, it has not been an easy task.

Chapter 4 discusses in detail how IS-K rolled out a structure to contain the different founding groups and make them work together.

Chapter 5 tries to unpack the reasons why IS-K was relatively successful in attracting members of well-established insurgent groups, like the Taliban, Tehrik-e Taliban Pakistan (TTP) and the Islamic Movement of Uzbekistan (IMU), among others. It also looks at evidence of social support for the group in some quarters.

Chapter 6 follows IS in Khorasan after January 2015, when IS-K was formally established. As it recruited and spread, IS-K expanded to incorporate more groups, as well as to gradually establish 'alliances' with more and more organizations which stopped short of their merging into IS-K.

Chapter 7 focuses on the funding of IS-K in its multiple aspects: local taxation, contributions of IS from the Middle East and donations by sympathetic individuals and states.

Much of the story of IS-K in 2014–16 is about its relationships with pre-existing, local jihadist organizations, such as the Afghan Taliban, the TTP and others. Chapter 8 is dedicated to this relationship, and tracks its ups and downs group by group. Inevitably, much space is dedicated to the relationship with the Afghan Taliban, for various reasons: in particular, IS-K has so far mainly operated on Afghan ground, interacting chiefly with the Taliban. The Taliban are a rather fragmented organization with multiple centres of power, each of which has its own approach to IS-K, which makes for a complex picture that requires in-depth analysis.

Chapter 9 discusses the difficulties met by IS-Central in turning IS-K into a capable organization capable of meeting its goals and contributing effectively to IS's global campaign, as well the difficulties faced by IS-K in establishing a firm hold. The initial impact of the crumbling of the Caliphate compounded such difficulties, undermining the momentum that IS-K seemed to have gained in 2015–16.

Chapter 10, which is entirely new to this second edition, takes full stock of the collapse of the Caliphate and of the string of defeats suffered by IS-K in 2018–20. It also looks at efforts to set the IS-K on new footing in 2020–1 and provides an initial assessment of its response to the change of regime in Kabul.

The conclusion looks forward to what we may expect from IS-K in the future, based on trends so far.

The IS model: what was being exported?

Most accounts of the rise and expansion of IS focus on the pre-IS roots, starting from Al-Zarqawi himself and the group he formed. The predominant view is that Al-Zarqawi left a strong imprint on what would become the IS, building into it his own inclination towards extreme and indiscriminate violence. The extreme interpretation of the *takfir*, or excommunication of all Muslims who do not follow the right Salafi practices, justified considering almost everybody a legitimate target. This interpretation of *takfir* went far beyond what even Al-Qaida itself had been practising.[12] As Fishman summarizes, 'although bin Laden endorsed the notion of killing an unjust regime's supporters, Zarqawiism claimed that anyone who "refrains from carrying out any obligation of shariah" could be declared an infidel'.[13] Still IS-Central has demonstrated considerable pragmatism at times, for example in its economic and military relations with the Assad regime in Syria.[14]

Polarizing violence was used to force large portions of society to take sides and turn to the organization for self-defence:

> dragging the masses into the battle such that polarization is created between all of the people. Thus, one group of them will go to the side of the people of truth, another group will go to the side of the people of falsehood, and a third group will remain neutral, awaiting the outcome of the battle in order to join the victor.[15]

Al-Zarqawi believed that 'his organization could take advantage of the resulting chaos to cast itself as the defender of the Sunni community'.[16] In Gerges' words:

> Firmly rooted in power politics as well as the politics of identity (Sunni versus Shia) and the construction of rival national identities (Arab versus Persian), this regional war by proxy is a godsend for ISIS and other Al Qaeda local factions in general. At the beginning of hostilities in Syria and Iraq, al-Nusra and ISIS obtained funds, arms, and a religious cover from neighboring Sunni states, precious social and material capital that proved decisive. ISIS's rebirth was facilitated by this geostrategic and geosectarian rivalry between Sunni-dominated states and Shia-led Iran.[17]

Al-Baghdadi developed this further after he took over the leadership:

> In his few pronouncements after his appointment as the newly anointed caliph in the summer of 2014, Baghdadi presented ISIS as the sole guardian of Sunni interests worldwide, not just in Iraq and Syria. He went on to accuse Saudi leaders of forfeiting their responsibility to defend Sunni Islam.[18]

An 'exaggerated show of force' is also a feature of IS's 'deterrent strategy'. It is usually seen as being rooted in Abu Bakr Naji's doctrine *Management of Savagery* and may serve two purposes: deterring local forces from rebelling and enlisting IS as the 'paramount conflict resolver'.[19]

Strategically, IS drew on Ibn Taymiyyah's fatwas to prioritize fighting the 'near enemy', not the 'far enemy' as in the case of AQ. This meant Iran and the 'empious' governments of Muslim countries, or even rival insurgent movements, rather than the Americans.[20] Despite the focus on the 'near enemy', al-Baghdadi decided to challenge the United States and other world powers and drag them into the conflict, in order to strengthen his ideological narrative and consolidate the hegemony over the worldwide jihadist movement. Nonetheless this should just be viewed as a diversion or a tactical shift from the prioritization of the near enemy.[21] Inviting Western or in any case foreign intervention in order for IS to then present itself as the defender of Islam against the invaders is a tactic that IS affiliates outside Iraq and Syria also seem to be using, for example in Libya.[22]

What this literature does not explain is why al-Zarqawi first and even more so his successors later found fertile recruitment ground in so many different locations. Al-Zarqawi's group had a limited constituency, but the Islamic State is an altogether different matter. What did attract recruits to it?

> New converts to ISIS say they were impressed by its military might, resilience, and financial solvency; in contrast, their own groups did not regularly pay their petty salaries, despite obtaining plenty of foreign assistance, and did not build a sustainable organization or potent identity. These personal testimonies point to structural defects, such as factionalism, parochialism, and warlordism, that hindered the ability of Syrian rebels to offer a viable ideational alternative to the Assad regime, as well as to provide for the material needs of its fighters.[23]

Ideology per se would not have sufficed to boost ISIL to success without the display of military prowess.[24] The extreme and inflammatory rhetoric of al-Baghdadi attracted youths 'socialized into a political culture of sacrifice, blood, and martyrdom'.[25] The appeal of IS speaks to the type of youth who is not attracted to the lure of a consumerist society, but is instead seduced by the offer of a life of fight, risk, adventure. IS aims to channel the youth's inclination towards rebellion, their energy and idealism and aspiration to sacrifice.[26] In this IS has already overtaken AQ.

> Even for the angriest young Muslim man, this might be a bit of a hard sell. Al Qaeda's leaders' attempts to depict themselves as moral—even moralistic—figures have limited their appeal. ... ISIS, in contrast, offers a very different message for young men, and sometimes women. The group attracts followers yearning for not only religious righteousness but also adventure, personal power, and a sense of self and community. And, of course, some people just want to kill—and ISIS welcomes them, too. The group's brutal violence attracts attention, demonstrates dominance, and draws people to the action.[27]

In contrast to most other jihadist organizations, IS insists on the professionalism of its 'officer corps'.[28] This is necessary for IS to achieve its trademark ability to concentrate and disperse quickly, and to take tactical decisions immediately:

The forces are organized in a way that grants them maximal flexibility, with a notable absence of rigid, fixed frameworks. This looseness allows them to realize their doctrine, which requires mobility and rapid reinforcement. ... The command and control structures are similarly decentralized to enable the same flexibility and mobility. Commanders thus take local initiatives with no need for a multilayered, complex command hierarchy. In fact, the Islamic State has inverted the entire structure of command and control so that it operates from the bottom up. A hierarchical division of command and control dependent on strategic, systemic, and tactical commanders no longer exists; instead, the decision making process has been flattened to allow junior commanders greater freedom of action so that they can swiftly respond to operational opportunities.[29]

Also functional to the exceptional tactical capabilities of IS is the extreme degree of discipline that it imposes on its members. All this is in stark contrast with other jihadist groups, including to some extent even Al-Qaida, and IS prides itself in its military capabilities.[30] IS represents according to Moubayed a break with the 'no organization' approach which he believes had predominated among the jihadists from the 1990s onwards:[31]

That same year, Mullah Omar of Afghanistan invited him to edit the Taliban's official newsletter, *al-Shari'a*. From the airwaves of Radio Kabul, Abu Musaab called for leaderless jihad: 'global jihad without any tanzim' (order). It was the duty of each and every Muslim to take up arms, regardless of hierarchy and party structure or affiliation. ... This would only work if the mujahideen pursued 'nizam, la tanzim' (order, not organization). It was the religious duty of every individual to strike out on his own, without waiting for orders. In other words: 'Centralization of thought and decentralization of execution.' This would be the only path towards the creation of an Islamic state with a proper caliph. And only then would real Muslims be on the right track towards paradise.[32]

In practice the centralized approach mixed with extreme discipline required very effective management from the top, which certainly the IS and its precursors have been trying to achieve, but not always successfully. Finding adequate local leaders turned out to be particularly challenging.[33] A commonly held opinion is that the turning point was the absorption of hundreds and maybe thousands of former Ba'athist officers and cadres, well trained in operating under a strong discipline. The view that ISIL owes much to the input of former Ba'athists officials and officers is shared by Baczko et al., in particular deriving its idea of the state from them.[34] An alternative view attributes ISIL's military proficiency to having drawn:

lessons from the experience it acquired in the decade-long battle against the US-led coalition in Iraq, and, as a result, it succeeded in forming a solid military command and control in both Syria and Iraq.[35]

Organizationally, therefore, IS turned out to be the opposite of AQ. As Fishman puts it, 'Al-Qaeda's core operated as a small, elite organization with a big-tent ideology. It aimed to work with a wide range of Islamist militants, even those with whom it disagreed on key issues', and was 'built as a special operations task force'. Al-Zarqawi and his successors by contrast objected to working with militants who did not meet that very high standard of what a good Muslim should be, but they 'also imagined a more accessible, populist organization than al-Qaeda had been traditionally'. They 'aimed to build a conventional army'.[36]

An important point made in particular by Fishman is that

> Zarqawiism argues that religious and political legitimacy is primarily a function of participating in war. Although Zarqawi held out the possibility of truces, he also argued that Muslims could not truly fulfill their obligation to God without fighting. As a practical matter, it means that the Islamic State will always remain at war.[37]

Quoting a publication of the Islamic State of Iraq: 'the state of war is a natural state in the life of the Islamic state, whether in the beginning of its development, before, or after'.[38]

Although IS tries to provide welfare to its subjects, its ability to do so is limited, and the overall level of the services it provides falls well below what either the Syrian or the Iraqi government have been providing.[39] Indeed, Fishman points out that Islamic State's first priority has always been imposing Shari'a, not providing services.[40] Contrary to Al-Qaida, IS 'places the use of violence and immediate, coercive implementation of the Shari'a at the centre of its governance policies'.[41]

> For Baghdadi and his lieutenants, persuasion (hegemony) and domination are two sides of the same coin, extracting loyalty and submission through fear and naked power. ... The significance of Adnani's statement lies in prioritizing action (violent jihad) over theory (theology), a distinctive characteristic of ISIS.[42]

The governance model of IS is one of control from the top, with little interaction with the subjects.[43] A related characteristic is the Islamic State's militarist approach to governance: there is only the military solution, with diplomacy and politics both seen as redundant. The literature tends to attribute this to the inflow of former Ba'athist officers when Al-Baghdadi took over the leadership.[44] Noteworthy is the refusal of ISIL (as it was then called) after it consolidated its power to recognize any role for tribal elders and for the tribes as interlocutors. After having initially co-opted the tribes by empowering ISIL loyalists within the tribes, ISIL rapidly centralized all power in its hands after taking Raqqa.[45]

The governance style of IS has been described as completely patrimonial and clientelistic, but IS proved to be apt at playing 'a divide-and-rule policy to ensure that social and tribal rivalry and hostility are more pronounced than any unified enmity to ISIS'. IS proved 'to be a more adaptable and entrenched opponent today than its predecessor was in the mid-2000s, deploying a potent mix of extreme violence and soft power to both coerce and co-opt the tribes'. According to one analyst, IS distributed government offices and departments, and even tasks like tax collection, throughout Iraq among the different tribes. Its relationship with the tribes remained unstable, however, as IS's policy of fighting on multiple fronts against immensely superior forces did not seem to be a good recipe for the Caliphate lasting a long time. The strict implementation of Salafi rules also kept the tribes from fully aligning with IS even when their interests might have temporarily aligned.[46] Overall, IS invested relatively little in the building of state structures. In this regard, the Caliphate has been described as a 'shell state', or 'light totalitarian state'.[47]

A particularly interesting model of the functioning of the IS is proposed by Matthieu Rey:

> The main function of the troops remains to control the flow of goods and people: therefore, the space is covered with checkpoints. These have become a new kind of institution that works more or less autonomously: every checkpoint can enforce its taxes, defend its position, govern the surrounding area; Each checkpoint is connected to others through symbolic means, such as the display of the same flag and the circulation of its militants. ... IS also transfers checkpoints from one place to another, using a modular system that allows the Organization to expand into territories as well as retreat quickly if needed. ... This political structure explains how and why IS can unify such diverse and far-off provinces as Sinai, Nigeria, Iraq and Syria: control points networks that show a common identity through their own flag ...[48]

Another major innovation of IS was of course the idea that time was ripe for establishing first an Islamic State and almost immediately afterwards the Caliphate, again in contrast to Al-Qaida, which postponed that second phase to an undetermined but very distant future. Al-Qaida was not in principle opposed to the idea of the Caliphate. Bin Laden mentioned the need to re-establish the Caliphate no later than 1997, in an interview, and was echoed by Ayman Al-Zawahiri in 2001, in his book *Knights Under the Prophet's Banner*. Initially, both stopped short of advocating jihad against Muslim governments, but, at least since Al-Zawahiri's audio statement in 2005, AQ espoused an ideology of fighting any Muslim government which did not fully implement a Shari'a-based system. However, AQ applied it more carefully, prioritizing some struggles, including that of the Taliban, and postponing the exporting of jihad to neighbouring countries until after a Taliban victory. In fact, it is not fully clear, according to AQ's ideology, what exact role was played by the 'far enemy' (the United States) as opposed to the 'near enemy' (Muslim regimes).[49]

The IS-Central position by contrast has been summarized as 'indiscriminate in its clash with a multitude of enemies, taking on all adversaries at once in a conspicuous and incredibly risk-tolerant manner that is anathema for AQ'.[50] The AQ counterargument was to describe this as a premature step which would expose the Caliphate to massive retaliation by its enemies. AQ believed it needed more time to awaken the Muslim masses and mobilize them to its side. The proclamation of the Islamic State and then of the Caliphate should be read not as an obsession with territorial control per se, but as a strategy for establishing the hegemony of the organization over the wider jihadist movement, and a necessity in order to deploy governance and Shari'a-related projects, in the hope of demonstrating the legitimacy of IS in leading global jihad.[51] In this regard, Fishman usefully notes that IS 'rejected the notion that [it] must defend a specific, static territory in order to be legitimate. Although controlling some territory was necessary, the [Islamic State in Iraq] was conceived as a flexible entity with validity based on collective allegiance to its leader, rather than a fixed set of borders'.[52] In other words, the Caliphate could in fact take the shape of a well-organized mobile insurgent organization.

Another specificity deriving from the proclamation of the restoration of the Caliphate is its implicit dramatic strengthening of the idea of global jihad that Al-Qaida already had. In IS's claims, global jihad was to be brought under the wings of the Caliphate, where it would be managed in a more disciplined fashion.[53] At the same time:

> the IS mode of expansion is pragmatic and flexible, able to adapt to different local contexts, facilitated by its 'thin' ideology, which is not constrained by a goal of attacking the far enemy, as was the case for AQ Core. Being largely tribal and Sunna [*sic*] in identity, with a focus on territorial control and expansion, this gives IS more leeway to operate in external contexts. One could argue that the 'IS model' is less at odds with the agendas of local jihadi groups. In this regard, IS is better attuned to (and is itself a product of) the changing nature of jihadi insurgencies since the mid-2000s. Those were rooted in changing political

economies and the rise of jihadi groups operating in the grey zone between smuggling networks and jihadism.[54]

Consistent with its claim to statehood, IS has made a point of applying its own rules wherever possible, and as strictly as possible, as 'the Caliphate's legitimacy is predicated on IS' ability to implement laws and otherwise function as a state'.[55]

The reaction of the jihadist constituency worldwide to the declaration of the Caliphate is a matter of debate. One view is that on the whole IS did not manage to replace AQ as the dominant jihadist influence in the world, with just thirty groups pledging alliance by August 2015.[56] The alternative point of view is more inclined to recognize the strength of the challenge posed by IS to AQ.[57] There is even some evidence that both AQ and IS have been growing.[58]

Even in terms of the more general implementation of the Salafi interpretation of Islam, IS was much stricter than AQ and its branches, like Al-Nusra.[59] The approach to modern education was strictly negative, despite the need to produce educated fighters for its armies.[60]

IS was described by most sources as wealthy because of its control of oil smuggling and other sources of revenue, at least until US and later Russian air campaigns reduced its ability to export oil and hit some of its cash storage centres.[61] Donations by private donors, by contrast, are often reported to be low, and from foreign governments even non-existent.[62] But is this the result of IS's ability to attract massive levels of funding from donors around the Arab world being understudied, or of genuine self-reliance? For sure, there is clear evidence of weapons bought by Gulf countries reaching IS in large numbers.[63]

Finally, despite the media hype and its popularity in the social media, 'The success of IS expansion has also been due to the importance it places on personal networks. In both Libya and Egypt, socialization in IS networks in Iraq under al-Zarqawi proved crucial in IS transmission'.[64]

IS appears, therefore, to have managed to reconcile personal networking and meritocracy, at least in the military field.

In summary, the main characteristics of the 'IS model' have been identified so far as:

- The practice of 'ultra' *takfir* (excommunication) to delegitimize rivals and legitimize violence against fellow Sunni Muslims;
- Engineering sectarian chaos in order to cast itself as defender of Sunnism, or failing that generating polarizing violence in order to force large portion of society to take sides;[65]

- Inviting foreign intervention in order to justify its existence in terms of acting as a force of opposition to the invaders;
- Coercive implementation of own strict interpretation of Shari'a;
- Militarism: belief in military victory as the only solution and in permanent warfare as the existential condition of the Caliphate;
- Military professionalism: enacting strict criteria for selecting military commanders and rejecting nepotistic and clientelistic practices, but at the same time relying on personal networking within jihadist circles for political recruitment;
- Peculiar combination of different systems of command and control:
  o Belief in the importance of an extremely centralized *political* organization;
  o decentralized *military* command and control, with the ability to concentrate and disperse;[66]
  o Top-down *governance*, with subject communities allowed very little say over rigid rules imposed on them;
- Strong discipline enforced among rank-and-file;
- Stress on global jihad, under the Caliph;
- 'Apocalypticism';[67]
- Emphasis on the unique capability of IS to defend Islam from its enemies;[68]
- Stress on the 'near enemy' as a priority over the 'far enemy';
- The refusal in principle to 'sequence' its adversaries, resulting in IS fighting against multiple enemies at the same time;[69]
- Rejection of AQ's new strategy of supporting popular demonstrations and 'seeking popular support' at the expense of armed jihad;[70]
- Acceleration of the timeline leading to the creation of the Caliphate;
- Dependence on generous funding for sustainability of strategy;
- 'Deterrent strategy' with exaggerated show of force;
- Skilful co-opting of local communities as IS expands (followed by the imposition of top-down governance).

This list incorporates some organizational features, some strategic choices and some ideological traits. It was worth noting, of course, that the IS model is not being exported only to Khorasan. Even in Syria, IS is often viewed as an alien implant, and originally it was mainly foreign fighters who decided to support it against Al-Nusra. ISIL started recruiting Syrians, who were seen as less ideologically motivated and more opportunistic than the foreign fighters or the Iraqis who constituted the core of ISIL, and increasingly disillusioned after experiencing domination by ISIL.[71] The rationale for Syrians joining ISIL and IS was that

ISIS's brutal clarity allowed it to monopolize the identity narrative (deliverance of the Sunnis from Shia domination) and appeal to downtrodden and marginalized Syrians. Ideologically and militarily, ISIS was seen as a powerful force that could deliver Syrians from bondage by toppling Assad and establishing a centralized Sunni rule in Damascus and Baghdad, a feat that none of its Islamist rivals could accomplish.[72]

Outside Syria, information about the relationship between IS-Central and the '*wilayats*' is even scanter. IS in Libya is believed to be closely connected to IS-Central, as shown by the despatch of operatives to advise and manage it.[73] Similarly, the predominant view about IS Sinai is that it is closely connected to IS, despite the obvious difficulty in transferring cadres and leaders back and forth (as Sinai borders only Israel). Even those authors who doubt the impact of direct IS-Central assistance to IS Sinai recognize an attempt by the latter to adopt the tactics and the style of the original IS.[74]

In the case of IS Yemen, the link to IS is even more obvious, as it was initially led by non-Yemeni cadres deployed by IS itself.[75] IS Yemen started gaining ground once its leadership was taken over by a Yemeni, but little is known about its actual relationship with IS, which must be logistically complicated. The group has not yet adopted the indiscriminate violence tactics of IS-Central, but it has taken a militarist approach, with no effort to establish any kind of welfare system for the population. It seems clear, however, that IS Yemen positions itself as the defender of Sunnis against the growing preponderance of the Zaidis.[76]

IS's expansion should be expected to make the viability of its centralized model more and more problematic. One observer predicted that:

> As more groups and individuals pledge allegiance to the Islamic State in a bid to gain power, notoriety, and resources, and as the Islamic State embraces more and more such entities and incidents to assert its global influence, it will be forced to change from a centralized organization into a franchise similar to al Qaeda.[77]

Methodology and research ethics

This book is primarily based on a RUSI research project and various other smaller projects carried out between 2014–18, as well as on smaller projects taking place in 2019–21. The project relied primarily on oral sources, with a total of 174 interviews having been carried out with IS-K members, advisers to IS-K and a range of external observers and participants to the conflict. Other sources, such as IS media and secondary sources, have mainly been used to corroborate or triangulate the information provided by interviewees. The breakdown by type of interviewee is the following:

- Members of IS-K (leaders, cadres, commanders and a few fighters): 91;
- External observers and participants: 61 (donors, suppliers, taxpayers, community elders, members of other insurgent organizations or armed groups such as Taliban and Al-Qaida, and members of intelligence agencies of various countries);
- Members of organizations allied to IS: 22 (IMU, ETIM, Lashkar-e Taiba, IMT, Jamaat Ansarullah, IJRPT, Hizb-i Islami).

The interviews were carried between late 2014 and mid-2021 by a mixed research team of Afghan and Pakistani interviewers. Most of the interviewers have a background in journalism and have been involved in previous research projects led by the author, covering mostly the Afghan Taliban. They were therefore already a battle-tested team before the project began, well versed in ensuring that interviews took place safely for all those involved. Access to IS-K, usually not the most accessible organization, was obtained by leveraging existing contacts with members who had participated in research projects when they were still with the Taliban, TTP or other groups. Once contact was re-established, it became easy to access other members of IS-K through introductions provided by the original contacts. The research team has established a reputation for the safe handling of interviews over several years of research activity, a fact that has facilitated access.

Many interviewees were remarkably frank in their answers, discussing IS-K's problems and flaws, or releasing detailed information about IS-K's finance and membership. This raises the issue of why some of the cadres and leaders of IS-K would collaborate with the interviewers to such an extent. In some cases, and particularly with regard to information concerning disputes within IS-K, the interviewees might have been motivated by the desire to communicate with the external world about aspects of IS-K they were not happy about. In addition, particularly when introduced by some individual they respected, when asked direct questions interviewees might not have wanted to deny facts and circumstances that seemed to be already known to the interviewer. The first wave of interviews was intended to gather sufficient information to help framing more detailed questions for the successive waves. By learning a little about IS-K, the team was able to convince successive waves of interviewees that it was already well informed about IS-K, and that interviewers could not easily be misled.

The willingness of some interviewees to share detailed data can be explained in different ways. Much of the data provided turned out to be essentially propagandistic in nature, and has not been used in this study. The author reviewed the data and determined which of it had at least some analytical value. Membership numbers could be triangulated with estimates provided by various intelligence agencies. Financial data was harder to make sense of, in the absence of ways to triangulate it except for comparisons that could be made with other insurgent groups. The overall level of funding available to IS-K therefore cannot be confirmed, but the author decided to use the data anyway because the breakdowns of funding and budgeting provided by the sources told an interesting story of how IS-K functions. This story is not particularly flattering to IS-K, and that is the main reason why the author decided that it was not likely to be manufactured in order to mislead. Funding figures will nonetheless strike many readers as high and should be taken with a pinch of salt.

In addition, the research team tried to obtain written IS-K material through the contacts developed during the interviewing process. Not much of it is accessible, but the most valuable find was the notebook of a senior IS-K member, which contained much factual information and a chronology of events. Secondary sources were also collated, such as the few analytical reports issued so far on IS-K and press reports.

As it will be noted, because this is the first extensive study of IS-K and the authorities release little in the public domain, it is heavily reliant on information provided by IS-K members. In those cases where external sources (media, elders, intelligence officials) were not available to confirm the plausibility of the information provided by IS-K members, the authors relied on cross-referencing between different IS-K sources, interviewed at different time and in different places. We also considered the sensitivity of the information provided; we focused on cross-checking the most sensitive information, while we adopted lower standards of cross-checking for information which was not very sensitive or not sensitive at all. The sources of all the information included in this book are documented in the footnotes. Each footnote covers the text included between it and the previous footnote. This means that in several cases a footnote may cover several sentences.

In this type of research work there is an obvious risk (or perhaps even a certainty) that much of the information provided will be essentially propagandistic in nature. While this is inevitable, the research project handled the risk by relying on:

a. interviews with external observers as well as IS-K members, allowing us to check a number of statements made by IS-K interviewees;

b. multiple interviews in different places and at different times, with different interviewers and interviewees contacted through different channels; this was meant to minimize the risk of collusion among interviewees in providing misleading information and to allow cross-checking among different IS-K interviewees;

c. the inclusion in the questionnaires of questions to which the answer was already known to the authors, in order to check to what degree interviewees were being honest in their answers; in three cases, it was decided not to use much of the material included in the interviews, due to doubts about the genuine character of the information provided;

d. structuring the interviewing process in successive waves, with a first 'exploratory' wave used to strengthen the questionnaires and to insert more test questions, based on the newly obtained information;

e. cross-referencing factual information provided to verify its internal consistency; thanks to previous research projects carried out on Taliban, TTP and Central Asian jihadists, it was also possible to compare the data obtained with similar data about other organizations.

The initial group of interviewees was selected on the basis of existing contacts; snowball sampling was used to reach out to a large number of interviewees, but the research team made sure that interviewees were distributed across the span of groups making up IS-K and across the different levels of membership.

Given the type of project, research ethics were a major concern. One of the criteria for selecting the members of the research team was their proven ability (from previous projects) to preserve confidentiality. The interviews were anonymized at an early stage, and nobody but the people directly involved in the research effort knows the actual identities of the interviewees. Interview transcripts were handed by hand (typically in small USB drives) to the author (the principal investigator), or sent through encrypted email.

1

HOW IT ALL BEGAN

Jihadism in 'Khorasan' before IS

Jihadism in 'Khosaran' has multiple sources and origins. The Afghan jihad was largely the retaliation of the Taliban Emirate, which was overthrown by a US-led operation in 2001. The Taliban were seeking to return to power, or at least force the Kabul government—supported by the Western powers, India and several other countries—to cede a share of power to them. No other jihadist groups had ever been in power: the Baluchi jihadists were fighting against the Islamic Republic of Iran; the Central Asian jihadists wanted to overthrow the regimes of their own countries; Pakistani jihadist groups had different aims, ranging from forcing the establishment of a Shari'a regime in Pakistan to fighting jihad abroad (mostly in Afghanistan), to eradicating Shi'ism from Pakistan. With the partial exception of the Afghan Taliban, these groups were to various degrees committed to the cause of global jihad, which sometimes even overrode their own national jihads.

After 2001, the Afghan jihad had become largely central to the world of jihadism in Khorasan, to the extent that few organizations had not taken part in it to some extent. The withdrawal of Western combat forces from Afghanistan at the end of 2014 was widely expected to lead to the successful conclusion of the Afghan jihad, which instead was rapidly bogged down in personal and factional disputes. The Taliban's reputation as the lead jihadist organization in the region had already started being questioned before that. The Taliban's 'jihadist legitimacy' suffered from 2010 onwards, as evidence started emerging that its political leadership were seeking a negotiated solution of the conflict. The appearance of another major 'cause célèbre' of jihadism, the Syrian civil war (2011 on), also caused a relative decline of importance of the Afghan jihad in the eyes of jihadists and sympathizers worldwide.

By the time the Syrian conflict was beginning in 2011, what IS calls Khorasan was already host to a myriad of jihadist organizations (see Appendix 3). Afghanistan had the largest of these organizations, the Islamic Emirate of Afghanistan, popularly known as the Taliban. By 2011, the Taliban had already been fragmenting for some time into different factions, such as the Miran Shah Shura (Haqqani network), the Peshawar Shura and the original Quetta Shura, which still claimed to represent the leadership of all Taliban. In 2014, a new faction had emerged—the Mashhad Office, which from being a dependency of the Quetta Shura became autonomous—and in 2016 the Peshawar Shura split, with half of it establishing the Shura of the North.[1] Alongside the Taliban, by 2011 the Hekmatyar faction of Hizb-i Islami had also been fighting a small-scale insurgency for several years, eventually signing a reconciliation agreement with the Kabul authorities in 2016.

In Pakistan, literally hundreds of jihadist groups big and small operated in 2011–17, among which the largest ones were Lashkar-e Taiba (LeT), Sepah-e Sahaba (SS), Tehrik-e Taliban Pakistan (TTP) with its various splinter groups (primarily Jamaat ul-Ahrar), Jaysh Mohammad (JM), Lashkar-e Jhangvi (LeJ), Harakat-e Mujahidin and Jundullah. All of these groups had relations with AQ (see Appendix 3).

In Iran, at least six groups were active, all in Baluchistan: Jundullah and Harakat-e Ansar-e Iran were active in 2010, and Jaysh ul Adl, Harakat-e Islami Sistan, Wilayat Khorasan Iran branch and the West Azerbaijan Islamic Movement were added after 2011. With the exception of Jundullah, all of these groups linked up in varying degrees with global jihad groups such as AQ or IS.

In Tajikistan, Jamaat Ansarullah was active in 2011, and three more groups emerged later: the Jihod Hizbi Nahzati Islamii (Islamic Jihad Renaissance Party [IJRPT]), Harakati Islamii Tajikistan (Islamic Movement of Tajikistan) and Harakati Islamii Gulmorad Halimov (Islamic Movement of Gulmorad Halimov). All of these groups had had close relations with AQ and/or IS.

In addition, several other groups operated in Khorasan, largely outside their home countries, like the Islamic Movement of Uzbekistan (IMU), the Chinese (Uyghur) Turkestan Islamic Party (TIP) and East Turkestan Islamic Movement (ETIM), the Chechens of Kavkaz Emarat and several smaller ones, such as the Islamic Movement of Turkmenistan (IMT) and others. All of these groups were closely connected with AQ and/or IS, and participated in their global jihad efforts in Afghanistan and Pakistan.

Finally, some groups which were international in nature operated in Khorasan, such as Al-Qaida (AQ) and the Islamic Jihad Union (IJU). AQ had several local fronts operating under its de facto control. In their case, the commitment to the cause of global jihad is obvious. AQ's role was much greater than might be suggested by the few hundred core members it had in Khorasan, as it acted as a hub, supporting almost all the jihadist organizations in Khorasan, facilitating their fundraising and providing advice. Appendix 3 shows how the jihadist web of relations in Khorasan was organized around 2011.

Volunteers for Syria: why they were invited and why they went

As the Syrian civil war was dragging on and different insurgent organizations were competing for a greater stake in the campaign against Assad's regime, in 2012 Al-Qaida's branches in Afghanistan and Pakistan lobbied their Taliban allies to start sending volunteers to fight in Syria.[2] Al-Qaida was probably intent on marketing its commitment to 'global jihad' to its donors and perhaps also in the longer term expanding its influence in Afghanistan and Pakistan. While there were some Afghans and Pakistanis with AQ in Syria and Iraq, the new development was the organized despatch of hundreds of volunteers for fighting there. The only known precedent of sending a group to Iraq is the Afghan Taliban's Mullah Dadullah, who despatched a small team to al-Zarqawi in early 2004 for training in suicide bombing.[3] Small numbers of individual recruits were already flocking to al-Zarqawi's *Tanzim Qaidat al-Jihad fi Bilad al-Rafidayn* and AQ-linked organizations from at least 2003. In April 2012, the Russian security services were already estimating the presence in Syria of 200–250 Afghans and 250–300 Pakistanis of the TTP.[4] In May 2012, the Syrian authorities released a list of 'foreign terrorists' killed in combat, which already included eleven Afghans.[5]

The new development was the decision to have AQ-linked organizations in Afghanistan and Pakistan (and possibly elsewhere as well) to form contingents for the Levant, which would remain under the banner of the original organization, with a contingent commander appointed from the original outfit. Clearly the intent was to get them back at some point, and not allow them to disperse among different IS units. According to one of the leaders of IS-K, the first contingent for Syria was formed under the initiative of a TTP

21

leader, Hafiz Saeed Khan, who on 14 July 2012 agreed to send volunteers to AQ. Reportedly, he rapidly gathered a contingent of 143 volunteers (Afghans and Pakistanis) and despatched it to Syria to fight in Al-Nusra's ranks.[6] More contingents followed from then onwards.

The impact was noticeable. In December 2012, the Syrian authorities already reported the killing of seventy Afghans and Pakistanis fighting for AQ. The build-up continued: in 2013, news agencies and specialist media reported on TTP getting involved and sending 'hundreds' of volunteers to Syria.[7] By June 2014, a source in ISIL claimed that there were already 575 Afghans and 714 Pakistanis in its ranks in Syria and Iraq.[8] As the end of 2014 approached, the TTP had already sent 1,000 volunteers to Syria, with plans to send hundreds more, as claimed by the TTP itself and confirmed by the Pakistani authorities.[9]

At the same time, efforts were also taking place to attract volunteers from 'Khorasan' without going through the Afghan Taliban and the TTP. This is the account of a volunteer's recruitment by a future senior leader of IS-K:

> In 1999 I graduated from ... madrasa. After graduation I started teaching in this same madrasa in 2003. I taught in this madrasa for 9 years. There was one Syrian teacher, I went with him to Syria in the month of June 2012. When we went there, we joined with Al Nusra, whose leader is Abu Mohammad Al Julani. We were with this group up to the month of June of 2013, after this we joined Daesh and with the senior commander of Daesh, Abu Omar Shishani.[10]

Hafiz Saeed Khan was not the only one in the region to have been co-operating with AQ on Syria. From 2010, the relations of Al-Qaida with the Taliban's Quetta Shura were quite cold, and its leadership council (Rahbari Shura) effectively refused to send volunteers to Syria. However, the two largely autonomous branches of the Taliban which existed at that time—the Miran Shah Shura (better known as the Haqqani network) and the Peshawar Shura—both reportedly agreed to co-operate in the recruitment of volunteers, in exchange for contributions to their coffers from Al-Qaida. One account is that it was actually al-Baghdadi, at that time still aligned with AQ, who contacted Serajuddin Haqqani in April 2013 asking him to send a group of volunteers to Syria. According to the source, Serajuddin agreed to send a contingent of 400, in exchange for a contribution of $12 million to the coffers of the Miran Shah Shura, in addition to another $20 million spent to pay, equip and maintain the contingent. The Haqqanis, with their large reserves of fighters waiting to be mobilized, could easily sacrifice 400 for Syria.[11] These were generous offers by Al-Qaida: the volunteers sent by the Haqqanis, for example, were paid $800 per month, about four times what full-time Taliban fighters were getting in Afghanistan.[12] There are, however, no sources that confirm the size of such deployment outside IS-K itself. Why would AQ and al-Baghdadi offer such generous rates of pay, when there was no shortage of cheaper local recruits?

One explanation could be AQ's desire to highlight to the world (and particularly to its donors) the global jihad dimension of the conflict. But another possible explanation is more relevant to this book: AQ and *ad-Dawlah al-'Irāq al-Islāmiyah* (Islamic State in Iraq, IS-I) might have already been viewing the Syrian conflict like an opportunity to gain new influence over local jihadist movements well beyond Syria, including 'Khorasan'. Attracting volunteers, who would then one day return home, was a way of spreading influence and skills of proven effectiveness (as had been done in Afghanistan in the 1980s and 1990s). The Syrian conflict represented a golden opportunity for AQ to relaunch its operations: it was relatively easy to raise abundant funding for that conflict, compared to older conflicts such as the Afghan one.[13] Indeed, once the first contingent sent by Hafeez Said was in Syria, the Military Commission of IS-I, as it was known at that time, reportedly offered ten of the TTP and Taliban commanders who were leading the first contingent to Syria $1 million to proselytize among other jihadist groups once back in Pakistan. From November 2013 onwards, they started approaching members of the TTP, IMU, Lashkar-e Taiba, Lashkar-e Jhangvi and others, as well as the Afghan Taliban.[14] Many of them emerged later as influential figures within IS-K, such as Sheikh Mohsin who became Amir of Kunar, or Saad Emarati who became Amir of Logar.[15]

Two training camps were reportedly set up in Waziristan and Kunar, by the Haqqanis and the Peshawar Shura respectively, with the purpose of imparting notions of Arabic language to the volunteers and providing some military education as well. Many of the recruits were not from the Taliban, but were Afghans or Pakistanis attracted by the promise of glory and the comparatively high salaries. This seems to suggest that the Taliban had an opportunistic streak: take AQ's generous payments and send fresh recruits. IS-K sources claimed that the recruitment system included an 'exam' to assess the motivations and attitudes of the volunteers, probably to weed out individuals attracted exclusively by the high pay. Those who became commanders and cadres of the contingent tended to have a rather strong background in Islamic studies.[16]

The flow of volunteers from Waziristan and Kunar brought hundreds of Afghans and Pakistanis to Syria and Iraq, where they typically joined the ranks of Al-Nusra and IS-I. According to IS-K sources, a large majority of the volunteers travelled through Iran, disguised as asylum seekers and economic migrants in order not to be detected by the Iranian authorities, then crossed into Turkey before reaching Syria. Senior figures and Arabs would mostly travel via the Arab Gulf and then into Pakistan, taking commercial flights with genuine or faked passports, or ships from Saudi Arabia to Karachi.[17] Quite a few of these volunteers were therefore operating under al-Baghdadi from the beginning of their arrival in Syria/Iraq; others entered into contact with him or his organization after it entered Syria in 2013.

Other groups of volunteers joined Al-Nusra from Pakistani or Pakistan-based jihadist groups such as Lashkar-e Taiba, Lashkar-e Jhangvi, Aseem Omari Front and Jaysh ul-Adl. Afghans and Pakistanis aside, the IMU was an early supporter of jihad in Syria. A senior IS-K source claims that IMU leader Osman Ghazi sent the first group of volunteers from North Waziristan on 19 December 2013. At the head of the group of 200 volunteers he placed one of his senior commanders, Sadullah Urgeni. The IMU volunteer group joined the IS precursor in Iraq: IS-I, not Al-Nusra.[18] The IMU by then was already developing doubts about its relationship with the Taliban.[19] By 11 May 2013, the group sent by Hafiz Saeed had already switched its loyalty to al-Baghdadi, and so did the Lashkar-e Taiba contingent on 18 November 2013. Lashkar-e Jhangvi followed suit on 1 January 2014, as did the Aseem Omari contingent on 3 August 2014 and the contingent of Jaysh ul-Adl on 25 October 2014.[20] It is not clear whether the decisions taken by these contingents were endorsed by their respective leaderships. It is also likely that the contingents did not join in their entirety, with minorities refusing to follow the contingents' leaders and instead opting to stick with AQ.

It would, therefore, appear that IS was beginning to attract Afghans, Pakistanis and Central Asians even before its big military successes of 2014. One senior Afghan member of IS later commented that the attractiveness of IS derived in part from the impression they gave of financial wealth, which particularly appealed to groups which were otherwise not doing very well financially, but also from the fear that the leaderships of TTP and Afghan Taliban would eventually sign peace deals with their respective governments and thus marginalize their own internal hardliners. Another factor which made the seemingly burgeoning IS so appealing an option was the first sign of unreliability of the Taliban's donors.[21] As a senior IS-K member commented: 'Many Arab countries are supporting Daesh like Saudi Arabia, Qatar, UAE and others. They also have a lot of natural resources under their control, like oil wells and others'.[22]

IS was not committing to Khorasan resources comparable to what the Taliban had. But for disgruntled Taliban members who had been cut off from funding, or who were not receiving enough in the first place, for the first time there was a seemingly plausible alternative.

The volunteers start returning to 'Khorasan'

Even before the proclamation of the Caliphate by al-Baghdadi, according to an authoritative source, al-Baghdadi, Muslim Turkmani and Abu Omar al Shishani of what had already changed its name to the Islamic State of Iraq and the Levant (ISIL) were encouraging the volunteers to set up a branch of the ISIL in Afghanistan and Pakistan, and later on in Central Asia and Iran.[23] As early as 3 April 2014, al Shishani appointed Qari Wali Rahman, an Afghan from Baghlan who had arrived in Syria in 2013, as IS's special representative for Afghanistan and Pakistan.[24]

As mentioned already, the commanders of the first group of 143 despatched to Syria by Hafiz Saeed, of Serajuddin's and the Peshawar Shura's contingent in Syria and Iraq, were used to spread the word and start recruitment efforts independently of the Taliban and TTP leadership. By the second half of 2014, their proselytizing was bearing its first fruits. For example, among the Haqqanis, Azizullah Haqqani (not to be confused with one of the brothers of Serajuddin, but a senior figure nonetheless), who led the contingent in Iraq, reportedly recruited about ten field commanders from the Haqqani network, convincing them to join what had in the meantime finally become the Islamic State (IS). He also reportedly established relations with some relatively senior Haqqani figures, who agreed to look the other way when it came to IS recruitment efforts in exchange for funds. Later, some of these figures joined Azizullah openly: Rauf Zakir, military leader for Sabari district; Khan Wali Zadran, military leader of Paktia province; Marouf Ibrahimkhel, responsible for IED operations in northern Afghanistan; Yousaf Zadran, military leader of Shawak district (Paktia); and Mullah Jamal, responsible for Wardak province. Reportedly, once Serajuddin Haqqani, the leader of the Haqqani network, became aware of this attempt to bypass his authority, it would lead to the first friction between him and al-Baghdadi. Initially, however, Serajuddin seemed unaware of what was going on behind his back. According to IS-K sources, as late as August 2014, after the formal split from AQ and the launch of the IS, Serajuddin even agreed to expand the size of the contingent in Iraq from 400 to 700. According to the same sources, the funds transferred by IS or spent on the Haqqani fighters in Syria rose to $42 million in 2014.[25] If these numbers are correct (and there is no way to verify this), it would suggest that IS was quite keen on hooking the Haqqani network to itself and expanding its influence within its ranks.

The Peshawar Shura was also co-operative with IS: in its territories, the amirs of the first groups declaring allegiance to IS and the governors/military leaders of the Taliban were effectively tasked to co-ordinate between the two organizations.[26]

According to Azami, IS emissaries tried repeatedly to reach an understanding with the Quetta Shura, even asking for a meeting with Mullah Omar (unaware that he was already dead) in August 2014. Failing that, IS would later approach individual leaders and commanders of the Quetta Shura, such as Mansur Dadullah, who were believed to have some ideological leaning towards IS.[27]

The arrival of the first returnees from Syria, IS's efforts to attract more volunteers and the first signs of their intent to establish a local branch of IS attracted little attention initially. In June 2015, the Pentagon still claimed that IS-K had just a 'limited' connection to IS. It was only in June/July 2016, for example, that the NATO mission in Afghanistan, Resolute Support (RS), acknowledged that groups calling themselves IS-K in Afghanistan had indeed financial, strategic and communications connections with the core organization of IS in Iraq and Syria.[28]

The press did detect IS propaganda activities, such as leaflets, pamphlets and other publications. In August 2014, a twelve-page pamphlet written in Pashto and Dari appeared in the frontier areas of Pakistan, announcing the imminent expansion of the IS into 'Khorasan'.[29] That alone would mean little, but the summer of 2014, according to all IS sources consulted, was when local networks of sympathizers started getting organized.

In November 2014, there were insistent reports about the existence of a training camp in Kunar. The first evidence of IS activities in Afghanistan emerged in January 2015, when a group of thirteen men was arrested in Bagram (Parwan). In the following weeks, Afghan army intelligence reports indicated the presence of a group of seventy IS-K members in Khoki Safed (Farah), a mix of Afghans and foreign fighters.[30] In February, finally the Afghan authorities admitted that groups identifying themselves as IS were active in their territory. The acknowledgement followed the killing of the deputy governor of 'Khorasan', Khadim, on 9 February in Helmand.[31] In March, there were reports of propaganda material being distributed even in parts of Kabul.[32]

A fragmented start: the 'coagulation points' before IS-K

During 2014, dispersed groups associated with IS started coalescing around some main leaders and forming organizations. This was done either under the direct impulse of emissaries sent by IS-Central, or on the groups' own initiative and later recognized by IS. None of the interviewees mentioned these groups as offering a formal submission (*bay'a*) to IS-Central, so it might well be that the recognition remained informal.[33] Several different 'coagulation points' started forming, reflecting the segmentary character of the Taliban and other local insurgent groups. These 'coagulation points' then established a relationship with IS-K which resembled that of the Taliban's autonomous fronts, called *loy mahaz*. These fronts formally depended on one of the main Taliban councils (shuras), mostly the Quetta one, but enjoyed a considerable degree of autonomy with regards to doing their own recruitment and fundraising, and they maintained separate chains of command. Each of the founding groups of IS-K had different origins.

Tehrik-e Khilafat Khorasan (TKK)

In Afghanistan, the various leaders and groups linked to IS started coalescing around three organizations. The Tehrik-e Khilafat Khorasan (Movement for the Caliphate in Khorasan, TKK), which appeared to be preferred by IS-Central, was the first of the officially IS-recognized groups to appear.[34] It largely gathered Afghans connected to IS, mostly in eastern Afghanistan. The original leader of TKK, Abdul Rahim Muslim Dost, was rapidly replaced by Mawlavi Nasratullah Popalzai, and Muslim Dost then set out to create a separate group with Khadim (Khilafat Afghan).[35]

Why exactly Muslim Dost was removed from the top position is not clear, but given his behaviour over the course of 2015 he might have displayed a tendency towards independent-mindedness that IS-Central found inappropriate.

Khilafat Afghan and Muslim Dost Group

The second coagulation point emerged around the figure of Abdul Khadim Rauf, a relatively senior former cadre of the Quetta Shura of the Taliban, who was accused by the Taliban of having absorbed Salafi ideas while in Guantanamo, because he printed and distributed Salafi texts. One of the early Afghans to be sent by Hafiz Saeed to Syria, Sa'ad Emarati, was close to Khadim and drew him into IS. An Alizai Pashtun from Helmand, Khadim had among other roles been provincial governor of Kunar under the Taliban emirate. When he was arrested, he was sent to Guantanamo until his release in 2007. After that, he fought for some time as group commander in Kajaki, in the ranks of Dadullah Mahaz. Both Emarati and Khadim had trouble with the Taliban, although for different reasons: the first exhibited undisciplined behaviour, while the second allegedly had ideological (Salafi tendencies) and tribal differences (he was Alizai while Ishaqzais were then dominant in the Quetta Shura).[36]

Thanks to Sa'ad Emarati, Khadim was one of the early recipients of al-Baghdadi's invitation to join IS, and he set out to form a group, starting among his own personal followers in Helmand. According to a senior IS-K source, in 2013 Khadim already had about 200 men. The group formally joined IS on 19 January 2015, significantly later than TKK. At that time, its membership had grown to 1,400, if we believe sources within Khilafat Afghan.[37] Khilafat Afghan split in early 2015, as friction between Khadim and Abdul Rahim Muslim Dost led to the former expelling the latter, who took some hundreds of men with him when he left. Khilafat Afghan's membership reportedly fell to 750 men (of which 600 were fighters) before it started recovering.[38] It is worth noting that this was the second clash Muslim Dost had with his colleagues in a matter of months.

By October 2015, Khilafat Afghan had reportedly partially recovered to 1,140 members, of which two-thirds were former Taliban, one-fifth fresh recruits and the rest veterans from Syria and Iraq. The former Taliban members came from a variety of Taliban groups. Of Khilafat Afghan's 240 support elements (as of October 2015), about 100 were said to be in Pakistan, working in logistics and finance.[39] In 2015, the main office of Khilafat Afghan was reportedly in Doha, marking its close relationship with Qatar. Subsidiary headquarters existed in North Waziristan, Kajaki (destroyed at least temporarily in 2015) and Nawa (Ghazni), in addition to a small base in the UAE. Khilafat Afghan had eighty staff in these offices outside Afghanistan.[40]

The main focus of operations for Khilafat operations was initially Helmand province, Khadim's home province. When Khadim was killed in Helmand in February 2015 in a US drone strike, his nephew Wahidullah Wahid replaced him at the top of Khilafat Afghan.[41]

At the time of its split from Khilafat Afghan and joining IS-K as a separate group on 6 March 2015, the Muslim Dost Group reportedly had about 250–300 members, rising to 500 by June. Three months later, thanks to abundant funding from private Saudi donors, the claimed membership had risen to over 1,100. Muslim Dost mostly recruited from the ranks of the Quetta Shura, at least initially, due to his association with Khadim, even if he personally hailed from Kot district of Nangarhar. Later he expanded recruitment towards Nangarhar. Muslim Dost has long-standing links to a Salafist organization.[42]

Azizullah Haqqani's group

The third initial coagulation point of IS sympathizers was around Azizullah Haqqani, the senior cadre of the Haqqani network who led the Haqqani contingent with al-Baghdadi. His group unsurprisingly drew its original strength from the ranks of the Haqqanis and did not recruit at all among other Taliban factions (a deliberate decision of Azizullah himself), but also tried to recruit green members and members of Hizb-i Islami.[43] When he went back to Waziristan in 2014, Azizullah reportedly managed to attract to his group several Haqqani commanders who had not been to Syria, before he and his men were temporarily expelled from Waziristan by an angry Serajuddin. Initially, according to internal sources, Azizullah gathered about 600 men around him, formally announcing their joining IS on 11 August 2014. Azizullah continued negotiating with more Haqqani commanders, but also started expanding recruitment beyond the original network. He also started despatching his group beyond his original area of influence in Loya Paktia, particularly towards southern Afghanistan.[44] By early 2016, the group started deploying combat groups to other areas, such as Helmand and Zabul.[45]

After the original brush with Serajuddin, Azizullah reconciled with him and was able to keep his job as head of the Miran Shah Shura's Fedayin Commission as well his membership of the Miran Shah Shura, the leadership organ of the Haqqani network. This lasted until October 2016, when Azizullah's renewed (and successful) efforts to 'steal' Serajuddin's commanders led to his being expelled from the Shura and sacked from his job.[46]

Tehrik-e Khilafat Pakistan (TKP)

In Pakistan, by contrast, there was initially a single 'coagulation point'. The TKP (which has nothing to do with a pre-existing group called Tehrik-e Khilafat and based in Karachi) was established by a group of TTP leaders and commanders, among which the most senior one was Hafiz Saeed Khan. Hafiz

Saeed, mentioned above as the first to despatch a contingent to AQ in Syria, had personally already joined IS on 11 May 2013.[47] Some sources describe Hafiz Saeed as holding Salafi tendencies and having been involved in attacks on Hanafi madrasas in Orakzai when he was still in TTP.[48] He and his associates formed the TKP on 15 July 2014; however, its existence was only publicly announced on 14 August 2014. TKP was essentially the merger of eight armed groups, led by their commanders:

1. Khalid Mansoor, TTP commander in Hangu;
2. Shahidullah Shahid, spokesman of TTP;
3. Mufti Hassan Swati, TTP commander in Peshawar;
4. Gul Zaman Fateh, TTP commander in Khyber Agency;
5. Hafiz Dawlat Khan, TTP commander in Kurram;
6. Hafiz Saeed Khan, TTP commander in Orakzai;
7. Abdul Bahar Mehsud, TTP commander in Waziristan;
8. Abu Bakr, commander of the TTP in Bajaur.

Each of these senior TTP commanders brought a few hundred men with him into TKP. Initially, TTP sources dismissed the defections as being in the 'hundreds', not in the thousands, and therefore of little consequence. Later, however, they admitted that the split had significantly dented TTP's membership.[49]

The commander of the largest group, Abdul Bahar Mehsud, was initially appointed representative of al-Baghdadi in Pakistan as well as leader of TKP, while another one of the commanders with the largest following, Hafiz Dawlat Khan, was appointed his first deputy. Of the lot, however, it was Hafiz Saeed Khan who was the closest to al-Baghdadi, having organized the first group of volunteer fighters for Syria back in 2012. As a result, he was the one chosen to be governor of Wilayat Khorasan in January 2015. Some of the volunteers who returned from Syria were also appointed to top positions in TKP, despite not having been senior before. Notably, all the leading figures of TKP were former TTP commanders; similarly, the majority of the fighters formerly belonged to TTP, even if some Lashkar-e Jhangvi and Lashkar-e Taiba fighters also joined after coming back from Syria. Although they were reported in the press as separate groups, according to TKP sources all these cells joined TKP. Similarly, some other small groups declaring their allegiance to IS were brought into TKP, including *Ansar-ul-Khilafat Wal-Jihad* (Partisans of the Caliphate and of Jihad).[50]

Of the about 2,000 fighters and commanders TKP sources claimed it had in the summer and autumn of 2014, over a fifth were reportedly returnees from Syria. Another fifth were new recruits, and the large majority of the remaining ones were former TTP. In other words, a substantial majority of TTP and LeJ members joined without going through Syria, while the new recruits are mostly freshly graduated madrasa students. Geographically, the recruits come from North and South Waziristan, Bajaur, Peshawar, Quetta, Karachi, Islamabad, Lahore and Kashmir.[51]

Essentially, TKP was formed by a particular sub-type of anti-Fazlullah dissidents within the TTP, angry that TTP leader Fazlullah was cutting them off from funding and resources. While other anti-Fazlullah dissidents formed splinter groups such as Jamaat ul-Ahrar and the Mehsud faction of the TTP, those coagulating into the TKP appear to have been characterized by Salafi or near-Salafi views, as well as by stronger-than-average (for TTP) sectarian inclinations. TKP sources claimed that pressure from the Pakistani army in North Waziristan was a decisive motivation that pushed many TTP members to join the TKP, perhaps in protest at the lack of support they were receiving from TTP leadership.[52] Fazlullah himself had some communication with IS, which was still going on at the time of the announcement of the establishment of TKP, but does not appear to have been seriously considering joining.[53] Most of the original members of TKP were Orakzais and Mehsuds, but TKP was later strengthened by the arrival of a large group of Afridis, mostly from the ranks of Mangal Bagh's *Lashkar-e Islam*. Some local sources suggested that TKP recruited Afghans in Nangarhar, particularly Bati Kot and Chaparhar, mostly to fight at the orders of Pakistani commanders.[54]

The birth of IS-K

Until the end of 2014, the different groups which had linked up to IS talked of each other as separate entities.[55] From January 2015 things changed. On 26 January 2015, the establishment of Wilayat Khorasan was announced by Abu Muhammed al-Adnani, IS-Central's chief spokesperson, in an audio statement.[56] From that moment onwards, IS-K teams visiting the villages identified themselves as 'Daesh' or as Daesh Khorasan, or sometimes 'Khilafat Islami'.[57] At the bottom of the IS-K structure, discussing membership in the individual component groups was strongly discouraged.

> My boss is Mullah Abdul Khadim, he is from Orakzai tribe of Pakistan and who is above my boss I don't know that and we don't need to know that. I only know that who is my boss and who is the leader of Khilafat-i-Islami that is Amir-Ul-Muminin Abu Bakr al-Baghdadi. Daesh is not open like Taliban that everyone knows about the Taliban system.[58]

Relations between IS-Central and IS-K: a franchise?

Some analysts and policymakers describe IS-K as a 'franchise' of IS-Central, although rarely do they clarify what they mean by this term.[59] By calling it a franchise, analysts seem to imply that beyond receiving a formal authorization to bear the 'Islamic State' brand, IS-K remains nothing more than a loose network. As Rani describes it, IS-Central is 'drawing weaker local players under its "brand" and into a loosely constituted network of radical actors'.[60] As discussed above, this description fits what IS-K looked like in its early days. But is this the end state as far as IS-Central's plans are concerned?

As explained by one of its leaders, IS-K was authorized to make autonomous decisions about military operations, procurement, salaries, recruitment and budgeting, without having to consult with IS-Central. Instead, IS-Central had to be involved in any change to laws, rules and regulations, and leadership selection.[61] Most importantly, IS-Central selected the Special Representative, who operated as a kind of political commissar, representing Central's interests with IS-K and making sure that guidelines and directives were being respected. IS-Central also exercised some direct supervision and monitoring of IS-K not only through its advisers but also by sending inspection teams. The IS-K Finance Commission, for example, would receive teams in Dubai, Pakistan and even Afghanistan. The inspections could happen every 1–3 months and would involve checking invoices and receipts, and making enquiries about how the money was being spent.[62] All this seems to suggest something more than a franchised structure. This seems also implicit in the adoption of the term 'wilayat' (province) to describe IS-K by IS-Central. Clearly, IS-Central wanted to highlight a hierarchical relationship between itself and IS-K.

IS-K's ideology: global jihad for jihad's sake

One important benchmark of the relationship between IS-Central and IS-K is the comparison of their respective ideologies. Strong ideological variance would suggest a loose relationship between IS-K and IS-Central, while by contrast the wholehearted adoption by IS-K of an ideology alien to the Khorasan region would suggest a closer relationship. As discussed below, on many points IS-K was undoubtedly fully aligned with IS-Central, whereas on some others it was not. Mielke and Miszak describe Sheikh Abu Yazid Abd al-Qahir Khorasani as the main IS-K ideologue, but little is known about his actual thinking apart from that he was previously involved with Salafi groups in eastern Afghanistan.[63]

Global jihad and Caliphate

IS-K was described by recruits as a movement genuinely committed to global jihad against all 'empious' governments, in particular the Pakistani one. In this regard, IS-K like IS-Central has been quite effective in establishing a reputation for an uncompromising attitude towards jihad, despite evidence of relations with foreign donors.[64]

> I understood that [Taliban were] not doing Jihad in Afghanistan, in fact we were fulfilling the plans of [the Pakistani] ISI in Afghanistan. Daesh is project to implement Shari'a in the world and that what we want to raise up one day the Islam flag in Washington. Daesh program is very big and I think it would be only Daesh Khorasan in Afghanistan who can really bring Shari'a law in Afghanistan.[65]

IS-K indeed showed its commitment to global jihad by carrying out or at least claiming to have carried out bloody attacks in Pakistan, disregarding pressure from some of its main donors. It is worth noting that despite AQ's support for groups opposed to the Pakistani authorities, such as TTP and IMU, it too appears to have been able (in some circumstances, at least) to enlist the co-operation of the Pakistani authorities, as evidenced by the protection it reportedly afforded to Bin Laden.[66]

In addition, IS-Central adds of course the proclamation of the Caliphate, the most distinctive feature of IS. But the IS-K interviewees, while fully picking up the 'global jihad' propaganda point, barely discussed the topic of the Caliphate, or even of the state dimension implicit in the name of IS-K itself. These members of IS-K did not seem to take the 'state' dimension of IS's claims too seriously, or perhaps they saw it as too distant a prospect to bother.

This, however, is what AQ has always emphasized in their argument against IS: the 'Caliphate' experiment is premature, as the 'global jihad' movement should lay the foundations for it first. Does IS-K break from the ideology of IS-Central with regard to the Caliphate? According to IS-K sources, a lot of indoctrination took place from the summer of 2015 onwards (see Chapter 3), but still none of the thirty-six members interviewed in 2016–17 (that is, after indoctrination had been ongoing for several months) spoke about the Caliphate. Three possible explanations come immediately to mind.

IS-Central might have downplayed the Caliphate in its indoctrination operations in the expectation that its Iraq/Syrian territorial base would collapse in the near future. Already in 2015 (well before the Iraqi government forces began their offensive on Mosul), IS-K seemed to be preparing to face the collapse of the core Caliphate territorial domain in Syria and Iraq, and high-level cadres were being told that soon Khorasan would replace Mosul as the centre of all IS.[67] A second explanation is that the IS-K commanders, cadres and leaders interviewed were simply uninterested in this dimension of IS. A third possible explanation has to do with the expectations of donors to IS-K, who also likely contributed to shaping the ideological message packaged for IS-K by IS-Central. These expectations were not about IS-K establishing state-like structures in Khorasan (see *The role of regional rivalries* below and Chapter 7), but about challenging Iranian and Russian interests in the region. It is worth reminding the reader of the prediction of Lina Khatib, that IS would gradually turn into something more like a franchise worldwide (see *The IS model* in the Introduction).

War as a natural state

The militaristic ideology of IS-Central was discussed in the Introduction. Baczko and Dorronsoro stress the 'lack of political work' in the expansion policy of IS-K.[68] When asked to describe the differences between IS-K (and in particular TKP, which was largely composed of ex-TTP) and TTP, a TKP source commented:

> There are many political differences between TTP and TKP. One difference is this that TTP does not fight against Afghan Taliban but TKP fought against Afghan Taliban. Another difference is this that TTP is not against Shi'a, but TKP is against Shi'as. Another difference is this that TTP is fighting against Pakistan government in Pakistan but we are fighting in Pakistan against Pakistan's government, in Afghanistan against Afghan Government, foreigners, Shi'as, and the same we plan to fight against Shi'as in Iran and Central Asian countries.[69]

The source focused his answer on the enemies of the two organizations, which is revealing of a nihilist militarist 'ideology' of war without end and as a way of life, trying to achieve ever-expanding and completely unrealistic aims, such as expanding the Caliphate to rule the whole world.[70] In this regard, IS-K and IS-Central therefore seem aligned.

Salafism

If militarist nihilism and uncompromising jihadism is the main trait of IS-K's ideology, it is not the only one. Interestingly, it is not uncommon for

IS-K members to reject its characterization as a Salafist group.[71] In the words of a commander:

> No no it is not true, we are following the Shari'a and we are against Salafi ideas. Those people who are thinking that we are following the Salafi ideas, in fact they don't have any idea of Shari'a.[72]

This denial suggests a degree of pragmatic awareness about the unlikeliness of Afghan and Pakistanis being attracted to Salafism as such. IS-K even rejects the idea that its main source of support might be Salafis, numerous in Nuristan, Kunar and Nangarhar, which is instead what analysts like Mielke and Miszak have argued.[73]

TLO described some of the cornerstones of the ideology of IS-K as:

- The need to remove occupying foreign forces from Muslim lands at any costs;
- Future generations should be raised purely in accordance with the Quran and Sunna;
- Secularism is an illness spread through the educational system.[74]

Osman pointed out how the 'inclusivist' approach of IS-K is important in the eyes of many members of ethnic minorities who joined it.[75]

> Interviewees saw the group's belief that 'there are no borders but Islam' reflected in the presence within ISKP's ranks of Afghans from many different ethnic groups and regions, as well as fighters from other nations. Those who had spent time in ISKP's territory in eastern Afghanistan were impressed by the 'egalitarian' behavior of members. ... They contrasted this with the Taliban movement, within which power is monopolized by leadership from Kandahar. The Taliban leaders were also accused of betraying their muhajir (immigrant) jihadist brethren from Central Asia when the movement turned to nationalism for the sake of international recognition after the death of Mullah Omar. ISKP was viewed as the only jihadist force active in Afghanistan with an 'open arms' policy toward jihadists from across the region ...[76]

In part it is true that some of the more extreme ideological features of IS-Central's Salafism have for now not been imported to Khorasan, such as *takfir*. Still IS-K made a serious effort to implement principles very alien to Afghanistan whenever it was in control, regardless of the environment. Particularly after the arrival of the Special Envoy from IS-Central, Abu Yasir Al-Afghani (see Chapter 9), IS-K for example enforced its ban on the drug trade very strictly; the leadership informed all farmers that if they were found to be growing poppies they would face fines, detention or even execution.[77] By

June 2016, IS-K was claiming to have eradicated 1,200 hectares, collected fines for $3 million and seized 20 tonnes of drugs.[78]

At least as of January 2016, a source in Haji Zahir's militia believed that IS-K was still being paid by drug smugglers to allow free movement through their areas. The TLO also reported allegations that opium seized by IS-K was then sold on to smugglers.[79] However, the weight of evidence points in a different direction, even if the existence of corruption within IS-K's ranks cannot be ruled out.[80] The justification for the very unpopular ban was that the drug trade is forbidden in Islam, but there might be other, more pragmatic, reasons for it (see Chapter 7, 'Taxation').[81] The ban on drugs was lifted in southwestern Afghanistan in January 2017, in what was described as only a 'temporary' move, probably in an effort to save face ideologically. In any case, IS-K moved swiftly and aggressively to compete with the Taliban, particularly those of the Quetta Shura, over taxation of the narcotics trade.[82]

IS-K interviewees also describe forcing people to give food and indulging in 'cruel behaviour' as abuses that were forbidden because there was no justification for them in the religious texts.[83]

> Taliban are doing everything against Islam, they are collecting taxes on drugs. ... They are taking money from people houses by force, but we are not doing such activities. They allow music but we do not.[84]

As will be discussed in greater detail in Chapter 5 below, a whole range of strictures were imposed on the villagers, even in areas where IS-K had some roots in the community. Abdul Rauf Khadim did not endorse *takfir* and did not spread anti-Shi'a rhetoric, which would have been redundant anyway in Kajaki (where there are no Shi'as).[85] He did, however, have a reputation for Salafi inclinations—in particular that he objected to the Taliban's tolerating Pashtunwali justice in their areas of control and condoning the drug trade—even if a source close to Khadim suggested that tribal marginalization might have been the main reason for splitting from the Taliban. The result was that even in Kajaki IS-K attacks on shrines and their imposition of Salafi-style prayers turned many against it.[86]

> I am one of these villagers and I prefer Taliban to Daesh. Taliban are a bit aggressive regarding their behaviour but they are Muslims and never ask people to follow Salafi rules.[87]

While some sources claimed that only collaborators of Iran are supposed to be targeted,[88] others were more frank: Shi'as must be killed, whether civilians, military or government staff, unless they bow to the Salafis:[89]

We are not against Shi'a but we want them to accept Shari'a and follow our rules. We know that Shi'a people believe a lot in shrines and some old traditional ceremonies, which is against Shari'a. For example, Moharam and other rituals. The way of their praying is different; we have to follow the style of Prophet Mohammad, Prophet Mohammad never prayed with open hands. If the Shi'a people really change these things, they are all our brothers.[90]

In sum, IS-K might have not been a coherent Salafist or jihadist-Salafist organization in the way its mother organization is. Nonetheless, it had at its core hardline former Taliban and TTP members who were influenced by Salafism, attracted by global jihadism or had at least some superficial sympathy for the assertive, uncompromising Salafist jihadism of IS, guaranteeing that this class of professional insurgents will have wars to fight virtually forever.[91] While some of the cadres and leaders with stronger clerical backgrounds seem to have been supportive of Salafism as such, by far the biggest component of IS-K's ideology was militarist nihilism wrapped in Salafist clothes. Hence the tendency of interviewees to indulge in listing their many enemies, emphasizing how they are not bothered by the fact that they had essentially been fighting another jihadist (although not global jihadist) organization, the Taliban.

By 2021, however, IS-K was turning more and more into a Salafist insurgent organization. The Salafists, who are very numerous in Kunar and Nuristan especially, but also in Nangarhar, account now for the majority of its Afghan members. Among the TTP members the Panjpiris predominate; Panjpiris are closer to Salafism than Deobandis, who mostly stayed in the TTP.[92]

Sectarianism

In fact, IS-K members easily contradict themselves with regard to the targets of their violence. For example, they claimed to having killed 'volunteers for Syria' while at the same admitting that three of seven victims were women.[93] For many former Taliban, another ideological shift they experienced when they joined IS-K that goes hand in hand with anti-Shi'ism is the extreme hostility to Iran, which turned it into a primary target. Although there had been serious friction between Taliban and the Iranian regime in the 1990s, and Shi'a were discriminated against in the Taliban Emirate of 1996–2001, from 2005 there was a rapprochement after which most groups of Taliban at one point or another had relations with Iran.[94] In many cases, however, more than convincing former Taliban recruits that Iran was now an enemy, IS-K attracted Taliban elements who were already hostile to Iran, but who rarely had been able to express their hostility while members of the Taliban. This was particularly the case of all the volunteers who had been to Syria, of course. In general, among Pashtuns there is an undercurrent of hostility to Iran for cultural reasons, which is likely to have made it easy for IS-K recruits to agree to serving under a leadership that denounced Iran.[95]

The role of regional rivalries

Whether or not and to what extent Saudi Arabia and Qatar supported IS-Central in the various phases of its history remains a matter of debate, as discussed in the Introduction. Saud Feisal is known to have stated to John Kerry that 'Daesh [an Arabic acronym for ISIS] is our [Sunni] response to your support for the Da'wa [Shi'a group in Iraq]'.[96] It is also known that US intelligence believed for years that Saudi Arabia and Qatar supported IS in Syria.[97]

Whatever the case for IS-Central, all IS-K sources and several external observers insist that IS-K received Saudi and Qatari support. Why would the Saudi government support an organization believed to have carried out attacks within Saudi Arabia itself, and believed to have planned more? Wouldn't the Qatari feel endangered too? When asked this question, Saudi, Qatari and IS sources converge at least in highlighting the traditional Saudi strategy of buying jihadist organizations off as discussed below. After all, AQ waged a campaign against the Saudi monarchy after the fall of the Taliban's emirate in Afghanistan, but by 2013–16 the Saudis and Qataris were back supporting Al-Nusra according to numerous reports.[98] It is even more realistic to believe that the Saudis would support IS-K, operating mainly in a remote country bordering Iran. The Saudis might be hoping that, by keeping IS-K busy far away from their own borders, they will reduce the chance of it becoming interested in doing serious damage at home. They might also be hoping to redirect IS anger against their own enemies.

A single source in the Saudi intelligence, although insufficient to build a strong case, provides a glimpse into Saudi rationales for supporting IS-K.[99] Interviewed in December 2014, the source summed up Saudi Arabia's aims in Afghanistan as establishing there an Islamic type of government which would have friendly relations with Pakistan, a Saudi ally, and unfriendly relations with Iran. Parallel aims included hampering the work of all groups linked to Iran, hurting Iran's interests, maintaining influence over the various jihadist organizations and supporting the aims of Pakistan. The Saudis started perceiving a growing Iranian encroachment in Afghanistan around 2013. They viewed the Iranian Revolutionary Guards as supporting Shi'as, but also as supporting one of several Afghan branches of the Muslim Brotherhood, Jamiat-i Islami, and as trying to co-opt Taliban leaders and groups, and they decided to become more active to counter that. Saudi intelligence also discovered forms of Pakistani–Iranian collaboration with regard to the Taliban that it did not like, and came to the conclusion that it was not wise to completely sub-contract its Afghanistan policy to the Pakistani authorities.[100]

The same Saudi intelligence source admitted providing support to IS-K was one of several tools in the struggle against Iran. The discovery of Iran having close relations with the Taliban appears to have shocked the Saudis and driven them towards seeking out more reliable jihadist groups. The Saudis did not believe that IS and particularly IS-K represented a real danger to them, as long as they were able to keep it financially dependent on Saudi support.[101] One IS-K recipient of Saudi funding thus explained their motivation for providing the funding:

> They helped so much the Taliban and now those Taliban are good with Iran. [The Saudis] mean to take those Taliban groups back from Iran and unify them with Daesh. In fact they want to end the Taliban movement completely and replace it with Daesh.[102]

An IS-K source involved in managing funding from the Gulf indicated in March 2017 that the Saudis had broken relations again with IS-Central, but were continuing to support IS-K.[103]

Similarly, the Qatari authorities appear to have lost faith in the Taliban because of its relations with Iran, which were becoming increasingly clear in 2013–14. According to a source in Qatari intelligence, while supportive of Taliban reconciliation with Kabul, in 2013 the Qatari authorities had already started supporting what would become IS-K, viewing it as a trusted anti-Iran actor at a time when Doha still viewed Iran as a likely threat. The source admits to hosting representatives of al-Baghdadi and IS-K in Doha. The Qataris intended for IS-K to eventually replace the Taliban as the dominant insurgent force in Afghanistan; the more moderate Taliban would reconcile with Kabul and the hardliners be absorbed into IS-K. The Qataris did not want IS-K to emerge as a dominant player very rapidly, however, and particularly not before the reconciliation between the Taliban leadership and Kabul government, which otherwise would derail.[104] IS-K also appeared to this Qatari officer to be an ideal platform for expanding support and improving the capabilities of Baluchi insurgents in Iran. Like the Saudis, the Qataris seem to think they have IS or at least IS-K on a leash, having made it dependent on their funding. He stated that the only possible way to bring Qatar's support for IS-K to an end would be if what the Gulf Countries perceive as Iranian expansionism were to come to an end. Like some other donors to the Taliban, the Qataris also had a sense that the Taliban were offering modest returns for the large sums received.[105]

Of course, the Iranians have not yet shown any intention of appeasing the monarchies by downscaling efforts to increase their influence. In Chapter 8 we discuss how it was Iran-supported Taliban who were at the forefront of clashes with IS-K in most provinces. It can be added that, from 2013 until mid-2015, the Haqqani network had relations with the Iranian Revolutionary Guards and not with the Saudis, according to sources within the Haqqani network, IS-K and the Quetta Shura Taliban. The Iranians started low-scale support to the Haqqanis in 2008, according to sources inside the network, and gradually increased it until 2013, when the Saudis discovered it and cut off their own funding to the Haqqanis. The Iranians then also despatched a few advisers to Waziristan and put pressure on Serajuddin to adopt a more confrontational attitude towards IS-K, contributing to the freeze in relations of late 2014. Relations between the Haqqanis and the Saudis were at their nadir at that time because of the arrest in Bahrain of Anas Haqqani, brother of Serajuddin, in which the Haqqanis suspected the Saudis had a hand. Only in the summer of 2015 was Saudi funding to the Haqqanis restored, as they cut off relations with the Iranians.[106]

According to an IS-K source, the Qataris are also pushing IS-K to open a new front in Central Asia. The rationale for that would appear to be a form of retaliation against Russia for its intervention in Syria, and an effort to force Russia to split its dwindling resources among several fronts. The Qataris' assumption is clearly that the Central Asian states, if threatened, would request Russia's assistance.[107]

2

THE ORIGINAL AIMS AND STRATEGY, 2014–17

If IS-K is not a mere exercise in opportunism and was indeed organically linked to IS-Central, it should be expected to produce and follow a relatively coherent strategy, based on aims going beyond the mere self-interest of its members. Aims and strategy should in turn be expected to match on the whole those of the parent organization, or at least be compatible with them. In this section, we discuss first of all IS-K's aims, which inevitably had different levels of priority. Because of the way IS-K has been operating, as a branch of IS and largely funded separately, it has had to rank fundraising first among its aims. IS-K's priority was therefore 'making itself useful', but this should not be taken as an indicator of 'opportunism' vis-à-vis IS-Central. Indeed, IS-Central itself pushed IS-K in this direction, as it could not afford to fully foot all its bills.

Moreover, IS-K's aims went beyond offering to fulfil whatever geopolitical aims its donors had. Aside from the fact that some of those aims were also IS-Central's own (such as retaliation for Syria), IS-K also tried to create a social base for itself by re-launching and expanding sectarian conflict in the countries of Khorasan. The establishment of safe haven(s) for IS leaders and a command centre in the region also implies that IS-K was more than an opportunistic imitation of the original IS-Central, exclusively focused on achieving or protecting local aims and interests.

The various aims of IS-K inspired the formulation of the organization's strategic choices. As discussed below, Afghanistan was chosen as the ideal platform for the landing of IS in Khorasan, being the weakest state in the region, with the least territorial control, but at the same time the most strategically placed, potentially giving access to Central Asia. In order to expand and consolidate its presence in Afghanistan, IS-K adopted a mixed approach: small groups spread around to mostly do recruitment, with a few strongholds where IS-K could build up its army. Although IS-K sources were evasive about military tactics and strategy, their operations as discussed in the coming sections suggest that it might have in mind replicating IS-Central's favourite 'blitzkrieg' approach to insurgency—concentrate force to achieve local superiority and rapidly conquer the enemy (see *The IS Model* in the Introduction).

In this strategy there was room for some flexibility. The trademark 'blitzkrieg' strategy, applied in northern Iraq as well, could not possibly apply to Iran, whose predominantly Baluchi insurgents could never plausibly represent a serious military challenge to the country's army and Revolutionary Guards. The same applies to China, no matter how many Uyghurs and Huis would join the ranks of IS. As for Central Asia, the prospect of anything approaching a 'blitzkrieg' was a distant one even as of early 2017. Finally, Pakistan mainly played the role of logistics hub for IS-K, at least until mid-2017. In all these cases, IS-K seemed intent on using terrorist and guerrilla tactics, at least for the foreseeable future.

IS-K's short-term aims

Establishing a beachhead in Khorasan: prioritize recruitment

IS-K's first priority was of course to establish a sufficiently solid presence in pockets of Khorasan, on which to start building a more sophisticated structure and from which to spread. The 'beachhead' metaphor catches well the character of this enterprise: a largely alien entity that needs to somehow disembark and gradually establish roots and organize itself. The 'landing' stage saw IS-K at its most vulnerable. The Taliban, the TTP and the Afghan and Pakistani security forces could have easily wiped it out if they had wanted or bothered to. This vulnerability was not just the result of IS-K's small initial numbers, or of its lack of consolidated safe havens. It also had to demonstrate its viability to prospective recruits and donors, some of whom were just advancing some funding to a new 'experiment'. An early failure could have compromised the venture for good.

In this context, it is perfectly natural and understandable that the leaders of IS-K and IS-Central might have set out some highly pragmatic initial goals and avoided advertising the 'landing' with too much fanfare. In particular, as will be discussed in detail in Chapter 8, IS-K initially sought forms of co-existence with the Taliban and TTP, even if it was already lobbying commanders and cadres of these two organizations to defect to its ranks. Also, IS-K's propaganda efforts were subdued, and even efforts to raise local taxes were banned for some months, possibly to avoid generating friction with the Taliban and TTP (see Chapter 7). Moreover, IS-K stayed well away from militarily challenging the authorities of any of the countries of Khorasan (see below, 'The primary theatre of operations: Afghanistan' and The 'Place of Pakistan').

Making itself useful: IS-K shops around for funding

As a newcomer in the crowded jihadist environment of Khorasan, IS-K's first and foremost aim has been finding a permanent place for itself in this environment. That meant in practice making itself useful or necessary to sectors of the local population, and perhaps more importantly to some of the regional powers. For IS-K and IS-Central, 'making itself useful' in practice often meant shopping around for funding aimed at any jihadist cause. IS-Central, for example, promised the radical Chinese Muslim groups it was negotiating with that it would start operations in China soon, and that it was making preparations for establishing a direct presence on Chinese territory.[1] IS-K sources link this effort to funds made available by private donors in the Arab Gulf specifically for this 'project'.[2] This plus the familiarity with the handful of Hui jihadists present in Syria and Iraq nonetheless prompted IS-Central to conceive the opening of a new front for jihad in Han China (as opposed to Xinjang). At the same time, IS-Central was getting closer and closer to the Uyghurs of ETIM, thanks also to the attraction IS had been exercising on the IMU and other Central Asian groups, with which ETIM mixes. Indeed, the input for opening a Chinese theatre of operations came direct from IS-Central:

> The leaders of Daesh have talked many times of China. They are telling us that we will do operations in Central Asia and China. 'You will work there on behalf of Daesh.' Our joining with Daesh is also for this purpose, that Daesh wants to perform operations and attacks in China. They said first we will go to Tajikistan and Central Asian Countries and then we will start operations in China.[3]

IS-K played an important role in attracting Chinese Muslims, as many of them were in Afghanistan and Pakistan when Wilayat Khorasan was announced. Although China itself falls beyond the area of responsibility of IS-K, Chinese Muslims based in Khorasan were supported and nurtured by

IS-K, and low-scale infiltration of China was organized mostly from Afghanistan and Pakistan. A large portion of the funds IS-Central mobilized for the cause of Chinese Muslims was therefore spent through IS-K. In particular, despite the close relationship with the TIP, IS was keen on galvinizing Huis and invested considerable resources in order to create a jihadist Hui movement inside China.[4]

Retaliating for Syria

A third aim of IS-K was retaliating against Iranian intervention in Syria and Iraq. One mid-rank commander admitted that, despite the rhetoric, Western targets ranked well below Iranian and Iranian-related targets in terms of priorities, because of Iran's role in fighting IS in Iraq and Syria.[5] Plans were made for targeting any group linked to Iran wherever it might be, including groups of Taliban linked to Iran.[6]

Targeting Russian interests in Afghanistan and Central Asia was a similar aim, due to Russia's intervention in Syria. Advisers sent from IS-Central were constantly pushing to start operations in Central Asia, as were donors.[7] Targeting both Russian and Iranian interests served not only IS-Central's purpose but was also again a way to make IS-K useful to donors, who had similar reasons for wanting to retaliate against these two countries.

Establishing safe havens

Another key aim of IS-K has been to develop in the short-term sufficient strength to establish at least one new spare safe haven in the region. This aim covered in fact two purposes: for IS-K to insure itself against pressures or repression by regional actors (as the Taliban were exposed to in Pakistan) and to be able to host leaders from IS-Central should the need arise.[8] By late 2016, elders in Nangarhar were hearing from IS-K fighters that Kunar was being turned into the organization's primary safe haven, where perhaps in the future even senior leaders from IS-Central might stay.[9] As part of this effort, IS-K tried to establish relations with local communities and elders, in order to create a safer operating environment.

IS-K's long-term aims

IS-Central and IS-K do not seem in principle to be satisfied with 'making themselves useful' as a long-term aim. They have greater ambitions than that.

Even if the premature launch of the Caliphate might well have been a trick to gain hegemony over the global jihadist movement, the establishment of the Caliphate is not mere rhetoric—it gives a real measure of IS's long-term ambitions. In the context of Khorasan, that means laying the conditions for the long-term sustainability of IS-K: gaining as much financial autonomy as possible; replacing or marginalizing all other insurgent movements in the region; and generating new types of conflict more in line with IS-K's 'mandate', such as sectarian conflict.

Forming an army

In line with the 'strategic culture' of IS-Central, IS-K appears to have intended to develop the facilities for shaping up a centralized and hybrid military force, well trained and led, capable of deploying quickly, outmanoeuvring its adversaries and concentrating and dispersing at will (see Chapter 4, 'Military organization').

Mobilizing local support for the IS-K's causes

Beyond the professional jihadists and some clerical networks, there was little or no social base of support for IS-K in Khorasan. A priority for the IS-K leadership was thus creating that support ex novo. That could be done by choosing sides in local disputes among communities, or by re-invigorating or starting anew conflicts, such as sectarian ones. Once established as a major insurgent organization, IS-K could also try to 'steal' the causes of competing jihadist organizations, for example taking the lead in the struggle to overthrow the 'puppet' Kabul government, the impious Pakistani one and the authoritarian Central Asian regimes (see Chapter 5, 'The local communities').

Taking over the jihad in Khorasan

IS-K also had the strategic aim of ultimately replacing the Taliban, TTP and other insurgent groups in Khorasan, establishing its own monopoly as it has been trying to do in Syria and Iraq. The original preferred path was a smooth co-opting of Taliban commanders and leaders, with violent confrontation to be postponed until IS-K achieved military superiority (see Chapter 8 for a detailed discussion of IS-K's early 'smooth' approach). In the early days of IS-K, a senior Pakistani in TKP candidly commented that IS-K's top priority was to absorb all other jihadist groups before setting out to seriously challenge the main enemy: Americans/NATO and Shi'as in Pakistan and Afghanistan.[10]

> Our strategy will be the same like Daesh strategy in Syria and Iraq. For example, in Syria there were many groups by different names like Al Shams and Al Nusra but now their fighters joined with Daesh. The same we want here all Afghan Taliban and Pakistani Taliban to become one group and our leader should also be Khalifa Abu Bakr Al-Baghdadi. We must be united not that they belong to TTP Maulana Fazlullah or Mullah Omar.[11]

The idea of absorbing the other insurgent groups derived also from the conviction that competitors like the Taliban and Hizb-i Islami would reconcile with Kabul, leaving many of their fighters and commanders free to splinter off and potentially be co-opted into IS-K. An officer in the Iranian Revolutionary Guards noted that one of the reasons why Tehran is against reconciliation between Kabul and the Taliban is that this would strengthen IS-K.[12] Indeed, Hizb-i Islami reconciled with Kabul in 2016–17, but with little apparent benefit for IS-K. As the prospect for Taliban–Kabul reconciliation seemed to fade during the first half of 2016, IS-K sources viewed their own prospects for fast growth as compromised:

> If Taliban do not do peace with Kabul Government, it brings a lot of changes to our plans. If Taliban did peace with the Kabul Government, maybe a lot of Taliban would join us.[13]

> It damages our plan because people do not join with us, but at that time when there were rumours of Taliban peace with Kabul, a lot of Taliban were joining with us.[14]

It might seem odd that, of all these aims, IS-K ended up putting so much focus on fighting the Taliban, as discussed in Chapter 8, even if IS-K has also made an effort to attack Shi'a targets in Afghanistan and Pakistan. However, as explained in Chapter 8, IS-K does not appear to have intended to spend so much of its energy and resources fighting the Taliban. Rather, it got entangled in local conflicts between rival Taliban commanders, some of whom joined IS-K and dragged it into their own fights, distracting the organization from its true strategic aims. The fight with the Taliban, as it actually developed in 2015 and 2016, can be described as tactical and ad hoc, while IS-K's strategic aims are regularly described by interviewees as very different.

Gaining financial autonomy

One of IS-K's subsidiary aims was to achieve a degree of financial autonomy, for example, by acquiring control over mining operations as a potential source of revenue.[15] An allegedly secret document recovered in Pakistan would also seem to support the idea of IS-K targeting sources of revenue in Afghanistan, which is confirmed by actual developments in 2016–17 (see Chapter 7).[16]

IS-K's strategy

IS-K's very ambitious aims, to be achieved against all odds, required a coherent strategy, formulated on the basis that maximum pressure should be exercised where resistance was expected to be weaker: Afghanistan. Although IS-K knew this would involve confronting the Taliban, Afghan army and at least Resolute Support (RS) air assets, Afghanistan with its many ungoverned spaces was still a better option than Pakistan, where the Pakistani army had been expanding control into the tribal areas for years. IS-K probably also expected to be able to navigate the Taliban's internal divisions, and to avoid facing American air assets by staying away from Afghanistan's main cities and highways (although this ultimately would not be the case).

IS leadership heard stories of Taliban weakness and internal divisions from the volunteers coming from Afghanistan, quite a few of whom had joined the Syrian/Iraqi adventure because they were unhappy with what was going on within their organizations (Taliban and TTP). It was expected that the Afghan authorities would not survive long after the withdrawal of the NATO combat mission. The choice was therefore an easy one to make: Afghanistan would become the keystone of IS-K's strategy. By contrast, jihad in Pakistan would be put on the back burner, with Pakistan to be used as logistical rear and safe haven for the early phases of IS-K expansion into Afghanistan and Iran.

The primary theatre of operations: Afghanistan

The grand picture of IS-K's strategy saw Afghanistan as its primary theatre of operations and future safe haven, while Pakistan only played a subsidiary role as a logistical hub.

> We want to transfer IS headquarter to Afghanistan, because Afghanistan is a mountainous country and we can defend ourselves very easily.[17]

Having secured a solid foothold in Afghanistan, IS-K would then export jihad to Central Asia and Iran, and later even to China and India. Most IS-K interviewees claimed that the organization's views of the Pakistani government did not differ from its views of the Afghan government: 'slaves of America', as a senior IS-K figure put it.[18] Despite the rhetoric against the

Pakistani government, a Pakistani ISI source admitted that no attack against Pakistani government targets had been carried out by IS-K as of January 2016, although there was an expectation that such attacks might start soon. All IS-K operations up to that point had been aimed at Shi'as in Parachinar, Charsada and Quetta.[19] Despite the 'jihad now and everywhere' rhetoric, therefore, IS-Central and IS-K have priorities; even a senior member of the Omar Ghazi component group, which had joined IS-K because of its promise to start a jihad in Central Asia as soon as possible, still rated Central Asia third in terms of the priorities of global jihad:

> We can say that Jihad is the duty of Muslims in the whole world. First in Afghanistan because it is captured by Americans, second in Syria, it is also important there because many Muslims are being killed. Third it is necessary in Central Asia.[20]

Within Afghanistan, IS-K would establish its presence by establishing bases in a number of strategic pivots and 'ink spots', from where it would spread its activities (see below). IS-K's influence beyond the 'pivots' and 'ink spots' (with the exception of parts of the north and north-east, where it was able to mix with the Taliban) was to be exercised mainly through small underground teams operating from hidden bases.[21] These underground teams would contact Taliban, elders, mullahs and others, laying the ground for future IS-K advances. Around the pivots, there would also operate IS-K groups trying to bring locations of economic interest (such as mining areas) under control while asserting control over areas not contested by IS-K's enemies.

The Nangarhar distraction

The main area of IS-K operations in 2015 and much of 2016 was Nangarhar province of Afghanistan. But was this a deliberate choice by IS-K? IS-K sources did try presenting this conflict throughout the second half of 2015 (after attempts to negotiate a smooth entry with the Taliban had ended in failure)—and in some cases up until spring 2016—as part of a grand strategy in which Nangarhar province was the first target in an ambitious plan to cut off Taliban supplies to Logar, Laghman and the north, as well as Taliban tax revenue from Nangarhar. In addition, control over Nangarhar would allow IS-K forces to cross easily from Orakzai to Tera and Bara, and vice versa.[22] These claims had some plausibility at the height of IS-K's offensive in Nangarhar: even a source in Haji Zahir's militia believed that IS-K had the aim of turning Nangarhar into its command centre and of relocating all its command and training assets there from Pakistan.[23]

> We want to make [of Nangarhar] a centre like North Waziristan. We could commute so easily from Afghanistan to Pakistan and Pakistan to Afghanistan.[24]

In reality, the Nangarhar conflict started in a haphazard way, and not as part of any ambitious plan. Even IS-K sources admitted that the close relationship with Shinwari elders (discussed in detail in Chapter 5) was a reason for IS-K's involvement in the province:[25] so one ad hoc reason, rather than a predetermined strategy to take Nangarhar. IS-K seemingly identified Mohmand Valley in Achin as one suitable pivot, because, on top of IS-K having some local support there, it is easily defensible from external attacks. Then other factors started driving this local conflict further. An IS-K cadre from Nangarhar, for example, reported pressure from donors to take Nangarhar, not least because important local (Nangarhari) actors were seen as being supported by Iran and Russia and thus needed to be humiliated. The same source also insisted that orders to continue fighting came from the very top of IS-K.[26]

As IS-K's fortunes in Nangarhar began to decline, a very senior IS-K source abandoned the claim that the Nangarhar fighting was part of a grand plan to seize the province, stating instead in January 2016 that the organization had no plans to capture whole provinces of Afghanistan for the coming 18 months. The source claimed that IS-K planned to expand it strength in Afghanistan to 20,000 before engaging in major operations. Then it would try to capture areas of the country which could produce high levels of revenue, and/or deny it to the Taliban, in Nangarhar, Badakhshan, Helmand and Kandahar. Until then, IS-K would limit its forays to some raids against Shi'as and small operations against the Americans and the Afghan government.[27]

In May 2016, a provincial-level leader admitted that IS-K did not plan a major offensive for 2016 and that Al-Afghani had ordered the prioritization of recruitment and establishing relations with the local population; that is, in practice they were to consolidate the beachhead established up to that point and work on the creation of safe havens.[28] This sounded like IS-K's original short-term aims (see *IS-K's short-term aims* above), to which IS-K reverted once enthusiasm for the easy successes of the summer of 2015 petered out. Two other senior sources in Azizullah Haqqani's group and Kunar's IS-K indicated that the top short-term priority of the group was to build up strength before starting operations against a whole range of enemies, such as the Americans, Iran and Shi'as, and the Afghan government.[29] According to IS-K sources, operations against US and Afghan government forces were withheld because of the conflict with the Taliban, confirming once again that the Nangarhar campaign and the conflict with the Taliban were not part of the original plan.[30]

An Arab adviser to IS-K communicated in December 2015 (before the rollback of IS-K in Nangarhar) a more realistic understanding of the organization's capabilities and prospects:

> There is such a gap between IS Khorasan and IS in Syria and Iraq. ... The IS which are in Syria and Iraq, they are very powerful, they have a lot of heavy weapons, tanks, anti-tank rockets, missiles, heavy artillery and a lot of cars. The number of the fighters of IS in Iraq and Syria are a lot. They are very powerful. Their income is also so much and they also have oil wells under their control. But IS-K is very weak; they started their activities recently. The IS-K does not have a lot of fighters; they did not have a lot of money here. They also have shortages in other fields for example they do not have modern weapons. Because IS-K in Afghanistan cannot collect tax easily like they are collecting in Syria and Iraq.[31]

No 'blitzkrieg' to Jalalabad and beyond, therefore, at least not in 2015–16.

Strategic pivots and ink spots

The ink spots of IS-K were essentially small strongholds in easy-to-defend positions. One example in Sherzad, Nangarhar, saw a force of 150 IS-K fighters take over three villages initially and then gradually expanding, depending on the human resources available. The group of 150 was mixed in composition: mostly Afghans with some Pakistanis, Central Asians and Chechens, and Arabs. The Afghans were from all over Afghanistan, very few being from Nangarhar, although the detachment commander was. Clearly a force of this kind was meant to establish and defend a stronghold, not operate around Nangarhar and mix with the population. The gradual recruitment of locals into the organization was meant to provide that capability at some point in the future (see also Chapter 5, 'The attraction of IS-K's wealth').[32]

The strategic pivots were large bases, usually acting as command centres and logistics hubs for hundreds of IS-K fighters. Contrary to the ink spots, which were only able to support small cells operating underground, the pivots were meant to enable large-scale conventional offensives. One of the first pivots was Mohmand Valley in Nangarhar, as discussed above. IS-K also initially chose Ghazni as another strategic pivot for carrying out operations against Shi'a enemies in Ghazni itself and Wardak.[33] The other pivot provinces were Badakhshan, Helmand and Zabul, to which the plan was added later to establish another one in either the southern districts of Jowzjan or in Sar-i Pul.

At the end of June 2017, IS-K captured its first district centre in the south of Jowzjan (Derzab), although it held it only briefly. Helped by Taliban defections, by mid-2017 IS-K controlled virtually all the rural areas of Derzab.[34] By the end of 2015, after Abu Yasir Al-Afghani had taken over as Special Representative of IS-Central (see below), IS-K was reverting to the short-term aims described above; the Nangarhar rollback helped IS-K re-assert more realistic goals. The next stage after setting up the ink spots and pivots and spreading out from them was meant to be the gradual absorption of all other jihadist groups sharing Khorasan with IS-K. The United States' assessment of IS-K's aims in late 2015 points in the same direction: the organization was trying to establish 'little nests' in various locations in Afghanistan. However, the United States also assumed that IS-K was serious about taking Jalalabad, and they missed the fact that some of the 'nests' were not that small (that is why we call them 'strategic pivots' here).[35]

In trying to establish its 'pivots', IS-K showed remarkable resilience. Compared to Helmand and Nangarhar, IS-K presence in Zabul was for a long time much more discrete. The first reports of IS-K presence in the province date back to January 2015, and concerned the districts of Khak-e Afghan, Daychopan and Arghandab.[36] The first attack claimed in Zabul on 23 February 2015 was dismissed by observers as belonging to an unclear perpetrator, even if local authorities attributed it to IS-K. Thirty passengers of a minibus, mostly Hazara returning from Iran, were kidnapped.[37] In May, the Afghan army reported a major operation and the seizure of a training camp, but seemingly these had little lasting impact.[38]

The second significant attack, with the beheading of seven residents of Khak-e Afghan, also caused little reaction, even with several residents reported to have fled the area due to IS-K activities, which included seizures of homes. An inflow of foreign militants, mostly Uzbeks, was also reported at this time.[39] In November 2015, the Taliban fought bitter battles against IS-K and IMU in Zabul—killing IMU's leader, Osman Ghazi—while the Afghan government and RS were still scratching their heads over whether IS-K was in Kabul at all.[40]

By mid-August 2016, RS sources were still claiming not to have seen any IS-K presence in Zabul province, despite locals reporting recruitment and training camps in Khak-e Afghan and Deh Chopan. The militants were reportedly well funded, were buying properties and were well equipped with satellite communications technology and in contact with Iraq.[41] At this stage, IS-K was mostly concentrated in the districts of Daychopan, Arghandab and Shajoy.[42] At the end of August 2016, Mawlavi Haibatullah Akhund, the

Taliban's supreme leader, ordered a large-scale offensive against a concentration of Wilayat Khorasan forces in the northern districts of Zabul province (Shahjoy, Deh Chopan and Arghandab) in Afghanistan's south. Haibatullah threw in all his reserves, which were, according to a Quetta Shura source contacted in September, as many as 8,000 men. IS-K accused Haibatullah of having enlisted Iranian help for the operation, including the direct participation of Iranian Special Forces. Taliban sources contacted in September confirmed that it was Iranian pressure that prompted Haibatullah to act, although he is likely to have seen the IS-K build-up as a direct challenge as well.[43]

Like the previous onslaught in late 2015, the offensive was successful. An IS-K source admitted that over 300 IS-K fighters and family members were killed. Among the victims were quite a few Uzbeks and Chechens. About twenty former Taliban commanders in Zabul, who had defected to IS-K, defected back to the Taliban, taking with them more than 180 men, according to Taliban sources in Quetta.[44]

Hurt but not wiped out, during November IS-K reinforced its positions in Zabul with deployments from all over Afghanistan. The IS-K reinforcements came from various places, such as Nangarhar, Paktia, Kunar and Pakistan, and from all the different sub-groups that compose Wilayat Khorasan. A source inside IS-K, contacted in November 2016, talked of 2,200 'members' in Zabul at that point, including 300 families (hence probably around 1,500 fighters or so), distributed between the districts of Deh Chopan, Khak-e-Afghan, Mizan, Naw Bahar and Arghandab. In addition to the 1,500 IS-K fighters, the source claimed another 300 IMU 'allies' also deployed alongside them. These figures are impossible to verify, but IS-K and IMU held these five districts against a Taliban offensive, by the Taliban's own admission. It is difficult to imagine this could have been achieved by a force much smaller than this. These forces have been placed under the orders of Wilayat Khorasan commander Qari Saifullah Kakar 'Al Khorasani', who as the name suggests is from the local Kakar tribe. Many Kakar tribesmen seemed to be flowing to the ranks of IS-K, a fact that might have contributed to the choice of north Zabul as one of the main bases of IS-K.[45]

Within the north and north-east, as of January 2016 IS-K was mostly concentrated in Warduj, even if the Afghan government's claims that IS-K's completely controlled that region were clearly overstated.[46] In April 2017, a source ranked the most important strategic pivots of IS-K as northern Zabul, Kunar and Mohmand Valley in Nangarhar. The northern pivots were still dependent on Kunar for supplies, a bottleneck that delayed their growth.[47]

Because the planned IS-K pivots were all in mountainous regions of Afghanistan, where Afghan government presence had disappeared during 2014, if not earlier, IS-K forces rarely clashed with Afghan security forces before late 2015. In line with the short-term aims discussed above, IS-K wanted to accumulate force before unleashing it against its enemies:

> In the future we will do such operations in Afghanistan as Daesh is doing in Syria and Iraq. It means most of our operations will be against foreign forces. The same we will have operations against the Afghan government. Like we will use bombs, suicide attacks, ambush and we want to capture areas.[48]

The timeline for the achievement of short-term aims and the transition to long-term aims fluctuated. In 2015, IS-K leaders were reportedly promising a massive offensive already in 2016, which would highlight the emergence of IS-K in Khorasan: 'Now we are sending the logistic supply to Afghanistan to start operations in the coming spring'.[49] Targets were supposed to be:

> Americans, Westerners, Afghan Government, Pakistan Government, those Shi'a groups who have link with Iran and Bashar-al-Asad. In Pakistan, Parachinar and Baluchistan areas and in Afghanistan those areas such as Bamyan, Daikundi, Herat, Midan Wardak and Ghazni. There are a lot of Shi'a groups which are helping Iran and Bashar-al-Asad.[50]

This would turn out to be an optimistic statement, as will be discussed below.

Stealing the Taliban's jihad

It is easy to note that, contrary to the plans mentioned in the previous paragraph, in 2015 IS-K efforts were concentrated against the Afghan Taliban throughout eastern, southern and western Afghanistan, even if the Taliban were not named in the two quotations above. It had always been understood that operations against Russian interests in Central Asia and Iran would require more preparation time. Meanwhile, IS-K sources claimed that their fight against the Taliban prevented them from starting operations against US and Afghan government forces, which remained their ultimate aim.[51] In reality, elders in Kot reported that IS-K teams entering their villages initially claimed that the Afghan government and people working for it were not their enemies, although that would later change.[52]

> It was around eight or nine months before that we heard that Pakistani Taliban belonging to Orakzai tribe who were operate in Kot district as Pakistani Taliban changed their flag and became Daesh Khorasan. When the Pakistani Taliban turned to Islamic Khalifate and raised up their black flag then spoke among the

villagers and elders and told the villagers that they have started a new Jihad against the Pakistan government. They told the villagers that they don't have any problem with the Afghan government and don't fight against the Afghan government. ... But later we were witness that they killed some schoolteachers, attacked Afghan government officials and later we understood that Daesh Khorasan or Khilafat-i Islami is established to fight against the Afghan government and Afghan people not Pakistan government.[53]

Early IS-K claims of being busy mostly with small-scale attacks against NATO and US targets in 2014 do not stand up to scrutiny.[54] IS-K in 2014–15 claimed many attacks in Kabul, Khost, Paktika (Yahya Khel), Pech and Nangarhar, in which it does not seem to have played any role.[55] In Kajaki, IS-K carried out a single attack on an Afghan army base before the Taliban overwhelmed them.[56]

The next large-scale attack against Afghan security forces in Nangarhar was in late September 2015, when IS-K forces assaulted the Achin district. Then, we have to wait until June 2016 before IS-K launched another large-scale offensive, this time against Afghan police in Kot, where the organization overthrew a few outposts. From then onwards, the Afghan security forces became IS-K's primary target in Nangarhar. In September 2016, IS-K launched a new offensive in Nangarhar, gaining ground in Achin, Kot and Haska Mina districts, exploiting the withdrawal of security forces from these areas.[57]

There are three possible reasons for this shift. One is an agreement of non-belligerence signed with the Nangarhar Taliban in May (see Chapter 8). Another is retaliation against the Kabul authorities for handing over TTP members—who might have entertained personal relations with former TTP members now in IS-K—to the Pakistani authorities. The third possible reason, and likely the most important one, is pressure from donors to show that IS-K was not just wasting energy fighting other Islamic groups like the Taliban, but was dedicated to aims more in line with its jihadist ambitions (see more on this in Chapter 8).[58] As IS-K was emerging from its infancy, it could no longer avoid the task that it had set itself, to take over the jihad against the 'Afghan puppet government' and the Western forces supporting it. Moving into that role was going to be essential to IS-K's efforts to establish a long-term constituency in Afghanistan.

IS-K's ability to carry out 'large offensives' was hampered in any case by its vulnerability to US air power. The drone strike that killed Khadim in Helmand in February 2015 could have been seen as a one off, as for some months no more noteworthy strikes were reported. The first unequivocal signal that IS-K was beginning to be perceived as a significant threat was the intensification of US air strikes against them in the summer of 2015, following IS-K's territorial gains in Nangarhar. The attacks were reportedly requested by the Afghan NDS, which was also improving its ability to track down IS-K targets. Hafiz Saeed Khan was targeted at this time but survived the strike. However, Shahidullah Shahid and Gul Zaman were killed during this wave of strikes.[59] At the beginning of 2016, US authorities publicly accepted at last that IS-K was growing, and they increased the pace of drone strikes against it, carrying out about twenty of them up to 11 February.[60] In June 2016, as IS-K forces amassed for attacking Kot district, US air strikes hit them hard again, this time actually succeeding in killing Hafiz Saeed Khan.

Despite the heavy losses incurred, carrying out these offensives against the Afghan security forces—and the of the fact that the Americans had gotten involved—allowed IS-K to present a more credible image of being a leading global jihadist organization than if it had kept fighting solely the Taliban. This would be in line with IS-Central's strategy, as discussed in the Introduction under *The IS model*'. The offensives might also have been meant to distract the Americans from IS-K's penetration of other areas, which were more viable for the establishment of safe havens and ink spots.

Spreading underground teams

IS-K calculated that low-profile underground groups would be difficult to detect and could therefore operate in challenging environments. For example, reports of an IS-K presence in Laghman, particularly in Qarghayi district, first appeared in December 2015 but were dismissed by the local authorities as unfounded.[61] In various locations, however, and particularly in the west and north, IS-K underground teams came under pressure quite soon. In Herat, for example, a local IS-K source claimed a presence in five districts of Herat as of December 2015, although it had not started operations yet, being busy building a support infrastructure.[62] Still, IS-K was promptly targeted in Herat by Iran's allies in the area, whether Taliban or local militias, and by December 2015 had lost about thirty men.[63] As of March 2016, IS-K was still in the early stages of penetrating the province of Balkh. In a raid of the security forces in Kishindih district, some militants and propaganda material were seized. Reportedly, there were signs of IS-K infiltration also in Zarai, Dawlatabad, Chaharbolak and Shulgara.[64]

When plans to establish a pivot or ink spot in a specific location failed, IS-K turned its presence in the area into a network of underground groups. An example of this is Helmand. Before the Taliban offensive, IS-K had four bases in Kajaki alone. There was a jail there as well, and patrols were visiting villages once a week. The forces of Mullah Naeem and Abdul Qayum Zakir, supported sometimes by Iranian special forces, destroyed the IS-K pivot along with its training camp in Kajaki in spring 2015. But IS-K did not disappear from Kajaki; it simply went underground and split into small groups. Reportedly, despite their withdrawal underground, IS-K still had a network of spies active, with cases of villagers being beaten on allegations of having links to the Taliban being reported.[65] By January 2016, IS-K's forces were still estimated at about 450 men dispersed around the districts of Kajaki, Musa Qala, Sangin and Girishk.[66] A year later, IS-K was still there, so much so that the Revolutionary Guards (Iran) had to put pressure on the Quetta Shura to clamp down on it again.[67] IS-K forces had camps in the mountains, mostly in Baghran, visiting villages perhaps once a month or once every 2 months, operating at night and staying in the mosque. Reportedly, they were discreetly recruiting local people in Kajaki, Marjah and Sangin, offering salaries of $400 per month.[68]

Taking over AQ's strategic safe haven

Initially not a primary focus of IS-K activities, Kunar rose in importance in spring 2016, after pressure on IS-K forces in Nangarhar reached the point where the leadership decided to withdraw most of the forces in favour of the more rugged terrain of Kunar.[69]

In Kunar IS-K established its main base in Sarkani district, with other smaller bases in Chapa Dara, Dara e Pech, Swaki and Marawara. Sources within the organization claimed to have brought 178 villages throughout Kunar under their control in the summer of 2016, up from 98 in January.[70] By September, IS-K was reported to be active in six districts of the province.[71] In December, IS-K forces in Kunar went on the offensive against the Taliban, significantly strengthening their positions in Nur Gul and Dara e Pech.[72]

IS-K sources admit that the migration of most forces from Nangarhar to Kunar from January 2016 onwards was dictated by the negative climate that had emerged in the former.

> In Nangarhar Province most of the people stood against us such as Haji Zahir, Taliban also and Afghan Government and the same the drones attacks increase against us and the number of our causalities were also a lot.[73]

The heavy losses inflicted by US air strikes on the IS-K leadership in Nangarhar spoke clearly: in 2015, Shahid Shaheed and Gul Zaman were killed; in 2016, Hafiz Saeed, Sa'ad Emarati and Mullah Bakhtwar; and, in 2017, Bakhtyar and Abu Yasir Al-Afghani. A devastating 21,000-pound bomb attack on a tunnel complex in Mohmand Valley (Achin) in April 2017, which was being used as command centre for Nangarhar, demonstrated that no fortification would hold if vulnerable to air attacks.[74]

In Kunar, by contrast, there was no such hostile environment (at least not yet). There were many hidden places for establishing training camps, and Kunar was also well placed to open a route to north-eastern Afghanistan.[75] Recruitment efforts in Kunar appear to have been bearing fruits, for example, in Sarkani. The truce with the Taliban, which only lapsed for a few months between September 2016 and early 2017, contributed to IS-K's successful penetration of parts of Kunar. At one point, its Kunar leaders were even negotiating with the Taliban the establishment of a shared courts system.[76] In all this, Kunar might not have differed too much from other emerging IS-K safe havens, such as northern Zabul. But there was a peculiarity to Kunar which made it attractive to IS-K as the main strategic safe haven, where even senior leaders from the Middle East might potentially find refuge. In Kunar, the village population, which had largely converted over the previous 40–50 years to Salafism, was supposed to be more sympathetic to IS-K, while the mountains and forests of Kunar were seen to be the perfect safe haven, even from drone strikes.[77]

> Here the drones cannot target us. From every point of view Kunar is a great place for us. Therefore, when we came to Kunar Province, we do not have any causality from drones or other sides.[78]

The place of Pakistan

IS-K sources usually presented the Pakistani government as an enemy, but for the first year and a half of existence of TKP no significant attacks were carried out against the Pakistani authorities.[79]

> Before they were creating problems for our logistics but now they are not creating any problems. Before they were seizing our goods and they said it is going to IS. But now they are not creating any problems. Even if they are creating problems, they are not a lot. They said you are using these goods against Pakistan so they seized our goods.[80]

In Pakistan, IS-K activities against government security forces were for the first 18 months of TKP's existence even more reluctant than against the

Afghan ones. In its early days, TKP leaders insisted that 'jihad in Pakistan' was one of their primary aims.[81] That had to be de-prioritized after IS-K came into existence. The merging of different groups into IS-K had the effect of making the component groups less parochial in their aims. For example, in the case of one of its small Pakistani component groups, Jaysh ul-Islam:

> Before the aims of Jaysh ul-Islam were Shi'as and Pakistan's Government but now our aims and targets are Shi'as, Pakistan's Government, Afghanistan's government and Iran's government. Our main enemies are Iran's Government and Shi'a.[82]

IS-K claims to have carried out several attacks against the Pakistani army in July–September 2015, and to have been targeted in army operations in Tera, Bajaur and Orakzai, but there were no reports in the media about them.[83] One of the few seemingly confirmed attacks was the decapitation of a Pakistani army prisoner, shown on a video released on 11 January 2015 which also featured Shahidullah Shahid (ex-TTP) pledging allegiance to IS.[84] The attack against the Pakistani consulate in Jalalabad in January 2016 also was attributed to IS-K.[85] Despite its high symbolic value, the attack was a rather isolated act. It might have been meant by IS-K to demonstrate active hostility against the Pakistani state (satisfying the demands of many members, former TTP hardliners), while inflicting only minor damage (therefore avoiding upsetting Arab Gulf donors or inviting stern retaliation).

As IS sources indicated in September 2014 that fighting the Pakistani authorities was a premature aim for them, the Pakistani authorities reciprocated by limiting themselves to 'monitoring' IS activities.[86] A source in Pakistani intelligence indicated that they were not taking the IS-K threat too seriously, at least as of January 2016:

> We do not worry about Daesh. These Daesh members are not the real ones who are in Syria. They are Pakistanis who raised the flags of Daesh. They will not become strong and we will also not allow them.[87]

An Afghan member of IS-K also believed ISI was adopting a neutral attitude towards the organization.[88] According to a source in the IS-K Finance Commission, the Pakistani authorities were aware already in early 2015 that IS-K was transferring money to Pakistan via the hawala system, but they did not move to prevent that from happening.[89] One source in Jaysh ul-Islam mentioned that after joining IS-K the group was ordered not to carry out attacks on Pakistani territory, but to help instead start operations in Iran.[90] Osman noted that the Pakistani army seemed to carry out operations against

IS-K with the purpose of pushing it across the border into Afghanistan, as opposed to crushing it or inflicting casualties.[91]

The self-evident restraint on both the IS-K and the Pakistani authorities' sides led to much speculation among Afghan observers, including Taliban, that the Pakistani security services were sponsoring IS-K.[92] Reconciled IS-K members in Afghanistan even claimed that equipment and funds were provided to IS-K by the Pakistani military.

> 'Pakistani military gave us weapons and used to tell us that Afghan forces are infidels and you must kill them,' said Zaitoon, a former Daesh fighter that joined the peace process. Arabistan, Zaitoon's co-fighter, said: 'I was tasked to fight in Nazian district [in Nangarhar]. We used to present our daily report to Punjabis and Pakistanis and they encouraged us to fight the Afghan government.'[93]

A Taliban source, who still had contacts in IS-K, reported in early 2016 that these contacts openly stated that the Pakistani ISI was supporting them.[94]

However, a donor to IS-K, contacted in January 2016, did not see any reason for the Pakistani authorities to adopt a soft policy towards IS-K other than the fact IS-K was not carrying out attacks against them. He insisted that he was keeping his activities secret from the Pakistani government.[95] The Pakistani authorities for their part claimed to have arrested numerous members of IS-K in Karachi and Lahore, including at least one Arab. They saw some risk of IS-K aggravating sectarian conflict in Pakistan, not least because the Revolutionary Guards (Iran) were expected to retaliate by arming Shi'a militias.[96] An ISI source denied ever having helped IS-K in Nangarhar and also denied bowing to Saudi pressure to let IS-K operate freely.[97] He admitted, however, that as of January 2016 IS-K had only been carrying out attacks against Shi'as in Kurram, Baluchistan and Quetta city, and never against the Pakistani government, although they were known to recruit and raise funds on Pakistani territory, with Westerners, Shi'as, Iran and Central Asia being their targets.[98] The Pakistani authorities also claim to have arrested a number of Pakistani citizens for supporting IS-K financially.[99]

The weight of the (limited) evidence discussed above is that for a good 18 months the Pakistani authorities oscillated between a wary tolerance of IS-K activities, with occasional efforts to contain them, and ad-hoc support when it suited their interest. A Revolutionary Guards (Iran) officer believed (in January 2016) that the Pakistanis did help and even train IS-K initially. The source pointed out that the Revolutionary Guards (Iran) passed on information about IS-K locations and individuals to the Pakistanis. That they failed to follow up, he believed, was because of Saudi pressure. However, by late

2015 the Pakistani authorities were turning against IS-K. The officer correctly foresaw that this would lead to IS-K starting operations in Pakistan soon.[100] Indeed, the Pakistani authorities did clamp down on IS-K's attempts to develop a network in urban Pakistan, attracting elements of other jihadist groups, particularly from Jamaat-ud-Dawa/Lashkar-e Taiba (JuD/LeT).[101] In January 2016, the ISI seemed to believe that they had dismantled IS-K networks in Karachi and confined it to the Pashtun north-west: Bajaur, Khyber, Lal Masjid, Lakki Marwat, Kurram, Hangu, Peshawar and Orakzay.[102]

Pakistani police sources consider the first serious IS-K attack in Pakistan to have been the May 2016 execution of forty-five Shi'as in Karachi, which was in fact claimed by Jundullah. Numerous targeted assassinations of police officers and a few attacks on schools and educational staff followed, all attributed to IS-K by the police.[103]

A source inside IS-K explained that the Pakistani authorities then started establishing relations with IS-K during 2016, as their relations with the Afghan government worsened again following the June 2016 border clashes.

> The relationship changed with Pakistan ISI after Torkham clashes between Islamabad and Kabul. Therefore Pakistan ISI's interest in us increased, they said, we will help you if your aim is only Afghanistan not Pakistan. They told us that they will also help us in logistics. Up to now we did not accept this offer. [Torkham] had a lot of effect on them and they are ready to help with us in every field. Before ISI was against us but now they do not do any operations against us in Pakistan.[104]

The Pakistani authorities at the same time started infiltrating IS-K to gather information about the goals and motivations of IS-K, and perhaps more. A source in Mullah Bakhtwar's group claimed to be receiving support from the Pakistani authorities and that the latter were trying to improve relations with IS-K in general. The source admitted that Mullah Bakhtwar's group was the only IS-K component group which had Pakistani advisers and made a point not to oppose (at least rhetorically) the Pakistani state.[105] Sources in the Haqqani network indicate that the Pakistani ISI also tried to use the network as another entry point for establishing its influence over IS-K, encouraging 'defections' from the network to IS-K. Haqqani network sources indicated in spring 2017 that Serajuddin Haqqani was using his former commanders inside the Azizullah Haqqani group as a lobby to influence IS-K towards dropping its jihad aims in Pakistan and China.[106] Then, as discussed in Chapter 6, there are some members of LeT that were allegedly encouraged by the Pakistani authorities to join IS-K in order to act as informants.

By mid-summer 2016, the picture was shifting again, with a series of bloody attacks claimed by IS-K against both civilian and Pakistani government targets. The August 2016 attack on the Quetta hospital, the October 2016 attack against the Quetta Police Academy and the attack on a Sufi Shrine in Baluchistan in November 2016 were all claimed by IS-K, and their participation was mostly confirmed.[107] The suicide bombing attack against a crowd at Quetta's hospital in August 2016 was carried out with the explicit aim of targeting personnel of the Ministry of Justice and the Pakistani police who were in the vicinity. Seventy people were killed.[108] Despite its main donors being opposed to destabilizing attacks in Pakistan, throughout December 2016 IS-K sources continued discussing plans to escalate attacks there. This might be the continuation of the empty rhetoric discussed above, or it might not.

By early 2017, a source in TKP pointed out that IS-K was making progress in building a presence in Pakistan's main cities, with about 1,200 members in Peshawar, 700 in Lahore, 240 in Islamabad and 750 in Quetta; according to this source, at least 40 per cent of IS-K members on Pakistani territory were in cities at that point.[109] Whether or not these figures accurately portray the reality, the general awareness of an IS-K presence in Pakistan began to grow, both in the media and in the state apparatus.[110]

However, this growing concentration of IS-K in cities, rather than being an indicator of the organization preparing for a sustained terrorist campaign, seemed to be more the result of the role of TKP in providing logistical support to the campaign in Afghanistan, and of the difficulty of holding groups in tribal areas due to the presence of Pakistani army operations. IS-K sources talk of planned future attacks against Chinese interests in Pakistan, of which there are plenty, and many of which are soft ones, such as schools, company sites, and so on. Reportedly, IS-K was pushed towards these targets by Uyghurs and Huis within its ranks, as well as by those it is negotiating with, who argued that there was no excuse for not attacking Chinese interests in Pakistan, where they are quite vulnerable. Some donors interested in a Chinese jihad threatened to reduce funding if IS-K did not fulfil its promises to carry out attacks against these targets.[111] IS-K, according to the sources interviewed, does not fear the Pakistani authorities, which have already worked to expel them from Pakistani territory.

IS-K might also have an interest in putting pressure on Pakistan with attacks not severe enough to destabilize Pakistan, but enough to remind its authorities and pro-Pakistan donors of the need to distract IS-K with incentives to focus its attention elsewhere. IS-K might have expected more toler-ance from the Pakistanis than they were willing to give, or it might have feared the long-term implications of Pakistan's alleged infiltration efforts (through 'defections' from Lashkar-e Taiba and some TTP factions).

The patient work of the ISI towards gaining influence within IS-K seemed to be paying off in May 2017, when a former commander of LeT, Aslam Faruqi, associated with the ISI was (controversially) chosen as new governor of Wilayat Khorasan (see also *Leadership rifts* in Chapter 9). The Pakistani do seem to have been pushing Faruqi towards finding a *modus vivendi* with the Taliban. Interestingly, a source in the Iranian Revolutionary Guard, when asked about the ceasefire between head of Quetta Shura Haibatullah and Faruqi's faction shortly before it actually collapsed, commented that the Iranians viewed it quite positively. Haibatullah was a major recipient of Iranian funding, so the Revolutionary Guards could easily have stopped the deal in the making if they had wanted to. Instead, the Guards accepted the view of the Pakistani ISI, that splitting IS-K was the most effective counter-insurgency technique and one, for that matter, which the Guards themselves had applied to the Taliban.[112] By weaning IS-K (Faruqi) off its dependence on Arab Gulf money, the Pakistanis would also reduce its need to actively target Iranian or pro-Iranian targets (real and presumed).

In any case, even with Faruqi in charge, IS-K's relationship with the Pakistani authorities remained somewhat unstable; some elements, especially within the ISI, supported IS-K, but most of the army was hostile, not least because of the presence of many former members of Lashkar-e Jhangvi in Wilayat Khorasan. In mid-2018, IS-K had resumed occasional attacks in Pakistan as well.[113]

By the end of 2018, according to one count, 10 'tier 2' leaders, 22 local leaders and 117 'tier 4' leaders (in fact cadres) had been killed or detained by the Pakistani security forces (mostly detained). According to such data, 2016 was the year characterized by the heaviest IS-K losses (84), followed by 2015 (32). Only 19 and 14 were lost in 2017 and 2018 respectively.[114] In 2015 alone, about thirty Pakistani citizens were reportedly detained for supporting IS-K financially.[115] Such data suggests a modest level of repression, although the fate of those detained is not known in detail.

Things calmed down in the latter half of 2018, but not for long. Taliban sources in the Quetta Shura, contacted in April, suggested that meetings with the Taliban during the first half of 2019 the attitude of the Pakistani army towards IS-K seemed to be hardening. This might be because in the US–

Taliban discussions, of which the Pakistani authorities have always been fully informed, the Americans were making clear that jihadism would have to be eradicated from Afghanistan as part of the peace process. Pakistan was betting on a successful peace process in Afghanistan achieving a rapprochement for itself with Washington and did not want to spoil its chances by being seen supporting IS-K in Afghanistan. In any case, IS-K cadres were saying in June 2020 that they still had access to their camps in Pakistan and could move freely over the border. IS-K still has camps in Pakistan in the areas of Jang, Muhmand Agency and Tira. It also shared some camps with Lashkar-e Taiba people in Lahore too. An IS-K source operating near the border admitted that it would be very hard for them to function if the Pakistani ISI blocked their access to military camps in Pakistan and their supply routes. Some IS-K sources attributed the tension with the ISI to its pressure on IS-K leaders to send volunteers to Kashmir.[116]

The alliance with the Pakistani ISI intelligence also suffered because of the pressure exercised by the ISI on IS-K to expel all Uyghurs from its ranks and even take action against them. IS-K steadfastly refused.[117] The ISI was also putting pressure on IS-K to improve relations with the Taliban, but they refused this also because of the Taliban's relations with Iran and Russia.[118]

IS-K's relationship with Pakistani intelligence was never approved by IS-Central. The Caliphate describes the Pakistani ISI as the 'colleague' of British intelligence. IS-K has been arguing that it needs to maintain this relationship temporarily, while it recovers strength and reaches the ability to operate in a more independent way.[119] The Pakistani intelligence services, on the other hand, push for a deepened relationship with IS-K, and the organization is divided internally about how to respond.[120]

Friction re-intensified in the late summer of 2020 when the ISI asked IS-K to ally with various other groups and splinters of the Taliban and Hizb-i Islami, in order to mount a campaign of targeted assassinations in Kabul. Eventually, the Pakistanis blocked the supply routes of IS-K and threatened action in Pakistan if IS-K did not agree, which in the end it did. The Pakistanis wanted IS-K to re-direct its military operations against the Afghan government, after they had been focused on the Taliban in 2015–19.[121] IS-K also agreed with the ISI's request to launch its campaign of targeted killings in Jalalabad.[122] The campaign gave IS-K visibility and allowed it to claim it had returned to Nangarhar, after pulling out at the end of 2019.

The relationship with Pakistani intelligence is controversial within IS-K too. As of early 2021, Wilayat Khorasan governor Shehab al Muhajir himself was reportedly opposed to the relationship with the Pakistani services, and Abdullah Orakzai agreed with him. However, the majority of the leadership council was in favour of the relationship because IS-K could not go alone and needed Pakistani support, especially as IS-K logistics remained dependent on Pakistan.[123]

Polarizing violence: the campaign against Shi'as

An approach which IS-Central adopted is setting off sectarian conflict in order to mobilize support among Sunni population by posing as their protector and saviour. This strategy is of course characteristic of IS-Central, as well as of its predecessor organizations, from the time of al-Zarqawi onwards. The strategy, however, could not always be implemented without facing serious obstacles. Although the Revolutionary Guards (Iran) consider IS-K to be aiming to incorporate all sectarian Sunni organizations in Pakistan and start a sectarian civil war, IS-K sources paint a picture of donors discouraging them from destabilizing Pakistan (see 'The place of Pakistan' above).[124]

Instead, from the beginning there appears to have been a strong slant towards attacking Shi'as. Setting off a sectarian conflict in Afghanistan at least is one of the IS-K aims identified above.

Already in January 2015, night letters bearing the IS logo appeared in the Hazara neighbourhoods of Kabul, denouncing Shi'as as infidels.[125] It is not clear whether this was the result of organized IS-K activity, or an action by sympathizers not yet connected yet with the actual organization. The first actual attack against Shi'a in Kabul occurred during the Ashura of 2015 (October); a small bomb was planted outside a Shi'a mosque, killing one and injuring several. It was also the first attack by IS-K ever in Kabul. Clearly, at this point IS-K operational capabilities in Kabul were very limited.[126]

Outside Kabul and in Pakistan, IS-K was able to carry out bloodier operations even in the early months of its existence. IS-K claims to have carried out several major attacks against Shi'as in Pakistan and Afghanistan, including one in Parachinar, where tens were killed; one in Karachi against a bus; one in Zabul; and one in Balkh.[127] Some of these attacks, however, were not confirmed by local authorities as having been carried out by IS-K.[128] In Ghazni, IS-K claimed in March 2015 the kidnapping of a group of Hazaras, accused of being on their way to Syria via Iran.[129] Another attack occurred in November 2015, in which seven Hazara civilians were killed. Typically, including in the Ghazni attacks, IS-K sources denied having hit civilians such as women and children, and claimed instead to have targeted only 'those Shia who were working for Iran government, and they were sending people to Syria and Iraq and they were fighting against us'.[130]

IS-K capabilities in Kabul had improved significantly by the summer of 2016. The attack against the demonstration of the Enlightenment Movement in July at least implied a relative sophistication in its preparation of explosives, even if IS-K sources admitted that it was a failure because two of three bombers could not reach their targets.[131] However, like the Ashura attack of October 2016 and the attacks against a Shi'a mosque in November 2016, the July bombing implied a modest capacity to organize complex attacks.

In comparison, the picture concerning attacks against the Shi'a community in Pakistan is murkier. The situation in Pakistan is complicated by the fact that most attacks claimed by IS-K have been claimed by other groups as well, making it unclear how much IS-K has really been doing on this front. But only a single major attack against a clearly Shi'a target was claimed by IS-K.[132]

As mentioned above, re-launching and expanding a sectarian conflict in Khorasan is one of the pillars of IS-K's strategy, as this would create for itself a large social constituency (among the Sunni population) and embed the organization in the social fabric of the region for the long term. It should be noted in this regard that Pakistan's social and political environment appears to offer much more fertile ground than that of Afghanistan for efforts to kick-start a sectarian conflict. Here IS-K's strategy seems to have had to adapt to the realities of funding and of donor priorities.

Co-opting the Baluchis

IS-K's aim of starting operations inside Iran implied a determined effort to gather Baluchi insurgents within the organization. This was seen as an easy task because the Iranian Baluchis were obviously eager to start or boost operations inside Iran. Even before IS-K came into existence the Baluchi insurgency in Iran was gaining steam, allegedly thanks to increased funding from the Arab Gulf. As of 2014, there were four separate groups fighting against the Islamic Republic of Iran, with a combined strength of about 2,000–2,500 men according to both a member of one of these groups and the Revolutionary Guards (Iran).[133] While this might seem a modest number compared to other jihadist organizations in the region, it is quite large relative to the population of Iranian Baluchistan (about 1.5 million). The trend in recent years has been moving away from a nationalist insurgency, towards a jihadist one. It was natural for IS-K to position itself as the ideal home for all these groups, offering expanded funding. According to a very senior source in IS-K, the big push towards Iran came from the advisers sent from IS-Central and IS-K obliged.[134] Donor sources also indicate strong interest in fostering the Baluchi insurgency inside Iran.[135]

Co-opting the Central Asians

IS-K's claims to have started laying the ground for a Central Asian jihad early on. Already in 2015, the Omar Ghazi Group reportedly sent reconnaissance elements to Central Asia, to lay the ground for operations, which were planned to start in 2016 in Tajikistan, Uzbekistan and Turkmenistan.[136] Recruitment activities were reportedly expanded to Uzbeks and Turkmen in Pakistan, Samarkand and Buchara.[137]

While these preparatory activities were going on, IS-K needed to attract the attention of potential Central Asian recruits and reassure its members that it was not fighting a phony war. The first actual attack carried out in Central Asia was against the Chinese embassy in Bishkek, and was for the most part intended to attract Chinese jihadists to IS ranks (see 'Co-opting the Chinese Muslims' below). Kyrghiz government sources described the attack as being the result of TIP co-operation with Fatah as-Sham (formerly Al-Nusra), the Syrian jihadist organization which until recently had called itself a branch of Al-Qaida. The Tajik authorities, however, linked the attack to IS and reported the involvement of Tajik IS activists in forging fake documents and supporting the operation logistically. Indeed, it is hard to see why Al-Nusra/Fatah as-Sham would want to sponsor an attack in such a remote location at a time when it was trying hard to distance itself from Al-Qaida, the more so as a Fatah as-Sham source denied any involvement.[138]

IS sources in Kyrghizstan suggested that the suicide bomber was an Uyghur operating within Al-Nusra's ranks until 6 months prior, when he switched to IS. This could explain the Kyrghiz interpretation of the source of the attack.[139] According to IS Kyrghiz sources, IMU and IS Tajiks and Kyrghizs also participated in both the planning and the supporting of the attack. IS-K sources in Kyrghizstan indicated at that time that IS was planning more attacks against symbolic targets, such as Russian embassies; other Chinese and Russian targets such as pipelines, businesses and schools; as well as assets of the Central Asian governments.[140] The sources indicated that the new IS-Central head of military operations, former Tajik security officer Gulmorad

Halimov, was particularly keen on starting operations in Central Asia.[141] IS-K sources alleged that in both Kyrghizstan and Tajikistan it could count on the complicity of government officials, who either had sympathy for IS or were being bribed.[142] These claims have some credibility, given that high-quality fakes of Tajik passports have been used by jihadists, including those involved in the Bishkek attack. How durable or widespread such support is, however, is impossible to confirm at the moment.

Co-opting the Chinese Muslims

The assertion that it would start a jihad in China (and not just Xinjang) was a big step to take for IS-K, given that at the time when it was starting to attract Chinese Huis no organization was anywhere close to acquiring the capacity to start violent operations in Han China. Within a couple of years, almost all sources within the Hui jihadist diaspora, both within IS-K and without, agreed that IS-K had indeed made some progress towards laying the groundwork for starting operations in China: in particular, recruitment cells were established, a few trained activists were smuggled back into the country and some basic infrastructure was being set up. IS-K was not even publicly advertising its Chinese branch, aware of its extreme vulnerability to a crackdown in these very early stages of development. It claimed that its strategy was to wait until the Chinese branch had 3,000–4,000 members before starting operations and open propaganda activities.[143]

In Afghanistan and Pakistan, the policy was to keep Chinese Muslims away from unnecessary risks; their presence in Afghanistan was so they could be trained and earn some battle experience. For this purpose, they were dispersed in very small groups accompanying IS-K around Afghanistan. Occasionally they would get caught in fighting; seven Chinese Muslims were killed in north-western Afghanistan in May 2016 during an offensive of the militias of Gen. Dostum and another one in Achin.[144]

While the preparations for a Chinese jihad were under way, IS-K started advertising its role in mobilizing Chinese Muslims by organizing the August 2016 attack against the Chinese embassy in Bishkek, as already discussed above. It had been a botched attack, launched without sufficient preparations, with part of the terrorist team failing to deploy and only minimal casualties inflicted. IS-K did not even openly claim it, and it was advertised to Chinese jihadists within and without IS-K as the first of a series of attacks that would demonstrate IS-K's capacity to support the cause of Chinese jihad.[145] IS-K expanded its Chinese membership rapidly by promising the rapid opening of a Chinese front, but it had to work out how to effectively start operations against Chinese targets.[146] At the end of 2016, Gulmorad Halimov, the successor to Shishani at the head of the IS Military Commission in Iraq, was reported to be putting pressure on IS-K to carry out attacks against Chinese targets as well. Uyghurs and Huis in IS were also putting pressure on IS-K to carry out attacks against Chinese interests, be they the embassy or business activities, in Afghanistan.[147]

3

EFFORTS TO 'SYNCHRONIZE' IS-K WITH IS-CENTRAL

IS-Central probably realized that mere sympathy for global jihadism and Salafism did not amount to a coherent ideology on which a solid and cohesive insurgent organization could be founded. Hence, the leadership hoped that the despatch of trainers, advisers and large numbers of volunteers to Syria and Iraq would help in upgrading the superficial shared ideology of most IS-K members to something more solid. Similarly, IS-Central acquired a non-homogenous set of affiliates in Khorasan who lacked a coherent organization. The only way IS-K was going to achieve anything in line with IS-Central's aims and strategy was by upgrading organizationally.

Vice versa, an increase in organizational skills compared to the standards of the region and the emergence of an ideology closer to that of IS-Central are possible indicators of external input, which in turn is another benchmark of a close relationship between IS-K and IS-Central. Evidence of the transfer of organizational skills would further confirm the source of this change. Were these new skills being imported from the Middle East? If so, how? In order to demonstrate the link between IS-Central and IS-K, it is necessary to have the presence of trainers and advisers, and/or the transfer of IS-K members to Syria and Iraq for acquiring skills locally.

The agents of organizational skills transfer: trainers and advisers

In the early day of IS-K's existence, the commitment of human resources by IS-Central was modest. As of April 2015, according to a senior source within

IS-K, there were just 30 advisers and 45 trainers despatched from IS-Central with IS-K, accompanied by protection teams counting in total 205 fighters and commanders. Mostly these advisers were from Iraq, Syria, Yemen, Libya and Egypt, as well as from Pakistan and Afghanistan.[1] Eight months later, the number of trainers and advisers had gone up to 250, if we believe one of these advisers (see Table 1).[2]

The number may appear high, but it is not altogether implausible if we consider that, according to sources in the Pakistani intelligence agencies, by mid-2016 200 'foreign IS activists' who had entered the country illegally were being sought (consider that quite a few of the trainers and advisers were Pakistanis and Afghans, sent back from Syria). In addition, an undisclosed number of individuals, also suspected of having something to do with IS-K, were entering Pakistan legally with Syrian travel documents.[3]

The number of trainers had been steadily increasing from spring 2013 onwards, when IS-IL was already sending trainers to Pakistan and Afghanistan to prepare the volunteers for deployment to Syria and Iraq, but there was a big acceleration in winter 2015. In part, this increase reflected the overall growth of IS-K, but it also reflected a greater commitment by IS-Central to build up the capacity ISK lacked in the financial, logistical and military fields. That was happening at a time when IS was under growing pressure in Syria and Iraq, highlighting how the IS leadership viewed 'Khorasan' as a strategic theatre of operations.[4] There seems to have been an expectation of even greater IS-Central involvement in training and advising IS-K: a source indicated in early 2017 that by the summer of that year the number of advisers and trainers from IS-Central were expected to reach 400.[5] It is not clear whether this target was actually reached, as movement between Iraq/Syria and Khorasan became very difficult from the second half of 2017.

In addition, some IS-K sources alleged that advisers were also sent by some of the donor countries. TKP, for example, had sixty-five advisers in December 2015, including many sent from Qatar and Saudi Arabia rather than from IS-K (Table 2). The Muslim Dost Group, Jaysh ul-Islam, the Bakhtwar Group and the Azizullah Haqqani group all had advisers from Qatar and/or Saudi Arabia, according to internal sources. The number of advisers fluctuated seasonally, so during the summer of 2015 their number might have been even higher. In the case of TKP just mentioned, the number of sixty-five was considerably lower than it would have been in the summer.[6] However, there is no confirmation of the presence of these advisers outside the claims of a single IS-K source.

Reportedly, advisers and trainers were distributed between the component groups and the top structures of IS-K. Each IS-K commission got two to three specialist advisers.[7] For example, the Logistics Commission had two Arab advisers in November 2015, as well as twenty trainers from Pakistan and Afghanistan who imparted two-month courses.[8]

Table 1: Deployment of IS-K advisers and trainers

Quarters	Number of trainers and advisers
I 2013	0
II 2013	10
III 2013	10
IV 2013	13
I 2014	13
II 2014	13
III 2014	13
IV 2014	18
I 2015	37
II 2015	45
III 2015	–
IV 2015	250

Sources: Interviews with IS-K cadres and commanders, 2015–16.

Table 2: IS-K advisers and trainers by origin, 2015–16[9]

	Qatar, Saudi Arabia	Syria, Iraq	All Arabs	Pakistan, Afghanistan	Others	Unknown
Trainers						
IS-K	–	7	–	28	–	5
Advisers	–	–	–	–	–	–
Shamali Khilafat	–	–	14	–	–	–
TKP	45	15	60	–	5	
Khilafat Afghan	–	–	37	–	–	–
Muslim Dost	8	–	–	–	–	–
TKK	–	–	38	–	–	–
Jaysh ul-Islam	13	–	–	–	–	–
Bakhtwar	5	–	–	14	–	–
Harakat	–	5	–	–	–	–
Azizullah	18	–	–	–	–	–

The advising effort

As of June 2015, the advisers corps was led by Abu Tahir Turkmani, from Iraq, with Abu Mohammad Al Tawani (another Iraqi) as deputy.[10] Reportedly, advisers mostly travelled to Qatar or Saudi Arabia from Iraq, then from there to Pakistan, flying on commercial flights with visa and passport, whether fake or genuine.[11] The typical shift for an adviser was 6 months; some would re-deploy there after a three-month break, while others would be replaced. Those re-deploying would benefit from an increase in salary.[12]

This intensification of the direct presence of IS on the ground allowed a much wider effort in transferring organizational skills to IS-K. IS-K sources claimed that in training and advising IS-K introduced a new concept, compared to the Taliban. According to internal sources, the advisers despatched by IS-Central tended to be specialists in a particular field, based on requestt send by IS-K to Mosul.[13]

> For example if we have problems in the field of logistics, the logistics adviser is sent to us and he is giving advice to us, if we have problems in the field of finance, the finance adviser is sent to us and he is giving advice to us in that field. In the recruitment field the adviser of recruitment is sent to us, in the field of military, military adviser is sent to us, in the field of planning, planning adviser is sent to us and the same for other fields.[14]

In reality, the Taliban too had specialist advisers, although in smaller numbers relative to their membership. Many former Taliban who switched sides and joined IS-K might never have met a 'specialist' adviser to the Taliban, so the sources were not necessarily lying when they claimed this to be a major IS-K innovation.

The advisers sent to train and mentor IS-K were reportedly stressing the need to train adequately before deployment, and to select people of adequate professional skills in senior positions, before deploying to battle.[15] Advisers would assist the military commanders in the field as well. One adviser interviewed for this project explained how the advisers accompany IS-K groups in battle in order to monitor their activities and their implementation of what they were taught.[16] That the advisers accompanied IS-K forces to the battlefield seems to be confirmed by their casualty levels. According to one of the advisers himself, up to December 2015, eighteen advisers were killed: fifteen in Afghanistan and three in Pakistan, with four more detained in Pakistan. All were combat losses (except the arrested ones) and nobody was lost en route to Khorasan, according to the source. The losses occurred in Zabul, Nangarhar,

Farah, Badakhshan, Orakzai and Bajaur.[17] In areas of intense American air operations, advisers had to be mostly pulled out to avoid casualties.[18]

The advisers seem to have assisted IS-K provincial-level leaders and were rarely seen at the bottom level of the IS-K structure. According to IS-K commanders in Kajaki, four to five Arab advisers were based in the district, but they visited the teams in the villages rarely.[19]

The training effort

The trainers instead provided basic courses to the mass of IS-K members. Typical profiles of a trainer/adviser are the following:

> The name of our trainer is *** and he is from Saudi Arabia, Riyadh. He was born in 19**. In 19** he went to king Abdu Aziz military Academy in Saudi Arabia. In 19** he was graduated from this academy. He had job there in military and in 20** he left the job and went to Syria. He was giving training to Daesh there. He has been with Daesh since 2013. In 2014 he was there in Syria. Now in 2015 he is in Afghanistan.[20]

> The adviser's name is ***. He was born in Homs City of Syria in 1965. In 1985 he came to Pakistan .... In 2005 he was an adviser with Taliban (Dost Mohammad front). In 2013 he went to Syria and I was also with him. In 2015 he joined Khorasan Province. He joined Daesh in 2013 and he is still with Daesh. Before he joined with Daesh, he was running a madrasa and he also worked as an adviser with the Taliban.[21]

As described by the sources, the typical course was 3–8 hours per day, every day, depending on the subject: military training was the most intensive, while in other fields like finance, recruitment and logistics the courses were usually 2–3 hours per day.[22] The courses taught by the advisers and trainers varied in length between 2 weeks and 4 months.[23] The standard 4-month course was divided in two parts. The first 3 months were called *Dura-e Khaas*, where the focus was on teaching IS rules and regulations and basic training. The fourth month was called *Dura-e Khatam* and was a course specializing in one of the military, training, logistics, finance, recruitment or other fields, chosen by the trainee.[24] Then, every month or two the advisers would also gather the commanders for seminars lasting up to 2 weeks to share new ideas.[25]

Training was mostly focused on military, logistics and finance, include tax raising.[26] The military training imparted included:

- bomb-making;
- tactics;

- weapon skills (particularly with US weapons, to which the former Taliban and TTP were not accustomed);
- communications;
- military intelligence (how to assess the weaponry in possession of the enemy, and their numbers, how to trace the source of artillery fire);
- personnel management—how to select qualified commanders.[27]

IS military advisers stressed the need to disperse combat groups and co-operate between different IS-K components.[28]

> The tactics of Daesh are different. They are professional. They are fighting in such a way as to have no causalities. Before Daesh wants to start fighting, they collect intelligence and assess how to perform the attack, which is the weakest point of the enemy, but Taliban are not doing these things. They are using mass attacks and they do not think about causalities.[29]

As of early 2017, IS-K had made sparing use of suicide bombing. The first main terrorist attack possibly involving IS-K was a suicide bomber hitting a branch of Kabul Bank in Jalalabad, on 18 April 2015. The attack took place at a time when soldiers and policemen were withdrawing their salaries, killing thirty-five. Although IS-K claimed the attack and the Taliban denied it, the attack was odd because at that time IS-K was not targeting Afghan government forces except in northern Afghanistan, and would not do so for some for several more months.[30]

The April 2015 suicide bombing in Jalalabad (Kabul Bank) was not attributed with certainty to IS-K. Further, RS sources claim that the attack on the 'Enlightenment' demonstration in Kabul in July 2016 was not a suicide attack at all, but rather a bomb hidden in the street; and the Ashura attack of October 2016 did not involve the attackers blowing themselves up. Only the January 2016 suicide attack against Obeidullah Shinwari's house in Jalalabad, the attack on the Pakistani consulate in the same month, the November 2016 attack on a Shi'a mosque in Kabul and the attack on Mullah Salam (Taliban governor of Kunduz) in January 2017 were unquestionably suicide attacks.

Given that IS as a whole showed no reluctance towards employing suicide bombing, the limited use made by IS-K in 2015–16 might be attributable to the technical difficulties and long lead time required to prepare 'efficient' suicide bombers, assuming IS-K failed to attract any of the suicide bombing teams which were part of TTP and Taliban. IS-K and Haqqani network sources say this was the case for the Afghan Taliban until autumn 2016 (see Chapter 4, 'Shahadat'). Interestingly, none of the interviewees, when asked about IS-K's main innovations in any field, volunteered indiscriminate suicide bombing (however described) as an answer, despite defending other IS-K techniques such as decapitations.

The training was reportedly more sophisticated than what the Taliban had been getting, although not all IS-K was being taught was necessarily of much use:

> They teach in training when we must use the mines, Taliban are placing mines under the earth, but we place in different areas like in the trees, in drains, and we also make small drones that carry mines and can be blown up.[31]

The advisers are also reported to be the source of the 'meritocratic' impetus which IS-K sources constantly discuss (see above).[32]

> [Our trainers] have worked in the logistics field in Iraq and Syria. We learnt so much from them in two months training. We also had advisers before but they were not as intelligent as these two are. They have experience, how to distribute supplies, how to keep the logistics and how to allocate the logistics and they gained a lot of professional skills in Iraq and Syria. ... The advisers and trainers who were working with Taliban were not professional and they did not have experiences in the field of logistics.[33]

Limitations of the training and advising effort

The training provided was sometimes rated very highly by interviewees.[34] Even local sources sometimes confirmed that IS-K's efforts to indoctrinate recruits were quite effective.[35] In reality, however, the training and advising effort was not exempt from problems. It is also not clear to what extent IS-K operations in the field were genuinely affected by the training. At the bottom of the IS-K structure, there was little sense of military innovation taking place in the early days at least:[36]

> They are doing training in the mountains but the way of fighting is same like Taliban. I haven't seen any changes on the way of fighting between the Taliban and Daesh Khorasan.[37]

> The way of fighting has not changed, only we were told to cover our faces when we are going to fight, we were told to take care of the civilians casualties during the fighting and to take care of our injured fighters during the fighting. When I was with Taliban, our senior commanders didn't care about our injured fighters, Taliban don't care about the civilians' casualties ...[38]

Some of the fighters at least seem to have believed that they did not need IS organizational skills to be transferred to them:

> No we haven't got courses for new tactics of fighting, we are not trained and we don't need to train because we know fighting, we know the area and district very well.[39]

Even among those receiving training, not every group was exposed to the same amount of training. A group commander in Kajaki, for example, received just 5 days of training, including a superficial description of the aims of the organization.[40]

One problem faced by trainers and advisers was language skills. Interpreters were used, but often were not up to par. Interaction between trainers and trainees was therefore often problematic. IS-K organized courses in local languages (at least Pashto and Baluchi) for the Arabs deployed to support them. Arabic language courses were also organized for IS-K members.[41] As of November 2015, according to IS-K sources, there were sixteen teachers of Arabic in Pakistan and more than fifty in Afghanistan tasked with teaching languages, and IS-K decided to send an additional sixty interpreters to Pakistan for intensive training in Arabic to resolve this problem.[42] These numbers may seem high, but not if we take into consideration other IS-K claims about the number of members and of trainers and advisers. In fact, there seems to have been shortages of interpreters, and they also appear to have been of poor quality:

> These advisers have language problems, we do not understand very well their communications. There are also not good translators and they cannot translate well. Yes what these advisers are instructing to us, we do not get the complete purpose of it.[43]

The advisers sent to Khorasan were first of all given 2 weeks of a cultural awareness course before deployment, where they were taught what they had to be careful about.[44] The advisers do seem to have done some preparatory work and made an effort to take local conditions into account, at least at the technical level:

> the geography of Afghanistan is different from the geography of Syria and Iraq. For examples the mines and bombs which IS [is] using in Syria and Iraq are not available here in Afghanistan, so we are showing them the way of new mines for which materials are easy obtainable here in Afghanistan. Second we show them different fighting tactics, because the tactics which we showed to IS in Syria and Iraq are not working in Afghanistan, because in Afghanistan there are a lot of mountains but in Syria and Iraq there are not. ... We are using both those models which IS is using in Iraq and Syria and we are also using new models in Afghanistan. For example the logistics which we are doing for IS in Syria and Iraq is different. There the weather is not very cold but in Afghanistan the weather is cold so the clothes, shoes and other things of IS Khorasan must be warmer than in Syria and Iraq.[45]

Still, regardless of formal denials by the advisers, there was some tension, as one cadre said, because 'these Arab Advisers are thinking that they know everything'.[46] This was despite the fact that at least some of the advisers had previous experience of Afghanistan or Pakistan, usually in the ranks of AQ, or were themselves Afghans or Pakistanis.[47] One such example was that of an adviser from Homs (Syria), who had been active as an adviser for some years after 2005 with the front of Dost Mohammed of the Taliban in eastern Afghanistan.[48]

According to an adviser sent from Iraq, the low average level of education of the trainees and (more surprisingly) their lack of experience were problems. It is worth quoting at length:

> IS people who are in Syria and Iraq, they are educated, and they have a lot of technical skills. Whatever is taught to them for new weapons and equipment, they are learning very soon. But in IS Khorasan, this problem is big, IS Khorasan members and fighters are not as educated and skillful as the members and fighters of IS in Syria and Iraq are. When we are giving training to the members and fighters of IS Khorasan, they cannot learn the lessons very soon. This is also the reason that the number of our advisers is high in IS Khorasan. ... [In Syria and Iraq] they also have good administration skills, like how to run an organized administration but IS Khorasan does not, therefore ... it will take time for IS Khorasan to reach to the level of IS in Syria and Iraq. ... For example IS Khorasan fighters did not know fighting tactics, they did not know how to make an ambush? They did not know how to coordinate and collaborate among groups. They did not know how to place a mine in the ground, they had problems and shortcomings in many fields. They also had problems in other fields for example in logistics, in finance, and others. They do not know how to do logistics and how to collect tax. Most of these problems have been solved after the coming of these advisers. ... Still there are some problems and shortcomings but these problems and shortages are not a lot and we are also trying to eliminate them very soon. For example before when we were not here as advisers with IS Khorasan, they did not have standards for anything, they were doing everything by their own choice, like what they wanted they were doing. They were doing logistics, finance, and other activities like common people are doing, but when we came to IS Khorasan, we made standards for all things.[49]

The major inflow of advisers and trainers may have had some substitution effect on IS-K's indigenous capacity. One adviser admitted that sometimes advisers sort out logistics for IS-K.[50] Some interviewees hinted that the advisers were in fact designing IS-K's structure for it.[51] A senior IS-K source admitted that decisions about the organization of IS-K are taken jointly by the leaders of IS-K and the advisers sent from Iraq.[52] The advisers could therefore be described also as supervisors, not least because they kept records of everything going on and submitted reports to IS-Central regularly.[53]

Alongside IS advisers, other foreign advisers are deployed from the donor countries, as discussed as the beginning of this chapter. The heterogeneous provenance of the advisers might have played a role in fostering divisions within IS-K. In early 2015, Qatari funding to Muslim Dost, in opposition to the Saudi funding to Khilafat Afghan, enabled him to split away.[54] Even within the corps of IS advisers, some were in favour of the component groups maintaining their existence, while others were in favour of an effective dissolution of the component groups into a completely unified entity. Al-Baghdadi was said to be in favour of the latter option.

In sum, language barriers, cultural differences and educational gaps were all factors affecting the transfer of skills from IS-Central to IS-K, and which certainly delayed its progress on the path traced for IS-K by its remote masters. This is not surprising, considering the environment. The trainees and advisees were approving all the know-how transferred, but it is not clear how much of it was actually absorbed.

The impact of the advising and training effort

Professed influence of IS-Central

Virtually all the IS-K interviewees insisted that IS was bringing 'new ideas, training, courses, lessons about Daesh's political views, military views and other views'.[55] In the courses taught by IS advisers to IS-K members in Pakistan, there was also a strong element of indoctrination, with political courses being taught every month or two.[56]

> The TTP did not give us such training about Shari'a, but TKP is giving us a lot of training like that Shari'a gives permission for whatever and we must learn it and implement it.[57]

When asked about the content of the ongoing indoctrination, the interviewees in general acknowledged they had been taught that Shi'as are enemies.[58]

> Even before we joined with Daesh we did attacks against Shi'as in Quetta, in Karachi but when we joined with Daesh, we became really opposed to Shi'as. Because Shi'as are always against Sunnis. We do not just want to start operations against Shi'as in Pakistan and Afghanistan. We also want to start operations against Shi'as in Iran.[59]

A Taliban observer confirmed the transformation of his former colleagues.

Those Taliban who joined with Daesh, they were not against Shi'as before, but now these former Taliban are also against Shi'as. ... Those Arab advisers who came to Afghanistan, they are telling IS-K that you should also start operations in Iran. You can see that Daesh has killed many Shi'a, Hazara men, children and women in Zabul province.[60]

A stricter attitude to Shari'a and the texts is another of IS's ideological exports to Khorasan, particularly after the arrival of the second Special Envoy of al-Baghdadi, Abu Yasir Al-Afghani, in November 2015 (see Chapter 9).[61]

We were told that praying at the shrine is against Islam, which is true. ... We are not trying to spread the Salafi ideas among the people. I agree that we have brought some difference in order to prevent people from some wrong traditional acts.[62]

As discussed in Chapter 5, IS-K's influence over madrasas in Pakistan and Afghanistan has been developing only gradually. It seems clear that IS-K has ambitions to develop a full-fledged madrasa network to supply ideologically prepared recruits. But this was a plan for the future. During 2014 and 2015, and to some extent during 2016, most of the recruits needed to be 'synchronized' ideologically after being brought into the organization. Indoctrination did not end with the courses taught at the camps by the advisers; group commanders were expected to sit with their fighters regularly and teach them about proper Islam.[63]

IS-Central's influence assessed

In reality, initially IS-K did not have the capacity to run full indoctrination courses for all its members. Throughout 2015, the indoctrination courses do not seem to have much affected the bulk of IS-K fighters and junior commanders. According to a junior commander,

Regarding getting lesson about the Daesh political views, we haven't got any courses or lesson. We have only told that Daesh is an international Jihadi group and its aim is bringing Shari'a to the world.[64]

Although even the external allies discussed in Chapter 6 were affected by IS attempts to influence them ideologically,[65] again not all of them were subjected to the same indoctrination process. For example, the IJRPT (Islamic Jihad Renaissance Party of Tajikistan) seems not to have been receiving anti-Shi'a propaganda, contrary to the IMT.[66]

Our view did not change about Shi'as and we do not have anything against Shi'as even now. Our mission and target is the government of Tajikistan. Up to now Khilafat Khorasan did not say anything about Shi'as nor Daesh says something to us to target Shi'as.[67]

As discussed in *The 'coagulation points'* above and Chapter 6 below, IS-K incorporated large groups of defectors from other organizations, with little evidence that significant numbers of aspiring members were vetted out. Over time, IS-K lowered its recruitment standards further, even bringing in people with no real jihadist background. Inevitably, the failure to apply its own recruitment rules made ideological indoctrination more problematic later on.

Given the fact that:

- advisers and trainers arrived in significant numbers only in the summer of 2015 and mostly left for winter before returning in the summer of 2016;
- the madrasa network of IS-K was still in its early stages of development in 2015;
- few recruits were really familiar with IS-Central's brand of Salafism;

in the short term IS-Central had to use other tools to keep IS-K more or less united and loyal to IS-Central. Among these tools were:

- the jihadist legitimacy and inspiration deriving from IS-Central's military successes in the Middle East;
- the funding granted by IS-Central to IS-K, even if during 2015 and even more so during 2016 IS-Central itself was embattled and soon running short of funds for its own operations (see Chapters 4 and 5).

Professed organizational improvements

Almost all IS-K interviewees stressed that there was little in common between their new organization and the old ones they belonged to, whether Taliban, TTP, Hizb-i Islami or what else. By their accounts, the discipline of IS-K was far superior to that of their old organizations, as were all the support structures, such as logistics, finance and administration. These interviewees all professed admiration for the 'professionalism' of IS-K.

A former Hizb-i Islami commander, for example, stated that IS-K's discipline was much tighter than in his old party, which had previously been known for being one of the most disciplined organizations in Afghanistan.[68] The former Taliban and the smaller groups were even more impressed with IS-K discipline:[69]

The commanders must accept the orders, and those commanders who are not accepting the orders, they must be seriously punished. All the fighters are under the orders of commanders, commanders are under the orders of district Amir, District Amirs are under the order of Provincial Amirs and Provincial Amirs are under the orders of Shura. ... Commanders have to follow the rules otherwise they will be punished. We punished twenty or thirty commanders who did not follow rules and regulations.[70]

It's not like Taliban that a thief can make a group and misuse from the name of Taliban but Taliban don't care and even sometimes Taliban support them, it's not like Taliban that one senior commander gives one order and other senior commander gives a different order to the same group. The commander of the group gets confused as to which order to follow.[71]

Particularly the smaller groups were likely to have a lot to learn from IS in terms of organization; for the first time they established groups dedicated to logistics, finance, health, military and recruitment.[72] A former commander of Jundullah (Iran), noted that

In that time we did not have a lot of logistics like we have it now. In that time our military skills were very weak compared to now. In that time our intelligence was very weak and our leader was also arrested by Iran. But now our intelligence improved a lot. Simply I'd like to say that in that time we were very weak in all fields, but now we are strong.[73]

A department was reportedly created by Special Envoy Al-Afghani for the specific purpose of supervision. This department, called Tahqiqat (Investigation), kept an eye on the members and investigated any suspected breach of the rules.[74]

IS has been trying to instil a stronger sense of institutional belonging than the Taliban might have had, doing away with the old patrimonial approach. For example, in the event of a commander getting killed, the group would not disband, but another commander appointed by the leadership would take over.[75]

Our military system is the same as government system. The commanders are changing. It is not like this that commanders are with their people and what they tell, their fighters are like his own people, like in Taliban.[76]

Professionalism is the other (claimed) main distinctive feature of IS-K, compared to the Taliban:[77]

We have professional people in every field and commission, such as in Military Commission, they can control their commanders and fighters well, the same in finance we have professional people who are graduated from economics, but Taliban do not have professional people to control and manage finance activities, in logistics and all other commissions.[78]

For sure, former members of other jihadist organizations reported IS-K to be much more meritocratic than what they were accustomed to:[79]

In the Taliban commanders were selected on friendship, relationship and those who could collect a lot of people in their areas, they became Taliban commanders but the commanders in Azizullah Haqqani Group are appointed based on experience, military skills, intelligence and other good qualities. The advisers are also getting them to pass exams. Those commanders who are weak, they are not appointed as commanders even if them are brothers of Azizullah Haqqani. In Azizullah Haqqani Group unprofessional commanders are never appointed such as in Taliban.[80]

Before Jundullah's people were selected on the basis of friendship and most of the people belonged to Rigi. By contrast, the commanders of Harakat Khilafat Baluch were selected based on the basis of military skills. In this group there is no recommendations and relationship. This thing is very good in Harakat Khilafat Baluch. If in any group there are no recommendations and relationship, that group is improving.[81]

In the Taliban those who are selected, they are selected based on friendship, of tribe, those who have a lot of men and recommendations, even if they are not intelligent. They cannot do great job and cannot control their men and cannot improve in their areas. On the other hand, Daesh is not selecting such people even if they have a lot of people, they are selecting those people who are intelligent, have military skill and spent a lot of time in military. In Daesh intelligence and experience is considered. If a person is very talented, he is given a senior position.[82]

Organizational improvements assessed

In reality, as we discuss in Chapter 6 and also in Chapter 1, the influence and number of followers of personalities joining did affect their appointments in IS-K. This is also confirmed by an interpreter, who stated that when IS-K selects its commanders, it takes into account the number of followers they have.[83] In Chapter 6, we discuss how IS-K recruitment rapidly started looking much more like the Taliban's, with whole groups co-opted without much vetting except of the leaders, rather than as a genuinely ideologically based effort. And IS-K itself has been accused by hostile critics of attracting criminal elements, much in the same way as IS-K accuses the Taliban of having done. For sure, some of IS-K's leaders had been sacked from the Taliban for misconduct (Faruq Safi, Sa'ad Emarati).

Despite these qualifications, the image of IS-K as a comparatively meritocratic organization (by the rather low standards of the region) is shared by several of the external observers contacted for this study. The impression of IS-K's organizational superiority was communicated by virtually all the members of Central Asian jihadist groups interviewed. NDS officers tended to agree:

> We have spies and people who are giving information to us, that there is difference between Daesh organization and Taliban organization. Daesh is really organized but Taliban is not as much organized. Like Daesh has good logistics, strong finance, they have modern and advanced weapons and their fighters are also trained well. They also have good advisers and trainers. On the other hand, Taliban are very weak. They do not have good logistics, they do not have modern weapons, their finance is not very strong. Their administration and administration activities are not organized well.[84]

> Daesh has an organization like government, but Taliban do not have organization at all. For example Daesh has specific person for logistic, for food, for medicine, for transferring the injured, for other things. They have special cars for transferring wounded people. Daesh is giving salaries on time and every one has ID that this is the member of Daesh but the Taliban do not have these things.[85]

An Iranian Revolutionary Guards source agreed, and also pointed out the higher-quality equipment owned by IS-K, although he was dismissive of the myth of IS-K's military proficiency.[86] A Nangarhari militia commander very hostile to IS-K also acknowledged their proficiency in finance, administration, logistics and all organizational dimensions.[87] Like the new IS-K converts, however, the NDS officers quoted above exaggerate the differences between IS-K and the Taliban. The Taliban has also developed dedicated structures for logistics and finance, and has had to supply a much larger number of people at per capita costs less than half of IS-K's, although it is true that the TTP had a more primitive organization than the Taliban. Moreover, as discussed below in Chapter 9, IS-K finance was far from perfect. Perhaps the impression of greater IS-K proficiency derives from its more cohesive character when compared to the Taliban (at least until spring 2017), which is divided in competing factions and has a convoluted organization with overlapping chains of command. A Pakistani ISI source provided a more sober assessment of IS-K when compared to the TTP:

> their logistics is better, administration like recruitment, finance, and other activities are very organized. They have good medicine; good weapons and they also have educated people. But TTP does not have educated people, they do not have good logistics, and simply it is not good from any side.[88]

The point of view of a Pakistani ISI officer is particularly interesting because, contrary to Afghanistan and Iran, it has never been the policy of the

Pakistani authorities to overstate the importance and power of IS-K for their own purpose, quite the contrary. Perhaps the most balanced view came from a senior Taliban cadre:

> The logistic of Daesh is better than ours, it is really organized, their military commission is better organized than ours, it means they are fighting better than us, their finance is better organized than ours, their discipline is better than ours and they are listening to their commanders. In their groups there is great coordination and collaboration. Simply I'd like to say that every commission of Daesh is more organized than corresponding Taliban commissions. ... One reason is also this that Daesh has a lot of money and there are also other reasons. They also have good advisers and trainers in finance, in logistics and in recruitment. They are giving four months professional trainings to their fighters.[89]

As in the case of the ISI officer, the Taliban interviewees do not have a vested interest in saying that the Taliban are organizationally weaker than IS-K. Hence, his point of view is particularly valuable.

It could be concluded that while IS-Central pushed IS-K towards an organizational upgrade, the achievements were mixed. One is tempted to conclude that, as of late 2016, IS-K still looked more like the Taliban than IS-Central would have liked, but were nonetheless better organized than them. Hard evidence of IS-K's capabilities is limited, as the organization was mostly busy setting up its structure and recruiting up to spring 2017. It could be argued that IS-K did give a hard time to the Taliban, despite the latter's large numerical superiority, but assessing whether IS-K's organization (as opposed to its tactics) performed better against the Afghan security forces or American forces is much harder. Arguably, IS-K demonstrated an ability to deploy far and relatively fast (for a force moving on foot), outpacing the Taliban and often capable of seizing the initiative against a potentially much larger force. At the same time, it remains questionable whether better logistics and a more effective centralized organization would have helped IS-K as much against a more conventional force than the Taliban. It should be taken into account, finally, that IS-K was barely more than 2 years old in spring 2017. In 2005 (2 years into their jihad against 'foreign occupation'), the Taliban had yet to make any major gain anywhere in Afghanistan.

Opposition to IS-Central inputs

IS-K leaders were not always passive adopters of IS-Central tactics and 'know-how'. One example is the debate about the use of large bombs against soft targets in urban areas, a 'trademark' established by the predecessors of IS, AQ in Iraq and ISIL. Some leaders—like Muslim Dost, Sa'ad Emarati and Amir Wahidullah—reportedly opposed the use of these bombs on the grounds that they would cause large casualties among bystanders. Others, particularly Pakistani IS-K, argued that big bombs are needed to show to the people the power of IS-K.[90]

The same is true of the use of gruesome tactics such as decapitations, another IS-Central trademark. Sources in IS-K diverge over what IS advisers told them, with some claiming advisers did not advocate decapitations and others claiming the contrary. This is probably an indicator of different views within IS-K itself.

> Shamali Khilafat did not advise us to perform actions like decapitations. The decapitations which took place in Nangarhar province, it was done by TKP of Hafiz Sayed Khan, we are strictly rejecting that action. We Shamali Khilafat group wants to have good relationship with people here in Kunduz province, we only kill those people who are against Daesh.[91]

These denials might have been dictated by the fear of negative publicity. However, several other sources admitted that IS advisers advocated decapitations and other types of exemplary punishments (executions by explosives, by setting people on fire and by running people over with cars) against enemies (but not civilians) in order to terrorize them and prevent further challenges.[92] That IS-K used gruesome execution techniques is not in doubt: the June 2015 execution by explosives of elders and villagers in Nangarhar was even documented in a video that was then circulated through the internet.[93] A Taliban cadre interviewee noted how his former friends who had joined IS-K were now verbally supporting its gruesome violence as well.[94] Several IS-K interviewees, moreover, did not avoid the question and instead explained the rationale of extreme violence:[95]

> They are telling you should use the hard formula of terror so that in the future no one will stand against us, like seating people on mines and blowing them up, like setting fire to people and simply give very hard punishment to them.[96]

> This mutilating and decapitating scares our enemies a lot. In Iraq and Syria also Daesh did decapitation and mutilation, which put pressure on enemies. So the advisers are telling to use the same strategy here in Afghanistan.[97]

> If we do not do these things, we will not be successful. ... If we do not do these things, they will stand against us. We did this, so that in the future no one will stand against Daesh.[98]

Undoubtedly, these terror techniques had some effect, although not necessarily the intended one:[99]

Always, from the time that Daesh has appeared in our district they are carrying out acts like beheading people in front of the villagers, killing people in front of the villagers and even blowing [up] villagers and elders with bombs, which has not happened in the history of our province before. This kind of acts really made the people very scared and forced the villagers to form a militia against Daesh.[100]

Perhaps because of these reactions, there was a U-turn, as IS-K realized extreme violence was counter-productive:

Now the advisers are telling us to decrease or finish violence against civilians because they think that this thing will create problems and mobilize tribes against Daesh.[101]

One source indicated that, given the small number of IS-K members, tactics such as decapitations would be counter-productive and arouse anger against the group.[102] The softer approach reportedly advocated by Special Envoy Al-Afghani during 2016, and eventually applied on a full scale after the death of governor Hafiz Saeed, was also about reassuring the tribal and village elders that the Nangarhar violence was an exception, the result of a group of rogue Pakistanis being in control (see Chapter 9).[103]

A tool of organizational skills transfer and ideological influence: the Syrian deployments

The importance of the despatch of volunteers to Syria is not limited to its representing an opportunity for IS to start reaching out to jihadist organizations in 'Khorasan', as explained in Chapter 1. A pool of future IS leaders and cadres were formed there, gaining experience and acquiring an esprit de corps. A statistical analysis of 72 biographical profiles (almost all cadres, leaders, trainers/advisers and unit commanders) provided by interviewees shows that during the research period (2015–16) the veterans of Syria and Iraq accounted for 54 per cent. This is in line with IS-K's claims about the presence of Syria and Iraq veterans in the ranks (see below). Within this sample of 72 IS-K members, the highest concentration of veterans of Syria was among the trainers (84 per cent), but they were also well represented among the sub-provincial and district amirs.

By contrast, few of the unit commanders interviewed had been to the Middle East, and quite surprisingly none of the deputy leaders and only a third of the leaders interviewed (Table 3). The different component groups were exposed to the Syrian experience in varying measure. In the case of the Azizullah Haqqani component group, according to one source, as of January 2016 60 per cent of the commanders and cadres had been to Syria.[104] Some other component groups had hardly been exposed to the Syrian/Iraqi experience:

> I don't know the other in other provinces of Afghanistan, but our leader Mullah Khadim and other senior commanders of Daesh in our district have not been in Syria for fighting.[105]

The percentage of veterans appears to have been much lower for IS-K's overall membership, if we accept data coming from sources within the different IS-K component groups. This shows that the percentage of veterans of Syria and Iraq varied between 10–30 per cent (Table 4). Note that this figure would include veterans who deployed to Syria in 2012–14, that is before IS-K was formed (hence the data is not comparable to the figures provided below in this paragraph).

The trend reported by IS-K sources in deployment to Syria/Iraq is shown in Graph 1. These numbers suggest that throughout mid-2015 to mid-2017 there were always 1,000–2,000 IS-K volunteers in Syria and Iraq. Are these numbers credible? IS-K and IS-Central sources reported much greater numbers of Afghans and Pakistanis in Syria and Iraq than was generally reported in Western studies of foreign fighters operating there, including those based on captured IS files, like CTC's.[106] However, these volunteers entered Syria and Iraq as groups and on the basis of pre-existing arrangements, probably bypassing normal procedures for the entry of individual volunteers (as they were 'guaranteed' by IS-K).[107]

In addition, media reports conflict with the extremely low numbers of Afghans and Pakistanis (twenty-two in all) reported among the foreign fighters in the captured files analyzed by CTC. The Iraqi media in particular often reports the killing of 'Afghan terrorists' fighting for IS-Central.[108] Michael Holmes, reporting from Mosul in October 2016, mentioned (based on security sources) Afghans among IS-Central's most 'capable' fighters, implying that they were a significant force.[109] Moreover, as discussed in Chapter 1, the Syrian, Russian and Pakistani authorities issued estimates of the numbers of Afghans and Pakistanis present or killed in Syria closer to the claims made by interviewees for the 2012–14 period. These figures are compatible with what IS-K sources have been sharing.

A final form of evidence of the presence of fighters from Khorasan in Syria and Iraq are videos released by IS-Central, of which there are several.[110] The fact that IS-K sources admitted to declining numbers from sometime in 2016 onwards lends some credibility to their claims: if they were lying, why would they admit to a negative trend?

US intelligence reported the flow of volunteers from all sources as drying up during 2016.[111] This seems to clash to some extent with the sources (Graph 1), although some of the growth shown between October 2015 and June 2016 is likely to have occurred before the end of 2015. It was possible to interview the commander of one group of thirty-five men travelling to Syrian in June 2016, a fact that suggests that the human pipeline was not completely shut yet.[112] By January 2017, an IS-K source admitted that the number of volunteers in Syria and Iraq had declined sharply during the second half of 2016, which suggested very few new arrivals in Syria and Iraq during this period. However, this does not rule out that a negative trend might have started sooner.[113] By April 2017, the flow of volunteers to Syria had stopped altogether, and IS-K was even struggling to get its volunteers back from there.[114]

In some cases, it was also possible to find some partial corroboration of IS-K figures.

In June 2015, IS-K sources reported the presence of 1,100 IS-K members in Syria and Iraq (Graph 1).[115] The Soufan group in August 2015 reported a non-official estimate of 330 Pakistanis having volunteered with IS-Central, which seems compatible with the above IS-K claim, as IS-K say the majority of volunteers were Afghans.[116]

What was the 2015–16 acceleration due to (Graph 1)? It could of course be that the IS-Central leadership, under growing military pressure, changed its mind about needing IS-K volunteers, but it seems more probable that Abu Yasir Al-Afghani might have advised the use of tours of duty in Syria and Iraq as a tool for 'synchronising' IS-K with IS-Central. This is a more realistic assumption, considering that Al-Afghani had been the head of the Afghan IS contingent in Syria before being sent to Khorasan as Special Envoy of al-Baghdadi.[117] The component groups that joined IS-K relatively late often had no record of involvement in the Syrian or Iraqi conflicts; they were, however, asked to start sending volunteers. On their return, the volunteers were expected to become the cadres of the different component groups (amirs and commanders).[118]

In terms of actual impact back in Khorasan, the same IS-K sources counted 383 volunteers coming back between January and October 2015 (excluding those who had gone back before IS-K was established).[119] The impact of the tours of duty in the Middle East was therefore not being felt that much. By April 2017, about 1,000 volunteers (about 600 Afghans and the rest Pakistanis) had reportedly made it back to Khorasan; if true, this would account for about 5 per cent of the total claimed membership.[120] Therefore, even after over 2 years from its launch, and assuming these figures are correct, the impact of rotating members through the Levant had had a modest impact on the membership of IS-K as a whole. However, according to IS-K sources, as of early 2016 the majority of the leaders and senior commanders of IS-K (up to 70–80 per cent) had been to Syria, and the percentage was expected to rise further.[121] If these figures are correct, they clearly show that the veterans were being appointed in command positions. IS-K sources claimed that veterans returning from Syria and Iraq displayed superior combat performances, an observation that reportedly contributed to the decision of increasing the number of deployments.[122]

Some advisers to IS-K were in fact Afghans and Pakistanis who stayed in Syria and Iraq and joined IS-Central, particularly before the increased flow of advisers and trainers of summer 2015.[123] In early 2015 at the Logar training centre, for example, of five trainers, two were former TTP commanders, one a former Afghan Talib and one an Afghan from AQ. The two Pakistanis had been in Syria for one and 2 years respectively, the former Talib for 4 years and the former AQ Afghan for over a year.[124]

Usually, the volunteers were deployed to Syria or Iraq for shifts of 6 months (plus about one month of travelling), renewable. The groups of volunteers were often of mixed nationality; one particular group which reached Turkey in June 2016 was composed of Afghans, Chinese and Uzbeks.[125] The volunteers would have not only excellent prospects of promotion once back in Khorasan, on the basis that in Syria they would get more advanced training and experience, but also a higher salary ($800 per month for fighters, plus a one-off premium of $3,000).[126] Some of the volunteers would spend more than 2 years in Syria and even refuse to return to Afghanistan/Pakistan.[127]

The 'volunteers' were selected on the basis of their physical fitness, their fighting skills and their knowledge of Arabic, but were still required to provide a reference by a senior member of IS-K.[128] Before deploying, the volunteers would receive a month training with Syrian, Afghan and Pakistani teachers, explaining mainly how to behave while en route to Syria.[129] On arrival in Syria, the volunteers received an additional month of training, including further language training, before deploying to combat areas.[130] The volunteers are accompanied by translators while in Syria.[131]

Table 3: Cadres of IS-K by experience, according to collected personal biographies

	Been to Syria/Iraq? % yes	
All	54.0	n=72
Trainers	84.8	n=33
Sub-provincial amirs	66.6	n=3
District amirs	75.0	n=4
Commanders	20.0	n=10
Deputy leaders	0.0	n=6
Leaders	33.3	n=6

Sources: interviews with IS-K cadres, commanders and leader, 2014–16.

Table 4: Veterans of Syria and Iraq by IS-K component group[132]

	Date	N=	Veterans of Syria and Iraq %
Azizullah Haqqani Group	January–16	1,680	16.6
IS-K Kunar	February–16	245	19.2
TKK	January–16	n/a	15
IS-K Herat	December–15	625	19.2
TKP	December–15	3,450	13
Muslim Dost Group	October–15	1,163	22.6
Shamali Khilafat	February–15	600	10–12
Khilafat Afghan	June–15	750	30

Legend: LeJ=Lashklar-e Jhangvi; LeT=Lashkar-e Taiba; JM=Jaysh Mohammad.

Graph 1: Afghan and Pakistani volunteers sent by IS-K to Syria and Iraq, according to IS-K sources

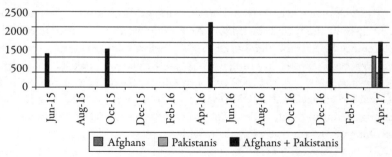

Sources: interviews with IS-K cadres, commanders and leader, 2015–17.[133]

4

HYBRID

IS-K STRUCTURE BETWEEN CENTRALIZATION AND CENTRIFUGAL TENDENCIES

The design of IS-K's structure

The political and leadership structure

The leadership shura of IS-K was one of the first structures to be established and is the top structure of IS-K.[1] Originally established by Abdul Rauf Khadim and presided over by Hafiz Saeed Khan with Khadim as first deputy responsible for Afghanistan, the leadership shura included thirteen members in 2015, among whom the known figures were:

- Mawlavi Faruq Safi, former district military leader of the Peshawar Shura who was sacked in 2013 and became one of the main leaders of TKK. He was said to be a favourite of al-Baghdadi;
- Shahidullah Shahid, ex-spokesperson of TTP;
- Gul Zaman Fateh, ex-TTP commander in Khyber Agency;
- Mullah Omar Mansur, former TTP commander;
- Sa'ad Al Emarati, a former Taliban commander expelled in 2012 for unauthorized activities. Was among the first group of volunteers sent to Syria in 2012;
- Qari Obeidullah, former TTP commander in the Peshwar area;

- Mullah (Qari) Jawad, another member of the original group of volunteers sent to Syria in 2012;
- Mullah Khalid Mansur, a former TTP commander who took refuge in Nangarhar before switching to IS-K;
- Mufti Hassan Swati, the former TTP leader in Swat;
- Mawlavi Bakhtiar, former district governor in Nangarhar, who quit the Taliban in 2015.[2]

Not all important leaders sat on IS-K's leadership shura; for example, Nasratullah Popolzai, one of the founders of Khilafat Afghan, did not.[3] At that time, the most powerful members were Hafiz Saeed Khan, Faruq Safi, Khalid Mansur, and Gul Zaman Fateh. Shahidullah Shahid, the spokesman, was described by some sources as another key IS-K leader, perhaps even closer to IS in Mosul and Gulf donors than Hafiz Saeed.[4] Usually the composition of the shura was based on a selection of IS-K senior leaders, appointed to the shura by the governor based on the recommendations of the emirs. A high-level internal source described the shura's task as being to debate current affairs, exercise critical decision-making and negotiate with the tribes. The shura's advice to the governor was described as non-binding, but it had the power to depose the governor. The source also stated that the decisions of the leadership shura had to be submitted to al-Baghdadi for approval.[5]

Internal sources reported that the leadership of IS-K was usually distributed between its main 'offices' (in fact private flats and houses used for financial operations and for hosting leaders and cadres) in North Waziristan, Qatar, UAE and Saudi Arabia.[6] Although it appeared to be a temporary role, the 'Special Representative' appointed by al-Baghdadi to lord over the IS-K was in a number of ways the most powerful figure in the organization. The Special Representative (Wali Rahman at first, then al-Afghani, then Abu Hamza and finally Abu Mohammad Zafar Safi) was the supreme authority who met with the leaders of the component groups once or twice a week if he was in Khorasan, or otherwise once or twice a month.[7] The deputy of one of the component groups stated:

> If he does not meet [them], then everything will go bad. He is controlling things from close quarters.[8]

At least three out of four Special Representatives had a record of spending a long time with IS-Central and its previous incarnations:

- Qari Wali Rahman was born in the district of Pul-i Khumri (Baghlan) in 1975. After graduating in 1999 from Al Haqqania madrasa in Pakistan, he taught in the same madrasa until 2012, when he travelled to Syria with one of his colleagues, a Syrian teacher, to join Al-Nusra. In June 2013 he moved on to ISIL. He was particularly close to Abu Omar Shishani. On 3 April 2014, he was appointed as a Special Representative for Afghanistan and Pakistan;[9]

- Abu Yasir Al-Afghani, whose real name is Qari Abdul Yasir, was born in 1977 in Achin district of Nangarhar. After graduating from a madrasa in Lahore, in 2004 he joined Jama'at al-Tawhid Wal Jihad, al-Zarqawi's predecessor of the Islamic State. He fought in Fallujah with al-Zarqawi and survived him to serve under al-Baghdadi. In IS he is known as particularly close to Abd al Rahman Mustafa;[10]

- Abu Hamza Al Khorasani was born in Kajaki (Helmand) and was previously active with Quetta Shura Taliban, particularly Mullah Dadullah. He volunteered for Syria, where he joined IS in 2014;[11]

- Abu Mohammad Zafar Safi: little is known of him.

While Wali Rahman kept a low profile in his days, Al-Afghani took a much more prominent role, presumably following a mandate explicitly given by al-Baghdadi. The governor of Wilayat Khorasan could potentially be removed from his job by the Special Representative.[12]

The organizational improvements sponsored and demanded by IS-Central (as discussed in Chapter 3) posed a series of major implementation issues for an organization like IS-K, which was born out of the alliance of four different groups (TKP, TKK, Khilafat Afghan and Azizullah Haqqani Group). Under IS-Central's advice, the first choice of IS-K's leaders would request the founding groups to disband into a single entity, which would take the name of one of the groups, TKK. The plan was that the other component groups would eventually be herded towards dissolving themselves into the TKK. The deadline agreed for that was initially 18 April 2015, but the process stalled in negotiating over the details (see *The IS-K structure as it turned out*, below).[13] The head of the TKK was given powers similar to those of the governor, below the Special Representative. This appears to have been a temporary position, and by 2020 nobody was talking of TKK anymore, the organization having been subsumed into IS-K.

IS-K sources mentioned that in April 2015 the name of Faruq Safi was already a likely choice for head of the TKK because of his close relationship with al-Baghdadi and because he was said to have the support of most main stakeholders in IS-K.[14] But as of April 2017 the appointment had not been yet made, and the whole TKK business was shelved.

Under the governor there were instead various commissions and departments, described below, the Shari'a Council and the Administrative Department. Later, a Health Council, an Education Council and an Intelligence Council were also established. Although at the time of writing some of these structures were still largely empty shells, waiting for IS-K to seize major chunks of territory before being rolled out, others appear to have had some substance, even the apparently less strategic ones. The Health Council, for example, counted on almost 300 staff as of June 2015, according to a senior source in IS-K.[15] In each of the provinces where IS-K operated (twenty as of January 2016), there would be a representative from each of these structures, working under the provincial amirs of Wilayat Khorasan (see *Governance structures* below).[16]

IS-Central insisted on keeping records of all IS-K activities, commission by commission, and for these records to be regularly transferred to Iraq and Syria.[17]

> Daesh is keeping records of all things, like the record of logistics, the same they keep the record of finance. Then they are sending the records of all these things to Iraq and Syria. Daesh are requesting from us the records of all the things like the supports that we get from companies, and the projects and contracts and the money that we spend, so we send these records to Al-Baghdadi to Iraq.[18]

Establishing the structure was a gradual process. In Ghazni, for example, only two commissions were operational in April 2015: Finance and Logistics.[19] As of June 2015, the provinces with the most developed structures were Nangarhar, Helmand, Kandahar, Zabul, Kunar, Kunduz and Badakhshan. Later, Kandahar was evacuated after the defeat in Helmand in early 2015, and IS-K forces only re-entered it in early 2017, despatching groups from Helmand and Zabul. These provinces represented a choice of a mix of strategic locations for spreading IS-K through infiltration and proselytizing (Nangarhar, Helmand, Kandahar, Zabul and Kunduz) and of provinces where safe havens could easily be established (Kunar, Badakhshan).[20]

Governance structures

IS divides the territory where it operates into provinces, which take the historical names they had under the original Caliphate, hence Khorasan for the region encompassing Iran, Afghanistan, Pakistan, Central Asia and parts of India. The governor is called *wali*, and under him operate a number of amirs. Of these, some are senior amirs and in charge of whole administrative units (confusingly also called 'provinces' in Afghanistan and 'agencies' or 'districts' in Pakistan), and some are sectoral amirs, responsible for each sector of activity: there are military amirs, a Shari'a amir, a security amir and so on. It should be noted that the sub-provincial amirs had a predominantly military role (see below). To avoid confusion, from here onwards we shall refer to 'Khorasan' as a province and to Afghan provinces and Pakistani tribal agencies as 'sub-provinces', and senior amirs will be referred to as sub-provincial amirs.

The first 'sub-provinces' and agencies to be see amirs appointed by IS-K were Farah, Zabul, Ghazni, Logar, Nangarhar, Kunar, Badghis, Kunduz, Badakhshan, Parwan, Baghlan, Faryab, Nuristan, Nimruz, South Waziristan, North Waziristan, Kurram, Khyber, Mohmand, and Bajaur.[21]

Besides the sub-provincial amirs, the various commissions and councils had the local branches. Initially, these local structures were not very active even when they effectively staffed. The Education Council, for example, had only 'plans' in January 2016 to open madrasas and schools for the common people (although the Health Council claimed at that time that IS-K doctors were already helping villagers), but the claim could not be confirmed.[22] Some basic administrative capability was built around these sub-provincial amirs, as shown by the fact that IS-K tried to implement population control, banning people from fleeing their areas of control and requiring written permits to pass IS-K checkpoints. Individuals had to make up excuses for leaving the area, such as visiting a doctor.[23] There were also reports of IS-K issuing ID cards, for which the population had to pay the hefty sum of $78.[24]

Part of IS-K's grandiose plans was the establishment of courts, under the Shari'a Council (see *The Shari'a Council* below).

The Finance Commission

Known within IS-K as Baytulmal Commission, the IS-K Finance Commission is in charge of fundraising from businessmen, mosques and governments; of receiving funds from IS-Central; of managing revenue from taxes and booty; of preparing a budget; and of distributing funds.[25] In total, between the HQ staff and those deployed around the area of operations, the Finance Commission employed 285 staff as of June 2015.[26] According to IS-K finance cadres, IS-Central taught IS-K how to collect taxes 'more effectively' and how to prepare a proper budget.[27]

IS-K sources describe the financial core of the IS-K as based between different locations in the UAE and particularly Dubai (also Abu Dhabi, Sharja, and

Jabal Ali), where it operated from privately rented flats. IS-K has also been saving money and keeping it invested in locations like Dubai as a financial reserve (see below), so not all of the $17,500 per member mentioned above would actually be spent. By mid-2016, the so-called Finance Commission was composed of a mix of Afghans, Pakistanis, Saudis and Iraqis. Afghans and Pakistani were mostly in charge of transferring money to Afghanistan and Pakistan, while the Arabs were in charge of getting the money to Dubai from the Gulf Countries.[28]

In February 2017, however, the offices of the Finance Commission in Dubai had to be closed after the authorities of the UAE cracked down on IS activities there and arrested twelve members of staff from that office. Two UAE-based donors to IS-K were also detained, while others (including Saudi-, Qatar- and Kuwait-based ones) were warned and blacklisted. The crackdown was reportedly the result of the discovery of an IS-inspired terrorist plot in the UAE, resulting in the decision to stamp out IS activities altogether, despite claims of non-involvement by IS-K cadres there. A mediation attempt by Qatari donors did not suffice to change the mind of the UAE's authorities, who gave IS-K 2 months' notice to vacate their Dubai offices.

IS-K's financial operations were seriously disrupted for months, and the organization had to arrange for donors to transfer funds directly to Pakistan and Afghanistan. As of March 2017, it was evacuating its staff from the UAE, with plans to re-open the Finance Commission offices in Qatar and Kuwait. The transfer of funds to IS-K within Khorasan was disrupted, not least because of the authorities clamping down on hawala activities, and emergency measures had to be taken, reportedly with the help of the intelligence agencies of some Arab Gulf countries. NGOs and private businesses in the other Gulf countries were used instead of the hawalas.[29]

By 2018, IS-K had managed to re-adjust and had found a suitable new base for its financial operations in Turkey. As had been the case in the UAE, the Finance Commission offices were split in half a dozen different physical locations (in Ankara and Istanbul's areas of Aviclar and Zeytinburnu), with a total of 110 staff as of 2021.[30] The staff was composed primarily of Afghans (some forty), Pakistanis (some twenty), Turks (more than twenty), Arabs (some twenty), and Uyghurs (ten).[31]

The Finance Commission offices were established with the support of donors from Qatar, UAE, Kuwait and Bahrain, who were probably worried about the traceability of operations from Kuwait, where only a few hawala traders are based and trade relations with Afghanistan and Pakistan are not so well developed. All the money paid to IS-K by the Caliphate and from foreign donors was coming through the office in Turkey, with only local taxes and contributions reaching IS-K directly. Led by a naturalized Afghan business-man (in fact an IS-K frontman), the office was well positioned to keep IS-K cash in Turkey without too many problems.[32]

In Turkey there are also a lot of hawala traders, and IS-K relies on them as conduits for transferring cash to Afghanistan. A special representative of IS-Central was tasked with inspecting the activities of the IS-K office in Turkey, visiting once or twice a month and reporting back to the Caliphate about how the money was being spent. The members of the office also visited IS-Central leaders in Syria and Iraq.[33] One major advantage for IS was that it enjoyed widespread support within the Uyghur community in Istanbul. In particular, it was Uyghurs who handled the money reaching the IS-K office in Turkey from Syria. The Turkish branch of IS was also helping IS-K, especially with providing advice on possible investments and moving money between Iraq and Syria and Turkey.[34]

As of 2016, the Finance Commission had autonomy with regard to how to determine IS-K's budget, which was not subject to the approval of the Finance Commission of IS-Central. Only in the case of some 'conditional' contributions by private donors was the Finance Commission bound in its allocations: that money could only go to a specific component group, or to a specific purchase or task.[35] The IS-K Finance Commission operated under the orders of the Special Envoy; Al-Afghani was reportedly particularly busy re-organizing it and spent much time in Dubai doing that. One of the Special Envoy's deputies was according to IS-K sources permanently based in Dubai and tasked to follow financial issues. The Special Envoy in particular had a big say, in conjunction with the Finance Commission, in deciding how to allocate budgets to the different component groups of IS-K, based on their membership and the number of operations carried out.[36] They might or might not consider requests and claims made by the groups, according to their discretion. The component groups were then bound to that budget.

> Whatever plan is made by the financial commission, the commanders must spend the money that way. If the commanders do everything by themselves, then corruption will happen again.[37]

All IS-K sources claimed that the payments to each group were perfor-mance-based, in particular rewarding each group's success in recruiting and expanding its ranks.[38] The system provided incentives to the leaders of the component group to come up with ambitious plans and recruit as much as possible in order to get funding. It could also potentially create incentives for IS-K component groups to cheat and inflate numbers, as it has sometimes been alleged of IS units in Syria and Iraq (a practice that IS has been fighting with determination).[39] As a member of the Finance Commission said, 'they are trying to make good plans to get a lot of money from us'.[40] At least one of the interviewees made a point that clearly implied the accumulation of personal wealth well beyond what his salary should have allowed:

> I have spent nine years with Miran Shah Shura but I did not have one rupee but I spent one year with Daesh and now I have 10 million Pakistani rupees. If we want to convert it to dollars it is 100000 USD.[41]

The Finance Commission would take into account the fact that the non-local IS-K groups faced high operational costs because they usually had to pay villagers in order to secure their hospitality. Food was sold to IS-K foreign groups at prices well above the market rate; the same applied to house rents.[42] Regardless, the fact that the various component groups were the recipients and handlers of funds distributed by the Finance Commission confirms that their leaders retained a substantial degree of power and have been able to negotiate a mechanism that allows them to retain the loyalty of their men.

The component groups were not authorized to 'save money' like IS-K did; they had to spend their entire budget. This was in part because of the lack of safe places for hoarding cash, in part probably because the IS and IS-K leadership did not want the component groups to gain too much autonomy, and in part to avoid corruption. Procurement money was assigned in response to specific requests for equipment and was therefore spent as soon as it was delivered.

In the early days of IS-K, cash stashes were kept in Afghanistan, ready to be used. However, it was soon evident that there was high risk to keeping the cash in vulnerable locations. Reportedly, after the seizure of $5 million of IS-K money in Hesarak (Nangarhar) by the militias of Haji Zahir on 17 February 2016, the decision was made to avoid this practice whenever possible.[43] Cash started being stored in locations considered to be very safe, although not always justifiably so: an IS-K source admitted that the strike against the IS-K tunnels in Mohmand Valley in April 2017 pulverized $8 million.[44]

Before the IS-K structure was in place, money would reach the leaders of the 'coagulation groups' discussed above, who would then pay their own commanders.[45] In 2015, the system became much more sophisticated and efficient. Salaries, for example, have reportedly been paid on time.[46] The typical senior IS-K finance officer had a background in financial studies or business as well as religious studies. Junior cadres were now posted everywhere to handle money once it reached the operational groups; they were the ones handing cash over to the field commanders.[47] This system was introduced by Al-Afghani in response to the corruption that he found in the previous one (see Chapter 9 below): until early 2016, cash transfers were made directly to field commanders. The junior financial officers were later reported to be obtaining receipts from the field commanders, which were then handed over to the provincial financial officer for the records.[48]

Each group had its own Finance Commission branch to handle the funds, and the original (early 2015) plan to merge all groups and their finance commissions into a single entity under the TKK denomination was never implemented.[49]

IS-K would also assign a budget to each sub-province, which, depending on the level of IS-K presence, ranged from a few millions to tens of millions of US$.[50] In principle, only the cadres of the Finance Commission had the right to collect taxes.[51] In reality, the budgets of the sub-provinces could be supplemented by locally raised revenue, which would then be spent locally: according to IS-K sources, in Farah in 2015 the $10 million budget was supplemented by $6 million of taxes,[52] while in Herat in 2016 a similar budget of $10 million was augmented by $4 million in taxes raised in just 4 months.[53] There was overlap between the budgets of the component groups and those of the sub-provinces: in practice, each sub-provincial budget would be split among the different component groups, with some funds remaining with the sub-provincial amir.

The Finance Commission, based until February 2017 in the UAE, transferred cash to IS-K in Khorasan mostly via hawala and sometimes through some complicit businessmen, particularly Pakistani ones (the Afghan hawala network is so thick and widespread that there is no need for additional channels).[54] The transfers were made to large financial centres in urban centres with hundreds of hawala traders active, in order to avoid leaving obvious traces. These included Peshawar Karkhano, Chaman, Quetta, Kabul Sara-e Shahzada, Spin Boldak and Jalalabad. In turn, smaller transfers were made from these locations to smaller locations around Afghanistan and Pakistan.[55] Kunar province, for example, received funds from the Finance Commission by collecting cash from hawala traders in Pakistan.[56] Farah province instead received the money through Chaman, from where it was taken through Kandahar.[57]

Some cash was also transported personally by agents directly appointed by the Finance Commission and assigned to specific areas.[58] IS-K in northern Afghanistan received the money from Kunduz, where it arrived after having first been transferred to Kabul.[59] Some of the hawala traders were linked to IS-K and were aware of the nature of the transfers they carried out for it; they transferred money without asking for any IDs and also charged higher percentages to cover the 'political risk'. Others are not aware, and they see the transfers as everyday business.[60] The closure of the Finance Commission's offices in the UAE in February 2017 forced the Commission to scramble for alternative locations, offering facilities to transfer funds to Pakistan and Afghanistan. It turned out to be quite problematic, as few available hawala traders were reportedly found in Kuwait and Qatar.[61]

A source in the Pakistani authorities confirmed that they tracked hawala payments to IS-K from Doha, Dubai and Kuwait City, resulting in the arrest of thirty hawala traders and employees in Pakistan.[62] Similarly, a source in the NDS reported the arrest of some hawala traders, who received IS-K money from Dubai.[63]

The Finance Commission saves some of the funds raised for rainy days. In 2015, for example, a source within it claimed that $30 million was earned from accumulated savings invested in Dubai.[64] The Commission reportedly had a team of sixty staff dedicated to investing IS-K savings in different fields, such as Afghan and Pakistani businesses, transport companies in the UAE and so on.[65]

Once the budget of a component group was assigned by the IS-K central leadership, the component group had to accept certain criteria imposed by IS-K. The salary of a fighter, for example, could not exceed $600 per month.[66] Within these constraints there was considerable variation. In Ghazni, for example, in April 2015 the fighters were reportedly getting 15,000 Afs/month (=$220), while commanders were getting 25,000 Afs/month.[67] In Mullah Bakhtwar's Group, in July 2016 fighters were said to be getting paid $400, commanders $600, district amirs $1,000, provincial amirs $1,500, and members of the commissions $2,000. The source acknowledged that the group's salaries were lower than the IS-K's average, perhaps because it had just joined IS-K.[68]

The Logistics Commission

IS-K central logistics has been handled in a very centralized way by the Logistics Commission, whose head in November 2015 was Mawlavi Ziaullah Shinwari, supported by five other members.[69] It is worth noting that the six members of the Commission were chosen from the ranks of the different component groups: as of November 2015, one was from Muslim Dost's Group, one from the Omar Ghazi Group, one from Khilafat Afghan, one from Shamali Khilafat and one from TKP, suggesting an attempt to represent the different groups.[70] This was probably standard practice in all commissions and councils. IS-Central was sending inspectors to Dubai to check the work of the Logistics Commission, how much it was raising and how much it was spending and to what use funds were being put, looking at the records.[71]

Among other things, the Logistics Commission is in charge of food supplies and even of organizing catering services for ongoing operations:

> When we have operations anywhere, our logistics commission go over there in that village and make the food there where we will start operations.[72]

IS-K members always pointed this out as being a remarkable difference from the Taliban, who were expected to obtain food from the villagers for free. By the standards of Afghanistan, therefore, IS-K had 'luxury' logistics. Its logistics were reported by all interviewees to be way better than the Taliban's. The quality of ammunition and weapons was similarly reported to be greatly superior.[73]

> We can say that when we were with TTP, we did not have logistics at all. In that time food was not given to us. We were eating it in the houses of the people. Our other equipment and logistics were not good. Now all of our things are special. Our food is special, our logistics is special, we have modern and advanced weapons etc. ... Our old logistics was very weak but now we have the best logistics like food, soaps, brushes, paste, shoes, clothes, shoes brush and shoes colour.[74]

> The logistics is not comparable with the Taliban's, when I was with Taliban we were like beggars and were begging food from the villagers, begging money from the villagers for buying ammunitions or other necessary stuff. But now our logistics is very good, we get clothes, we get food, we get weapons and ammunitions on time etc.[75]

There are also insistent rumours of helicopters delivering supplies for IS-K in the western part of Nangarhar, presumably contractors tasked for delivering to logistically impervious places. The rumours, reported initially by elders, were confirmed by IS-K sources, although they remain hard to believe given the very high costs involved.[76] Some sources including Afghan authorities even insisted that planes from an Arab Gulf country, delivering official relief aid, have also clandestinely delivered supplies to IS-K in Faryab.[77] Whether these allegations are true or not, the scale of IS-K operations suggests that support delivered in this way could only have had a marginal impact anyway. As a senior Taliban cadre acknowledges:

I can say that Daesh logistics is better organized compared to government logistics. Daesh has a much better organized logistics system, they are having contracts with companies, which are bringing things to Daesh. For everything they have specific people. For food specific people, for clothes specific people, for ammunition specific people, for weapons specific people, for shoes specific people, for medicine, for injured people to transfer them, and the same for other activities Daesh have specific people so it is clear from this that the logistics of Daesh is much better than the Taliban's.[78]

The IS-K Logistics Commission took over most of the logistics, but the component groups maintained a limited structure to liaise with IS-K logistics. As described by a source inside the Commission in November 2015, IS-K's logistics was a lean structure compared to the Taliban's, reportedly with just 85 people in headquarters and another 600 distributed among the component groups.[79] The Logistics Commission has representatives with each of the component groups, who receive supplies from the Commission and redistribute them within the groups.[80] In addition, each component group has its own small logistics structure. Bakhtwar's group, for example, reportedly had 30 men tasked with logistics out of 400; the source inside the group acknowledged that 80 per cent of logistics was provided by IS-K.[81] Another example is that of Harakat Khilafat Baluch, which reportedly had fifty men in its logistics.[82]

The internal logistics of the component groups was all the same, being dictated by the Commission. The logistics staff of the component groups in fact worked for the Logistics Commission. There were also inspectors sent by the Commission to inspect the work of representatives and groups, who checked how many men were effectively in the tactical units. One partial exception were Muslim Dost's people, said to be 'more experienced' at handling logistics than the other groups. In reality, this might be yet another sign of Muslim Dost's autonomy within IS-K. Every time supplies passed into a new set of hands required signatures by those delivering and those receiving. The component groups did not have autonomy when it came to handling the supplies, and their requests were assessed by the Logistics Commission on the basis of their recorded manpower.[83] Adapting or changing the system was not allowed, the rationale being:

if there were differences in the logistics of these groups like the logistic of one group is better but the logistics of another group is not good, this would have a really negative effect in the groups and it will create disunity in the groups. Like one group will say that why our logistics are not good but the logistics of another group is good.[84]

Still, this small central structure reportedly had $95 million to spend in 2015, and it did so by relying mostly on private contractors.[85]

Contracting out a large portion of IS-K logistics to private companies is another innovation of the IS advisers, although the Taliban might have also occasionally relied on contractors. IS-Central insisted that IS-K should develop functional and well-organized logistics, advising that private companies should be used as much as possible.[86]

> We can say that time we did not have any right logistics. ... We can say that time our logistic was equal to nothing before. At that time our goods and logistics were seized and we did not transfer it easily but now our goods are not seized and we can carry it easily even to Iran.[87]

Private companies were delivering supplies to the combat groups. The logistical units at the provincial level of IS-K were mostly busy liaising with the contractors and buying additional supplies on the black market.[88] Normally, private companies would handle soft logistics, such as deliveries of food, clothes, boots and medicines, while hard logistics (weapons, explosives and ammunition) was handled directly by the Logistics Commission.[89] The private contractors would normally bring the supplies to the provincial centres, and from there IS-K logistics would take over.[90] Some of the private companies were aware they were working for IS-K, and some were not.[91] Staff of one such company was arrested by the Afghan NDS inside Afghanistan.[92]

An employee of one of the companies providing logistics to IS-K stated that he had begun working with IS-K in 2014, when some Arabs visited the his company's office in Pakistan and signed a contract for him to supply clothes and shoes to IS-K. IS-K chose the company as a supplier because of its previous track record in selling supplies to the Taliban and its readiness even to deliver the goods to IS-K tactical groups in their operating areas, except when fighting is going on, in which case the delivery would go to the nearest safe place. There was inevitably no tendering out of supplying contracts; the companies had to be contacted by IS-K secretly.[93]

The supplying of medicines and electrical equipment was also contracted out.[94] The Logistics Commission signed formal contracts with the suppliers, but under the name of some businesses linked to IS-K. The sources provided the names of some Afghan and Pakistani companies based in the UAE, whose existence was verified by the authors. IS-K, however, pays a premium of about 50–100 per cent on the going market rate. The contractors' managements did not seem to harbour any particular sympathy for IS-K—they were simply looking to make a profit—but sometimes they employed Afghan IS-K sympathizers for making deliveries. IS-K appeared to pay its invoices on time.[95]

> We find easy dealing with Daesh because they are educated people who are working in the Logistics Commission and Finance Commission. In these commissions all the people are educated and no problems take place between them and us. Yes they are, they are difficult clients but not for us now but for other people it is difficult, because Daesh does not trust on any person or companies to start working with them. They do not trust anyone and they do not start working with everyone. They are working with people for whom they receive guarantee from a trusted person. Like Daesh started working with us when one Arab gave guarantee to them that we will not create problems for Daesh.[96]

Most of the supplies were purchased in Bara and Tera and other locations inside Pakistan. Some weaponry was donated by Arab sheiks to IS-K and smuggled through Pakistan.[97] Orders for better-quality weapons could be placed through some smugglers even in Central Asia. IS-K claims not to buy secondhand equipment, because it can afford to buy new. Whether this is true or not, the Taliban also claimed that IS-K was better equipped than Taliban combat groups. Efforts to buy anti-aircraft missiles have born no fruit, however, as these are in short supply in the regional black market. There was nonetheless pressure on the Logistics Commission to procure heavy and advanced weapons for future operations.[98]

The Recruitment Commission

Recruitment was of course one of the highest priorities for IS-K as a young organization. Efforts to build a widespread recruitment infrastructure, to be managed by the Recruitment Commission, started in earnest even before the Commission actually started its activities. A source claimed that recruitment offices existed in all of Pakistan's main cities, as well as the two Waziristans, Bajaur and Kashmir.[99] In Afghanistan, the first recruitment 'office' was opened in August 2014 in Dara e Pech (Kunar), with eight mobile teams travelling around Kunar's district for recruitment. From September 2014 through April 2015, seven more recruitment offices opened in Achin (Nangarhar), Shahjoy (Zabul), Gilan (Ghazni), Warduj (Badakhshan), Balkhab (Sar-i Pul), Kunduz and Helmand.[100]

In total, during the first year of its existence IS-K reportedly spent a total of $13.5 million in its Afghan field recruitment offices alone. Some of the teams set up small recruitment centres in the districts, for example in Kot.[101] Some sources also maintained that IS-K was recruiting schoolteachers to proselytize among students. In Nangarhar, by the end of 2015 there were, according to a former IS-K member, already two schools that were operating under IS-K influence.[102] According to TLO's research, the textbooks used in these schools were mainly Saudi ones, officially approved by the Saudi authorities.[103]

According to a senior source in IS-K, the organization always carried out selective recruitment and carefully vetted its volunteers, in order to avoid infiltration and keep the quality of the members high. Every month, 1,000–2,000 aspiring volunteers came knocking at its doors, most of whom ended up being rejected. In May 2015, for example, only 420 recruits in all of Khorasan were accepted, according to the source.[104] IS-K sources also claim that initially they set high bars in terms of madrasa educational requirements for recruits, and IS-K made a big vaunt of this:

> We are hiring and recruiting people who did Islamic studies complete and know Islam completely but Taliban are hiring and recruiting people who are not educated. Who did not do Islamic studies. Who are completely illiterate.[105]

The intelligence department

IS-K invested significant resources in the development of an intelligence apparatus. The intelligence department was formed in early 2015 and by June of that year already had according to IS-K sources 500 staff (as TKK members), distributed across the territories of IS-K activity.[106] Operational assets were controlled by IS-K and not by the individual component groups. Later on, numbers in intelligence grew. In Jalalabad alone, for example, IS-K sources claimed to have 250–300 members doing intelligence and recruitment.[107] Elders shared the view that IS-K indeed had a thick network of informers in the villages:

> Just three weeks ago in Khana Khil village, Daesh beheaded a villager accused of spreading propaganda against Daesh among the other villagers. When this villager said something negative against the Daesh, for sure there wasn't any Daesh people near him otherwise he wouldn't say something against Daesh. This shows that there was Daesh informers among the villager.[108]

Among other things, the IS-K intelligence apparatus was also tasked to infiltrate the Afghan security forces, which IS-K sources claimed it did effectively as far back as June 2016 in some areas of Nangarhar like Achin, Kot, Bati Kot, Shirzad, Ghani Khel, Hesarak and Shinwari.[109] At least one district governor in Nangarhar was reported to have an understanding with IS-K, while police checkpoints in Nangarhar reportedly had deals with the private companies taking logistics to IS-K units.[110] Such claims could not be confirmed, however.

Military organization

The top military structure of IS-K is the Military Shura or Council, composed of a varying number of members, ranging from twenty to twenty-five initially and then reportedly growing to forty as IS-K expanded. Its first head was Sayed Hafeez Khan. Within the Military Council sit sector commanders, each responsible for three so-called 'battalions' of 150–200 men each. This structure highlighted the fact that the military forces of IS-K at that time were in principle conceived as mobile conventional units, able to deploy where required. The structure might have been meant to kick into place when large operations were planned, such as the blitzkrieg attacks in Zabul, Kunar and Nangarhar, but it was not what IS-K units looked like on the average day (see below).

The Council also included a general staff, a commander of 'special commandos' and suicide groups, a commander of logistics, a commander of sniper units and a commander of 'ambush forces'. The Council was tasked with strategic planning, directing military operations, planning attacks, exercising oversight, supervising and advising field commanders, and managing weaponry and the 'spoils of war'. The Military Council had a representative in each province and in each district.[111]

Around 2020, a different model of military organization was adopted, based on groups or teams of five, ten, thirty and fifty men, which could then be combined in large fronts as required. All major operations were led by the amir and the other senior commanders; group and junior commanders could only lead local fights. This new organization appears to have been intended to fight a more hybrid type of warfare.[112]

IS-K members were, at least in the early years, kept under strict discipline and required authorizations from their commanders to do anything: 'Daesh Khurasan has a very good system, fighters and commanders cannot do anything without permission of their senior commanders'.[113] This is another indicator that the concept was not that of an insurgency being fought in a decentralized way. Although it should be noted that the trademark black dress often sported by IS-K members is not a compulsory uniform.[114]

IS sources claimed that, contrary to the established practice in the Taliban, the death of a commander of IS-K does not entail the disintegration of the whole combat group; IS-K retains 'ownership' of the fighters, and a new commander can be appointed by the military leadership without resistance.[115]

The command-and-control model was imported from IS-Central and featured a higher level of secrecy than what characterizes the Taliban or TTP. Even the average IS-K field commander knew little of the upper levels of the organization. According to one of them:

> I only understand that my senior commander is Mawlawi Janan, who is from Orakzai tribe of Pakistan, he is the one who give us logistics and weapons, he was the one who brought some teachers of Daesh for training us. I have no information about who is above Mawlawi Janan. Most of the leaders and important commanders are Pakistanis and they don't meet with their fighters or commanders a lot. As far as I know there is a leadership council in Swat of Pakistan and most of the orders are coming from Swat and Bajaur of Pakistan.[116]

Throughout 2014–16, IS-K did not use part-time militias, and all its fighters were on a 24-hour call-out system; they were banned from holding other jobs apart from fighting for IS-K.[117] Only towards the end of 2016, local part-time forces were established in Nangarhar, in order to boost IS-K mobile forces deployed there in the defence of some fixed assets in Mohmand Valley and nearby areas. A source quantified their strength at around 1,000 men in 2017.[118]

Like the Taliban, IS-K in principle allowed its fighters 3 months of leave each year,[119] although in Zabul as of October 2015 no leave system had been introduced.[120] With the leave system activated, 10–40 per cent of fighters would be in rest or recuperation at any time.[121]

The effectiveness of IS-K's military was only moderately tested during 2015 and 2016. In the first 6 months of its existence, IS-K was not very active; internal sources claim that, despite serious clashes with Taliban, only 183 men were killed, mostly due to drone strikes in Achin.[122] That would amount to around 4 per cent of IS-K's strength at that time (see Table 9), so not quite negligible over a period of just 6 months, but still well below typical Taliban casualty rates.[123] Independent data gathered over the first 18 months of IS-K's existence determined that up to June 2016, out of 52 IS-K commanders profiled, 6 had been killed, 3 had joined a pro-government militia and 2 had given up, with the rest still being active.[124] This represents a 11 per cent killed-in-action ratio over 18 months, quite similar to the one reported above by IS-K sources. Casualties started mounting in the second half of 2016, as IS-K engaged in semi-conventional fighting in Nangarhar. An IS-K source acknowledged that in July–August 2016 245 were killed in fighting in Nangarhar alone; the sources admitted that was the first time IS-K took 'heavy casualties', as this was the first time the organization was targeted in heavy airstrikes.[125]

When asked what were the sources of IS-K's apparent military proficiency, a source pointed out their terror tactics and the plentiful RPG and DSchK heavy machine guns which were available to them, as well their superior rganization.[126] IS-K sources have also been claiming to be in possession of anti-tank missiles, 'advanced rocket launchers, night vision scopes, mostly of Russian make, allegedly bought on the black market, and new rifles'.[127]

The Shari'a Council

Religious affairs are managed by the Shari'a Council, whose original head was Sheikh Bilal Ishaqzai. Apart from advising the IS-K leadership on religious matters, this Council was supposed to manage the courts, disputes and litigations; mediate disputes; and order punishments, 'promoting virtue' and 'punishing vice'. In the early days of IS-K, there was no attempt to co-opt or replace the mosque mullahs.[128] Later, however, through this Council IS-K paid mullahs to preach in the mosques in favour of the Caliphate. In Nangarhar, for example, a source hostile to IS-K claimed that as of January 2016 IS-K had its own mullahs in eleven districts. Often these were mullahs previously associated with the Taliban.[129] A Council of Ulema was also being planned as of 2015.[130]

The propaganda office

The propaganda operations of IS-K were initially managed by an office of Wilayat Khorasan, which reportedly relied on 60 staff members in June 2015,[131] and also by a propaganda office within the TKK, with 160 men claimed to be distributed in five locations as of June 2015—North Waziristan, Quetta, Peshawar, Nangarhar and Helmand—and plans to open in some Gulf locations as well. Mostly the members of this office were former Taliban and former TTP, with a sprinkle of cadres from Syria and Iraq.[132] The media unit of IS-K, Abtad-ul Islam, is probably part of this office.[133]

Later, the two propaganda units were merged and expanded, under the impulse of then newly arrived special envoy Abu Yasir Al-Afghani, who was also the first one to start recruiting university-educated people and internet specialists into the unit. Press sources reported efforts to recruit experienced journalists as well.[134] At the head of the merged structure was placed a former

Lashkar-e Taiba commander with 2 years in Syria in his curriculum, Abu Abdul Wahab Al Khorasani. It was claimed that by March 2017 the unit had grown dramatically in size to around 470 staff, the large majority (over two-thirds) of which were Pakistanis, with 20 per cent Afghans and 10 per cent Arabs. This figure purportedly includes staff tasked with face-to-face and other propaganda and proselytizing operations on the ground, with teams among other locations in Kabul, Balkh, Herat, Peshawar, Karachi, Quetta and Lahore. If this is right, the propaganda office in fact overlapped with the Recruitment Commission in its functions. About a hundred Afghans and Pakistanis had previous experience of working the propaganda apparatus for either the Taliban or TTP. Because of the nature of its activities, the department was entirely staffed by educated people: 19 per cent had university degrees, 40 per cent madrasa diplomas and the rest all had high school diplomas. About 10 per cent had technical training in web mastering and other related specializations. New offices were opened in the provinces of Kabul and Balkh, and in Karachi, Orakzai and Lahore. The budget for 2017 was reportedly still a modest $3 million, according to an internal source, but up 50 per cent on 2016, which in turn had doubled from that of 2015.[135]

Propaganda in its various forms distributed through the internet keeps more than half the staff of the propaganda team busy. The topics of videos distributed through Facebook included mainly portrayals of fighting, but also increasingly displays of non-military activities: courts hearings, education courses and others. By March 2017, IS-K claimed to have 200 Facebook pages, 60 Twitter accounts, and 40 Instagram accounts, as well as videos hosted on 20 other websites of sympathetic organizations and groups. Only blogs were not being used at that point.

Telegram and Facebook were also used for recruitment purposes, with the propaganda team targeting individuals who posted positive comments. The social media pages used by IS-K are continuously changing, so they are difficult to keep track of, but the author has visited at least some of them. Some of the videos directly attack the Taliban, singling them out for their involvement in the drug trade. As of March 2017, IS-K's propaganda team had issued eighteen videos, of which six were videos of fighting, two of training, three of religious propaganda, two of court activities, two of anti-Taliban propaganda, one of educational activities and two about IS-K's aims. The propaganda videos sometimes feature the leaders of IS-Central, and sometimes the leaders of IS-K. In early 2017, videos were being prepared to denounce atrocities by Iraqi government forces in the battle for Mosul and explain the anticipated fall of

Mosul as a 'tactical withdrawal'.[136] Osman described the social media effort of IS-K as 'agile and deft', and:

> outmatching the Taleban in terms of the quality and diversity of the media it employs, as well as the activeness of its loyalists in promoting the group's message—especially taking into account the differing size of the two groups and their level of establishment in Afghanistan. ISKP is most notably ahead of the Taleban in its usage of FM radio and social media. ISKP employs a dedicated team of broadcasters and reporters who produce reporting on military advances and life under the caliphate that is engaging to its audience. The radio reporters interview fighters, talk to local residents and record reportages featuring life under the caliphate. The language used by the broadcasters is brisk, energetic and focused on attracting listeners and new recruits. Similarly, in their use of social media, ISKP loyalists are dedicated and give the appearance of a well-connected community, although it is not clear if this is centrally coordinated. The Taleban's De Shariat Ghag [Voice of Sharia] Radio, that intermittently broadcasts throughout Paktika and Ghazni provinces, on the other hand, mainly plays tarane [Pashto plural for tarana, chants performed without instrumental accompaniment] and reads out articles that have been posted on its website.[137]

The propaganda team's activities were initially aimed at Afghanistan, Pakistan, Central Asia, Iran and India, but also Bangladesh, Burma, China and Russia, as the team was asked by IS-Central to cover those areas as well.[138] Among other things, the office operates the Voice of the Khalifat radio, which in 2015 was broadcasting from an area 15 km from Jalalabad.[139] The propaganda content of the FM station included accusations of the Taliban for being Pakistani puppets and of Akhtar Mohammad Mansur for being an apostate, but during 2016 it was only broadcasting for short periods of time each day.[140] TLO reported that the radio's broadcasts were popular in Nangarhar.[141]

> Some respondents explained that the radio channel was highly effective in building Daesh's popularity since it 'explained everything', including their own actions and those of others with reference to the Quran or the *hadiths*.[142]

Much of IS-K's propaganda activities have been carried out in Nangarhar: murals, CDs, posters, banners, flags, leaflets for distribution in schools and mosques.[143] Video clips and songs were also distributed via USB keys; according to one source, IS-K even convinced music shop owners to copy IS-K propaganda onto the USB keys and CDs of unaware buyers. Again according to TLO, these propaganda clips and songs were popular among the general population, and even fashionable for a time being.[144]

The first output of IS propaganda in Khorasan predated the establishment of IS-K and was a flyer titled *Fatah* (Victory), issued in Pashto and Dari but asking for support in establishing the Khalifate in Pakistan.[145] IS-K even composed a song (no music) about belonging to IS and their allegiance to al-Baghdadi, which they sing or play from tapes when they visit villages.[146]

As of March 2017, the IS-K propaganda team was planning to start a print magazine, but they never managed to obtain the machinery to print it.[147] IS-K also distributed videos in CD and DVD format to sympathetic mullahs and mawlavis, university teachers and village elders for further distribution. The main audiences of IS-K were ranked as madrasas, high schools, universities, mosques and common people. Madrasas were a priority because, as noted by the source, 'madrasa students are convinced very quickly'.[148]

The propaganda activities of the department have not been risk-free. As of early March 2017, twenty-two staff members of the unit have been arrested in Afghanistan and Pakistan. Six were caught in Torkham, Afghanistan, carrying videos and books from Pakistan, while sixteen more were detained in Pakistan where they were visiting a printer to discuss the publication of some booklets.[149]

The content of IS-K propaganda disseminated in the villages was similar to that spread by the Voice of the Khalifat: essentially diatribes against the Afghan government and in particular the Taliban, accusing both of being in the service of foreign intelligence services.[150] Local elders in Kajaki never heard IS-K commanders talking of Iran and Shi'as as enemies.[151] The ranking of priorities for IS-K are clear from its propaganda:

> Daesh is always saying propaganda against the Taliban and I think Taliban is the most important enemy of Daesh in the area. They are saying that Taliban has been around in Afghanistan for more than twenty years but haven't brought any change in spreading of Islam around the country, that Taliban are the dogs of Pakistan's ISI. After the Taliban America is the enemy of Daesh and they are saying that Americans are based in Afghanistan to control Asia and turn this Islamic country into a Christian country in the future.[152]

In general, IS-K propaganda cannot be said to have been effective among villagers. Despite the IS-K's constantly insisting on Taliban links to Pakistan, many villagers believe IS-K itself to be a stooge of the Pakistanis.[153]

The Shahadat (martyrdom) department

In IS-K there is a department under the Military Commission called Shahadat, which is charge of organizing terrorist attacks. In its shape (as of the end of 2016) it was established in February 2016. In December 2016, it was led by Sheikh Abdullah Adamkhel, who spent 2 years in Syria with IS. As of December 2016, according to IS-K sources, this department employed in total around 5 per cent of the overall claimed strength of IS-K (see Table 9), mostly organized in teams of about fifty men in each province where the department was active, except Nangarhar and Kabul where the groups are larger. Except for Kabul and Nangarhar, in late 2016 the structures of the Shahahdat were still being set up in Herat, Karachi, Lahore, Islamabad, Peshawar and a few other locations.[154]

This compares with the 1.5 per cent of total Taliban strength (but 10 per cent of Haqqani network strength) accounted for by the Haqqanis' Fedayin Commission, the Taliban's closest equivalent (but the Taliban also had other structures, beyond the Haqqanis', carrying out terrorist attacks).[155] In 2015, the department (in its previous incarnation as a simple unit of the Military Commission) reportedly operated with a budget of $10 million, which doubled to $20 million in 2016 when it was upgraded to a department. Sources claimed that the 2017 budget would be increased further, suggesting that the leadership of IS-K considered Shahadat to be a priority.[156]

As mentioned already, up to spring 2017 Kabul was almost the only theatre of operations for the Shahadat department. IS-K invested considerable resources in its Kabul Shahadat organization, but for the first 18 months of its existence was hampered by its inability to 'steal' significant numbers of skilled terror operatives from the Taliban. In October 2016, one analyst estimated that there were probably three IS-K cells in Kabul, with in total some dozens of operational members and around 250 members in total. One of the cells had probably 'defected' from AQ to IS, while another was composed of Salafis who had been in the Taliban before but had not been operating inside Kabul. After joining IS-K, this cell appears to have been involved in the distribution of propaganda material and perhaps in an attack on a Sufi mosque in west Kabul in March 2015. The third cell seems to be based in north Kabul and composed mainly of Tajiks of Salafi inclinations. Some members of this cell had been in Syria or had fought in Nangarhar.[157]

These forces mainly operated against very soft targets. Most IS-K attacks in Kabul were carried out against Hazaras. The exception might have been a relatively sophisticated attack in Kabul on 20 June 2016, against a minivan carrying Nepalese guards employed by the Canadian embassy, killing fourteen. The attribution to IS-K was not uncontested, however.[158]

In November 2016, IS-K capabilities were dramatically enhanced by the defection of 150 members of the Haqqani network, who had operated in

Kabul. The defection, admitted by the Haqqanis themselves, was triggered by the breakup in relations between Serajuddin Haqqani and Azizullah Haqqani, which led to the latter cutting ties and taking his loyalists with him to IS-K.[159] Apart from the numerical strengthening of IS-K capabilities, these 150 men brought into Shahadat capabilities that were not there before: the Haqqanis had the best expertise within the Taliban in carrying out complex operations in Kabul. By early 2017, IS-K still had yet to put these new human resources to use and some re-organization seemed to have been going on. In November 2016, a source in IS-K believed that it would take 1–2 years to mount attacks similar in complexity to the ones carried out by the Haqqani network in Kabul. At that time, IS-K sources claimed to be working on developing car bombs to breach the city's protective concrete walls.[160]

By the end of 2016, the total strength of the IS-K Kabul unit was estimated by Taliban at 300–400, while IS-K sources put it at around 450 men. Of this, about 100 were in operations and the rest in various support roles: 50 in logistics, 20 in finance, about 50 in recruitment and over 200 in intelligence. These figures seem to match the estimates mentioned above.[161]

The IS-K structure as it turned out

The failed fusion of the component groups

In practice, the planned merger discussed in 'The political and leadership structure' above did not happen, and the TKK's military wing continued being just one component group among the others.[162] By 2016, there was no longer any talk of a complete merger of the different component groups within the TKK, but rather of the groups persisting indefinitely with the TKK acting as an umbrella organization. However, as the component groups failed to merge into the TKK, a compromise had to be worked out. On top of the governance structure developed separately from the component groups (that is, Wilayat Khorasan), TKK would develop support and administrative services to be used by all the component groups. To make those structures work, the component groups would have to standardize their structures and practices according to a single model imposed by the leadership.[163]

The original intent of making TKK a 'party' pendant of the Wilayat is betrayed by the oversizing of its non-combat structures, when compared to other components of IS-K. By October 2015, 43 per cent of TKK's strength were non-combatants, including finance, logistics, recruitment, health, intelligence and education cadres. This was because TKK as the supposed 'container' in which all the other component groups should merge took over partial or full responsibility for providing these support activities. This also resulted in other component groups having much leaner support structures: 14 per cent for the Muslim Dost Group, 16 per cent for Shamali Khilafat, 21 per cent for Khilafat Afghan and 13 per cent on average for all of IS-K (according to internal sources).[164]

According to a senior figure in IS, the IS-K leadership also established the principle that each component group's leader had to be recognized by the leadership in order to be legitimate. The source might be referring to the acceptance of *bay'a* by al-Baghdadi, but as it will be discussed below IS-Central also played a key role in selecting leaders for vacant positions, such as leader of the TKK.[165]

Probably in order to prevent the consolidation of the component groups into personal fiefdoms of their leaders, during 2016 the IS-K military leadership decided to start mixing up groups of different component groups in the same sub-province, but keeping them in distinct districts. Maps 1–3 show the situation in Kunar in February 2016, in Nangarhar in the second half of 2015 and in Farah in December 2015.

In order to manage the component groups after the aborted merger, it became necessary to establish under the TKK leader a so-called 'Hamahangi' office, where a representative of each component group sits and is allowed to exchange information, plans and so on.[166] Each component group had its own Leadership Shura—usually smaller than the top one, with just a few members—under which small replicas of the main commissions and councils operated. Finally, each component group would have its own amirs in the provinces, liaising with other component groups and with the Wilayat's amirs. The support structures of the various component groups account for a relatively substantial share of their membership, around 13 per cent on average. Muslim Dost's Group, for example, claimed to have about 160 men in its support structures as of October 2015, 50 of whom were based in Pakistan.[167]

The lost 'code of conduct'

It is worth noting that the IS-K code of conduct—which in April 2015 a senior figure said would be ready 'very very soon', and in January 2016 was said by another senior figure in the organization to be 3–4 months away from completion—was still not ready as of November 2016.[168] Abdul Bahar Mehsud and Hafiz Saeed Khan were reported to be leading in the preparation of the wider code of conduct. 'It will be different from that of the Taliban', promised a senior IS-K cadre.[169] There were clearly varying opinions within

Map 1: IS-K component groups in Kunar, February 2016[170]

Legend: MD=Muslim Dost group; KA=Khilafat Afghan.

Map 2: IS-K component groups in Nangarhar, second half of 2015[171]

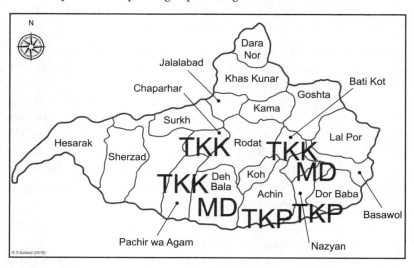

Legend: MD=Muslim Dost; TKK=Tehrik-e Khilafat Khorasan; KA=Khilafat Afghan.

Map 3: IS-K component groups in Farah, December 2015[172]

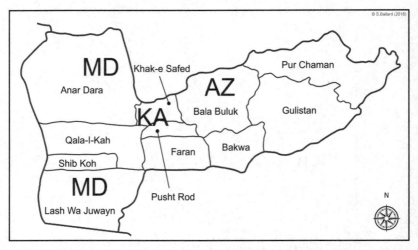

Legend: MD=Muslim Dost group; KA=Khilafat Afghan; AZ=Azizullah Haqqani.

IS-K on the content of the code of conduct. Moreover, not all IS-K members were convinced that written rules were needed:

> I think we don't need a code of conduct, we know everything, we know our enemies, we know how to fight and we know our aims.[173]

The failure to issue a code of conduct reasonably quickly is certainly surprising given IS-K's great stress on discipline. It also begs the question of how discipline was maintained.

Instead, at least the TKP released its own short code of conduct, authored by its leader, Abdul Bahar Mehsud, and consisting of some basic points (see Annex 1). Apart from discussing relations with the TTP and the Taliban, the Code of Conduct insisted that defections would not be forgiven (except if so requested by the highest authority within the TKP), banned the collection of taxes and insisted on recognizable and distinct uniforms for its men and on the display of the Caliphate's Black Flag.[174]

The missed target of revenue centralization

Original groups around which pro-IS commanders coalesced, like Muslim Dost's, were entirely funded directly by foreign donors; in Muslim Dost's case, it was Saudi Arabia. When IS-K launched, it banned its own members in principle from getting any funding from third-party sources. All foreign funding had to be received through the Finance Commission.[175] The various donors agreed to stop directly funding the component groups in May 2015.[176] In reality, this ban was never fully implemented, and most component groups continued to receive funding directly from donors, although presumably in most cases with IS-K's consent and approval. Table 5 shows the budgets of the different component groups. The various component groups could also use local tax revenue to supplement the budget allocated centrally.

A source in the Finance Commission acknowledged that some of the component groups received funds bypassing the Finance Commission; he did not believe such funds would account for more than 5–10 per cent of the total raised. IS-K authorized these exceptions to the rule, as otherwise these donors might simply not pay.[177]

The above 5–10 per cent estimate provided by the source in the Finance Commission might be understated, if information provided by other sources is considered. Table 5 summarizes the cases of five IS-K component groups, for which detailed information was obtained from sources within those component groups. In addition:

- IS-K sources claim that several of the component groups received direct funding from Saudi Arabia to the tune of $18 million in 2013, $23 million in 2014 and $35 million in 2015. Among the main recipients were Muslim Dost's Group, Khilafat Afghan, and TKP (included in Table 5) but also Harakat Khilafat Baluch;[178]
- Some extra funds were also reportedly accruing to Azizullah Haqqani from Qatar and the UAE. The Azizullah Haqqani component group had a finance officer posted to Saudi Arabia to raise funds with private and state donors.[179]

The most commonly cited sources of funding were Saudi Arabia, Qatar and Pakistan, but it is not clear whether the sources were private or government donors.[180] This fundraising autonomously from the Finance Commission is likely to have negatively affected the leadership's efforts to merge the different component groups together, even if all the component groups seem to have been primarily dependent on handouts from the Financial Commission.

Table 5: IS-K Finance Commission (FC) contributions to some IS-K component groups vs other sources of funds, according to IS-K sources[181]

$ million	2015		2016	
Component groups	From IS-K FC	Direct contributions bypassing FC and locally raised taxes	From IS-K FC	Direct contributions bypassing FC and locally raised taxes
TKP	30	14	35	25
Khilafat Afghan	18	16	25	15
Muslim Dost	14	6	20	10
Shamali Khilafat	8	10	28	2
Bakhtwar Group	–	–	0	32

The lack of recruitment centralization

IS-K recruitment was in practice carried out by both the central recruitment commission, by the recruitment commissions of the component groups and by individual commanders. Commanders, however, had to report all recruitment to the commissions before receiving permission, getting a IS-K ID issued and training would take place.[182] Recruitment by the different component groups was still a free-for-all activity as of July 2016: there was no division of labour, and each group competed with the others for the same pool of potential recruits.[183] The component groups therefore had their own recruitment facilities. The Bakhtwar Group, for example, claimed to have 50 recruiters out of about 400 members in mid-2016, that is, over 12 per cent of its strength. Some mullahs also sent recruits without being on the IS-K payroll. They were operating in refugee camps, madrasas and mosques. There were at least four madrasas closely connected to Bakhtwar Group in Pakistan as of July 2016.[184]

An example of how IS-K recruited in its early days was provided by one of the organization's rare deserters, from Nangarhar. Having been with the Taliban for many years, this fighter followed his commander into IS-K. The fighter's personal motivation was a dispute with the cousin, also in the Taliban. The commander was attracted by IS-K's hardline and anti-Pakistani rhetoric, made all the more convincing by the fact that it was accompanied by a good financial offer.[185]

Not-so-selective recruitment

Claims of selective recruitment cannot be substantiated with other sources, and this might just be part of a wider IS-K propaganda effort to present itself as a more professional and ideologically oriented organization than the Taliban. It is clear, for example, that new groups joining IS-K after its formation, like Jaysh ul-Islam (see Chapter 6), were admitted into IS-K as a block. The account provided by an IS-K commander in Bati Kot also casts serious doubts on this narrative:

> I have ten fighters, all these fighters were with me when I was with Taliban, they are all my friends and when I decided to join with Daesh, they were all agree with me. Now all my fighters are the same fighters that I had when I was with Taliban, there is no other fighter from other groups with me.[186]

Perhaps in the early stages of recruitment, when it mostly operated underground, IS-K was indeed selective in its recruitment efforts; as it started expanding rapidly, however, it had to open its doors. Even a source at senior level admitted that there came a point that these 'high bars' were lowered. Illiterate or poorly educated recruits were given lessons after recruitment. The requirement for commanders to be madrasa-educated, however, stayed, according to the source.[187]

By 2017, there were clear indications that IS-K recruitment standards had been lowered further. At least two groups with no serious jihadist background were allowed to join. One was the Sangari, a militia funded with Afghan security services funds in Helmand, that defected to IS-K in part because funding had temporarily dried up. Another was an armed group of perhaps 200 men in Faryab province, previously loyal to Jamiat-i Islami (a party member of the National Unity Government in Kabul) and led by Commander Ajmal.[188]

Not much military innovation

There is some evidence to support claims that IS-K successfully fostered a sense of organizational identity and esprit de corps, as the fighters of Khadim (Khilafat Afghan) did not desert or disappear after he was killed (see 'Khilafat Afghan and Muslim Dost Group' above in Chapter 1). However, there is also some evidence of the contrary, as the few defectors from IS-K were mostly men following their commander out (see *Enter Abu Yasir Al-Afghani* in Chapter 9). The desire of IS-K leaders to strengthen the esprit de corps of the organization can therefore perhaps be described as a 'work in progress'.

In operations, all component groups were supposed to mix and operate together, although at the beginning, at least, this was not often the case.[189] As we have seen at the beginning of this chapter, pragmatically the IS-K leadership assigned the component groups to different districts, so that they would not normally have to work together on the average day. All component groups had to obey the sub-provincial and district amirs. The groups, whose size should in theory have been standardized as twenty to twenty-five, are the tactical unit on the group.[190] The group and the two or three teams that compose it are what IS-K forces look like almost all the time when they are away from their bases, except when large-scale operations are launched. IS-K forces are found most of the time. In practice, while some component groups, like Muslim Dost's and all the component groups in Zabul, did have twenty to twenty-five men in each group,[191] others—in Kunduz, for example—had thirty men.[192] The fighters of Bakhtwar Group were organized in combat groups of thirty men each,[193] and a high-level source even described the IS-K groups as having sixty men each.[194]

Despite IS-K doing a good deal of talking up of its military capabilities, up to the end of 2016 there were few signs of any major IS-K innovation in military tactics. There were also reports of IS-K using horses for mobility and operating like a 'professional army', presumably a reference to their having a higher degree of discipline than the Taliban.[195]

After being drawn into the unplanned confrontation with the Taliban over Mohmand Valley in Achi (see Chapter 8), in June 2015 IS-K achieved their first major breakthrough in Nangarhar by relying on a fleet of pickups, equipped with heavy machine guns. The tactic surprised the Taliban, who fled, but it was of course nothing new, as the Taliban had already used it in the 1990s.[196] The IS-K also used other tactics that had previously come from the Taliban. In at least a few occasions, IS-K claimed to have carried out a suicide attack against the Taliban, including one in Zabul province, in which the shadow governor Matiullah and military leader Pir Agha were killed,[197] and one against Mullah Salam in Kunduz in 2017 (see 'Negotiations and agreements' in Chapter 8).

Examples of where IS-K practised 'blitzkrieg' tactics of suddenly taking over relatively large areas include Nangarhar in the summer of 2015 and again in the summer of 2016, Zabul province in autumn 2016 and Kunar at about the same time. Except for the summer 2016 offensive in Nangarhar against the Afghan security forces, which were repelled by the intervention of US Special Forces and Air Force, these blitzkriegs were successful. However, IS-K's superiority to the Taliban appears to have been due mainly to the fact that crack Taliban mobile units were rarely deployed against IS-K. When they were—for example, Iran-trained Taliban 'commandos' in western Afghanistan and later in Nangarhar—IS-K usually has the worst of it. The local Taliban units, which IS-K mostly faced in the east, were usually poorly equipped with secondhand or cheap copies of Russian assault rifles, very few machine guns and RPG rocket launchers, and they lack an 'officer corps' able to manoeuvre large numbers of them.

The impression that derives from the process of organizational development as it unfolded in 2015–16 is that the leadership, probably under pressure from Mosul, tried to make IS-K more cohesive and efficient, but local conditions and resistance by the component group leaders limited the impact of its efforts. As of early 2017, the military organization of IS-K was still in hybrid form. IS-K appears to have been effective in gathering, quickly deploying and commanding concentrations of forces of 1,000–2,000 men. This suggests that the structure described at the beginning of this chapter is not 'on paper only', nor is it mere propaganda.

At the same time, IS-K has clearly had greater problems in controlling its groups when they are deployed sparsely around the villages to recruit, scout or secure territorial control. Clearly, not all the component groups got on well with each other, hence the decision to partition their areas of operation by territory. As the component groups raised their own taxes and recruited separately, having overlapping territorial control would inevitably result in friction between them. As discussed in Chapter 8, much of the fighting with the Taliban was the result of unplanned actions by such groups, whose commanders often had personal issues with local Taliban and/or local communities. Enforcing discipline among dispersed combat groups is of course a classical problem of any armed organization.

Shari'a courts almost only on paper

Baczko and Dorronsoro noted that IS-K did not do much to establish a shadow state.[198] As of June 2015, a senior source admitted that there were still no operational IS-K courts anywhere; the source explained that they 'will be created very soon and we will make department for it. We will bring professional judges for them who did religion studies'. Later, the existence of IS-K mobile courts was at least mentioned in Kajaki, where IS-K brought in its own mullahs to staff its courts with ideologically suitable clerics, as well as in Nangarhar and Kunar. Sources external to IS-K, however, did not see any trace of IS-K courts or judges of any kind, even in Kajaki.[199] In 2017, a video of an IS-K court in Afghanistan was circulated on Facebook.[200] In practice, disputes were being dealt with by IS-K commanders, who sometimes even had jails at their disposal; according to one source, some twenty villagers were jailed by IS-K in Kajaki for having had arguments or a dispute.[201] Such dispute resolution and administration of justice in any case appears to have happened on a small scale: even in Kajaki, elders were not aware of IS-K having tried to resolve disputes and administer justice on a significant scale.[202]

Window dressing or work in progress?

It is clear that as of early 2017 IS-K had only had partial success in building up the structure mandated by its remote patrons in Mosul. The question is whether that structure was ever really meant to be built: was it largely a propaganda or window dressing exercise, or was IS-K struggling through various difficulties but nonetheless striving to make it really happen?

The first consideration is that 2 years for building up a structure as ambitious as the one laid out in early 2015 is not a long time, particularly in a context where IS-K was active militarily and being actively targeted in response. IS-K lost all its main leaders during those 2 years, a fact that must have slowed its development.

There are signs, moreover, that the IS-K leadership and IS-Central were really trying to forge a united, cohesive organization. It is worth noting, for example, that in centralizing intelligence collection in the hands of TKK, the one component group it directly controlled, the leadership earned an additional tool of control over the other component groups. IS-Central also seems to have a policy of keeping propaganda activities as concentrated as possible, with the various component groups forbidden from having their own propaganda activities. The opening of a website dedicated to IS-K and operated from Khorasan was a matter of controversy between IS-K and IS-Central. IS-K's leaders and propaganda department demanded it, but IS-Central objected to the idea and insisted on having all IS-K media releases, videos and pictures posted on the IS-Central website. IS-K was only authorized to distribute propaganda material directly on Facebook, Twitter and any existing website or social media outlet where videos are also posted, as well as through their radio.[203]

On the whole, therefore, it should be concluded that IS-K strove to make the structure happen, but it had to face the hard reality of a complex and non-conducive environment, which delayed progress and might well ultimately condemn to failure at least some of the leadership's efforts. To some extent the leadership implicitly recognized this, as shown by the fact that they worked out alternative solutions: for example, they got the component groups to work together in as synchronized a fashion as possible.

5

DRIVERS OF SUPPORT FOR IS-K

IS-K made sufficient impact and demonstrated enough resilience in Khorasan, demonstrating at least the ability to establish a beachhead there. But what kind of base of support did IS-K find? Did it establish social roots at least in some pockets? Did it attract some social strata? Or did it merely attract members of the already existing numerous and large jihadist organizations of the region? The type of support IS-K found is of course important for assessing its future potential in Khorasan.

Exploiting the crisis of other insurgent organizations

Of the seventy-two IS-K cadres and leaders whose biographical details are known, in terms of previous affiliations more than a quarter of the interviewees were former Taliban and a similar percentage former TTP. Only 4 per cent had been in AQ, and a surprising 33 per cent had no previous affiliation, which suggests that new recruits (typically mullahs) were already making their way to the mid-ranks of the organization. These were in their large majority Afghans, with one Chinese and one Arab. The average age of the seventy-two interviewees was forty, and just slightly lower among those with no previous affiliation (thirty-eight).

Many clerics and madrasa teachers who had not been attracted to any other jihadist organizations found the appeal of IS-K irresistible (Table 6). This could be read as a sign of growing radicalization among the clergy. It could also be interpreted as a sign of the Taliban/TTP's lack of credibility among radical clerics, who were waiting for a more credible organization to appear. Among the Taliban cadres who defected to IS-K, there was a strong concentration in east and south-east; even many Quetta Shura cadres who went over to IS-K were based in the east, a region where the Quetta Shura's foothold has always been weak and there were tensions between Quetta Shura and Peshawar Shura Taliban (Map 4). This already suggests that friction and conflict within the Taliban was one driver of recruitment into IS-K, as will be further elaborated below.

Table 7 instead summarizes data about the whole membership of the different IS-K component groups, as provided by IS-K sources. TKP appears to have had by the end of 2015 a surprisingly low number of former TTP among its ranks (33 per cent), despite all its dominant figures being former TTP with former LeJ members accounting for about half that number. All the Afghan component groups had in excess of 50 per cent of former Taliban in their ranks, except Muslim Dost's Group, which had a relatively modest 43 per cent of them. In any case, even if the interviewees' sample is not a random one, the difference between the two sets of data seems to suggest that there are more former Taliban among the rank and file of IS-K than among the cadres, while the contrary seems true of TTP (Table 7).

After a strong outflow of Taliban towards IS-K in late 2014 and through 2015, in the first 6 months of 2016 the flow slowed considerably. According to internal IS-K sources, a modest 342 Taliban joined IS-K in the first half of 2016, mostly in the east from the ranks of Taliban fronts badly affected by the financial crisis of the Peshawar Shura, which would in fact even disband temporarily in August 2016, before resuming operations in November (see also Chapter 5 on the financial crisis of the Peshawar Shura).[1]

The emergence of hardline factions

There were substantial numbers of hardline Taliban, especially in eastern Afghanistan, often very close to AQ (particularly Dost Mohammad Mahaz), and the arrival of IS-K offered them the chance of switching to an organization that was more aligned with their uncompromising views. IS-K's hope was always that the leadership of competitor jihadist organizations would sign peace deals with Kabul. This in their mind would allow IS-K to attract towards their organization hardline commanders who did not see a role in peace for themselves. This applied to Hizb-i Islami too, at least in IS-K's hopes:

If the deal between Kabul and Hekmatyar goes ahead, some of the commanders of Hizb-i Islami will join us. Some donors have good relationship with them and they said that they will join us. ... We are negotiating with a lot of Hizb-i Islami commanders and the same Arab donors are also negotiating with them ...[2]

A senior IS-K commander thus summarizes the appeal of IS-K to hardline Taliban, of whom he used to be part:

First reason is this that Taliban started peace talks with Afghan Government and Taliban. The second reason is this that Taliban morale decreased in fighting against Afghan Government and Americans. The third reason is this that Taliban were not independent. It means they were under the control of Pakistan ISI. What ISI was telling and instructing to Taliban leaders, they were doing. ... We were also telling to Taliban leaders to expand Jihad in Pakistan, Iran and Central Asia but they did not accept this.[3]

Within the Taliban and the TTP, there had previously been groups who had issues with Shi'as and Iran, and who did not appreciate the growing warmth between the Taliban and Iran, particularly after 2012. IS-K offered a suitable venue for these groups to express their frustration openly.[4]

Similarly, particularly in eastern Afghanistan and particularly in Chaparhar and Kot, many Salafis who were with the Taliban before joined IS-K, for reasons of ideological affinity.[5] Some of the Salafi networks within the Taliban even had separate appearance and manners:

Daesh sympathizers and Salafi Taliban were reportedly distinguishing themselves from ordinary Taliban and jihadis by their appearance and manners. Interviewees admired their handsome looks (clean and smart), their fashionable clothes and modern equipment (computers, mobile phones and the latest weapons), and their language skills (Arabic) and education (computer literacy). Accounts described them as modern, civilized, honourable and respectful, yet uncompromising regarding the rules and regulations dictated by Islam and their Salafi organization.[6]

A TLO survey of thirty-three IS-K commanders in Nangarhar found that twelve of them were Salafis, even if their Salafism did not appear to be the main reason why they joined IS-K.[7] In general, Afghan Salafis are split into many small groups, mostly not militarily active; some of these groups which are mentioned include Haji Atiqullah's Salafi Group and Mawlavi Nasrat Salafi Group, both from in Kunar province, and Qari Afzal Khan's Salafi Group in Nangarhar.[8] Local sources also reported how IS-K appeared attractive to Salafi groups in Badakhshan.[9]

The originally Arab character of IS-K is one factor that made it attractive for some Taliban, as was the string of victories it achieved in 2014–15 in the

Middle East. IS-K's Arab background had a legitimizing effect. While the Taliban was riddled with personal and tribal rivalry, IS seemed to project a much more appealing image.[10]

IS-K's comparative wealth

With al-Baghdadi having already denounced Mullah Omar as 'an illiterate warlord', IS-K then exploited the crisis affecting the Taliban in the wake of funding cuts and later of the 'Mullah Omar' affair. The financial crisis of the Peshawar Shura, which would lead to its collapse in August 2016, was a great boon for IS-K. The Peshawar Shura had until then controlled most of the Taliban in the east, in the Kabul region and in the north-east.[11] In eastern Afghanistan, IS-K sources claimed to have initially attracted mainly commanders and fighters of Atiqullah Mahaz and Dost Mohammad Mahaz, two Taliban fronts which were running through heavy financial difficulties in late 2014 and early 2015. Some members of Tora Bora Mahaz, also not well funded, also joined.[12]

> When Atiqullah's Mahaz [one of the Peshawar Shura's fronts] faced with a financial crisis, they told us that you should go home. We were in the village, then the people of Sheikh Muhsin came to us and they told us, come and join Daesh. The recruitment representative of Daesh for Kunar Province was Maulana Abdul Sattar Safi. He took us to Sheikh Muhsin who is the Amir of Kunar Province. Sheikh Muhsin told us 'leave Taliban, our Jihad is good jihad'. We are ready to support you in finance, in logistics etc. We accepted his proposal. There were fifteen people with me. He also gave us 2 million Afs with fifty weapons.[13]

The fact that the Taliban struggled to pay and supply its fighters reinforced the attractiveness of IS-K: from late 2015, IS-K took good advantage of deteriorating relations between the Taliban's Peshawar Shura and the Pakistani authorities, which started further reducing the flow of supplies and funds.[14] In this sense, there is not necessarily a contradiction between an individual's claimed ideological sympathy for IS-K and their being attracted by its financial wealth: the latter enabled hardline Taliban to make the switch that they had long dreamed of. Even when the Peshawar Shura was resurrected in November 2016, it had shrunk in size and did not have anything comparable to the level of funding it had enjoyed in its peak years.[15]

Virtually all the IS-K interviewees acknowledged that IS-K offered better conditions than their old organizations. For example:

> Daesh has better financial condition then Taliban, we have good uniforms, we have good money for eating and we get salary on time from Daesh. But when we

were with Taliban, Taliban told us to get food from the villagers, Taliban asked us to fund ourselves by collecting *Zakat*, etc.[16]

When Taliban joined with Daesh, a lot of changes came. When they were with Taliban, they were hungry and their families had financial problems, but when they joined with Daesh, their financial problems were solved.[17]

By contrast, the fact that IS-K was perceived as being bankrolled by powerful and wealthy sponsors also helped a great deal in attracting recruits to IS-K.[18]

Daesh is very strong financially, second Daesh succeeded so much rapidly, the Muslims and Jihadis of seventy-seven countries are in Daesh and in the future Daesh want to establish its capital in Afghanistan. If they come to Afghanistan, we will be their big commanders.[19]

It is commonly alleged that one key factor in attracting Taliban to IS-K is higher salaries and better conditions and equipment.[20] According to elders in Kajaki, many young villagers sympathized with IS-K because of its financial incentives.[21]

There are lots of dodgy boys who are doing anything for money, yeah of course there are boys in our district that still they are sympathizers of Daesh and if Daesh again come on power and start their recruitment openly, lots of boys from our district will join them. In the beginning when Daesh came to our district and start recruitment because Daesh paid a good salary for the fighters, lots of boys from our district joined the Daesh.[22]

Elders in Nangarhar alleged that it was the most venal, mercenary-minded Taliban commanders and young villagers who joined IS-K for money.[23] While the amount of money saved by the cadre quoted above is surely out of the ordinary, IS-K does appear to have offered a better financial deal to those joining it than what they could expect elsewhere. According to the finance commission, the salary it paid to fighters was $600 per month, to which allowances such as food ($150 per month) and clothing ($100 per month) were added.[24] Another source in 2015 put the salary range at $500–800.[25] Sources in various component groups mentioned significantly different figures, usually $200–300 per month for fighters plus 'hazard pay' of 1,500–2,000 Afs per each deployment, with commanders getting $300–500.[26] One IS-K interviewee even denied being paid a regular salary,[27] but the wealth of evidence is that IS-K offered at least 50–100 per cent better pay than the Taliban. In addition, the families of 'martyred' fighters received a one-off payment of 1 million Afs ($15,000), while injured fighters received good treatment and were often sent abroad.[28]

IS-K sources of course completely deny that venality might come into play.[29] More noteworthily, a Taliban cadre from Kajaki admitted that most of the IS-K recruits were not primarily motivated by money.[30] An NDS officer moreover observed:

> We have captured more than sixty-five people from Daesh. Yes these people were trained for four months from Daesh side and they believe in Daesh. Some people also said that we were jobless and we joined with Daesh for money. The number of this kind of people was very low.[31]

Another NDS officer volunteered the somewhat different view that 'The small fighters are working with Daesh for money but the senior people really want to work for Daesh.'[32] A commander of the Nangarhar militia claimed in January 2016 to have captured thirty-three IS-K members up to that point, some of whom they handed over to the Afghan authorities, while executing others. Based on their interrogation, a militia commander stated:

> These people were the real believers in Daesh and they were the real members of Daesh. They did not join with Daesh because of the money. Money is not important for this kind of people.[33]

The fact that these IS-K members developed a real belief in the organization does not necessarily rule out financial or in any case opportunistic reasons for joining, as was shown to be the case for the Taliban.[34]

A small glimpse into the way IS-K establishes its pockets of support is provided by the account of an elder, interviewed shortly after his escape from his village in Sherzad (Nangarhar). When a group of 150 IS-K fighters took over his and two neighbouring villages in May 2015, IS-K established a stronghold in this mountain valley, which it would later defend against half a dozen Taliban attempts to retake it. Apart from the usual imposition of IS-K strictures, IS-K immediately set out to recruit villagers. Some joined, but others were conscripted in non-combat roles, so that 8 months later the group had grown by 50–100 members and had taken over three more neighbouring villages. The conscripts were paid the same salary as the volunteers ($500–600 per month), and very quickly IS-K became popular with the local youth as the only source of well-paid jobs in the range of tens of kilometres. The elder, who is hostile to IS-K, acknowledged that 60 per cent of the village youth supported IS-K by January 2016. The indoctrination by the IS-K cadres in the group and preaching by the only mullah left in the village (co-opted by IS-K with the help of a $150 per month salary) helped gradually turn the recruits into Salafis. According to the elder, IS-K was trying to bring in new, ideologically close mullahs to provide imams for the other two mosques of the village.[35]

Factional and personal rivalries

A different set of people joined IS-K because of intra-Taliban rivalries, such as Mullah Abdul Khaliq and Mullah Batkhiar and their men in Nangarhar, who belonged to the Quetta Shura and were ill at ease with the hegemonic role of the Peshawar Shura in that area.[36] In Helmand, it was initially mostly commanders of Mansur Mahaz and Rahbari Shura who joined IS-K in order to fight without restraints their rival Abdul Qayum Zakir, who was at that time close to the Revolutionary Guards (Iran). Allegedly they were encouraged by Abdul Manan, the shadow governor of Helmand.[37] But IS-K was also able to recruit some of Abdul Qayum Zakir's commanders, after Zakir was sacked from the Taliban's Military Commission and before he became a major recipient of Iranian support. So, for example, Khilafat Afghan ended up recruiting from a heterogenous lot of Taliban, belonging to a variety of Taliban groups.[38] Similarly, a TLO survey of IS-K commanders in Nangarhar found that 'many commanders seemed to have switched allegiances for personal reasons—particularly to gain power and resources within their immediate communities', often also because they were not well connected within the Taliban.[39]

> There were a lot of opposition and disunity within the Taliban, which divided Taliban in groups such as Peshawar Shura, Quetta Shura, Miran Shah Shura and Mashhad office. Another reason is this that Taliban do not have the same financial support that they had before. They face a financial crisis.[40]

These were also the findings of Ali and Gaharanai in Kunar.[41] In the same way, IS-K managed to make inroads among the ranks of the Pakistani TTP. An ISI source believed that the TTP defectors to IS-K had essentially been marginalized by the TTP before they defected, except for a few who had actually been to Syria.[42] The appointment of Fazlullah (the TTP leader in Swat) as leader of the TTP in November 2013 was controversial and alienated quite a few senior TTP figures, like Hafiz Saeed who had hoped to get the job. The Mehsud TTP members were among those disgruntled, because Fazlullah was not appointing many Mehsuds to senior positions as he had in the past. In July 2015, the group of Baitullah Mehsud, at that point led by Maulana Mehsud Baryalai, Mawlavi Jamal Waziri and Qari Bilal Ahmed, joined IS-K. In December 2015, several more commanders were reportedly negotiating with IS-K.[43]

Table 6: Cadres of IS-K by previous affiliation

	Previous affiliation (n=72)
AQ	4.2
Taliban	27.8
TTP	26.4
None	33.3
Other groups	11.1

Sources: interviews with IS-K cadres, 2014–16

Map 4: serving senior Taliban cadres who joined IS-K, by Taliban Shura[44]

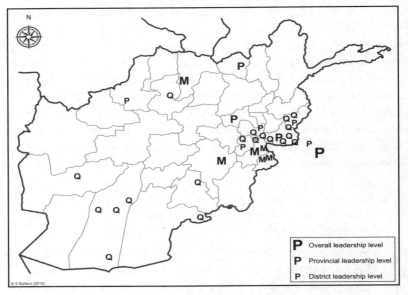

Legend: Q=Quetta Shura; P=Peshawar Shura; M=Miran Shah Shura. Each letter represents an individual, the size of the letter represents his seniority.

The emergence of the professional jihadis: jihad as a way of life

The idea of being part of a worldwide movement also had its appeal among insecure Taliban, who were beginning to question the viability of their cause in the longer run.[45]

> I joined Daesh because it is a powerful network throughout the world, there are Muslims of every country in this network such as countries in Europe, America,

Table 7: Rank and file composition of IS-K by background and component group, according to IS-K sources[46]

	Date	N=	Former Taliban	Former Hizb-i Islami	Former members of other Afghan groups	Former IMU	Former ETIM	Former TTP	Former JeJ	Former LeT	Former JM	Fresh recruits	Veterans of Syria and Iraq
Azizullah Haqqani Group	Jan-16	1,680	58.0	6.3	5.3	–	–	–	–	–	–	13.7	16.6
IS-K Kunar	Feb-16	245	40.0	–	–	–	–	–	–	–	–	40.8	19.2
TKK	Jan-16	n/a	55.0	10.0	–	–	–	–	–	–	–	20.0	15.0
IS-K Herat	Dec-15	625	29.6	–	–	–	–	–	–	–	–	51.2	19.2
TKP	Dec-15	3,450	–	–	–	–	–	32.8	16.2	8.7	3.5	25.8	13.0
Muslim Dost Group	Oct-15	1,163	43.0	–	–	–	–	–	–	–	–	34.4	22.6
Shamali Khilafat	Oct-15	1,260	48.8	–	–	4.9	2.4	–	–	–	–	46.3	–
Khilafat Afghan	Jun-15	750	60.0	–	–	–	–	–	–	–	–	10.0	30.0

Legend: LeJ=Lashklar-e Jhangvi; LeT=Lashkar-e Taiba; JM=Jaysh Mohammad.

Africa, Asia and Australia. ... We want this network to work in the whole world and bring an Islamic regime all over the world.[47]

IS-K forces present themselves proudly as a global jihadist movement (despite oddly never mentioning the Caliphate, see *IS-K's ideology* in Chapter 1), the 'only one that can bring justice and Shari'a to the world' (see also Chapter 1, *IS-K's ideology*).[48] IS-K patrols in the villages would also display this pride and talk of global jihad.[49] The proclamation of the Caliphate in June 2014 was in this regard a public relations masterstroke, because it made IS-K's global jihad message much stronger, overshadowing AQ and its own version of global jihad.

With such an aim, the future of the jihadist fighters was guaranteed. The fact that it provided a weapon and the status of a fighter added to the lure of IS-K.[50] To many former Taliban, it did not really matter which organization they belonged to; they vaguely wanted to fight for what they could perceive as a 'just cause', and had few qualms about fighting their former colleagues:[51]

> For us Jihad is important, not the old friends, we know that our way is the right way for jihad and if anyone stands in front of us and tries to stop our jihad, we kill him. Before I came to Daesh I told all my close friends who are with Taliban now to come and join with Daesh but they didn't accept this. Now they are not my friends and they are my enemies and if they oppose me during the fighting, I don't care if they will be killed by my fighters.[52]

> Two months ago there was fighting between Daesh Khorasan and Taliban in Zamendawar, you won't believe but I was fighting with the same group of Taliban to which I belonged before. Now we have different ideas and different missions, if anyone tries to interfere with our ideas and mission we will fight against them even if they were our family.[53]

A sense of moral nihilism, which probably emerged within Taliban ranks as a result of many years of fighting and killing, meant that some just followed their Taliban leader into IS-K:

> The man whom we trusted a lot and was a respectful man in our district, Mullah Abdul Rauf Khadim, became the senior commander of Khurasan Daesh in Afghanistan, he asked many Taliban commanders in Kajaki district who had relation with him before to join Daesh Khurasan. ... We accepted his offer and joined him.[54]

Often Taliban commanders and cadres were brought into IS-K even by former colleagues, with whom they remained in personal contact.

> I contacted Daesh on 7 February of 2014. Yes, I approached them and I also knew Mokhtar Khorasani, because he was group commander before with Mansur and I knew him from that time.[55]

Jihadist frustration

IS-K, like IS in general, was particularly successful in recruiting members and groups of émigré jihadists, who had been fighting somebody else's jihad for long years and saw no alternative opportunities for finally bringing jihad back home. The Central Asians in particular were motivated by IS-K's promise of starting jihad in Central Asia very soon, with preparations getting under way almost immediately.[56] This was in contrast with AQ's policy of prioritizing jihad in Afghanistan before launching jihad in Central Asia. The Omar Ghazi Group recruited from the IMU and from Afghan Uzbeks, from Turkmen from both Afghanistan and Turkmenistan, and from Uzbeks flocking to Syria and Iraq and from there to Afghanistan and Pakistan. Only Kazakhs were missing in the Omar Ghazi Group, at least as of spring 2015.[57]

Likewise, Chinese Muslims were anxious to return to China, where they alleged the denial of religious rights by Beijing, which included obstacles to the construction of mosques, discouragement of fasting, closure of some mosques, bans on the use of Islamic names and repression against clerics.[58] IS-K therefore succeeded in attracting Chinese Muslims impatient with Al-Qaida's of postponing the start of jihad in China by several years. The Gansu Hui Group claimed to be planning to start launching attacks in China by 2018.

A Hui militant who stayed loyal to AQ doubted the ability of Gansu Hui to start a serious jihad in China on these timelines. He feared that the group would end up carrying out a few isolated attacks, with the only result being to attract further repression from the Chinese authorities and to make recruitment and infiltration in Hui communities in China more difficult.[59] The jury is necessarily still out in the case of the ability of IS's Central Asians and Chinese Muslims to actually start the jihads they are planning. However, the interviews carried out with both IS-K members and members of various Chinese and Central Asian groups suggest that IS has been able to convince them that these targets are achievable.

Similarly, many TTP members were angry that the Afghan Taliban was constantly asking for jihad in Afghanistan be prioritized, at the expense of jihad against the Pakistani government. This disillusionment with the Taliban for having sold out to Pakistani interests was constantly repeated by former TTP members, who joined IS-K.[60]

> I learned that the only motive of the Taliban is the program of Pakistan's ISI. I learned that Taliban are not doing Jihad in Afghanistan and their motives are not Jihad, then I was looking for a way to leave the Taliban. Of course I couldn't

join the government because my view on Afghan government is negative and I am fighting against them. When the Daesh Khorasan started its operation in Kajaki district, it was a good way for me to join Daesh Khorasan.[61]

Baluchi insurgents (particularly, but not only, those of Iranian nationality—see Chapter 6) were also desperate to mobilize sufficient funding to upgrade their jihad against the Islamic Republic of Iran; before IS entered the scene, resources available in the fight against that particular enemy were far from sufficient for having an impact. A Revolutionary Guards (Iran) source estimated in January 2016 that by that point 600–700 Baluchi rebels had joined IS-K from Pakistan and Iran, and maintained that many Baluchis linked to IS-K had already been arrested in Iran.[62] Baluchi anxiety to upgrade their jihad coincided with IS-K's ambition of starting operations in Iran (see also Chapter 6).[63]

The Islamic State and the societies of Khorasan

Data on the ethnic background of IS-K is far from complete, but suggests a strong Pashtun predominance, despite the presence of non-Pashtun groups such as Shamali Khilafat (Tajiks and Uzbeks) and the Baluchi and Central Asian groups, of course (Table 8). Since the large majority of IS-K's original recruits came from organizations which were themselves largely Pashtun in composition, this is hardly surprising. Unfortunately, there is no data on TKP, which leaves the ethnic breakdown of the Pakistanis in IS-K in the shadows. While Pashtuns should be expected to be there in great numbers, significant numbers of Punjabis should also be there.

The poor and disenfranchised

According to elders in Kajaki, many young villagers sympathize with IS-K because they have issues with both the Afghan government and the Taliban, such as a criminal record, or because of the financial incentives.[64]

> There were around three or four people who were criminals and escaped from the government and from the Taliban. They joined Daesh because they didn't have any other way but to join Daesh. Two of them were killed in the fight against the Taliban, but two others still are with Daesh, living in unknown areas.[65]

Does this amount to some kind of IS-K social agenda? IS-K's radio propaganda claims that wheat and other agricultural produce collected as *zakat* are

Table 8: Composition of IS-K by ethnicity[66]

	IS-K all	IS-K all	IS-K all	Gansu Hui Group (Chinese Muslims)	IS-K Kunar	IS-K Farab	IS-K Herat	Khilafat Afghan (Afghanistan)	Muslim Dost Group (Afghanistan)	Shamali Khilafat (North Afghanistan)
Date	Apr-20	Jun-20	Aug-18	Jul-16	Feb-16	Dec-15	Dec-15	Jun-15	Jun-15	May-15
Pakistanis	–	42	–	–	–	–	–	–	–	–
All Pashtuns	38	–	–	–	66	59	60.5	100	100	–
Afghan Pashtuns	–	–	–	–	–	–	–	–	–	–
Afghan Tajiks	–	–	–	11.6	12.1	29.4	–	–	43.9	–
Afghan Uzbeks	–	–	–	–	–	10.1	–	–	27.5	–
Afghan Uzbeks and Tajiks	4	–	–	–	–	–	–	–	–	–
All Central Asians	9	–	–	–	–	–	–	–	–	–
Pashais	–	–	–	–	11.6	–	–	–	–	–
Nuristanis	–	–	–	–	6.1	–	–	–	–	–
Arabs	–	–	–	–	4.8	–	–	–	–	–
Huis	–	–	–	40.7	–	–	–	–	–	2.6
Uyghurs	–	0	–	59.3	–	–	–	–	–	–
Baluchis	–	–	6	–	–	28.9	–	–	–	–
Others incl. Bangladeshi, Indians, Arabs …	5	–	–	–	–	–	–	–	–	–

redistributed to poor families by IS-K. The main thrust of IS-K's propaganda is, however, aimed against the village elders (the *maliks*) and their power and influence in the villages; they are accused of looking after their own interests, and not that of the villagers.[67]

The community elders: claims and reality

The elders' claims that IS-K attracts socially marginal elements appears to be an understatement of its influence. In the early months of IS-K's existence, the group tried to cast itself as more moderate and respectful of religious traditions than the Taliban:

> We do not have opposition with common people, even those people who are in Afghan Police or Army or Afghan Government staff. It means if one of them is dead or killed, his funeral prayer must be performed openly. Problems must not be created, but Taliban do not let the funerals of such people happen. We do not create problems for those staff of Afghan Government who are working in education, health, and other welfare activities, but Taliban do not let them. They are killing everybody.[68]

> Daesh are very friendly with the villagers and don't want to disturb the villagers, but Taliban are very aggressive and they want to fulfil their program forcedly and many others different. Because of these different I left the Taliban and joined with Daesh Khorasan.[69]

The exaggerated characterization of the Taliban as indiscriminately violent and opposed to any kind of welfare activities would not hold for long, given how IS-K forces behaved themselves, but it seems to have bought some tolerance for IS-K initially, as discussed below.

In some locations like Kajaki, IS-K had a large number of local recruits, due to relatively senior Taliban (or TTP) joining the organization. Did these former Taliban bring their tribal contacts with them? In Helmand, because of Abdul Rauf Khadim being an Alizai from the Hassanzai sub-tribe, his men were largely Hassanzais, with a sprinkle of Achakzais and Ishaqzais. They mostly came from the Loy Naicha area, in particular Zamindawar, where the local population is still reported to harbour IS-K sympathies.[70] According to Borhan Osman, Khadim played explicitly on tribal grievances in his 23 January 2015 speech in Gandum Rez Bazaar, in front of hundreds of Alizais.[71] Another account of one of his speeches, this time in De Babab Bazaar, provided a different picture:

> Mullah Khadim was taking about Daesh Khorasan with us and was saying that it's only Daesh who can bring Shari'a and an Islamic government in Afghanistan.

He told us that he got permission from Daesh leader Al Baghdadi to become as the leader of Daesh in Afghanistan. There were many fighters who were taking the security of the meeting and they had black flags and were with uniform and mask. ... Mullah Khadim was asking us to not let other groups like Taliban misuse the name of Islam but work for Pakistan ISI. He also asked us to not support the government people and inform them as soon as they are seeing any government activity or Taliban fighters at our area.[72]

It is not clear, therefore, to what extent IS-K played the tribal card. For sure, many IS-K interviewees claimed that the organization had extensive relations with the elders:

- In southern Afghanistan, a senior source in Muslim Dost Group claimed that the group had relations with tribal elders of the Ishaqzai, Alizai and Noorzai tribes;[73]
- Another senior source in Khilafat Afghan mentioned tribal elders of the Kakar, Noorzai and other tribes as being linked to the group;[74]
- In Ghazni, a local IS-K source claimed relations with the Qarabaghi, Maquri, Ibrahimkhel, Andar and other tribes;[75]
- In Achin (Nangarhar), Shinwari sub-tribes such as Ali Shir Khil, Abdul Khil and some Pekha clans reportedly supported IS-K and contributed many young men to its cause;[76]
- In Kot (Nangarhar), it was the Lortia, Shabdany and Saa Pay sub-tribes that reportedly were closer to IS-K;[77]
- In northern Afghanistan, a senior Shamali Khilafat source claimed having relations with Safi, Ahmadzai and Turkmen elders.[78]

In sum, IS-K sources claimed to have close relations with the elders of several tribes.[79] Such claims are, however, dismissed as unfounded by the elders themselves:[80]

There are two reasons why there is no contact between the elders or villagers and Daesh. One is that Daesh asked people to follow Salafi rules. We and the villagers are Muslim and never accept other religions, which would be against Islam or Shari'a. The second reason is that Daesh commanders and fighters themselves didn't want to visit the elders or meet elders in the villages.[81]

Daesh never come for getting advice or talking, they always coming to warn the villagers.[82]

The fact that IS-K recruited from some sub-tribes did not necessarily imply that they had agreements with the tribal elders; commanders who joined IS-K would recruit mainly in their own sub-tribe anyway.

As long as Hafiz Saeed was governor, there were few exceptions to elders' claims that they kept their distance from IS-K. For example, in Kajaki at least one elder in Khadim's home area admitted to having entertained close relations with him.[83] Still, while IS-K might very easily and understandably exaggerate the extent of tribal connections the organization had, it is also true that elders might have had an interest in downplaying any relationship. An NDS source estimated that in the east IS-K had connections with tribal elders of the Shinwari, Mohmand, Dawlatzai, Alizai, Zadran, Ibrahimkhel, Sharif Khel, Safi, Batokhel, Adamkhel and Albekhel tribes.[84]

After the death of Hafiz Saeed, there were indications that IS-K was making efforts to improve relations with community elders. In some cases, these efforts at least seemed to have achieved a degree of success. An example was in October 2016, when the Zazai tribe (Paktia) went from supporting the Haqqani network and elders for their privileged relationship with the Zadran tribe, with which they have agreements allowing development projects to take place, with operations by the Haqqanis only to take place with the consent of the tribal elders. Meanwhile, the Haqqanis were permitted to enter Mangal and Zazai territory and fighting there as they pleased. According to an internal source, IS-K was negotiating with other south-eastern tribes, trying to lure them away from the Haqqanis as well.[85]

Another example is that of the Kakar tribe of northern Zabul; at least some of its elders opened the door to IS-K, as the tribe felt marginalized by the Taliban.[86] According to Baczko and Dorronsoro, Mullah Dadullah's front with its strong Kakar links, after flirting with IS-K for some time, eventually gave up joining after coming under heavy pressure from the Taliban. But some of those contacts might have benefited IS-K nonetheless.[87]

That Hafiz Saeed might have been a key factor in driving IS-K's ruthless violence seems confirmed by the fact that IS-K atrocities were rarer in the north-east and also in the north, where Hafiz Saeed's influence was much weaker (because his Pakistanis would not venture there). Here IS-K forces entertained better relations with the Taliban and worked in close co-operation with the IMU, a group which still maintains relations with many Taliban commanders and has many years of experience in northern Afghanistan. There was a single report of an elder executed in Faryab.[88]

With regard to Pakistan, a senior TKP source identified elders in the Orakzai and Wazir tribes as supportive, followed by others in the Afridi, Shinwari, Mehsud, Yusufzai and Bajauri tribes, but there is no confirmation of this from external sources.[89]

The mullahs

IS-K did not sit idly waiting for the wind to blow its way. Of the sample of seventy-two biographies gathered for this project, 93 per cent were madrasa-educated. Aware of the importance of madrasa networks in generating cadres and members for Taliban and TTP, IS-K started working hard to establish its own madrasas. IS-K sources claimed they had the support of some senior *ulema* in Afghanistan and Pakistan.[90] More generally, in many madrasas in Pakistan and remote districts of Afghanistan there was sympathy for IS-K, according to an NDS source.[91] As discussed in *The Shari'a Council* (Chapter 4), IS-K, not unlike the Taliban, pays mullahs to preach in its favour. In general, however, IS-K does not appear to have tried hard to co-opt mullahs in Afghanistan, beyond some existing Salafi networks.[92] Even there, many Salafi mullahs are quietists and have not been willing to collaborate with IS-K.[93] Moreover, in Helmand there was little effort to get the mullahs to preach in favour of IS-K or to advocate respect of its rules, possibly because IS-K did not believe they would support Salafi views.[94] Indeed, some elders whisper that the mullahs opposed IS-K's Salafi views and sympathized instead with the Taliban. Only in areas where IS-K had solid territorial control—as, for example, a pocket of a few villages in Khogyani (Nangarhar)—did it sometimes appoint its own mullahs to the village mosques.[95]

This is not to say that evidence of clerics supporting IS-K is completely lacking. The Afghan security services, for example, detained in Nangarhar alone ten mullahs and three *ulema* for supporting IS-K.[96] Madrasas were said by an internal source to be the primary ground for recruitment for at least the Azizullah Haqqani group.[97] A Saudi NGO source estimated that, of the mosques the NGO supported, about sixty mosques in Afghanistan were connected to IS-K.[98]

At the same time, IS-K rarely dared cracking down on the mullahs in most locations where it took control.[99] There were nonetheless reports of *ulema* and mullahs detained in IS-K's prisons in Achin, and of a mullah executed.[100] In Kot, local sources mentioned the execution of six mullahs, while another five were assassinated in Jalalabad.[101] In Kot, when Panjpiri madrasas were asked to transfer their students to IS-K, some even chose to relocate to Jalalabad.[102]

In the Zamendawar area of Kajaki, where Mullah Khadim was from, in some mosques I heard that one or two times Mullahs asked the villagers not to pray the Sunnat part of the praying, but people became angry. Regarding the Sunnat part of praying, Daesh was not too serious and did not force the people to do that, but was giving advice.[103]

IS-K might have been more successful in Pakistan. In September 2014, there were already reports that 'In the madrasas of Lahore and Karachi, a debate is going on about the legitimacy of ISIS and Abu Bakar Baghdadi'.[104] An ISI source confirmed links between madrasas and IS-K in Bajaur, Orakzai, Waziristan, Baluchistan, Lahore, Karachi and Peshawar. Some madrasa principals were arrested for these connections.[105] In Pakistan, most recruitment was indeed reported to be taking place in madrasas; the second-most important types of recruits were villagers and students.[106] In total, in June 2015, according to IS-K sources, twenty-eight Pakistani madrasas were closely linked to the organization in Kohat, North Waziristan, South Waziristan, Lahore, Karachi and Peshawar, but none in Afghanistan. Most of these madrasas appear to have been established ex novo by IS-K. There were furthermore plans to establish closer connections with more Pakistani madrasas by funding them.[107] As one IS-K source explained, funding usually determines which organization is supported:

> Different madrasa and mullah networks play a role in the division between TTP and TKP. For example TTP has their own mullahs and scholars and TKP has their own mullahs and scholars. Those madrasas which get financial supports from TKP, they are working for TKP but those madrasas which get financial supports from TTP then they are working for TTP.[108]

A source in an NGO based in the Arab Gulf and working extensively with madrasas and mosques estimated that just among the madrasas they were supporting at the end of 2016, nine major madrasas had linked to IS-K, and another hundred or so small madrasas networked with these nine. The source also estimated that, of the mosques the NGO supported, about 150 in Pakistan were connected to IS-K.[109] These figures, if correct, imply an expansion in the support IS-K received from clerical circles. In some cases, however, there was also resistance. IS-K has targeted Hanafi *ulema* in KP province of Pakistan, particularly ones known to be supporting the Taliban and opposing Salafism. Of these, Mawlawi Ghulam Hazrat was the best known.[110]

The students

IS-K has also been targeting radical student groups for recruitment; in 2016, it reportedly allocated $5 million (450 million Pakistani Rupees) to such groups in Pakistan.[111] In Pakistan, IS-K was reported to have significant influence among the students, primarily (but not only) those of Karachi University, as well as among their teachers. A group called 'the Islamic Students'

Movement of Pakistan' claimed to have links to IS, but there is no confirmation from IS-K that this is the case. The group claimed to be spreading propaganda through leaflets and study groups, and to be attracting not religious zealots but 'modern girls, modern boys'. A lecturer in Karachi University was arrested in March 2016 under the accusation of having tried to establish an IS cell. A *Times* journalist met several IS sympathizers in the campus. An IS-K cell accused of various attacks in Karachi was dismantled in May 2015 and included members of the graduating class.

In addition, a small splinter group of Hizb-ut Tahrir, called Saut-ul Ummah, with a following among students and educated professionals in Lahore, also declared allegiance to IS. Seventy of its members were arrested in the summer of 2015. However, this group was not integrated into the IS-K structure, and it is not clear whether it had fully merged with IS. According to a police officer, militants previously linked to TTP, faced with the crackdown on TTP in urban areas, had started drifting towards IS. Other similar cells were discovered in Sialkot and Lahore.[112]

One analyst also reported the presence of mainstream Hizb-ut Tahrir activists (as opposed to the small Saut-ul Ummah splinter group) in IS-K, attracted by the idea of establishing a Caliphate.[113] Other sources, however, question how ideologically close IS and Tahrir might be. In Pakistan, for example, the local spokesperson of IS-K described Hizb-ut Tahrir and IS-K as 'poles apart', probably referring to the fact that Hizb-ut Tahrir rejects violence.[114] In 2020, an IS-K commander reported that there was a significant inflow of Hizb-ut Tahrir members into IS-K, with the tacit tolerance of the leadership of that group. According to the commander, himself a former member of Hizb-ut Tahrir, the majority of IS-K recruits from Badakhshan were in fact from that group.[115] Cases of IS-K recruitment among university students continued to be reported throughout 2017.[116]

In Afghanistan, IS-K invested significant human resources towards recruiting, at least in Nangarhar University, where by mid-2016 they claimed to have sixty-five recruiters, mostly in the faculties of Shari'a and literature.[117] In November 2015, the IS flag was raised at a student demonstration, while students were chanting pro-IS slogans.[118] A source in the security services confirmed that there is some sympathy for IS-K in schools and universities, and fifty teachers and 110 students have been arrested for this just in high schools in the provinces of Nangarhar, Zabul, Herat, Farah and Badakhshan.[119] In Nangarhar University alone, thirty-five people were arrested in the Shari'a faculty.[120] Some of the arrests at Nangarhar University were reported in the media in November 2015.[121] Sources in the Afghan security apparatus even accused senior members of Jamiat-i Islah, a student organization gathering a mix of Muslim Brothers and Salafis, of supporting IS-K. Sympathies for IS-K were also said to be common among mullahs and *ulema*. The involvement of Islah in supporting IS-K is also confirmed by a former member of IS-K.[122]

IS-K also wanted to carry out recruitment in Jalalabad city, although as of June 2016 they were still talking of it as of something that was still in the planning stage.[123] More evidence of successful IS-K recruitment of university students emerged in 2019, after some students (and teachers) were detained. One of the detainees, under interrogation, claimed hundreds more had been recruited.[124] Overall, the security forces of the Islamic Republic detained hundreds of urban youths in 2017–19 on allegations of being members of IS-K. Mostly Tajiks, but with a significant Uzbek presence, students recruited were largely male but with a significant group of females. Many of them were from the Shari'a faculty, but others came from faculties such as law, chemistry, engineering and literature.[125]

6

THE EXPANSION OF IS-K, 2015–17

The social support IS-K found in Khorasan might have been limited to certain pockets of the region, but its popularity among the ranks of existing jihadist organizations has been enough to allow it to expand considerably during 2015 and 2016. This expansion was both numerical (that is, more members) as well as geographical. It was also political: IS-K attracted whole jihadist organizations to its fold, although mostly small ones, and it established alliances with a wider range of organizations, including some fairly established ones.

IS-K growth and spread

Overall growth

In the public domain, no official source has provided estimates of IS-K's overall size and growth trends. At the peak of IS-K operations in eastern Afghanistan, local sources estimated 3,000–5,000 IS-K insurgents there.[1] RS sources put their estimate for the same area and time substantially lower, at 1,000–3,000.[2] By mid-2016, US sources estimated the total number of IS-K members in Afghanistan at 3,500, of which 1,500 were fighters.[3] These figures appear to largely underestimate the overall presence of IS-K even in Afghanistan alone. Western assessments of IS-K numbers remained low even as late as December 2016:

> They have a presence in three—in two to three districts in southern Nangahar, so Achin, Deh Bala, et cetera. We've also detected they have a small presence up

in Kunar as well. We don't think that's because they're trying to expand, or that they have the capacity to expand, we think that they're trying to survive. So as all of this pressure has been put on them in southern Nangahar by the Afghan security services and the US counter-terrorism strikes. We think they realize they have to find a new place and so we think there is a small presence up in Kunar, and we're beginning to try and address that as well. But all told, we think there are probably, approximately 1000 members of Daesh in Afghanistan.[4]

The intelligence agencies of the region diverged from these 'official' estimates substantially. Russian and Iranian propaganda regularly attacked RS for doing little to contain the threat represented by IS-K, sometimes even accusing them of conspiring with IS against rival powers. While this propaganda is indeed as crass as it looks, Taliban sources indicate that the Iranians first and the Russians from late 2015 onwards have been seriously concerned by IS-K, as their intelligence showed the group in constant and rapid expansion. The Iranian Revolutionary Guards have entertained relations with the Taliban for a long time,[5] but according to the Taliban by early 2016 the Iranians were putting pressure on the Taliban for the first time to downscale or abandon altogether operations against the Afghan security forces and NATO forces, in order to concentrate on IS-K.

The same applies to Russian engagement with the Taliban, which had been a taboo for Moscow for many years. The taboo was broken in late 2015, when Russian diplomats started engaging with the Taliban diplomatically (as they acknowledged publicly) and reportedly even offering them funds and weapons to fight IS-K, first in eastern Afghanistan and later in the north (according to Taliban and Afghan government sources). Taliban sources report their contacts in the Russian diplomacy and military insisting that they engage IS-K aggressively, particularly in northern Afghanistan.[6]

As discussed in detail in Chapter 2, the Pakistani authorities too were becoming worried about IS-K's aims and expansion by the second half of 2016. They intercepted communications between IS-K and illegal Pakistani jihadist organizations, but also with the legally registered SSP. Up to June, 425 Pakistanis had been detained on allegation of working for IS-K.[7] By early 2017, the Indian government was also assessing IS-K as a serious threat to Afghanistan, among others.[8]

For sure, the estimates of IS-K's strength by regional actors were much higher than Resolute Support's. In January 2016, a source in the Revolutionary Guards (Iran) estimated 3,000 IS-K members in Pakistan alone, and 8,000–8,500 in Afghanistan,[9] while a Pakistani ISI source estimated their numbers in Afghanistan at about at 5,000–6,000 and in Pakistan at 2,000.[10] An NDS officer estimated IS-K forces in Afghanistan to be at 7,500.[11] Later, in June 2016 another NDS officer mentioned to Hekmatullah Azamy an estimate of 4,500–5,000 IS 'fighters' in Afghanistan (as opposed to total IS-K membership, as the first NDS officer had estimated).[12] None of the sources consulted provided figures for other parts of 'Khorasan': all IS-K interviewees acknowledged that the presence of IS-K members in Iran, Central Asia and India was modest or very modest, entirely underground and therefore difficult to estimate. It is worth noting that both TTP and Afghan Taliban admitted to having lost thousands of their own men to IS-K.[13]

Information provided by IS-K sources put the size of the organization in terms of paid and active members at 9,800 in January 2016, implying that Revolutionary Guards (Iran) figures were definitely somewhat inflated. ISI figures were lower, and NDS figures were about the same as IS-K's (Table 9). Indeed, as Resolute Support and the US military might have had an incentive to undersell IS-K presence, the Iranians had an interest in upselling it. The Pakistani authorities were also inclined towards understating (in fact, denying) IS-K's presence—in Pakistan, at least. The Afghan authorities had by January 2016 given up on their efforts to upsell IS-K, having managed to get the Americans firmly engaged on the ground during the previous months. On the whole, IS-K's claims about its membership do not appear to be much out of line with the intelligence assessment, the more so as they include a support element, which tends to be much less visible than the fighting component and is therefore harder for intelligence agencies to detect. The exception is the January 2017 claim of 20,000 members, which appears to be quite propagandistic and out of line with previous IS-K claims.

IS-K sources show an upward trend for IS-K until early 2016, essentially doubling over the last 6 months of 2015, then stagnation for the following 6 months. In January 2016, two Afghan intelligence sources confidentially agreed with this trend and expressed the view that IS-K was still growing and that it could one day replace the Taliban and become a significant force in Central Asia.[14] Indeed, as Table 9 shows, 2016 represented the peak of IS-K's strength. A long decline followed, with the nadir reached in April 2020 (see Chapter 10 for the background to this decline). A modest recovery took place in late 2020 and early 2021, as IS-K re-organized and a concerned IS-Central increased funding somewhat (see Chapter 7).

The core areas of IS-K settlement can be identified through Map 6, which shows the location of the training camps. In 2014, the future component groups of IS-K seized control over the training camps that had been used to train the volunteers for AQ, then in 2015 set out to establish new ones. Graph 2 shows the progression in the establishment of the training apparatus, with a big acceleration in the first quarter of 2015. The announcement of Wilayat Khorasan in January 2015 was therefore not just a mere formality, but a turning point in terms of the deployment of funds and human resources. After June 2015, more training camps were established in Pakistan, reaching a total of eight by January 2017.[15]

Table 9: claimed and estimated IS-K membership[16]

Date	Total membership of IS-K according to internal sources	Total membership of IS-K according to external observers	Of which support staff
Apr-15	4,500	–	–
Jun-15	5,200	–	–
Jan-16	–	7,000–11,500	–
Jun-16	9,500	–	1,200
Jan-17	20,000	–	–
Dec-17	–	10,000	–
Sep-18	6,900	–	–
Oct-19	–	2,500–4,000	–
May–19	–	5,000	–
Apr-20	6,000	–	–
Jun-20	6,500	–	–
Jan-21	7,500	–	–
Mar-21	7,650	–	–
Aug-21	–	4,000–5,000	–

Geographic Spread

Alongside claims of growth in numbers, IS-K sources also claimed to be spreading geographically. In June 2015, they claimed to be present in seventeen provinces (Map 5); by January 2016, they claimed to have a presence in twenty provinces.[17] The same sources indicated that in June 2015—apart from a concentration of forces in Nangarhar, where the conflict with the Taliban was just starting—IS-K forces were rather spread out (Map 5). Afghan NDS sources estimated in January 2016 that IS-K was present in sixty-five districts, mostly in Nangarhar, Zabul, Herat, Farah, Helmand, Nimruz, Paktika,

Badakhshan, Kunduz, Baghlan, Faryab and Laghman.[18] The presence of IS-K in Pakistan as of the end of 2016 is illustrated in Map 8.

As mentioned above, information about IS-K's presence in Iran and Central Asia is much harder to corroborate. The Iranian authorities regularly reported discovering and destroying IS guerrilla groups, but there seemed to be at least two distinct infiltration paths, one via Kurdistan, which is unrelated to IS-K, and one through Baluchistan, which is related to IS-K. Given that IS-K had only a few hundred Iranian Baluchis in its ranks as of 2015–16, as discussed in 'Harakat Khilafat Baluch' below, and since they were divided between Iran and Pakistan, its presence inside Sistan should not have been more than 200–300 men.[19] The attack on the Iranian parliament and the Khomeini shrine on 7 June 2017 showed that IS-K's capabilities in Iran were not limited to Sistan. According to a source in IS-K/Iran, there are three separate groups that constitute it:

- Harakat Khilafat Baluch;
- Khorasan Branch of Iran;
- West Azerbaijan Islamic Movement.

According to the source, these groups counted on over 800 members in total, more than half of them Baluchis and the rest mostly Kurds, with some Arabs, Farsi speakers and Azeris. All the members were of the Sunni religious minority. Around 200 foreign fighters support this small number of local recruits. IS-K/Iran was originally led by Abu Hafs Al Baluchi, who was then replaced by Sheikh Hamza Rigi, a former member of Jundullah who had served in Syria. According to the source, IS-K Iran grew quickly from the 300 members it had in 2016 thanks to abundant funding, but suffered in 2017 due to the cancellation of all Qatari support (although Saudi funding quickly made up for that). The Qatari authorities allegedly even shared intelligence on IS-K with the Iranians.[20]

As in Central Asia (see above), by the time it consolidated in a single entity IS-K/Iran was only technically under IS-K, while in reality it was de facto autonomous. For this reason, its later developments are not covered in detail within this book.

There is also some evidence that IS-K was trying to attract Indian jihadists as well. The Indian authorities reported killing a IS-K suspect in March 2017 in Lucknow and in the months leading up to May arresting a total of fifty-two suspects in various locations.[21] IS-K sources indicated that the bombing of the tunnels in Mohmand Dara by US forces killed eight Indian members, including two commanders.[22] There were also early reports of an IS presence in Kashmir.[23] However, it is overall obvious that the presence of IS-K in India and among Indian *mujahidin* was very marginal. Then, in 2019, Wilayat Hind was established (see Chapter 10), absorbing whatever Indians might have been there.

In Central Asia too, groups affiliated with IS were initially divided between those depending directly on IS-Central (Tajikistan) and those depending on IS-K (Kyrghizstan, Uzbekistan, Kazakhstan). In both cases, members who crossed into Afghanistan came under the authority of IS-K. IS-K membership within the Central Asian borders was estimated in January 2017 at 750 men overall by sources in IS-K and in Central Asian groups affiliated to it.[24]

In Central Asia, IS-K appears to have been able to establish a presence thanks to the flow of volunteers from Central Asia to Syria and Iraq. Some of these volunteers were sent back to their home countries, where they enlisted some initial support from networks belonging to IS's allies, such as the IMU and the ETIM. An IS source in Kyrghizstan estimated there to be 800 Kyrghiz members of IS-K as of August 2016, more than half of whom were in Syria or Iraq and about 250 in Kyrghizstan, with the rest divided between Afghanistan and Pakistan.[25]

In Kazakhstan, IS penetration was much slower than in Kyrghizstan and Tajikstan, with 135 Kazakhs reportedly recruited as of September 2016, of whom only forty-five were inside Kazakhstan. The route used in this case for smuggling volunteers and veterans back was Syria–Turkey–Georgia–Azerbaijan, then by sea to Kazakhstan.[26]

Tajikistan was a special case in that it was under the direct orders of IS-Central, and not of IS-K. Tajik official sources and IS sources differ with regard to their estimates of how many citizens of Tajikistan are fighting in Syria with IS, the former claiming 386 and the latter claiming 2,000.[27]

At a date that it has not been possible to establish, IS decided to establish a sub-branch in Central Asia itself, which it called IS-K/Bukhara. The sub-branch unified Tajikistan and the other Central Asian states into a single entity and was in theory responsible for managing all Central Asians within IS-K, even those in Afghanistan, although in practice the link appears to have been rather tenuous in terms of day-to-day business. Like the Iranian sub-branch (see above), IS-K/Bukhara was in fact essentially completely autonomous from IS-K, and hence it is not discussed in detail within this book.

Map 5: Spread of IS-K in Afghanistan according to IS-K sources, June 2015[28]

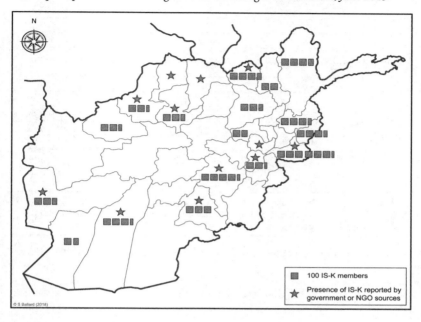

Graph 2: Growth of IS training capacity in 'Khorasan', 2013–15[29]

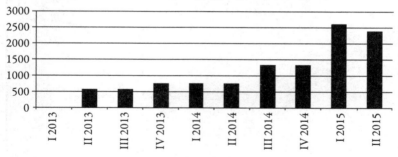

The incorporation of new component groups

The growth of IS-K occurred both through the expansion of the existing 'component groups' and through the incorporation of new groups (Graph 3). In some cases, these new groups had had relations with IS for some time before entering it, while others had not. As the component groups multiplied, the picture on the ground started looking increasingly complex (Map 7).

Graph 3: Claimed numerical strength of IS-K's component groups, 2014–16

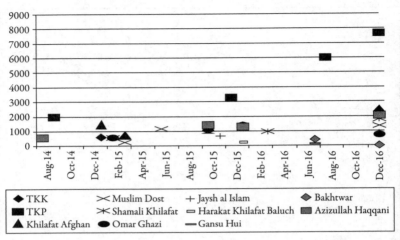

Sources: Interviews with cadres and leaders of IS-K component groups, 2014–16.

Map 6: IS-K training camps as of June 2015[30]

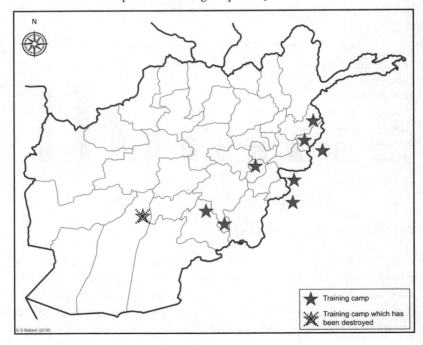

Omar Ghazi Group

As mentioned in Chapter 1, the IMU had a contingent in Syria, which had relations with IS from late 2013 at the latest. The Omar Ghazi Group split from IMU on 19 February 2015 after having been encouraged to form its own group by Abu Muslim Turkmani of IS-Central. It is led by Omar Ghazi himself and by an IMU commander posted to Syria named Sadullah Urgeni. Sources indicate that initially 580 IMU members gathered around Omar Ghazi, 200 of whom were based in Pakistan, 180 in Afghanistan, 120 in Syria and 80 in Iraq. Those based in Pakistan moved into Afghanistan the following summer. The main base of the Omar Ghazi Group was initially Faryab.[31] In January 2017, a source placed the number of Omar Ghazi's followers at 740.[32] As Osman Ghazi, leader of the mainstream IMU, increasingly leaned towards joining IS himself, the split was gradually healed. And, as of spring 2016, the Omar Ghazi Group was being described by IMU sources as once again 'part of the IMU', even if in the meanwhile a new, pro-AQ faction had emerged within the IMU (see also 'External clients and allies' below on the IMU's convoluted relationship with IS-K).[33]

Shamali Khilafat

In north-eastern Afghanistan, groups of Taliban sympathetic to IS were initially organizing themselves into a network within the Taliban, centred around Dasht-i Archi, near Kunduz. According to local sources, contacted by Mielke and Miszak, the Taliban leadership expelled the IS sympathizers only in late 2015, after they started supporting Daesh openly in the mosques and madrasas. However, some groups had organized themselves into a new branch of IS-K prior to that.[34] An altogether new 'coagulation point' emerged in early 2015 in northern Afghanistan, among Taliban commanders of Uzbek and Tajik ethnicity who had close relations with the former IMU commanders and who gathered in the Omar Ghazi Group. In the first 6 months of its existence, Shamali Khilafat attracted few veterans of Syria, only about 60–70.[35] This set it apart from groups like Omar Ghazi's, which had their roots in the Syrian war. IS-Central's relationship with this new coagulation point was therefore indirect: it was through contacts and relations with members of the Omar Ghazi Group that the leaders of Shamali Khilafat were dragged towards joining IS-K. Established by Mawlavi Hakimullah Baghlani on 13 February 2015, Shamali Khilafat claimed 600 members at the time of its founding. That number had reportedly grown to around 1,000–1,100 members as of May 2016.[36] Baghlani had briefly been with the Taliban, which he joined in 2013, as a member of Atiqullah Mahaz (linked to the Peshawar Shura).[37] Many other Taliban, most of them previously associated with the Peshawar Shura, also followed him into Shamali Khilafat.[38]

Gansu Hui Group

Similarly to the Omar Ghazi Group, Chinese jihadists in Syria and Iraq were joining IS, and some of them were eventually invited to coalesce in a formal group. While IS-Central was negotiating with ETIM over a merger, which would have brought the main Uyghur insurgent groups into IS (see below), the IS leadership seemed to have accepted the claim of some Hui militants that the time was ripe to mobilize Huis into the insurgency. The creation of an ad hoc group was seen as instrumental in exploiting this opportunity. The Gansu Hui Group was established by a Chinese Muslim known in jihadists circles as Abu Abdul Hamza Al Turkistani and some of his close associates. Al Turkistani was still in Syria, where he had deployed in 2013, when he was asked by Abu Ali al Anbari (deputy of al-Baghdadi) to travel to Pakistan and set up a new group aimed at recruiting Chinese Muslims. Particularly among Huis, opposition to the Chinese government has only recently emerged.[39]

Al Turkistani therefore gathered a number of Uyghurs and Huis who were already members of IS and asked the IS leadership to recognize the group, known within IS-K as the Gansu Hui Group, even if in reality the majority of its members are not from Gansu. The group was established (without any official announcement) on 26 July 2015 and formally recognized by IS on 14 August. However, it was not given the status of a 'component group' as discussed at the beginning of this chapter, probably because of its small size. As of July 2016, the group claimed a modest 118 members in Afghanistan and Pakistan, only forty-eight of which were actually Huis, the others being Uyghurs. This suggests that IS-Central was pushing for a 'Hui project' regardless of whether there was any sort of Hui 'pressure group' advocating for it. The group was involved in negotiations with other Chinese Muslims in IS-K, IS and external allies of IS, such as IMU, ETIM and IJU, but also with rivals such as AQ, in order to attract Chinese Muslims.[40]

By 2020, the ability of IS-K to attract Muslims from China had greatly reduced. From its peak of 300 Uyghurs (between Gansu Hui and IS-K proper), the number had fallen to 60–80 by June 2020, due to a slowing flow of recruits, heavy casualties and defections to other, pro-AQ groups. IS-K still collaborated closely with ETIM in Afghanistan, but ETIM too had seen a decline in strength. Donor support for Chinese groups was in decline due to these groups' lack of achievements. There is also a reduction in the flow of recruits.[41]

Harakat Khilafat Baluch

A major stream of funding into IS-K was dependent on the organization's claimed ability to reach out to the Baluchis and upgrade the insurgency within Iran:

> We are not very interested in the activities of IS in Pakistan, Afghanistan and Central Asia, but we are interested in the activities of IS in Iran. IS-K succeeded because they made relationship with Iranian Baluch and Sunni groups and they will start their activities very soon against Iranian Government.[42]

The IS-K leaders were keen to attract Baluchis, and they targeted Baluchi rebels of various descriptions, including characters such as Saleh Khan Regi—a Regi tribal elder (see also Chapter 2)—as well as existing organizations.[43] Iranian Baluchis were the main target for recruitment, but Afghan and Pakistani Baluchis were also important for IS-K to acquire influence and control over the border areas. It was Abdul Rauf Khadim who first reached out to Iranian Baluchis in 2014 through some Afghan Baluchi commanders; after that, some IS agents visited the Iranian Baluchi leaders in January 2015, probably in Pakistan.[44] In particular, two pre-existing groups of Iranian Baluchis, Harakat-e Ansar-e Iran (Movement of the Partisans of Iran) and Jaysh ul-Adl (Army of Justice), entered negotiations with IS-K with regard to merging into it.[45] These two groups were already being funded by the Gulf Countries and had Islamist leanings.

Harakat-e Khilafat-e Baluch (Baluch Movement for the Caliphate) was established on 13 July 2015 by a number of Iranian Baluchi commanders, coming from the ranks of the two groups mentioned above, as well as from the ranks of Jundullah, the third and original Baluchi insurgent group in Iran. Among those joining was the leader of Harakat-e Ansar-e Iran, Abu Hafs al Baluchi, who, however, could not carry the majority of the members with him. He became the main figure of Harakat-e Khilafat-e Baluch, alongside Muhammad Hassan Baluch.[46]

At its start, Harakat Khilafat Baluch only claimed 245 men, despite the fact that IS-K allocated quite a large budget to the organization. About a third of them were claimed to be from the ranks of Harakat Ansar Iran, a quarter from

Jaysh ul-Adl and a fifth from Jundullah. The group spent the first several months of its membership of IS-K recruiting and organizing logistically.[47]

Despite its best efforts, IS-K and IS-Central did not achieve a high degree of success in engineering the creation of a serious coagulation point for Baluchis. A large group of Baluchis from Pakistan and Afghanistan with about 800 men, called the Hassan Khan Baluch Group, negotiated with IS-K. However, negotiations were not successful, possibly because the IS-K ban on drug smuggling was discouraging to the group's leader Hassan Khan, a notorious heroin smuggler.[48]

Jaysh ul-Islam

As IS-K gathered speed and notoriety, a couple more groups joined in Pakistan. Jaysh ul-Islam (Army of Islam) was active for years in Pakistani Baluchistan and merged into IS-K on 4 November 2015. At the time of joining IS-K, it claimed almost 700 members. The group was targeting Shi'as even before this date, so there was a clear ideological attraction to IS-K. Like other Baluchistan-based groups, Jaysh was reportedly allocated an oversized budget by IS-K ($35 million in 2016), witness to IS-K's commitment to Baluchistan as a route into Iran, although Jaysh is not a specifically Baluchi group and is of mixed ethnic composition. Sources of funding were IS-Central, Qatar and Saudi Arabian private donors, as well as some taxes collected mainly from smugglers.[49] The leader of Jaysh ul-Islam was initially Mehmud Rahman, replaced after his death by Maulana Mohammad Tahir Baluch.[50]

Mullah Bakhtwar's group

The other group which was attracted to IS-K after its exposure in the media was called Khilafat Speen Ghar Bakhtwar Group, which was formed by Mullah Bakhtwar, a former TTP commander from the Afridi tribe who had previously operated in Bara. The group was created in early 2016, after Bakhtwar had split from the TTP in 2015 over differences with TTP leader Fazlullah. At the time of joining IS-K, Mullah Bakhtwar's group claimed 400 members, of which half were Pakistanis (mostly former TTP Afridis from Bara, Tera, Jamroad and Landi Kotal), a quarter freshly recruited Afghans and the rest Central Asians from IMT, ETIM, IMU and even some Tajiks.[51]

Mullah Bakhtwar maintained close relations with TKP despite deciding to form a separate group, as well as with Muslim Dost and Al-Afghani.[52] A source inside the group indicated that Mullah Bakhtwar was receiving support from Saudi Arabia and particularly from Pakistan, and both countries reportedly posted advisers to the group. The group was also against fighting with the Taliban.[53] In autumn 2016, Bakhtwar was killed in a drone strike in Nangarhar and his group merged into the TKP, ceasing to exist as a separate group.[54]

The Shamsatoo Group

All the groups described above were formally recognized by IS-K as semi-autonomous entities, with their own budgets and structures. A particular case is that of a large group of Hizb-i Islami members from Shamsatoo Camp in Pakistan, who joined as a whole but were not allowed to form a homogeneous component group. This was possibly due to IS-K fearing this could become a kind of Trojan horse for Hizb-i Islami's leaders. A group of reportedly 400 Hizb-i Islami fighters and commanders, led by Commander Mustafa and headquartered in Shamsatoo Camp, which has been a Hizbi stronghold since the 1980s, joined IS-K in 2015. According to one of his associates, he was encouraged by Hizb-i Islami leader Hekmatyar to do so, probably in an effort to 'park' some of the party's residual armed force somewhere, while negotiating reconciliation with Kabul and reintegration/disarmament of its fighters.[55]

A militia commander linked to Haji Zahir confirmed having personally arrested three IS-K members, who under interrogation confirmed that they were former Hizbis from Shamsatoo Camp and that many others had joined the organization as well. The terms of the agreement between IS-K were that the new recruits would be given a number of senior positions and be extended all the facilities available to other members of IS-K. However, the Hizb-i Islami group would not be officially recognized as one of the components of IS-K, and its members would be distributed among IS-K's various component groups, mostly TKK and Muslim Dost.[56]

The reasons for this decision are unclear; perhaps the IS-Central and/or IS-K leaderships did not trust the motives of Hizb-i Islami and wanted to disperse the recruits in order to control them more easily. Indeed, Shamsatoo training camp commander Mustafa reportedly had concerns about what he was hearing of IS-K atrocities against elders, the closure of NGOs and schools and so on, and he discussed the matter with Faruq Safi of IS-K in Shamsatoo, who promised that IS-K would work to prevent such abuses in the future. A source within the group claimed that after the meeting IS-K allowed some schools in Achin to re-open. Nonetheless, a number of Hizb-i Islami members left the group in protest of this agreement with IS-K.[57]

The same appears to have applied to a number of other Hizb-i Islami groups which joined inside Afghanistan (in Azra of Logar, Tagab of Kapisa, Hesarak of Nangarhar, Kohi Safi of Parwan, Nurgul and Dara e Pech of Kunar). Throughout its existence, IS-K and its component groups negotiated with individual Hizb-i Islami commanders for them to join. IS-K, Hizb and local sources all confirmed the presence of former Hizbis in IS-K. A source within the group of Hizbis who joined IS-K admitted that the inability of Hizb-i Islami to pay salaries and fund operations was a major factor in driving its members towards IS-K.[58]

This does not necessarily imply that ideological and political motivations were entirely absent: Hizbis had good reasons of their own to be hostile to Iran, after their dramatic expulsion in 2002.[59] Hekmatyar was also working hard on restoring his ties with Saudi Arabia, severed in 1991, with the aim of enlisting Saudi financial support. Eventually this paid off, as the Saudis agreed to support Hizb-i Islami's re-integration after the group's 2016 peace deal with Kabul.[60] The price to pay was the adoption of anti-Shi'a rhetoric, which Hizb-i Islami had always avoided in the past. Several other senior Hizb-i Islami commanders were reported to be negotiating with IS-K as well in January 2016.[61]

Map 7: Presence on the ground in Afghanistan and Pakistan's border regions of different component groups of IS-K, circa October 2015[62]

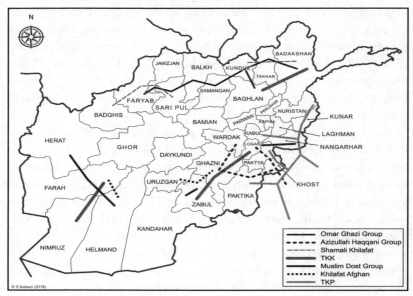

Map 8: Distribution of IS-K component groups in Pakistan, end of 2016

Sources: Interviews with TKP, Jaysh ul-Islam, Harakat Khilfat Baluch and Jundullah cadres.

External clients and allies

IS-Central and IS-K have been building relations with a variety of jihadist organizations operating within Khorasan, presumably with the aim of eventually absorbing them. As of December 2016, many of these organizations looked happy to receive funding and other forms of support from IS, while mostly merely talking of the possibility of merging into IS-K at some point in the future. IS-Central has been supporting allied organizations directly, outside of its IS-K budget.

The Central Asians

After 2010, Central Asian jihadists previously based in southern and south-eastern Afghanistan started moving north. By 2014, they started being presented by the Afghan authorities as a serious threat, while the authorities of some Central Asian states started issuing alarming figures about the number of their citizens fighting in IS ranks in the Middle East. The figures provided by the Afghan and Central Asian authorities might or might not have been inflated, but the upward trend is clear.[63] As discussed in Chapter 2, both IS-Central and IS-K made a determined effort to attract Central Asians. Above, we discussed the recruitment of individuals and groups into IS-K, but another important aspect of the process occurred between 2013 and 2016, when several Central Asian jihadist groups established close relations with IS, despite not fully joining and merging into it. These include:

- Ozbekiston Islamyi Harakati (Islamic Movement of Uzbekistan, IMU), the original Central Asian jihadist group, formed in 1998;
- Jamaat Ansarullah (Society of the Partisans of Allah), the main armed opposition group in Tajikistan;
- Ittehad al Jihad al Islami (Islamic Jihadi Union, IJU), a splinter of IMU, which later reconciled with it and attracted mainly non-Uzbek Turkic speakers;
- Turkmenistan Islamyi Hereket (Islamic Movement of Turkmenistan, IMT), de facto a sub-brand of the IMU tasked to penetrate Turkmenistan;
- Sherqiy Turkistan Islamyi Harakat or Partisy (East Turkestan Islamic Movement/Party—ETIM/ETIP), one of the two main Uyghur armed opposition groups to the Chinese government;
- Harakat Islami Tajikistan, a small group in Tajikistan;[64]
- Hizbi Nehzati Jihadi Islami Tajikistan (Islamic Jihad Renaissance Party of Tajikistan, IJRPT), a splinter of the Islamic Renaissance Party of Tajikistan, a once legally registered party, which was banned in August 2015.[65]

In some cases, like IJRPT, the relationship with IS-K became so close that AQ was cut off. IJRPT established relations with IS in 2013, as some members travelled to Syria as volunteers. By 2016, IJRPT was entirely funded by IMU, IS-K and some private donors from Saudi Arabia, with IS-K funding almost twice that of IMU, giving the IS quite a strong say in IJRPT's decision-making. According to a source inside IJRPT, the party was considering joining IS altogether.[66]

Our fighters are also with Daesh. So they also want we to join with them. In reality we already joined with Daesh and we do many things decided by Daesh. What Daesh is telling us we are performing it.[67]

The IMU also established a close relationship with IS, forged on the battlefields of Syria and Iraq. From mid-September 2014, the IMU's position has been one of support for IS and its aims, despite continuing to receive support from AQ and avoiding openly raising the issue of the role of Mullah Omar's disappearance in 2011 with the Taliban.[68] Then, in August 2015, Osman Ghazi, the IMU's leader, followed in the steps of fellow IMU member Omar Ghazi and swore allegiance to IS. In a video widely circulated on the internet, he announced that the IMU was now part of the Caliphate. This announcement was well received in IS media, suggesting that it was accepted without qualms.[69] At this point, many IMU commanders considered themselves to be part of IS-K.[70] One factor pushing many IMU members towards joining IS-K was the declining credibility of the Taliban's Quetta Shura as a jihadist partner.

We are tired of the Taliban, we have worked with them for thirteen years we did not see Mullah Mohammad Omar. Not only the leader was not known. The Peshawar Shura was giving the orders, Quetta Shura and Miran Shah Shura too were giving orders. ... Another reason is this that Taliban became weak and started negotiations with Afghan Government and foreign forces.[71]

However, not everybody in the IMU accepted the idea of a merger with IS-K, and two groups split from Osman Ghazi's IMU between 2015 and 2016, seeking to remain loyal to AQ. Osman Ghazi himself was killed in November 2015 by the Taliban, and IS-Central reverses in Iraq and Syria seemingly advised a growing number of IMU commanders to reverse their earlier choice and side again with the pro-AQ faction. As of February 2017, the IMU was split three ways, with the Omar Ghazi Group already incorporated into IS-K, the mainstream IMU semi-merged into IS-K and the two pro-AQ factions at large, plus Jamaat al Bukhari, a group which had split from the IMU in 2013 and had always stayed loyal to AQ.[72]

A Revolutionary Guards (Iran) officer described Osman Ghazi as 'a member of Daesh' and hinted that he was killed in an Iranian operation, with the collaboration of Taliban linked to Iran.[73] There appears to have been some disappointment among IMU members with regard to IS, as they were in a position to receive information from their colleagues in Syria and Iraq about the critical situation of the Caliphate. As the words of IS defector and former IMU mufti Abu Dher al Barmi suggest, IMU had forged close relations with the Taliban over the years, and some members did not approve of IS-K's hostile attitude towards them.[74]

The IJU is de facto a sub-brand of the IMU and similarly maintained close relations with IS-K.[75] Similarly, the ETIM closely co-operates with the IMU, maintaining close relations with IS-K and receiving funds from it in exchange for sending volunteers to fight in the ranks of IS in Syria and Iraq; IS-K has been trying to convince ETIM to merge with it. The pro-AQ element in ETIM was at that point (2016–17) largely concentrated in the TIP.[76] Later, however, the ETIM distanced itself from IS-K and re-established connections with AQ.[77]

With regard to the IMT, which had good relations with IS from 2014 and with IS-K from 2015, it also despatched volunteers to Syria and Iraq to fight alongside it.[78] A source in the Omar Ghazi Group stated that IMT was seen as the most likely to merge into IS-K in the future.[79] Asked whether IMT would choose Taliban or IS-K if forced to, a member indicated IS-K as the more obvious choice; the same answer applied when he was asked to choose between IS-K and AQ.[80] However, IMT–IS-K relations appear to have cooled down during 2016, and IMT edged closer to AQ again.[81]

Jamaat Ansarullah[82] too switched from having a very close relationship with AQ until 2014 to a rapid worsening of relations after Jamaat volunteers in Syria joined IS and the latter started supporting Jamaat financially. In 2015, Jamaat Ansarullah was receiving 50 per cent of its revenue from IS, 30 per cent from IMU and 20 per cent from AQ and others, according to an internal source. Jamaat continues sending volunteers to Syria.[83]

Jamaat tried to maintain a good relationship with the Taliban, despite its alliance with IS-K. Contrary to other Central Asian groups, Jamaat seemed to consider its relationship with the Taliban to be more precious than that with IS-K; the same did not apply to AQ.[84] Together with IJRPT and Harakat Islami Tajikistan, Jamaat Ansarullah reportedly negotiated a merger with IS-K, to be implemented in February 2017.[85] It later dropped the idea and, like other Central Asian groups, edged back towards AQ.[86]

All the Central Asian groups were attracted to IS primarily by the latter's commitment to supporting jihad in Central Asia straight away. As long as AQ was funding them, they had to prioritize jihad in Afghanistan, postponing the Central Asian jihad to an indefinite future.[87] It seems plausible that the Central Asians' hearts were yearning instead for jihad back home, the more so as they started hearing about the Taliban's interest in reconciling with Kabul and subsequently banning IMU from Afghan soil.[88]

Hizb-i Islami (Hekmatyar)

The Hekmatyar wing of Hizb-i Islami has also flirted with IS-K in 2015, not only in order to park some of the party's underfunded fighting force somewhere, as discussed above in 'The Shamsatoo Group'. Hizb-i Islami as a whole was also interested in collaborating with IS-K in an anti-Taliban function. Although not all sources agree about how good these relations really were, at least there are no reports of any clashes between them until the second half of 2016.[89] Hizb-i Islami as such was never a client of the IS in that it did not receive funds from it, but Hekmatyar openly advised party members on the party press to side with IS-K against the Taliban in Nangarhar.[90] The two organizations also shared a strong hostility towards Iran. However, in 2016 things changed as Hekmatyar entered serious discussions about reconciliation with Kabul, and eventually reached an agreement in September 2016. Even before that, after IS-K massacres started in Nangarhar and IS-K's school closures, Hizb-i Islami had to distance itself.[91] Some armed clashes between Hizb-i Islami and IS-K started occurring in Pachir wa Agam (Nangarhar) and Dangam (Kunar).[92]

Elements of Hizb-i Islami re-engaged later on with IS-K, in 2020, reportedly under pressure from the Pakistani ISI to contribute to IS-K's campaign against the Islamic Republic. Some 800 Hizb-i Islami members got involved, but never joined IS-K. Rather, they co-operated with it in an ad hoc alliance called Ittehad Dawat Islami (Islamic Invitation Alliance).[93]

The Pakistani jihadists

Among the Pakistani jihadist groups, IS-K had the closest relations with Lashkar-e Jhangvi and the Jundullah (Baluchistan). In its early months of existence, TKP had already attracted hundreds of men from Lashkar-e Jhangvi. Al-Baghdadi himself reportedly had direct, close relations with Lashkar-e Jhangvi, which turned into a client organization as it started receiving funds from IS.[94] However, negotiations over a merger of Lashkar-e Jhangvi stalled during 2016, as Arab Gulf donors reportedly warned IS-K that if a merger of Lashkar-e Jhangvi into IS-K took place they would retaliate and crack down on IS-K activities.[95] Relations with Lashkar-e Jhangvi worsened further in 2020–21, after the latter signed an agreement with the Taliban in August 2020 and then sent large numbers of volunteers to fight alongside the Taliban.[96][97]

In the early days, TKP also maintained good relations with TTP, the organization from which most of its leaders came.[98] But relations worsened rapidly (see Chapter 8 below). However, some internal factions and splinters of TTP remained or became much closer to IS-K. Lashkar-e Islam, for example, reportedly entertained good relations with IS-K, at least in Nangarhar, and often co-ordinated with them. Some sources also report that the Tariq Gidar Group, which is part of TTP, also collaborated with IS-K in Nangarhar, but a senior IS-K source firmly denied this.[99] Finally Jamaat ul-Ahrar also appears to have maintained close relations with IS-K and has appeared supportive of the 'Caliphate' in its media outlets. The former spokesperson of Jamaat ul-Ahrar commented that

> Jamaat ul Ahrar [a break-away group from TTP] was also made an offer by ISIS to become a part of ISIS Khorasan. This was also discussed within the organization [Jamaat ul-Ahrar]. The head of the Jamaat ul Ahrar, Omar Khalid Khorasani, wanted to join ISIS but three or four other people, including myself, opposed it. However despite this, we were ordered to start supporting ISIS in the media unannounced or at least not to oppose the group.[100]

According to Ehsan, the leadership of Jamaat ul-Ahrar proposed the formation of a new province—Wilayat Hind, to include Pakistan, India and Bangladesh—which would be led by Jamaat ul-Ahrar as a condition for merging into IS. Jamaat ul-Ahrar even sent a delegation to IS-Central in Iraq and Syria to lobby for this, but the request was rejected.[101]

In September 2014, Jamaat ul-Ahrar declared their support for Al-Baghdadi, but later rejoined the TTP before splitting from it again.[102] IS-K claimed the Quetta Hospital attack of August 2016; Jamaat ul-Ahrar, however, insisted it was the one to carry it out and rejected having collaborated with IS-K.[103] However, the October 2016 attack against the Quetta police training college was also claimed by both organizations, without prompting any reaction by Jamaat ul-Ahrar. Sources in TTP also believed a close relationship and military alliance was in place, even in Nangarhar.[104] Eventually, however, Jamaat ul-Ahrar and its splinter Hizb ul-Ahrar opted to rejoin the TTP and cut off relations with IS-K. This was after both groups suffered heavy casualties while fighting on IS-K's side in Nangarhar in late 2019, and was also in protest at the relationship between IS-K and the ISI.[105] The TTP also cut off negotiations with IS-K on the same ground.[106]

On the other hand, IS-K had poor or even non-existent relations with Lashkar-e Taiba (LeT) initially, 'because that is the private group of ISI. We do not want to have relations with them'.[107] Lashkar-e Taiba was described as 'the special representative of Pakistan Government' by a senior TKP figure, but the leadership of IS-K negotiated with it as well in order to convince it to join, or at least to co-operate.[108] IS-K tried to reassure LeT that its arrival in Pakistan was not meant to challenge their interests.[109] And according to a LeT source, its donors in Saudi Arabia and Qatar similarly put some pressure on LeT to co-operate with IS-K. Some form of co-operation indeed started in 2016, with LeT sending some trainers and advisers to IS-K.

In LeT, only a small minority of members held anti-Shi'a views, and some of these had already joined IS-K before relations between the two organizations improved. According to LeT sources, as of October 2016, 167 LeT members had gone over to IS in Syria and Iraq, and about 100 joined IS-K in Afghanistan and Pakistan. According to the same source, the flow was encouraged by the Pakistani authorities, which wanted to use the former LeT members as sources of information about IS. Among those who joined were some relatively senior figures, including Abdul Wahab, former chief of LeT in Kunar, and Mufti Iqbal Lashkari, senior commander in Kashmir.[110] Subsequently, Pakistan's police did raid some LeT (Jamaat ud Dawa) cells, which had defected to IS-K.[111]

In fact, TKP sources were already claiming in late 2014 that 300 or so members of LeT had joined their group, and a senior IS-K source claimed that the LeT contingent in Syria had joined IS there already as of November 2013.[112] These could of course be unauthorized defections, with the more recent ones instead being part of an infiltration plan, but there is no hard evidence to back up the LeT source's claims.

Later, however, relations with LeT as such certainly intensified. IS-K even started using some LeT camps near Lahore for training. The Pakistani authorities reportedly gave their agreement to IS-K and LeT strengthening relations, and there began a new inflow of LeT members into IS-K.[113] Such close relations did not last long, however, and after the fall of Kabul to the Taliban in August 2021 Lashkar-e Taiba suddenly turned on IS-K, and the bulk of former LeT members inside IS-K moved back to their mother organization (see also Chapter 10).[114]

The Baluchis

Despite their head-hunting of Baluchi commanders within existing organizations—and despite their ban on drugs—IS-K leaders claimed to have been able to maintain good relations with pre-existing Baluchi groups, who were in awe of IS-K's financial resources.[115] The January 2017 lifting of the ban on drugs might be related to renewed efforts to push for a merger of Baluchi insurgent organizations with IS-K.[116] Those Baluchi groups which proved difficult to absorb into IS-K were, however, offered attractive deals to incentivize their co-operation.

IS-K has been particularly targeting for recruitment Harakat Islami Sistan, one of several Baluchi insurgent groups in Iran which had established relations with IS early on and was already sending volunteers to Syria in 2014.[117] Baluchi militant group Jundullah, particularly active in enacting violence against Pakistani Shi'as from 2014 onwards, was reported to have pledged allegiance to IS. In November 2014, Jundullah's spokesperson Marwat described IS as 'a brother to Jundullah' and offered support. Reportedly, Jundullah met an IS delegation in Saudi Arabia.[118]

During 2015 and 2016, IS-K also worked towards the merger of the Iranian and the Pakistani Jundullah, which it ultimately sponsored in August 2016. According to an IS-K Baluchi commander, the unified Jundullah collaborated closely with IS-K, which provided it funding, allowing it to expand its ranks. Significantly, Mohammad Dhahir Baluch, the leader of the Iranian branch, was chosen as leader of the unified Jundullah, despite the Pakistanis being much more numerous. The choice highlighted what role IS-K had figured out for the new Jundullah: infiltrating Iran.[119] After 2019, Jundullah shifted its 'alliance' to the newly formed IS-P.[120]

7

THE FUNDING OF IS-K

One Revolutionary Guards (Iran) officer perhaps unsurprisingly commented that the real source of IS's power is its financial wealth: they can afford better equipment and pay their members higher salaries.[1] This officer might underestimate the organizational capital accumulated by IS over the years, but undoubtedly IS-K would not have been able to establish multiple beachheads in Afghanistan and Pakistani in just 2 years if it had not been well funded. But where did their money come from? There are only three possible sources of funding for IS-K: taxation and local 'contributions', payments from IS-Central and funds donated by external donors.

Taxation

In its first few months of operations, IS-K commanders were told not to raise their own funds and to rely instead on the logistics provided by their structures. This might have been part of an effort to avoid clashing with established insurgent organizations (Taliban and TTP) at a time when IS-K was still very weak. After initially banning the component groups from raising taxes, in 2015 IS started insisting that IS-K raise some of its own funding locally in the form of farm taxes, taxes on economic activities and taxes on smuggling, except for the poppies after their ban in November 2015.[2]

> Daesh is telling to us that we must find some local source of money, which can help us. We are trying to extract from some mines and we are collecting taxes

167

from the people. They are telling to us that you can make a lot of money for your future. You must have budget for yourselves to buy weapons and ammunitions for yourselves. Before we did not have permission for this to collect the money.[3]

Zakat and *Ushr* were levied in accordance to Shari'a, usually one animal per herd or 10 per cent of crops.[4]

Prior to the ban on poppies, there were allegations that IS-K was aiming to assert control over heroin refineries, and many of these actually fell during the period of IS-K control in the districts of Achin, Mohmand Dara, Shinwari, Chaparhar and so on.[5] For sure, originally IS-K even imposed a special tax on smugglers, at 15 and sometimes even 20 per cent.[6] At that time, IS-K had dedicated 'agents' tasked with raising funds from the smugglers, who were appointed by virtue of their close relations with them.[7] The ban on poppies was justified on ideological bases. The Taliban were painted as drug smugglers who disrespected Shari'a. However, IS-K sources acknowledged that the ban on opium poppies cost them a lot in potential tax revenue.[8]

However, why did the ban only come into play in November 2015? The ban coincided with Abu Yasir Al-Afghani's efforts to bring order in IS-K, so one reason might have been to eliminate a source of contention within IS-K (over who should control the drug revenue). Another reason might have been to deprive the various component groups of a major source of revenue, which had they been in possession of might have made them less likely to respond to orders from the leadership. This interpretation is reinforced by the fact that the ban was lifted in the south-west of Afghanistan and in Baluchistan in January 2017, possibly in response to requests from IS-Central to raise more funds at a time of financial difficulties in Syria and Iraq. It is also worth noting that even during the implementation of the ban, IS-K kept using cadres with a background in the drugs trade, like Abdul Zahir Brahawi, whose family members continued to trade opium and heroin. Brahawi and others like him reportedly lobbied IS-K to lift the ban, as it impeded IS-K's progress in areas of intense drug trafficking like Helmand, Nimruz, Nangarhar and Bakuchistan.[9]

In 2019, a group of Nangarhar-based drug traders approached IS-K and invited them to revise their ban on drugs, which was still in place in eastern Afghanistan, probably hoping that given the organization's financial difficulties, this time it would prove more reasonable. The leadership of IS-K refused to lift the ban on the cultivation of poppies, but agreed to allow smugglers to use routes into Central Asia that went through territory held by IS-K in Kunar, Nuristan and Badakhshan. That, of course, was in exchange for the smugglers paying substantial protection money to IS-K.[10] After that, drug smuggling remained a major source of revenue for IS-K, especially after the Taliban started challenging IS-K's control over some mines in Badakhshan.

In 2019, all IS-K's ability to tax mining operations in Nangarhar was lost. In reality, after the defeats of 2019–20 in the east, relations with smugglers were poor too, as IS-K was no longer in a position to be of much help to many of them. IS-K's finance and military commissions set off working on a plan for rebuilding relations with the smugglers, and most importantly to get them to start paying taxes to IS-K again. The plan included checkpoints on the Afghanistan–Pakistan border, intelligence cells operations and proper co-ordination among IS-K units with regard to tracking the smugglers. In practice, IS-K did not have the manpower to implement the plan at that time.[11] As of April 2020, several Afghan drug-smuggling gangs active on the drug route to Central Asia were reportedly paying money to IS-K. Sources in the smuggling world stated that IS-K was trying to expand its alliance with drug traders and was negotiating with smugglers in southern Afghanistan.[12]

Other sources of revenue existed as well. Trucks stopped on the roads were charged up to $9,000. There are also widespread reports of kidnappings for ransom, with as many as 300 reported up to the end of 2015, with ransoms of as little as $20,000.[13] Some sources even indicated that IS-K was actually bringing machinery to wooded areas to increase timber production, either for profit or for taxing the output.[14] That IS-K forces were raising taxes locally has been confirmed by military intelligence sources too.

> Rather than relying on external funding, IS-K is attempting to develop its funding streams within Afghanistan, which has put it into conflict with the Taliban and other groups vying to raise revenue from illegal checkpoints and the trade of illicit goods.[15]

In mid-2015, a high-level source in IS-K put the yearly revenue collected at $25 million, excluding taxes in kind.[16] A different source in the Finance Commission indicated that in the first half of 2016 IS-K collected $33 million in taxes, according to the Finance Commission's records. He described this amount as a decrease from the previous year's tax collection due to the ban on opium poppies imposed by Al-Afghani.[17] Assuming these two bits of information are both correct, they would suggest revenue collection reached its peak in the second half of 2015, which is not implausible given that this is when IS-K first laid its hand on significant drug revenue in Nangarhar.

IS-K's main sources of tax revenue came in autumn 2015 from the Nangarhar, Helmand and Zabul opium trade (until its ban in late 2015), and from some mines in Badakhshan and Achin of Nangarahar.[18] During 2016,

IS-K laid its hands on a number of other mining industries such as marble, talc and luminous stones in Nangarhar (Hissarak, Achin, Kot, Ghani Khel) and elsewhere, such as uranium and carbonium mines in Khaneshin, Helmand. In some cases, IS-K took direct control of the mining activities, including transporting stones and selling them. In other cases, it contented itself with taxing the mining businesses at the rate of 200–500 Pakistani Rupees per tonne (depending on the material), 1,500 Pakistani Rupees per horse carrying timber or 20 per cent of the value of precious stones and minerals. They also started collecting taxes on electricity, water and all business activities.[19]

The pressure to raise funds clashed with the fact that in many cases IS-K could not raise revenue through taxes because of competition from other groups:

> Up to now we did not collect any money from tax, meaning we did not start the collections of tax in Iran. Powerful groups can collect tax, but we are not powerful and the number of our people are also small now. There are Baluch and many other mafia groups that do not give permission to us to collect tax.[20]

Another reason that IS-K raised relatively little in taxes centrally was that all of its component groups continued to raise their own taxes and contributions. What they could collect varied widely from place to place. Over the course of 2 months in autumn 2015, Muslim Dost's Group alone reportedly collected $5 million in in Helmand and Kandahar, including through a 15 per cent tax on smugglers and a 10 per cent tax on farmers.[21] Jaysh ul-Islam collected $10 million in taxes in Baluchistan in 2015, according to an internal source.[22] TKP raised almost $3 million in taxes from Orakzai Agency during 2015, again according to an internal source.[23] In principle, at least, the IS-K component groups are asked by the leadership to establish a transparent taxation system, with computerized records and receipts.[24]

Sources converged in saying that IS-K was not taxing the poorest farmers, but rather focusing on shops and the wealthy.[25] One possible reason for IS-K renouncing taxes on agricultural produce, aside from its financial wealth, is the fact that most areas where it operated were sparsely populated and poor.[26] Tax collection among shopkeepers and the wealthy only took place in areas where IS-K's control was already consolidated.[27] When it was implemented, however, collection was very thorough: 'all the shops at Da Baba bazaar and Ab Dara bazaar were giving taxes for the Daesh'.[28]

> Not from the villagers and elders, but they were collecting tax from the businessmen, shopkeepers and drug traffickers. This way of Daesh was completely differ-

ent with Taliban. Taliban were collecting *Zakat* from the villagers but Daesh was taking *Zakat* or Tax from shopkeepers, drug traffickers and businessmen.[29]

IS-K's fearsome reputation meant that 'all the people are ready to give tax to us'.[30] Because of the wide disparity in wealth between provinces, tax collections were also very uneven (Table 10).

In general, tax revenue fell from 2019 onwards, due to IS-K's loss of control over the richest province where it had a foothold, Nangarhar.[31]

IS-K constantly tried to identify new sources of revenue. In March 2019, it established an NGO department within its Finance Commission, tasked to register non-government organizations that wanted to operate in areas under IS-K control. IS-K sources did not hide the fact that one of the main reasons for establishing the NGO department was to raise taxes from NGOs, although they also argued that the IS-K leadership wanted to improve relations with the population as well. The new department was established against the advice of the majority of IS-K's central shura, a fact that suggests that the leadership's concern for fundraising was greater than the opposition of most military commanders.[32]

Table 10: Example of tax collection by IS-K[33]

Province	Year	Monthly collection rate ($ million)
Zabul	2014	0.5
Zabul	2015	1
Herat	2015	2.5
Farah	2015	0.5
Nangarhar	2016	4.7
Kunar	2016	1.5
Helmand	2016	1.9

IS-Central funding

At the time of IS-K being launched, and during the several months of IS-K's 'pre-history' in 2014, IS-Central was in all likelihood the main source of funding, although sources provided different figures for 2015 (see Table 11). Afghan intelligence sources confirmed the flow of funds from the Middle East to IS-K.[34] Usually IS-K would submit an annual budget to the Caliphate for approval. It could request additional funding during the year, but it had to justify it.[35] The Caliphate had to approve the IS-K budget proposed by the governor, and the Khorasan governor would then decide how to spend it.[36] IS-K sources indicated, however, that IS-Central reduced its commitment to IS-K in 2016 by about 22 per cent. This might be due to the fact that other sources of funding were taking off (see *External funding* below), or to the fact that IS-Central was not doing that well financially anymore.[37]

A source in the Finance Commission commented that he had not expected IS in Syria and Iraq to be able to increase its level of funding until it consolidated control over Syria and Iraq; until then, he argued, IS-K would be dependent on funding from the Gulf.[38] As of early 2017, the prospects of IS-Central control over Iraq and Syria were as remote as ever, with most observers expecting Mosul to fall to Iraqi government forces within months. In early 2019, there was a temporary upsurge in cash flows from IS-Central, allowing IS-K to go on the offensive in Kunar in March, but it was short-lived.[39] Year 2020 started badly, as IS-Central paused funding, and then once funding resumed it transferred the lowest amount ever to IS-K. Its funding levels fully recovered in 2021 (see 'How much' below).

External funding

Efforts by IS-K to directly raise funding in the Gulf were confirmed by Afghan intelligence sources.[40] Under the Finance Commission, a fundraising group was established in 2015, known in Pashto as Mujahideno Sara Da Marasti Tolana (Community of Support for the Mujahideen), with offices in Jebel Ali and Al Ain (UAE), Medina and Riyad (Saudi Arabia) and Doha (Qatar), and a total membership of about eighty.[41] The location of this group already tells us a lot about the location of the majority of donors.

Who pays

As discussed in 'The Finance Commission' above, the bulk of IS-K funding was money transferred by private and allegedly state donors abroad. NDS sources also indicated that Afghan intelligence sees money coming to IS-K from Saudi Arabia, Qatar and Pakistan, as well as from locally raised taxes.[42]

> They have a lot of sources because they are extracting from mines, they have relationship with big smugglers, they are collecting taxes, there are many donors from Arab countries who are helping Daesh.[43]

One source reports the existence of IS agents travelling the Middle East and South Asia, lobbying wealthy individuals and businessmen to support the organization.[44]

Private donors have privileged relations with specific IS-K leaders. At least one major donor, for example, was reported to have close relations with Hafiz Saeed, while at least two were close to Al-Afghani. Several donors were transferring funds to IS-K by virtue of their relations with ISIS leaders like Al Anbari, Abu Saleh al Obaidi and Abu Omar al Shishani.[45]

Aside from the main donors paying millions, there are a larger number of donors paying hundreds of thousands each year. One stated he had paid $200,000 in 2015 and $300,000 in 2016.[46] Private donors are typically wealthy individuals, businessmen and government contractors, allegedly even some members of royal families, mostly Saudis, but also Emiratis, Kuwaitis and Qataris.[47] On the whole, in 2015 $20 million paid by private donors was transferred from Qatar by IS-K to its Finance Commission.[48]

IS-K sources insisted that apart from private donors from Qatar, Kuwait, UAE, Saudi Arabia, Iraq, Syria and Egypt, three Arab Gulf governments also secretly contributed to IS-K's coffers: Saudi Arabia, Qatar and Kuwait.[49] According to a cadre from the IS-K Finance Commission, the government of Qatar started supporting IS in 2013, around the same time that they started supporting Al-Nusra; shortly thereafter, they started providing funds for what at that time was still the Khorasan project.[50]

The IS-K delegation in Doha as of April 2015 was reportedly led by Mawlavi Nasratullah Popolzai, one of the main figures in TKK, a fact that if true would signal the importance of Qatar for IS-K.[51] Whereas Iranians and Russians regularly and publicly accused Saudis and Qataris of supporting IS, even a Pakistani ISI source confirmed that IS-K was receiving funds from Qatari and Saudi donors, and that trainers and advisers were accompanying the money flow.[52] Whether these allegations should be believed or not (and confirming them with external sources was impossible), the question remains of whether private entities could really donate money to IS-K without some tacit consensus by the authorities. The UAE government was, according to a source in the Finance Commission, aware that some money for IS-K came from local donors, but otherwise IS-K tried its best to hide its transactions from the eyes of the UAE government.[53] However, after the February 2017 crackdown on the structures of the IS-K Finance Commission in the UAE, several UAE donors were warned by the authorities to stop funding IS, or face serious consequences.[54]

IS-K has continued to do its own fundraising, in addition to any funds sent by IS-Central. Its donors were located in the UAE, Bahrain, Saudi Arabia, Kuwait, Oman and Qatar. Sometimes IS-Central assisted in this fundraising with some lobbying and advice. One senior IS-K source alleged that there was tolerance for IS-K activities in the Gulf: IS-K offices and those of the single component groups in Qatar and Saudi Arabia were known to the authorities of those countries. Only the IS-K office in the UAE remained unknown to the local authorities until its discovery in 2017. However, by 2017 Qatari donors had deserted IS-K, except for a few small ones.[55]

How the funds are transferred

Most of the foreign money—probably 70 per cent of it—is transferred to the Finance Commission through the hawala system, while the rest is mostly transferred through legal businesses.[56] Private donors in particular typically transfer money through the hawala system in small instalments of tens or hundreds of thousands of dollars, in order to avoid attracting unwarranted attention. In many locations, cash can be transferred to IS-K representatives, who then transfer it via hawala to the Finance Commission, eliminating any risk for the donors.[57] Government donors prefer to transfer money to IS-K through businesses, although they can also easily deliver cash direct to the Finance Commission.[58] Those who raise funds for IS-K maintain regular contact with their donors, visiting them sometimes as frequently as every few weeks. These regular visits are necessary in the case of the businesses, which contribute to the IS-K cause depending on how much profit they made that month.[59]

Why donors pay IS-K

One private donor to IS-K, an oil businessman from Qatar, recounted how he used to fund IS in Syria before 2015, when IS itself told him to redirect funding towards IS-K. He denied having been encouraged by anybody, including his own government, to support IS, except for the Saudi government. He stated having paid $6 million to IS in Syria and Iraq, and then $3 million to IS-K in 2015. He was planning to pay $6 million throughout 2016. His aid, however, was conditional to IS-K demonstrating growth in numbers and capabilities.[60] A smaller Pakistani donor also told how IS encouraged him to focus on IS-K, and not to send money to the original IS.[61] These were the only two private donors whom it was possible to contact, and they do not represent a sample wide enough for drawing broad conclusions, but they both hinted that IS-Central might have played a role in re-directing donors towards IS-K.

One stated reason for supporting IS-K is of course religious piety.[62] Another one of the main reasons for funds accruing to IS in general is the fact that donors see it as a bulwark against Iran and its allies, where IS promised to focus its activities.[63]

> Iran is interfering in Syria and Iraq, so we are also interfering in Iran and we want to create problems for Iran inside their own country. IS is collecting a lot of money and funds from other Arabian countries such as Dubai, Kuwait, Saudi Arabia and other countries for talking about fighting Iran and Shi'as.[64]

A member of IS-K Finance Commission describes the motivation of private donors as follows:

> First of all they are rich people and they think that we must give 1–2 per cent to Jihadist to secure their place in heaven. The second reason is this that they are against Shi'a. They are saying that Shi'as have relationship with Iran and IS is against Shi'a so they are supporting IS. These people who are from Saudi Arabia, Qatar, and Kuwait, they are encouraged by their governments to support IS, but in the UAE the private donors are acting without government support.[65]

The second most popular concern among the donors after Iran was Central Asia.[66] As one donor said,

> Our interest increased after Russia sent its military into Syria and they are fighting us there. This is the reason why we want to start our operations in Tajikistan, Uzbekistan, and Turkmenistan, to bring pressure to bear on Russia and force it to withdraw its forces from Syria and stop its intervention there. ... This is the reason that we are giving fund to IS Khorasan.[67]

According to some sources, several donors to IS-K had previously funded the Taliban and Al-Qaida and then either diversified their beneficiaries or completely dropped those two organizations in favour of IS.[68]

> Some of our donors stop their support for Taliban because they did not get as many achievements as it was expected from them. Now they are giving money to Daesh.[69]

To the extent that government donors were interested in supporting IS-K in Pakistan, they were said to view it as a tool to fight Shi'a groups there, not against the Pakistani government.[70]

> The donors do not have any interests in Pakistan, they are telling us that you can only do recruitment and you can buy weapons in Pakistan, but you can do operations in Afghanistan, in Iran and Central Asia. Especially they are telling us that now you can do operations in Afghanistan and later you can start operations in Iran and Central Asia.[71]

One of the donors indicated that another factor driving donors towards IS-K is the perception of IS as being better organized than other jihadist organizations:[72]

IS is more efficient compared to other groups in Afghanistan and Pakistan. The whole world knows how much IS is efficient. In a very short time it gained a lot. Before this no Jihadi groups made progress and succeeded as much and as quickly. It means IS is the only group in history, which achieved a lot. ... IS is very good in logistics, in finance, in leadership, in training, in supplying, they have very strong finance; it means they are having a lot of sources of money and funding. They also have a lot of advanced and heavy weapons but the other jihadi groups are not strong.[73]

This donor also saw IS as the only truly international jihadist organization, with a major presence in Syria, Iraq, Pakistan, Afghanistan and even to some extent in Iran.[74]

For another donor, IS's image of total commitment to its radical jihadist course, with no compromise with the ruling elite of any state (see the anti-Saudi rhetoric used by IS-Central) was a major selling point:

IS is different from other jihadi organizations. For example the other jihadi organization belong to some country but IS is independent. The Afghan Taliban belong to Pakistan and they did dealings with Americans and Iranians. The same TTP organization belongs to Afghanistan [a reference to allegations of Afghan government support for the TTP]. The same other groups belong to one country. But IS is independent. Their main target is doing Jihad.[75]

There is sensitivity among some donors about corruption in jihadist circles; one current donor to IS-K discussed how in 2010 he stopped funding the Afghan Taliban and the IMU because they 'were putting in their pockets or spending in other private interests'.[76] Another donor stopped funding the Taliban in 2008 after the TTP started going violent in Pakistan, but resumed support for jihadist groups when IS emerged in 2014.[77] Some donors started asking IS-K to report back about their expenses:[78]

They mention the price of every item they bought and the quantity of every item they bought with our money. They give report to us every month and show proof to us, if they do not do like this, then we will not help them next month. They are very transparent in these activities; they do not have any problems with this.[79]

As it can be noticed, if its donors' interests were indeed what the sources described, then IS-K has been unsuccessful or at least slow in delivering results. Many donors might realize that 2 years for starting one jihad (or, in fact, several of them) is not a long time span. But, as discussed in Chapter 7, there was already some nervousness among donors by mid-2016.

How much

As mentioned in the Introduction (*Methodology*), any precise figures about funding should be taken with a pinch of salt or two. According to IS-K sources, in 2015 private donors in the Arab Gulf contributed $66 million to the Finance Commission, while state agencies (also from the Gulf) were reported to have paid $63–115 million (see Table 11). In 2016, the picture changed considerably. State agencies reduced their commitments by at least 35 per cent, while private donors almost doubled theirs. If we accept the figures provided by IS-K sources, the declining support from the agencies of Qatar and Saudi Arabia was an inversion of a trend. According to this same source, this trend had seen, for example, Qatar support the recruitment and training of volunteers in 2013 with $15 million, which it then increased until 2015, when Qatari support reached $40 million.[80] The sources were not forthcoming on why this was the case, but it seems likely that government donors might have provided bridging funding while more private donors were being mobilized, if these allegations are true.

According to IS-K sources, in 2015 total revenue of the IS-K Finance Commission probably reached close to $300 million (see Table 11 and *Taxation*). This was a major increase on 2014.[81] The figure compares to about $1 billion that was accruing to the various Taliban 'finance commissions' around 2015. The Taliban's total paid manpower (fighters, support and administration) was around 200,000 at the same time, meaning that per capita IS-K's funding (at $57,200) was over ten times per capita the Taliban's (see Chapter 6 for IS-K membership figures).[82]

In reality, IS-K funding was meant to allow for rapid expansion of the organization, including by buying Taliban and TTP commanders, and during 2015 funds were not being spent on operations for the most part. As a source reported in early 2017, in 2016 revenue accruing to the IS-K Finance Commission increased further to around $350 million, at a time when revenue to IS-Central was in decline (see Chapter 7 for details).[83] This translates into per capita revenue of $17,500, or less than a third of what it was in 2015. This seems a much more accurate reflection of the actual cost of maintaining the IS-K structure. It is still over three times the Taliban's per capita funding, but it should be taken into account that the Taliban pay large numbers of local militiamen at very low rates ($100 per month), whereas IS-K does not. As discussed in this chapter, IS-K does indeed seem to have better (that is, more expensive) logistics than the Taliban, pay higher rates to full-time fighters and commanders and be able to afford advanced weaponry and various other luxuries, as described elsewhere in the book.[84]

After 2016, funding from most sources entered a declining trend, although with significant fluctuations. In 2017, there was a veritable collapse in funding, with a total budget of just $106 million, in part due to the declining finances of IS in general. After the 2017 decline, there was a rise in the first half of 2018, followed by another decline. The cash reserves accumulated in Syria had mostly been moved out, with little coming to Khorasan from there at this point, and fresh funding from the Arab Gulf was significantly reduced compared to its peak time (2015–16). There were also problems and delays in transferring funding to Wilayat Khorasan, as the financial support network was not the same as it used to be.[85]

In 2020, there was a pause in funding for the first few months of the year, while IS-Central assessed the situation after a string of defeats and the capture of Aslam Faruqi. By June 2020, the funding flow from IS-Central had been restored, but IS sources deemed the level of funding to be insufficient to go on the offensive and recapture territory. IS-Central promised IS-K $80 million, but in the end only transferred $42 million; another $18 million came from other sources. Not only that was the lowest point of IS-Central's support (see Table 11), but IS-K at that point was receiving little from other sources. A source in IS-K commented that as a result there was too little for IS-K to go on the counter-offensive and regain ground.[86]

In 2021, IS-Central allocated $100 million to IS-K, matching the previous highest level of 2015 (Table 11). Another $24 million was expected to accrue from other sources. At that time, IS-K expected further increases to the budget, because the Caliphate wanted it to expand its operations. According to a source, tax revenue was up 20 per cent from 2020.[87]

Table 11: External funding accruing to the IS-K Finance Commission by source, in $ million, according to internal sources[88]

	2015	2016	2017	2018	2019	2020	2021
Governments	63–115	40	–	–	–	–	–
Private donors in Arab Gulf	66	120	–	–	–	–	–
IS-Central	100	78	–	–	–	42	100
All other sources	–	–	–	–	–	18	24
TOTAL	300	350	106	–	–	60	124

How IS-K 'managed' the donors

Donor support to IS-K was mostly conditional on the organization achieving results.[89] For a period, IS-K was reporting wildly inflated assessments of its progress in Khorasan, in order to show its donors that it was meeting their expectations. For example, a Qatari donor was told that in mid-2016 IS-K controlled 28 per cent of Afghanistan and more than 60 districts; it also claimed to have been preventing the recruitment of volunteers for the Shi'a militias of Syria from Afghanistan.[90] IS-K propaganda videos refer a lot to the presence of Afghan Shi'a volunteers in Syria.[91] None of this bore any relationship with reality. IS-K sources also claimed to have killed more than 150 police in Kot in the summer of 2016 (a figure that appears much higher than the reality) and 500 Hazaras during the attack on the Enlightment demonstration in July 2016 (against an official death toll of 80).[92] A Pakistani donor believed what IS-K told him about 'large scale operations against foreign forces (Americans and British) and Afghan Government'; that was well before the first real offensive against Afghan government forces took place in the summer of 2016.[93]

As admitted by an IS-K source, by mid-2016 IS-K's donors were beginning to question its narrative of exceptional, ongoing success.

> The donors are telling to us that we must be more active. They are telling us that we must continue fighting and we are indeed increasing operations now. They are telling us that we must increase attacks. Rather than East Afghanistan, we are asked to give a lot of importance to Shi'a areas and Central Asia. They are telling us that we must do a lot of operations in the Northern Provinces of Afghanistan and from North Afghanistan we must enter Central Asia. So they bring pressure on us and they are telling us that we must increase the number of operations and capture many areas. The fighting which started in Nangarhar [in the summer of 2016] is because of the pressure of these donors.[94]

A common complaint from donors was that IS-K was busy most of the time fighting the Taliban, rather than the enemies they had committed themselves to fighting.[95] Some relatively small donors had already stopped funding to IS-K in 2016, including at least two from the UAE and three from Saudi Arabia. Other donors also threatened to stop their funding.[96]

The impact of disparate sources of external funding

In part, IS-K's difficulties derived from its disparate array of donors, with sometimes diverging interests. While the typical donor from the Arab Gulf would be horrified by the thought of destabilizing Pakistan, some private Pakistani donors were of a different opinion, and they pushed IS-K in a completely different direction. According to a source, the Saudi government promised the Pakistani one that IS-K would not cause trouble to the Pakistani government.[97] A private donor from Pakistan saw things differently:

> We also want their activation in Pakistan because Pakistan's government is also not good and it does not apply Islamic rules and regulation in their law and courts. We want such type of IS activation in Pakistan that is against Pakistan's Government not the common people. They must do operations against Pakistan's Government and they must also do operations against those people who are working against Islam. These kinds of people must be finished as soon as possible.[98]

IS-K was raising funds by speaking in different voices to each of them, a practice that in the long run led to much trouble. The same Pakistani donor stated:

> We do not support IS fighting against Iran and Shi'as, we are supporting IS to do Jihad against Americans and Westerners in Afghanistan. IS did not say that they want to fight against Shi'as and Iran. If IS wants to fight against Shi'as and Iran, then we do not want to support IS anymore in the future.[99]

Some of the IS-K component groups were said by internal sources to maintain privileged relations with Saudi Arabia and Qatar, although these relations seem to have been constantly in flux. For a period, TKK and the Muslim Dost Group were reportedly closer to Qatar, while Khilafat Afghan, TKP and Azizullah Haqqani were said to be closer to the Saudis. Then, the Qataris started supporting Khilafat Afghan and TKP (in particular Hafiz Saeed), while the Saudis turned to supporting the Muslim Dost Group. Khilafat Afghan, however, also had close relations with the Qataris, who according to sources paid it the largest amount of money.[100] It has been reported that Omar Ghazi Group and Shamali Khilafat do not have direct relations with any of the Gulf Countries.[101] As a result, more money was reaching certain component groups directly (see Chapter 4, 'The missed target of revenue centralization'). It is easy to understand how external funding bypassing the IS-K leadership and accruing directly to its component groups could only compound the problems highlighted above, deriving from the presence of disparate donors with varying interests and concerns.

By 2017–20, the main fault lines were no longer between the original component groups, but between the two large factions of Faruqi and Moawiya (see Chapters 8, 9 and 10). Moawiya remained more dependent on funding from the Arab Gulf compared to IS-K (Faruqi).[102] However, Saudi donors to IS-K (Faruqi) also remained important and reportedly pushed for an aggressive stance towards those Taliban linked to Iran, which included the Taliban's leader, Haibatullah. The Pakistani agencies, on the other hand, favoured a rapprochement between Taliban and IS-K, and would have liked to co-opt IS-K (Faruqi) among the groups they already sponsored and manipulated for their own ends.[103]

8

SHAKING UP THE WORLD OF KHORASAN'S JIHADISM, 2014–16

As already explained, IS-K entered an environment crowded with jihadist organizations of all descriptions. Some friction would have been inevitable even under the best circumstances, but Afghanistan and Pakistan jihadists have a tradition of hospitality towards foreign jihadists, which could have allowed the co-existence of IS-K and the others. However, from the beginning IS-K had been planning to offer co-existence only while it was trying to get established; even then, it was actively trying to attract members from the Taliban, TTP and other organizations. A clash was inevitable.

Although IS-K did not push Caliphate propaganda in Khorasan, probably in order to avoid immediate conflict while it was still weak, its allegiance to Caliph al-Baghdadi made co-existence with the Taliban, TTP and AQ difficult to sustain for the long term. It was always implicit that ultimately IS-K meant to absorb or expel them all.

In addition, in order to quickly establish a beachhead, IS-K focused initially on attracting commanders and members from all these other organizations, a fact which inevitably caused intense friction. As territory suitable for IS-K growth and development was already mostly occupied by its competitors, conflict over territory was also hard to avoid. IS-K could not accept becoming like other jihadist organizations hosted by the Taliban or the TTP, nomads without a stable home. It needed solid and stable safe havens where it could develop the comparatively sophisticated structure that is an IS trademark.

Finally, IS-K inevitably attracted members of the Taliban and the TTP who had issues with their comrades first and foremost; once separated organizationally (and sometimes even before that) these individuals and groups often started fighting against their rivals, those in the Taliban in particular, dragging the mother organizations with them into the fight.

Relations with the Afghan Taliban

Late 2014 through early 2015

By February 2015, one Iranian observer already had considerable foresight on what was about to happen in Afghanistan:

> The Taleban who separated their path from Daesh a long time ago, are incompatible with this group. They are preparing to confront Daesh should they emerge in the regions under Taleban influence. It is not unlikely that should such a thing happen and Daesh actually reach Afghanistan, we may witness battles similar to what happened among the terrorists themselves in Syria. ... However, the main concern of the Taleban is the reduction in their forces and the possibility of some of their commanders joining the newly emerged Daesh.[1]

In 'The volunteers start returning to "Khorasan"' above (Chapter 1), the early engagements of soon-to-become IS-K with the Afghan Taliban were described in detail. During the second and third quarters of 2014, IS messengers tried to convince the Taliban to accept them as jihadist guests, much in the same way as other jihadist organizations were doing. They even started paying a disguised 'tribute' to the Taliban, with a few tens of millions of dollars being paid to the Shuras of Miran Shah and Peshawar. The difference between IS and other organizations like AQ was that, because of its own claim to have established the Caliphate, IS-K could never swear allegiance to Mullah Omar, who at that time the Taliban still claimed was alive. Hence, the Quetta Shura in particular was hostile to entertaining formal relations with IS.

The leaders of the Quetta Shura might or might not have been aware that Al-Zarqawi had been influenced by a long stream of criticism of the Taliban, dating back to the 1990s with Abu Abdallah al-Muhajir, which he then transferred to IS.[2] However, as late as September 2014, their commentary on IS-Central's performance in the Levant was positive and supportive.[3] The 'tribute' IS offered was probably always meant to be a temporary measure, and it was paid before Wilayat Khorasan and IS-K were even formed. It was clear that a change was in the making when in the December 2014 issue of its *Dabiq* magazine authors Ash-Shamali and Ash-Shami accused Mullah Omar of 'nationalism', of insufficient implementation of pure monotheistic practices and of favouring good relations with India and Shi'a Iran.[4]

This type of accusation became standard fare in the way IS-K described the Taliban. For example, in *Dabiq* governor Hafiz Saeed would describe the Taliban as 'nationalists' who 'rule by tribal customs and judge affairs in accordance with the desires and traditions of the people, traditions opposing the Islamic Shari'ah', echoing previous accusations by Abu Jarir Ash-Shamali printed in the pages of *Dabiq*.[5] By January 2015, as IS-K started taking shape and challenging the Taliban more explicitly, all it could hope for was some kind of cool neighbourhood relationship, and certainly no longer a formal position within the Taliban-managed space of 'licensed jihad' in Afghanistan.[6]

According to Borhan Osman, the contacts between Taliban and IS rotated around the Taliban's desire to get IS-K to acknowledge their leadership in the Afghan jihad and IS-K's desire to see the Taliban disband and merge into IS-K itself.[7] However, as discussed above in the early months of Taliban–IS-K relations, this long-term desire of IS-K's was not openly stated. Quite the contrary, while the early approaches were going on, IS-K adopted a soft attitude towards the Taliban and TTP, as evidenced by their Code of Conduct (Annex 1). A senior member of TKP described relations with the Taliban and TTP in very positive terms in late 2014:

> We have a good relationship with the Afghan Taliban. ... Not only Afghan Taliban but also Pakistani Taliban allow Pakistan Daesh group to operate in their areas. There is no restriction or prevention for our group.[8]

Another TKP member stated that

> Whenever we want to do operations in Afghanistan, Haqqani network and Peshawar Shura are supporting us a lot. We are really happy with Peshawar Shura and Haqqani network. ... But we do not have relationship with Quetta Shura and we are not operating in their areas and provinces.[9]

The confrontation starts

Given the direct challenge to its legitimacy (which ultimately derived from Mullah Omar's supreme leadership), it was unsurprising that the Quetta Shura was the one to open up hostilities in public. In April 2015, the spokesperson of the Taliban's Qatar Office, Mohammad Naim, asked for IS-K not to interfere in Taliban internal affairs, possibly referring to IS-K's recruitment of active Taliban members. The Rahbari Shura, under Mullah Omar's stamp, issued a fatwa declaring any oath of allegiance to al-Baghdadi as being against

Shari'a, and therefore forbidden. This was probably in retaliation to al-Baghdadi describing Omar as 'uneducated' and unfit for leadership.[10]

IS-K did not give up its efforts to recruit Taliban. In April 2015, an Iranian source reported that twelve members of the Taliban had already been executed for having defected to IS-K.[11] By May, the Taliban were already circulating statements that called IS-K 'alien to the tradition and the desires of the Afghan people'. By June, an open letter from the Rahbari Shura already seemed to imply that 'non-interference' now meant for IS to stay out of Afghanistan altogether, and the Taliban threatened retaliation for the first time. The Taliban's *ulema* authorized the Taliban to 'defend' themselves against IS-K, legitimizing the use of violence against another jihadist movement.[12] Al-Baghdadi responded that IS-K was not going to restrict its activities to Afghanistan and wanted instead to use Afghanistan as a springboard for jihad in Central Asia.[13] Almost immediately, IS-Central propagandists started openly inviting all jihadists to transfer their pledge of allegiance from Mullah Omar to al-Baghdadi.[14] By August, the Taliban had started openly criticizing IS-K atrocities, such as the execution of pro-Taliban elders with explosives.[15] Once Mullah Omar was officially announced to be dead, it was even easier for IS-Central propaganda to hit out at his successor Akhtar Mohammad Mansur, who was in the middle of a succession crisis.[16]

While these 'diplomatic' negotiations were unfolding, fighting was already going on in some areas. According to an IS-K source, the first violent incident with the Taliban occurred in Bala Baluk district of Farah on 4 November 2014, even before IS-K was formed. A Khilafat Afghan commander called Qari Bilal was killed with six of his men. In Farah, by February 2015 there were already reports of 400–600 IS-K fighters distributed around the province, which was confirmed by the local authorities. IS-K fighters started to flow into Farah in December, initially settling in the mountains between Khak-e Safid and Shindand, in Golestan and Bakwa. The Taliban promptly mobilized the mullahs to preach against them, reportedly convincing a significant percentage to return to the Taliban. Then the Taliban attacked the training camp, capturing or killing many IS-K men.[17] Losses amounted to forty-three killed and forty captured, according to IS-K itself.[18]

Early clashes took place in Logar as well. There reports of an IS-K presence had already surfaced in January 2015, when the local authorities claimed to have spotted IS-K units in all districts of the province, mostly Taliban who had defected. Clashes with the Taliban were immediately reported, resulting in IS-K forces being expelled from Baraki Barak.[19] IS-K groups reportedly burned some houses and destroyed a shrine.[20] There were also attacks on the Shi'a population of Khoshi in April–June 2015, but even in this case the Taliban retaliated and pushed the group out, with Logar governor Sa'ad Emarati barely managing to get away.[21]

The most violent clashes were in Kajaki. Apart from Khadim being killed in a US drone strike, the Kajaki fighting also saw Mullah Basir (governor), Mullah Abdul Khaliq Zabed (IS-K district chief of Kajaki) and Mullah Bashir Akhund (military head for Kajaki) captured and executed by the Taliban.[22] IS-K went underground in Kajaki and for some time did not even replace the governor or district chief.[23]

> When our leader Mullah Abdul Rauf Khadim was alive, we had many permanent bases in Kajaki district. The bases were in different villages but when our senior commander was martyred by American airstrike, we became a bit weak and when we fought with Taliban in order to take the control of Kajaki dam, Taliban ambushed our convoy, it was very hard fighting, unfortunately Taliban asked for help from other provinces and brought lots of fighters from other province and districts to win the fight. They killed lots of our people including many of our commanders and high-ranking officials of Daesh Khurasan. Then we were told to stay quiet for a while till we reorganize our team. Now we are reorganizing our team and will come out soon.[24]

The prompt intervention of the Taliban in Helmand might have been due to several factors, one of which no doubt was the high priority that Helmand had at that time (2015) in the Taliban's battle plan. Another important reason were the rumours that for much of 2014 the most prominent Alizai Talib, Abdul Qayum Zakir, had been negotiating with IS over his potential defection to the group. Zakir had been sacked from the Military Commission in April 2014 and had been a rival of the Quetta Shura's de facto leader Akhtar Mohammad Mansur since 2010.[25] Eventually, the negotiations failed and Zakir turned into an enemy of IS-K. The fear might have been that Zakir and Khadim would link up and drag thousands of Alizai fighters with them into IS-K.[26]

It is clear that the Quetta Shura started perceiving IS-K as a competitor very early on, due to the proclamation of the Caliphate that implicitly delegitimized the role of the Taliban *Amir al Muminin* (the Taliban's supreme leader or 'head of the believers') even before al-Baghdadi openly declared him to be illegitimate. Once friction started, it rapidly escalated as each side tried to show it was more determined and wanted to have the last word.

The importance of the incompatibility between Caliph and Amir al Muminin is highlighted by the fact that the Peshawar and the Miran Shah

Shuras, not particularly bothered about the discussions about the supremacy of the Quetta Shura, were initially much friendlier to the emerging IS branch in Afghanistan and Pakistan, as discussed above. Serajuddin Haqqani's close relations with IS soon suffered a blow, as IS was found to be trying to attract a number of his senior commanders.[27] Still, Serajuddin's posture remained a restrained one vis-à-vis IS-K. Throughout his stay at the Quetta Shura as a deputy (August 2015–present), Serajuddin Haqqani threatened military operations against IS-K several times, but never ordered one.[28] In fact, for a long time Serajuddin allowed Azizullah Haqqani to continue wearing the triple hat of IS-K component group leader, member of the Miran Shah Shura and chief of the Miran Shah Shura's Fedayin Commission; Serajuddin also maintained close relations with IS-K's Chinese Muslims (a mix of Huis and Uyghurs organized in the Gansu Hui Group) and the Central Asian allies of IS-K. His decisions appear to have been dictated by his donors, some of whom he shared with the IS-K.[29]

The Peshawar Shura also turned against IS-K when it realized that its commanders and cadres were being head-hunted. Typically, IS-K would offer fast-track promotions to Taliban commanders; for example, a team commander could become commander of a large detachment of over a hundred men.[30] Even after relations between Peshawar Shura and IS-K started deteriorating markedly, several cadres of the Peshawar Shura were reportedly negotiating with IS-K over joining it. According to a senior IS-K source, these included at least three district-level military leaders, as well as several commanders.[31]

The relationship of the Peshawar Shura with the IMU and the Omar Ghazi Group was similarly damaged, to the point where Peshawar actually asked the Omar Ghazi Group to leave Afghanistan.[32]

In Nangarhar province in the first half of 2015, friction between Peshawar Shura and IS-K was particularly high, driven by local conflict between the Taliban and former colleagues now with IS-K, and between the Taliban and a former TTP commander who had switched to IS-K. In the summer it escalated into full-scale war. Clashes between IS-K and Taliban had already started in May, reportedly after the Taliban's warning in December 2014 to Pakistani TTP groups not yet affiliated to TKP that they were not needed in Nangarhar. After the confiscation by the Taliban of a weapons shipment to these TTP groups, negotiations between the two organizations went on from March to May 2015, but the TTP groups settled in Nangarhar refused to leave. Instead, they linked up with the emerging TKP.[33]

It's very strange, we never thought that Daesh would suddenly operate in our district because we haven't seen any sign of Daesh in our district before. There were Taliban operating in our district, there were Afghan Taliban and Pakistani Taliban. One day we have received news that Pakistani Taliban in Shinwar districts decided to join to Daesh and operate in our districts under the name of Khilafat-i Islami. It happened like that, after some days we were witnesses that those Pakistani Taliban who were active in our district under control of Taliban changed their flag from white to black, changed their uniform and announced their support from Daesh leading by Abu Bakr Al-Baghdadi.[34]

A partially different account, based on local tribal sources, sees groups of TTP fighters who took refuge in Nangarhar (in Achin, Nazian, Kot, Deh Bala, Rodat and Ghanikhel districts) becoming increasingly unruly and ready to mess around with local tribal rivalries, eventually forcing the Taliban to intervene to restrain them. The TTP fighters then joined IS-K so they could enlist its support in their local conflict with the Taliban.[35] Reportedly, the final straw was an attempt by the Taliban to crack down on a spate of kidnappings carried out by TTP groups, to which they reacted violently.[36] IS-K sources lay the blame on some local Taliban cadres, namely provincial military leader Mir Ahmad Agha and district governor of Bati Kot Mullah Kuchi, whom they accused of having tried to stop IS-K activities in the area. The fighting spread to several districts, not only in the eastern part of the province but in the western part as well.[37]

If they show opposition to us, we will show our reaction. On the other hand, if they do not show any opposition to us like Taliban leaders in northern provinces, we will not fight against them but even we will help them and we will do joint operations. We always requested Taliban not to show opposition to us.[38]

In the early stages of the Taliban–IS-K confrontation, the latter managed to kill two Taliban district chiefs. The Taliban withdrew from Nazian, Kot and Mohmand Dara, but IS-K pursued them into Bati Kot, Chaparhar, Deh Bala, Khogyani, Sherzad, Pachir Wa Agam, Rodat and Ghanikhel.[39] In June 2015, IS-K even managed to assassinate the Nangarhar military leader of the Peshawar Shura, Hashemi, in Peshawar.

Apart from the invading TKP force, IS-K co-opted at least twenty-seven small groups of Taliban in Nangarhar before and during its first main offensive, which started in June 2015.[40] By the end of June, IS-K was already reported to be present in seven or eight districts of Nangarhar.[41] Initially, IS-K was welcome in some quarters, even in Mohmand Valley, as they appeared to be intent on fighting the Taliban only and not Afghan government forces, and they even allowed members of army and police to visit their villages without hindrance. IS-K did not demand villagers feed them, contrary to the Taliban's practice, but it imposed a ban on poppy cultivation and drug sales (see Chapter 7 for a discussion of the ban on drugs).[42]

A Taliban counter-offensive in July initially pushed IS-K forces out of Pachir wa Agham, Khogyani and Deh Bala, in alliance with several tribal elders who mobilized their *lashkars* alongside the Taliban. In other areas, and particularly in Achin and Mohmand Valley, however, the IS-K fought back almost immediately and pushed the Taliban out. The subsequent crackdown on the tribal elders who had supported the Taliban was merciless, and it inaugurated IS-K's campaign of terror in Nangarhar.[43]

Support for IS-K in some Shinwari tribal segments at least seems confirmed by the Taliban's retaliation against villagers, which included the burning of houses and forcing alleged sympathizers of the enemy to flee their homes.[44] According to a former IS-K member, it was particularly the Shinwari of Pekha Valley who supported IS-K because of their rivalry with the neighbouring Mohmands of Mohmand Valley.[45]

At the peak of its expansion in Nangarhar, IS-K controlled or had a strong presence in eleven districts (Mohmand Dara, Dorbaba, Nazeyan, Bati Kot, Achen, Deh Bala, Rodad, Pachir Agam, Khogyani, Shirzad and Hesarak, corresponding to about 40 per cent of the province). Different hostile sources estimated that, of these, only 15–30 per cent were Afghans, with 60–80 per cent Pakistanis and 5–10 per cent other foreigners.[46] In each of the districts held by IS-K, its forces had several bases in key villages (four to ten of them), from where their patrols would cover the rest of the district.[47] In Kot, IS-K forces were able to patrol 50–60 per cent of Kot from ten village bases.[48] The Taliban were perceived as very weak and doomed at this point.[49] Plans by local strongman Haji Zahir Qadir to mobilize a local militia against IS-K were not taken seriously, although they indeed materialized later.[50]

Both Taliban and Afghan security forces were afraid of fighting IS-K forces. In June 2015, Taliban forces panicked in front of an IS-K onslaught and retreated, taking refuge in Pakistan and in some cases even surrendering to the government.[51]

Following a fatwa from the Taliban's *Ulema* authorizing full jihad against IS-K, in January 2016 the Taliban counter-attacked.[52] Militias linked to local strongmen, reportedly incensed by IS-K's ban on the drug trade, also contributed to increased pressure on IS-K. In the following months, IS-K pulled out of the main settled areas of Nangarhar towards the mountainous border areas and towards Kunar. From an estimated 1,400–2,000 fighters in autumn, numbers declined to less than 1,000 in early spring.[53]

As relations deteriorated, IS-K started describing the Taliban as 'servants of the ISI' and criticizing what they viewed as their soft attitude towards the Afghan government, in particular the Taliban's refusal to declare Afghan officials 'apostates',[54] their rejection of global jihad, their tolerance of tribal codes like Pashtunwali despite their clashing with Shari'a and 'polytheism' (the cult of the saints).[55] Another source of friction was the claim by IS that there cannot be 'two Caliphs'.[56] Osman noted in 2020 that young, urbanite IS-K members and sympathizers:

> accuse the Taliban movement of implementing a corrupted version of Islam that blends religious law and Afghan culture. Some ISKP members and supporters consider this to be a result of the unscholarliness of the Taliban's leaders while others regard it as a manifestation of the movement's inherent religious laxity. ... The Taliban was the target of heavy criticism, not least for focusing on consolidating power in the 1990s rather than on instituting and enforcing sharia; whereas the Taliban implemented sharia only 'casually,' the Islamic State followed a 'systematic implementation of sharia.' Some saw the Taliban under Mullah Omar as more sincere in its goal of establishing an Islamic system than subsequent Taliban leaders, but argued that his understanding of Islam was equally flawed. Al-Qaeda, although considered purer ideologically than the Taliban, was criticized for following the Taliban in not actively trying to establish its own caliphate and for being satisfied with 'random' attacks. Interviewees barely mentioned the Taliban's and al-Qaeda's refusal to pledge allegiance to the Islamic State as a key reason for their 'perversion.'[57]

Some component groups like Shamali Khilafat had better relations with the Taliban, with whom they did not fight. A source pointed out that the group had no plan to initiate a fight with the Taliban, although they would defend themselves if necessary.[58] Despite these differences in local approaches, by early 2016 IS-K had moved from statements issued by some of its senior figures to an orchestrated social media campaign to discredit the Taliban in jihadist circles all over the world, in particular stressing how the Taliban desired to reconcile with Kabul.[59] Their accusation of the Taliban having become a stooge of the Pakistani authorities rapidly became routine.[60] By spring 2016, the rhetoric about the Taliban sounded quite different from what it had sounded like in the early days:

> They are our enemies. We do not do any difference between Americans and Taliban. Both of them are the same to us. Still we are in fighting with Taliban in Kot District, in Bati Kot District and in Achin District and we inflict a lot of

causalities on them. As much we dislike Taliban, we do not dislike Afghan Government and Americans because Taliban are the sons of ISI. Taliban are not fighting for Islam, they are fighting for Pakistan and money. They stained the name of Jihad.[61]

The Taliban had evidently become IS-K's top enemy:

We do not want to fight against Taliban but if Taliban do not change their policy, then our first target is Taliban and our second target will be Afghan Government and foreign forces. If they change their policies, we want to have good relationship with them.[62]

Even Mullah Omar was not spared:

[The former Taliban who joined us] think very bad about Mullah Omar. Because he was Pakistan's and ISI's man and he did not fight for Islam, so many Taliban join IS. Those Taliban who joined IS now they regret having joined Taliban before.[63]

At this point, IS-K was even banning its members from entertaining personal relations with members of the Taliban.[64] The Taliban in turn were telling villagers to stay away from IS-K. They condemned Salafism as alien to Islam, describing it as an Israeli plot to give Islam a bad name.[65]

Aside from the Nangarhar conflict, which had local origins, most armed clashes between Taliban and IS-K involved groups of Taliban linked to Iran, such as Naeem Mahaz and Zakir Mahaz, which were trying to prevent IS-K from entering Helmand and Zabul.[66] For all of 2015 and the first few months of 2016, the Iranian Revolutionary Guards relied on the men of Abdul Qayum Zakir and Mullah Naeem to carry out operations against IS-K, primarily in Herat, Farah and Helmand. IS-K sources allege that Abdul Qayum Zakir's forces handed over forty IS-K prisoners to the Iranians.[67] A senior IS-K source admitted that operations against IS-K in Zabul and Helmand in 2015 caused significant loss of life in IS-K ranks, with tens killed.[68] Even in Nangarhar, during 2016 the conflict was largely with specific groups of Taliban like Sabir Kuchi Mahaz and Tora Bora Mahaz, which were particularly active against IS-K.[69]

Sometimes local causes of conflict merged with Iranian intervention to generate violence. In Kajaki, for example, the decisive Taliban offensive that uprooted IS-K, at least temporarily, from the district was in part the result of competition over controlling the electricity generated by the Kajaki Dam, as well as pressure from Iran to crack down on IS-K activities.[70] Map 9 provides a list of clashes between Taliban and IS-K for the period November 2014 through July 2015.

IS-K policies towards the Taliban

IS-K approached the Taliban in 2014–15 with a proposal for reciprocal non-belligerence with the Taliban:

> Taliban must not interfere in our activities and we will not interfere in Taliban activities. Abu Bakr Al-Baghdadi is sending one representative and he will visit Rahbari Shura and Peshawar Shura to talk with them and invite them not to create any problems for our people anymore.[71]

This seemed to imply some kind of territorial partition of Afghanistan, but in reality IS-K already envisaged replacing the Taliban altogether in the longer run: 'An agreement will be for the short time. We do not want the presence of Taliban forever. We want to finish them, because they have relationship with ISI and Iran'.[72] IS-K just wanted to buy itself time in order to establish itself firmly first:

> I know many Taliban commanders want to join Daesh because they have lots of problem with Taliban, problem of logistics, problem of leadership ... Most of the Taliban are now confused about who supports Taliban and what the aim of the Taliban in Afghanistan are. Due to Daesh being a new group and having started operations only in some provinces, now the Taliban don't take the risk to join Daesh, because they think that maybe Daesh will not be able to challenge the position of Taliban in Afghanistan, but I am sure that in a very short time, when we show our activities in different provinces too, then most of the Taliban commanders will join us. As soon as the Taliban commanders are assured that Daesh is something serious then they will join us.[73]

The Taliban of course objected to any idea of territorial partition of what they considered 'their' territory and were rightly suspicious of IS-K's longer-term intent, even if IS-K emissaries were of course not advertising their objective of replacing the Taliban altogether. As a result, IS-K appears to have been drawn itself into a large-scale conflict with the Taliban sooner than originally anticipated. Inevitably, the Taliban retaliated. In the words of a local elder,

> Now in Achin district and other Shinwar district, Taliban only target the Daesh, they don't think of the government a lot, they are planning for Daesh.[74]

Negotiations and agreements

When clashes started, IS-K's position was that a ceasefire with the Taliban was only possible if they accepted in principle the idea of IS-K being entitled to operate in Afghanistan alongside them.[75] Then, from its initial attempt to be accepted as good neighbours, once friction ignited with the Taliban the IS-K leadership went rapidly to an all-out clash, miscalculating its chances of winning. A province-level Taliban cadre admitted that there was pressure from Saudi Arabia and Qatar—particularly on Akhtar and the Rahbari Shura as a whole—not to fight IS-K. Mansur complied during November 2015 through February 2016, as we have seen, but then turned against IS-K after his relations with Saudi Arabia deteriorated, leading him to edge closer to Iran as a source of financial support.[76]

The Qatari authorities were also reportedly trying to mediate between the Taliban and IS-K, and they tried to organize a meeting in Doha between them during the early phases of the confrontation.[77] Although these top-level efforts were ultimately unsuccessful, even within the ranks of the Quetta Shura some figures continued to maintain relations with IS-K, according to a senior IS-K source.[78] While the source might have had some interest in being deliberately misleading, in January 2016 Taliban leader Haibatullah sacked sixteen shadow provincial governors and other Taliban officials, accusing them, among other charges, of having relations with members of IS-K.[79] The same source, in fact, listed several Taliban cadres of the Quetta Shura as negotiating with IS-K over joining it. These included three provincial governors, a deputy governor and several lower-rank cadres and commanders.[80]

The Revolutionary Guards (Iran) identified Akhtar Mansur, the controversial 'supreme leader' of the Taliban (July 2015–June 2016), and more in general the Leadership (Rahbari) Council of the Quetta Shura as being in co-operation with IS-K in late 2015 through early 2016, despite their original commitment to fight IS-K.

> At the beginning Akhtar Mansur wanted to deceive us and he was taking support from us and he was only saying that he was against Daesh. When we understood, we stopped support for them. Akhtar Mohammad Mansur and Rehbari Shura are always helping Daesh. Our relationship has not been good with Akhtar Mohammad Mansur and Rehbari Shura for the last eight months.[81]

This Iranian assessment was probably the result of the few months of Quetta Shura–IS-K co-operation between November 2015 and February 2016 (the interview was carried out in January 2016). First they co-operated against Mansur Dadullah, head of a front allied with the Taliban breakaway faction of Mullah Rasool, known as High Council of the Islamic Emirate. They also co-operated against Akhtar Mansur's arch-rival Abdul Qayum Zakir, at that time based in Iran. An IS-K cadre in Farah confirmed that IS-K–Quetta Shura co-operation was aimed against the Iran-based Taliban of Abdul Qayum Zakir and Mullah Naeem.[82] A source indicated that IS-K forces even fought alongside the Taliban of Akhtar Mansur, at least in Marjah and Nawzad.[83] Although by March 2016 Akhtar Mansur took a 180-degree turn and ordered his men again to crack down on IS-K, there remained a strong lobby in the Quetta Shura, even among close allies of Akhtar Mansur, advocating accommodation with IS-K; a prominent member of this lobby was Helmand governor Abdul Manan.[84]

This erratic attitude towards IS-K did not just characterize the Quetta Shura's behaviour. When Qari Baryal was still head of the Peshawar Shura Military Commission, he ordered the crackdown on IS-K, which eventually led to the Nangarhar war.[85] After he set off to form his own Shura of the North in early 2016, despite his close relations with Iran and reportedly even Russia at that point, Qari Baryal maintained good terms with IS-K, perhaps remembering his costly mistake from earlier.[86] A source within IS-K indicated that Qari Baryal in fact had signed a non-aggression agreement with Shamali Khilafat on 11 July 2015.[87] A second agreement with Abu Yasir Al-Afghani on behalf of all of IS-K followed on 13 January 2016.[88]

For much of 2015, IS-K forces (Shamali Khilafat, Omar Ghazi Group) in northern Afghanistan even supported Taliban operations in Badakhshan, Takhar and Kunduz, until Faruq Safi, a member of the IS-K leadership, banned IS-K forces from carrying out joint operations with Taliban under any circumstance.[89] According to an internal source, this co-operation with the Taliban of Qari Baryal had not been authorized by the IS-K leadership, but was a personal decision on the part of the leader of Shamali Khilafat, Abdul Shakoor Baghlani, following his being approached by Qari Baryal. Baghlani's decision was, however, reportedly endorsed by the 'advisers' who accompanied his forces in the north.[90] Another IS-K source inside TKP, however, seemed to recognize the ceasefire when asked about it in January 2017; he predicted it would not last because of Iranian and Russian pressure on Qari Baryal to move against IS-K in the north.[91]

Throughout the north, until the last quarter of 2016 only a few commanders linked to Iran were actively pursuing and fighting IS-K groups; in Sar-i Pul, for example, only two commanders of Abdul Qayum Zakir were active.[92] Shaikh Mawlavi Abdul Rehmani, shadow governor of Jowzjan, seen by the IS-K as a bitter rival, was another protagonist of many clashes.[93] Towards the end of 2016, as Taliban leader Haibatullah was growing closer to Iran and Russia, his closest ally in the north-east, Mullah Salam (shadow governor of Kunduz), started attacking IS-K forces in Kunduz. Baryal, still committed to a ceasefire with IS-K, sacked him from the position of Military Leader of Kunduz for the Shura of the North.[94]

In January, as Salam was discussing further operations against IS-K with envoys from Haibatullah, a suicide bomber struck, killing the envoys and severely injuring Mullah Salam, who died of his injuries a month later. The attack caused a significant worsening in the relations between Baryal and Haibatullah: Haibatullah wanted to intensify operations against IS-K, while Baryal—who attributed the attack to the TKP faction of IS-K—exempted the north-eastern IS-K component groups of Omar Ghazi and Shamali Khilafat from culpability and refused to retaliate against them. Regardless of whether Baryal genuinely believed that TKP, the most hardline component group within IS-K, was trying to undermine the ceasefire between Shura of the North and local IS-K component groups, he certainly wanted to preserve the ceasefire for as long as possible.[95]

In Kunar, one of the provinces under the Peshawar Shura, IS-K and Taliban managed to keep up good relations for a long period. From mid-2016, relations worsened following an offensive ordered by the Peshawar Shura against the TTP, to which IS-K objected. The Taliban groups most active against IS-K in Nangarhar from January onwards started deploying to Kunar at the end of that year. This pushed relations between Taliban and IS-K in Kunar towards open war, which broke out in December 2016. The Taliban suffered significant territorial losses as well as the defection of several commanders to IS-K. A ceasefire was re-established in early 2017.[96]

Similarly, for a period IS-K entertained friendly relations with Atiqullah Mahaz, a front affiliated with the Peshawar Shura. Many of its members joined IS-K. Even its leader Atiqullah for a period negotiated for a senior appointment with IS-K, before being denied it and breaking relations with the organization.[97]

Regardless of the status of relations between IS-K and Taliban shuras, IS-K seems to have been constantly negotiating with potential sympathizers among the ranks of the Taliban. The IS-K amir (leader) of a north-eastern district, for example, claimed to be negotiating with several district-level governors and military leaders of both Quetta Shura and Shura of the North.[98] Despite maintaining relations with Serajuddin Haqqani, Azizullah Haqqani continued negotiating with at least four relatively senior Haqqani commanders.[99] A source close to Azizullah Haqqani indicated that these senior Serajuddin Haqqani commanders received funds from IS-K during 2015, in the range of $2–3 million each. While these seem hefty payments, it should be considered that IS-K had an important presence in North Waziristan at that time, and it needed to lobby Haqqani network members for their tolerance if not support.

Azizullah Haqqani was probably also hoping that his clients within the Haqqanis would eventually join him in IS-K.[100]

After Al-Afghani took over, IS-K's tendency was to revert to the original approach of keeping a low profile and avoid insofar as possible conflict with the Taliban. In practice, IS-K had to adopt a policy of local ceasefires, as it was too late to keep up the charade as long-term good neighbours of the Taliban. By the summer of 2016, this new approach was fully fledged:

> We told to all the Taliban whether Peshawar Shura, Quetta Shura, Miran Shah Shura or others that we do not have any opposition with you and you must not do operations against us.[101]

The Taliban's reactions varied. On 19 July 2016, IS-K and the Taliban agreed to a ceasefire in Nangarhar and to re-orient their energies towards fighting the Afghan government instead of each other. Omar Khorasani for IS-K and Mullah Shireen for the Taliban's Quetta Shura signed the deal. The initiative appears to have come from IS-K, which accepted that it was not worth getting stuck in a permanent fight against superior enemy forces in Nangarhar against the advice of its donors, who were not particularly interested in funding a war against the Taliban.[102] Clashes with the Taliban continued, however, in other parts of the country, particularly Zabul in

Map 9: Known Taliban-IS-K Clashes November 2014–July 2015[103]

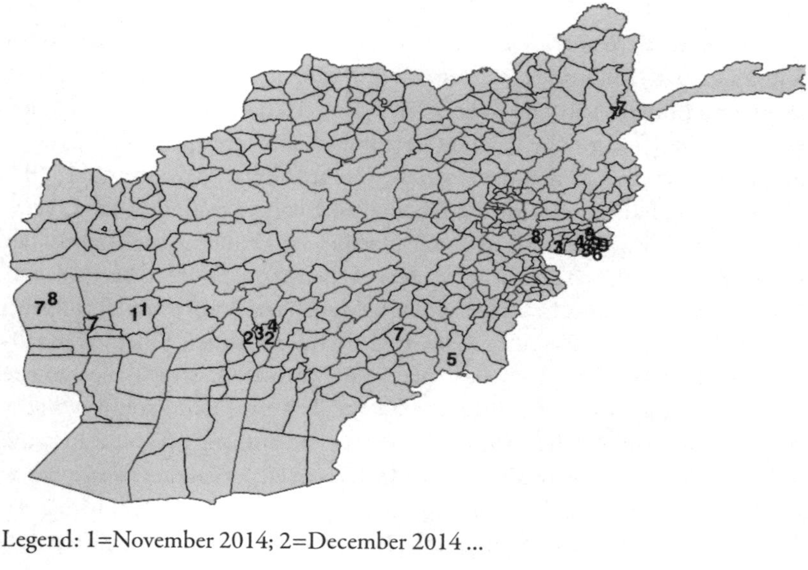

Legend: 1=November 2014; 2=December 2014 ...

August–November 2016, Zazai (Paktia) in October 2016 and Kunar in December 2016.

Relations with Mullah Rasool's Shura and Obeidullah Ishaqzai's faction in the Quetta Shura

For a period in late 2015, IS-K appeared to be tempted by an alliance with the group opposing Akhtar Mohammad Mansur within the Quetta Shura, in particular Dadullah Front leader Mansur Dadullah and the son of Mullah Omar, Mullah Yakub.[104] Mansur Dadullah indeed came very close to joining IS-K, and for a short period in Zabul in late summer/early autumn 2015 he actively co-operated with it, causing press reports that he joined wholeheartedly.[105] However, the selection of Mullah Rasool to the top of this group of dissidents, which called itself the 'High Council of Afghanistan of the Islamic Emirate', marked the establishment of a relationship with Iran as well as the transfer of funds from Iran. Rasool was chosen by the leaders of the Taliban opposition because Iran, the only available source of funding left available, trusted him, as they had been entertaining relations with him since 2012. This development also marked the end of all relations with IS-K, whose legitimacy was rejected entirely. Mansur Dadullah aligned himself with Rasool, while Yakub dropped out and temporarily withdrew from active life. The Rasool Shura, as it was mostly known, described IS-K as '*fitna*' (sedition) in July 2016.[106]

In autumn 2016 there was a relative rapprochement between the Rasool Shura and IS-K, following the detention of Rasool in Pakistan and his replacement with Mullah Arif, who did not have good relations with Iran. Arif allied with the IMU and reached a good neighbourhood agreement with IS-K in order to resist their common enemy, the Quetta Shura.[107] By early 2017, the Rasool Shura had allied with the Obeidullah Ishaqzai faction of the Quetta Shura, which was opposed to the leadership of Haibatullah. Obeidullah shared the view of Arif and other leaders of the Rasool Shura, that it was not in the Taliban's interest (nor in that of Obeidullah's or Arif's donors) to spend energy fighting with IS-K. On that basis, the Rasool Shura–Obeidullah alliance quickly negotiated a co-existence policy with IS-K, which allowed the group to re-establish a significant presence in western and south-western Afghanistan in areas where these two groups had a strong presence. In some cases, the Taliban of Obeidullah and IS-K even negotiated agreements for sharing narcotics revenue, for example in Sangin and Musa Qala (Helmand). In Farah, according to internal sources, IS-K's presence skyrocketed from 300 at the end of 2015 to over 900 in March. In Helmand, IS-K's presence almost doubled from 450 in January 2016 to 850 in March 2017.[108]

Relations with the TTP

The official statement of the TTP at the announcement of the establishment of the Caliphate is telling:

> Oh our brothers, we are proud of you in your victories. We are with you in your happiness and your sorrow. In these troubled days, we call for your patience and stability, especially now that all your enemies are united against you. Please put all your rivalries behind you ... All Muslims in the world have great expectations of you ... We are with you, we will provide you with Mujahideen [fighters] and with every possible support.[109]

Initially, Fazlullah reportedly stated to his TTP colleagues who aspired to join IS that 'it is your choice whether you want to stay here with us or join with Daesh'.[110] In reality, tension appears to have existed even in the early days, if in the summer of 2014 the TTP leadership expelled Khalid Khurasani, the chief of the Mohmand Agency branch, for having advocated joining IS. Reportedly, his expulsion was the result of pressure from AQ.[111] Several senior TTP commanders' defection to IS-K in 2014–15 was the final straw, eventually leading to serious deterioration in the relations between IS-K and TTP. Talks between Fazlullah and IS-K ended abruptly, even if there were never serious clashes between the two organizations.[112]

By 2015, IS-K's assessment of TTP had turned much more negative:

> The Pakistani Taliban had sincere people in their midst fighting to raise the word of Allah and apply its pure Shari'a. After the proclamation of the Caliphate, many sincere members of the movement joined it and made allegiance to the Caliph. In this way, only the corrupt remained in the Pakistani Taliban and they and the Afghan Taliban resembled each other more and more. The only difference is that the Afghan Taliban is fighting the wilayah according to the direct instructions of the Pakistani intelligence services. We also see divisions emerging within the Pakistani Taliban: at present, the faction that follows Fazlullah has pledged allegiance to Akhtar Mansur, that is to say, actually, to the Pakistani intelligence services.[113]

By June 2016, relations between IS-K and TTP had taken a new turn, as a result of worsening relations between TTP and Quetta Shura. On 18 June, Fazlullah and Al-Afghani signed an agreement of non-belligerence, which according to IS-K sources was a result of Taliban operations against both IS-K and TTP in Afghanistan.[114] Overall, the relationship remained hostile, even though large-scale clashes were averted. The agreement worked better in Afghanistan, even if skirmishes still occurred in Nangarhar. In Pakistan, the implementation was patchier, as TTP was burning the houses of those joining IS-K, and frequent skirmishes between the two organizations occurred in Bajaur, Mohmand Agency and Orakzai Agency. Only some local commanders among the Mehsud and in North Waziristan maintained relations with IS-K.[115]

The rivalry between TTP and TKP might also reflect tribal rivalries. TTP continued to attract commanders from the Yousafzai, Wazir, Afridi and Mohmand tribes, while TKP drew mainly from the Mehsud and Orakzai tribes, although at a later stage many Afridis joined.[116]

Relations with Al-Qaida

AQ was almost as troubled by the proclamation of the Caliphate as the Taliban, given its declaration of allegiance to the Amir al Muminin. Like the Taliban, however, AQ was fully aware of the potentially delegitimizing impact of being seen as fighting another jihadist organization, in the eyes of its donors first and foremost. In the early days of IS in Khorasan, AQ tried to maintain good relations with them.[117] As of late 2014, IS-K sources were describing even their relations with AQ as friendly, outlining the differences between AQ and IS as follows:[118]

> This is the difference between Al Qaida and us, that Al Qaida is only targeting Americans and British and they are controlled by Yaman Al Zawahiri. We are targeting Americans, NATO and Afghan Government, and also those groups which are against Sunni.[119]

Reportedly, the leader of AQ in Afghanistan and Pakistan, Faruq al Qahtani, co-operated with IS for a period, training (together with about fifteen other AQ cadres) Afghan and Pakistani volunteers to be sent to IS-Central in Syria.[120] Al Qahtani then dropped his co-operation with IS-K, but some of his men joined IS-K altogether.[121] An AQ source admitted that, of AQ's members in Afghanistan, about eighty in total joined IS-K over the years, mostly in 2014.[122]

IS-K's relationship with Al-Qaida worsened markedly during 2015.[123] However, in Kunar in the summer of 2016, IS-K and AQ reached a ceasefire and non-interference agreement between themselves, as well as with TTP. The agreement banned IS-K and AQ from recruiting each other's people, but not from entering each other's areas.[124] An AQ source indicated that TTP played a role in the ceasefire, putting strong pressure on AQ to negotiate, despite AQ being disinclined to do so. The ceasefire was controversial within AQ because of the fear that IS-K would exploit it to consolidate its presence in Kunar before challenging AQ again.[125]

Indeed, in early 2017 the ceasefire collapsed, as new IS Special Representative Abu Hamza decided to abolish it and demand AQ either ally with IS-K or flee Kunar. The killing of al Qahtani—who had close personal relations with IS-K and IS-K Central, which probably facilitated the two groups reaching an understanding—in a US drone strike in November 2016 might have precipitated the worsening in relations. IS-K sources indicated that AQ started relocating its forces in Kunar as a result of Hamza's ultimatum, allowing IS-K to take over several valleys in Ghazi Abad, Pech, Chapa Dara, Sirkanay, Marawara and Nari. One AQ cadre confirmed the losses.[126] An AQ source contacted in January 2018 reported that IS-K had started moving against AQ even in some areas of Badakhshan, such as Zebak and Keran wa Munjan.[127] Only in the later months of 2018, after IS-K started losing steam (see Chapter 9), did negotiations with AQ and TTP resume.[128]

For AQ, the emergence of IS in general was a major challenge. It tried to address it by strengthening its allegiance to Mullah Omar, the Leader of the Faithful (as he started calling himself in 1996). Until al-Baghdadi proclaimed himself Caliph, AQ's leader Al-Zawahiri, like Bin Laden before him, had not paid much attention to Mullah Omar's fatwas. Al-Zawahiri had stated clearly in 2008 that Mullah Omar was just the leader of the Afghan Taliban:

> Zawahiri, for instance, had argued the opposite case. In 2008, asked the same question posed to Bin Laden above, Zawahiri responded: 'Mullah Muhammad 'Umar—may God protect him—is the emir of the Islamic Emirate of Afghanistan and whoever joins it, Shaykh Osama Bin Laden—may God protect him—being one of his soldiers. As for the commander of the faithful across the world, this is the leader of the caliphal state that we, along with every faithful Muslim, are striving to restore, God willing.' Here Zawahiri denied that all Muslims must give *bay'a* to Mullah 'Umar, the caliph-inwaiting having not yet emerged.[129]

Only in July 2014, Al-Zawahiri started portraying Mullah Omar as a kind of proto-Caliph.[130]

> Al-Qaeda's media wing released an old video of Bin Laden explaining his decision to give his oath of allegiance to Mullah Omar as commander of the faithful. A questioner asked Bin Laden if his oath implied that he considered Mullah Omar to possess 'supreme leadership,' the prerogative of the caliphs, which Bin Laden affirmed. Later that same month, al-Qaeda released a newsletter that began with a renewal of the oath of allegiance to the 'Commander of the Faithful Mullah

Muhammad Omar' and 'affirm[ed] that al-Qaeda and its branches in all locales are soldiers in his army, acting under his victorious banner.'[131]

In subsequent occasions, AQ continued to portray Mullah Omar as leader of the 'call of jihad' and the Taliban as the 'the hope of the [Muslim] community for the revival of the caliphate'.[132] The revelation in July 2015 that Mullah Omar had in fact died 2 years earlier and that Akhtar Mansur had deliberately kept his death secret was therefore widely perceived as a terrible blow for AQ.[133] The situation was only made worse by the fact that Akhtar Mansur, who managed to get himself elected as successor to Mullah Omar, had an agenda of reconciliation with the Kabul government, which of course did not suit AQ. Al-Zawahiri had no option but to recognize Mansur as leader without too much fanfare. Relations with the Quetta Shura started worsening again, and soon, according to an internal source, AQ was cutting all funding to Mansur and re-orienting it towards hardline Taliban in Quetta and elsewhere.[134]

9

THE DEAD END OF SALAFISM
AND IS-K ADAPTATION

IS-K's resilience to the American 'decapitation' strategy, which by 2017 had killed at least twenty members of its founding circle according to one count, and sixty 'tier 1 and tier 2' leaders in Afghanistan alone according to another, has been noted.[1] It is possible that IS-K faced bigger challenges from its own internal divisions. Despite some noticeable improvements in IS-K's capacity compared to the pre-existing jihadist organizations of 'Khorasan', the organization was dealing with an extremely fragmented social and political environment which encompassed nine different states. Some of these states were in turn characterized by considerable internal social and political segmentation, Afghanistan more than any other. Inevitably, such fragmentation and segmentation would be reflected somehow inside IS-K. In addition, IS-K was perceived in Khorasan as a carrier of a new political and organizational model, at odds with local political cultures. This too was bound to create some backlash. Within a few months of its launch, IS-K entered a crisis that lasted at least 16 months, despite attempts (originating in Mosul) to resolve it.

Leadership rifts

From its early days, IS-K was ridden by multiple rivalries among its leaders. The first rift to emerge was between Muslim Dost and the leadership of TKK. In January 2015, Muslim Dost had been 'parked' in the leadership shura, with the plan being to absorb his men into TKK.[2] Then Muslim Dost quit to join Khadim in Khilafat Afghan. A second rift then occurred between Muslim Dost and Abdul Rauf Khadim (see also Chapter 1, 'Khilafat Afghan and Muslim Dost Group'). A senior IS-K source so explained the reasons of the rift:

> Mullah Abdul Rahim Muslim Dost was not listening to Abdul Rauf Khadim and he was doing things independently, so this was the reason that Mullah Abdul Rahim Muslim Dost was taken out from his position, so Mullah Abdul Rahim Muslim Dost made his own group.[3]

According to the same source, interference from Iraq played a role in the splitting of Khilafat Afghan, with the head of the Military Shura of Iraq Abu Suleiman inviting Muslim Dost, whose men were mostly veterans of Syria, to set up a separate group which Suleiman offered to support.[4] This rift resulted in the end of the alliance, as Muslim Dost set up his own group. It seems clear that rifts were being resolved through the multiplication of component groups inside IS-K. Although a source within one of the latest component groups to be recognized by IS insisted that al-Baghdadi had no objection towards the creation of new groups,[5] the enemies of IS saw the the organization's persistent division into multiple component groups as an opportunity.

> This is a problem for them. We are also trying to make different groups and oppositions between them. Now there are oppositions between Afghan Daesh and Pakistani Daesh. ... We want the Taliban of Atiqullah's *mahaz* to enter Daesh to create problems and divisions inside Daesh. The people of Atiqullah's *mahaz* who were entering Daesh, we told to them to do such things. We do this to increase oppositions in Daesh. The fighting which is in Taliban and Daesh in Nangarhar Province, it is because of Taliban of Atiqullah's *mahaz*.[6]

Whether or not the Iranian officer's claims were founded or not, al-Baghdadi surely realized the dangers of IS-K's internal divisions, given his personal experience and that of IS-Central. However, for all his own centralizing tendencies, he had to accept the multifaceted character of IS-K as an inevitable evil for the short term. His attempts to push the founding groups into a full merger by April 2015 failed miserably despite repeated efforts, as discussed in Chapter 4. The rift between the Afghans and the Pakistanis in IS-K was catalyzed by the 'cruel activities' of two former TTP commanders in Mohmand Valley, Obeidullah Peshawari and Mawlavi Khalid Mansur.[7]

Local sources all agree that IS-K had committed major abuses in Nangarhar and particularly Achin and Kot, looting, burning or seizing houses; kidnapping villagers for ransom; forcing local families to marry off widows and unmarried girls; and carrying out gruesome executions. At least 17,000 villagers were displaced.[8] IS-K also punished allegedly hostile elements (those who fled its domination) by allowing Daesh supporters and sympathizers to cultivate their land.[9]

One episode mentioned in the press concerned the execution of a woman for working in a private university.[10] Kidnapping of women to be exchanged for IS prisoners was also reported.[11] Some sources external to IS-K did not see much difference between Afghan and Pakistani IS-K fighters in Nangarhar.[12] However, one former member of IS-K indicated that Muslim Dost's groups in Chaparhar had a good relationship with elders during his stint in the organization, contrary to what was going on in the neighbouring districts under TKP and TKK control.[13]

Whatever the case, external sources confirmed the seriousness of the rift between Muslim Dost, Faruq Safi and Omar Khorasani on one side and Hafiz Saeed on the other.[14] Muslim Dost and Safi demanded the replacement of Hafiz Saeed, but TKP refused and even threatened to split off if their leader was indeed replaced. Muslim Dost and Safi also demanded the withdrawal to Pakistan of TKP forces within a month.[15] Muslim Dost had already been at odds with Hafiz Saeed, whose governorship he coveted and while also resenting Saeed's attempts to marginalize Muslim Dost. At the peak of this rift, rumours started circulating in Helmand that Muslim Dost had rejoined the Taliban.[16] Even some low-level IS-K sources stated that he had rejoined the Taliban.[17] Muslim Dost even went public with his opposition to Hafiz Saeed and accused IS-K of being just another stooge of the Pakistanis.[18] TKP's violent behaviour might have been a useful opportunity for him to press for Hafiz's replacement. A senior TKP commander commented:

> The replacement of Hafez Saeed is not acceptable for us. If he is changed, then it is for sure that we will be divided by two groups and two provinces. But this is not possible.[19]

TKP and Afghan commanders close to it rejected Muslim Dost's accusations and refused to admit to having killed any innocent civilians. Rather, they insisted that all the gruesome executions it had carried out were the actions of spies and Taliban.[20] TKP sources described the rift in these terms:

> TKP people did not do any violence against the villagers in Nangarhar Province. TKP is doing violence against those people who are against Khorasan province whether they are in Afghanistan or in Pakistan. On the other hand, if someone is not against us, then we do not say anything to him or her. The people that we killed in Nangarhar province, they were against Wilayat Khorasan. This action is both beneficial for us and also beneficial for Muslim Dost. Muslim Dost showed

opposition to this. He said why you killed these people. Saeed Hafiz said that if anyone is against us we will kill them. Nothing else, only this is the problem.[21]

We have very good behaviour with the villagers, we know how to behave with villagers, don't need for anybody's advice, with innocent villagers we don't have any problem but of course when we capture a spy among the villagers or arrest someone accused of having link with Taliban, government or other enemies then we will give him a very strong punishment, that would be beheading him, hang him or shoot him. From the time we have started our activities in Nangarhar province, I don't remember that we killed any innocent villagers.[22]

At one point, Muslim Dost made an attempt to claim the governorship for himself, and, according to his supporters, in October 2015 his appointment was supported by at least some of the other component groups. It was opposed by TKP, of course.[23]

Now Wilayat Khorasan belongs to Muslim Dost, not Hafiz Saeed. The head of Wilayat Khorasan will be Muslim Dost. Muslim Dost does not have good relationship with Hafiz Sayed. Therefore, Hafiz Sayed must do operations in Pakistan not in Afghanistan, he committed cruelty on Afghan people, like he killed a two-month-old child, damaged schools, killed elders and innocent people. Not only Muslim Dost but all the groups in Khorasan accept Muslim Dost as a head. TKP is not part of Khorasan anymore. Therefore, Farooq Safi and our head Muslim Dost are talking with Baghdadi and he will take out Hafiz Sayed and Tehrik Khilafat Pakistan from IS-K.[24]

According to a source, Muslim Dost actually expelled some TKP commanders from Nangarhar, forcing them to return to Pakistan with their families.[25] Omar Khorasani of TKK ordered that TKP should not carry out operations in Afghanistan without being accompanied by Afghan IS-K units, but TKP did not comply.[26] Muslim Dost's and Omar Khorasani's criticism of Hafiz Saeed and his men undoubtedly had a wide influence among IS-K Afghans of various tendencies, including senior ones such as Faruq Safi. However, by no means did all Afghan IS-K commanders agree or dare to criticize Hafiz Saeed.[27] As the number of Afghans in IS-K kept rising, TKP's involvement in Afghanistan became less necessary, leading to demands that TKP should focus solely on Pakistan.[28]

For several months between the end of 2015 and spring 2016, the majority of the Afghan IS-K leaders refused to recognize Hafiz Saeed as the governor of Khorasan.[29] This rift paralyzed IS-K to a large degree. According to one source, the rift between the Pakistanis and the Afghans was one of the reasons why IS-K reduced its operations in Nangarhar and pulled out most of its forces in the first 5 months of 2016.[30]

The killing of Hafiz Saeed Khan in August 2016 ended the leadership rift, but it might have started new ones.[31] Hasibullah Logari was appointed temporary governor of Khorasan. As the name suggests, he was an Afghan from Logar (Azra district), who studied in Pakistani madrasas. He had spent 14 months in Syria with IS, before returning to Pakistan. He was considered personally close to al-Baghdadi's Special Envoy to Khorasan, Al-Afghani, as well as to Muslim Dost, Omar Khorasani and Sa'ad Emarati (who was killed shortly after Logari's appointment in a drone strike in Nangarhar), among the most important Afghan IS-K figures.

Logari was a member of TKK. A long-term replacement was supposed to be chosen later, but at last (if temporarily) the Afghans in IS-K seemed to have gained the upper hand, controlling the governorship too. Indeed, several senior Pakistani figures in IS-K objected to Logari's selection. According to an IS-K commander, among them were spokesman Shahidullah Shahid, Omar Mansur (chief of IS-K in the Lal Masjid area), Obeidullah Peshawari (head of IS-K in Peshawar) and Hassan Swati (head in Swat), objecting to Logari's appointment on the ground that IS-K recruitment in Pakistan continues to run faster than in Afghanistan. Some other senior Pakistanis in IS-K kept silent, however, including Hafiz Dawlat Khan (head in Kurram), Khalid Mansur (head in Hangu) and Abu Bakr (head in Bajaur). The situation was temporarily pacified by making clear that the appointment was a temporary one, but the wound would inevitably be re-opened at some point.[32]

Indeed, the killing of Logari in May 2017 in a US Special Forces raid started the biggest row over leadership within the ranks of IS-K. Probably as a result of the ongoing extermination of the IS-K leadership by US strikes, on 22 May the Military Shura of IS-K chose Aslam Faruqi, a former LeT commander, as the new governor of Khorasan.

A Pashtun Afridi born in 1977 in Bara, Faruqi joined LeT in 2004 and operated in Afghanistan in 2007–14, before deploying to Syria in 2014. There he joined IS, before returning to Pakistan in 2016. An IS-K source indicated that his choice as governor was due to his contacts with the Pakistani ISI, which suggested to IS-K the possibility of a tradeoff: the appointment of a leader linked to the ISI and the subsequent cessation of attacks against Pakistani government targets, in exchange for access to safe havens in Pakistan. The rapprochement with the ISI was in line with the lobbying that the Haqqani network was carrying out thanks to its links with the Azizullah Haqqani group. Faruqi had reportedly been close to both Abu Yasir Al-Afghani and Logari. He received the support of his own group,

TKP, as well as three Afghan component groups: TKK, Azizullah Haqqani's and Muslim Dost's.[33]

However, Faruqi's main selling point, his closeness to the ISI, was also the source of strong opposition to his appointment within the ranks of IS-K. The Central Asians of the Omar Ghazi Group, the Chinese Muslims of the Gansu Hui Group and the Afghans of Shamali Khilafat all rejected Faruqi, with the encouragement of the external allies of the IMU and other Central Asian and Chinese Muslim groups. An Uzbek commander recently returned from Syria, Moawiya, was chosen as the leader of the IS-K opposition to Faruqi. Moawiya was reportedly sent from Syria to act as Logari's deputy and was close to Gul Morad.

The tension between the two groups was running very high in June 2017, and at least one armed clash between them was reported in Nangarhar (Chparhar and Achin). Moawiya started pulling out all his men from eastern and southern Afghanistan, concentrating them along the Central Asian border. The leadership of IS-Central tried to mediate between the two factions, sending two representatives to Khorasan for this purpose.[34] Negotiations were suspended in the late summer, as Moawiya had ruled out recognizing Faruqi as governor under any circumstance, and Faruqi and his supports would not surrender his governorship. Apart from the Central Asians, Moawiya had the support of some Afghan Tajik and Uzbek commanders of IS-K and a few others. Overall, about two-thirds of IS-K's strength was under Faruqi, and one-third under Moawiya. The central leadership of IS-K kept neutral throughout the dispute and did not formally recognize Faruqi.[35] Mawlawi Zia ul-Haq, also known as Abu Omar al-Khorasani, was officially acting governor as far as IS-Central was concerned.[36]

Hardliners like Moawiya and his supporters believed that Faruqi could go so far as to become completely independent from the central leadership. They cited Faruqi's warming relations with the Pakistani authorities (despised by Moawiya and other Central Asian jihadists) as one piece of evidence. They also cited Faruqi's ceasefire with the Quetta Shura in October 2017 (see below in Chapter 9) as another piece of evidence of an unacceptable drift, although that ceasefire collapsed quickly.[37]

Moawiya and his supporters positioned themselves as a purer IS group. In reality, sources within the group (and confirmed by Taliban sources) acknowledged that they too had ceasefires with various Taliban groups linked to Iran and Russia in the north-east, so they were not exempt from making pragmatic choices.[38] Still, Moawiya and his men might not have been wrong in being suspicious of Faruqi's relationship with Pakistan (see 'The Place of Pakistan' in Chapter 2).

The alienation of the villagers

From the point of view of the local communities affected by IS-K's emergence, it was like a bolt out of the blue.

> It was around eight or seven months before that Daesh suddenly appeared in Achin district and started their activities. Daesh did not appear like Taliban, which started from ten fighters and slowly grew up, Daesh suddenly appeared in our district with hundreds of fighters. The commanders and fighters of currently Daesh in Achin were with TTP and they were fighting against the Pakistan government, I don't know that why suddenly they changed side and turned to Daesh.[39]

Although this sudden appearance in strength did not require it to seek local support, from the beginning IS-K's instructions to its units were to behave nicely to the villagers, and it made an effort to implement these orders. In particular, fighters were asked by the leadership not to take food from villagers, and to rely instead on what IS-K logistics provided for them.[40] Only occasionally would IS-K teams, arriving in a village late at night and unable to buy food, ask villagers who could afford it to bring food for them to the mosque.[41] The state schools were initially left open.[42] Even IS-K's practice of not taking food from villagers did not apply to Nangarhar, or at least not always and not everywhere.[43] Of particular interest was the case of TTP fighters, whose abusive behaviour towards locals in Nangarhar changed overnight once they joined IS-K (before turning abusive again):

> When these people were operating under the name of TTP, at that time they were very aggressive and didn't have a good behaviour with the villagers. Because most of them were Pakistani people and they didn't care about Afghan villagers. When they turned to Daesh and met with the villagers and elders, at that time they were very kind with the villagers and told the villagers that they joined Khilafat-i Islami and their aim or mission is only to fight against the Pakistani government and Americans. They told us that they don't have any problem with the Afghan government staff and the villagers. But after around one month after they joined Khilafat-i Islami their attitude changed and became very aggressive against the villagers and Afghan government staff.[44]

For a period, IS-K also behaved nicely with shopkeepers:

> Around nine months ago I was in De Baba Bazaar that saw a group of ten people with black masks and black dress, I understood that they might be

Daesh. They stopped at a shop and were shopping there. After they left the bazaar, I went to the shopkeeper and asked about the group, the shopkeeper told me that he asked them to introduce themselves, they told him that they belonged to Daesh. The shopkeeper told me that after they bought their stuff, they left 500 Afs as gift.[45]

In their areas of control, IS-K would regularly patrol the villages—and particularly the bazaar, which they visited two to three times a week—also to collect tax.[46] There appears to have been little communication between the villagers and the small IS-K teams patrolling. Even in Kajaki, according to local elders, IS-K teams did not speak to villagers much, and if they did it was to deliver their propaganda against Taliban, Americans and ISI, or to remind them of the rules of behaviour. They would also stop vehicles on the road to deliver the same message, that they were there to bring real Shari'a.[47] They would play messages on the loudspeaker, saying that they belonged to the Islamic State and that their leader was al-Baghdadi. The villagers were not particularly interested, but not upset either by this propaganda.[48]

All was well when IS-K were offering villagers better conditions than the Taliban, despite the heavy presence of foreign fighters in its ranks in some areas. However, at the same time IS-K groups were told to fully implement Shari'a as understood by the Salafis: this meant implementing bans on the drug trade, on television, on music, on smoking; compulsory praying in the mosque five times a day; marrying girls as they reach puberty; plus the usual punishments for theft and murder. Transgressions were swiftly and very seriously punished. Moreover, the initial 'honeymoon' period in which schools and clinics were left open soon ended and they were shut down. There were also reports of IS-K destroying shrines.[49]

Even in Helmand, where Khadim had a good understanding with local elders, his forces implemented the ban on music, watching TV, smoking and visiting shrines.[50]

> In this regard they were very aggressive, more aggressive than Taliban. If the Taliban caught villagers listening music they would only beat that villager and release him, but when the Daesh caught a villager listening to music, they beat and also jailed them for one month and twenty days.[51]

There was in fact a commander in Kajaki, Hafiz Nurullah, whose task was to implement IS-K's rules for behaviour.[52] IS-K spies in the villages were also instructed to report on fellow villagers who broke IS-K's rules.

> A few days ago one of the Daesh commanders by the name of Mullah Mansoor called a villager and told him that they have reports that he is watching TV. He threatened him and told him that very soon they would come to see him.[53]

The ban on the drug trade was effectively and ruthlessly implemented, despite the loss of revenue it resulted in for IS-K.[54] A senior IS-K source linked the ban on the poppies to the arrival of Al-Afghani and direct instructions that he carried from al-Baghdadi.[55] Transgressors were fined 50,000 Afs and were also jailed.

IS-Central and IS-K alike appeared to have considered that bringing 'real Islam' to Afghan villagers would have been a welcome initiative. Indeed, these strictures did not prevent some Shinwari sub-tribes and clans from supporting IS-K, but they rescinded their initial support after the atrocities that IS-K organized from July onwards, according to external observers.[56] However, clearly much of the population objected strongly to IS-K's strict rules.[57] Here are several examples:

> People are not happy with Daesh because of their Salafi ideas. People are saying that Daesh came to Afghanistan to change the religion of Afghan people. Daesh came to Afghanistan to spread the Salafi ideas among the Muslim people and most of the villagers think that Daesh is a project of Israel. I told you that villagers are happy to accept Taliban with all their bad behaviours because Taliban at least follow Shari'a and Holy Quran way but not Daesh with all their good behaviour.[58]

> People hate Daesh a lot because Daesh prevented people from indulging in their traditions, like praying at shrines.[59]

> Daesh has some laws, which are against the Islam and against the villagers' traditions. Daesh don't let the people to go to shrines to pray, don't let the people give charity (food, clothes and money) for the poor people, if someone is to give *Zakat* or charity, they should give them to Daesh not to the poor villagers.[60]

> People didn't like the Daesh, people think that Daesh is not Muslim and we think Daesh is belonging to Wahabi religion.[61]

> Taliban are very aggressive as always but Daesh group has very friendly behaviour. Taliban are following the Shari'a, which is acceptable by Muslim people but unfortunately Daesh group is following Salafi ideas which are against Islam and not acceptable to Muslim people.[62]

The villagers perceived the Taliban's imposition of Shari'a as much more tolerable than IS-K's version of it. Gradually the initial welcome started wearing out as IS-K men used extreme coercion every time somebody violated one of the rules it was imposing. In one village of Helmand, a villager was jailed for 15 days because they found a cigarette in his pocket.[63]

> People or villagers were happy from the behaviour of Daesh, when I saw them in the first time in our bazaar, while they were talking with shopkeepers, they were

looking very friendly with the shopkeepers and also heard from other villagers who are living in Loy Naicha and Naicha areas that Daesh were friendly .... But when I saw Daesh fighters arresting a villager, they were very aggressive people. ... Totally Daesh as I saw them and heard from other villagers they were better in their behaviour than Taliban. But I have to also mention that they were forcing people to follow some acts, which were against Islam and against our traditional rules.[64]

Things got even worse after IS-K began being regularly targeted in air strikes.

When there is any air strike on their fighters and their fighters are killed because of the air strike, then they become more aggressive with villagers, they think that these villagers reported to the Americans or Afghan government about their bases. Then they come to the villages and arrest some villagers. Daesh is not like human to learn a little bit humanity from other people, they are like brutal animals that only know attacking and killing.[65]

For example, after the killing of Khadim, IS-K's behaviour became more aggressive, with frequent jailings (up to fifty arrests in Kajaki alone) and extortion of money from local wealthy families.[66] Elders also suggested that IS-K was too reliant on the information provided by its spies, who might have been providing inaccurate information that damaged local rivals.[67] Gradually IS-K patrols became more and more aggressive:

I witnessed Daesh people beating up a motorbike rider who for some reason couldn't give way for Daesh vehicle to overtake him in the street; the Daesh fighters got out and beat the person very badly.[68]

Compared to Helmand, IS-K left a far worse impression among the elders of Nangarhar, who viewed it as a bunch of lumpen Pakistanis with no honour or respect.[69] The strong presence of Afghan Salafis in the area also might have strengthened IS-K's tendency to adopt a heavy-handed approach towards the population. As a former member of IS-K pointed out, the Salafis had always been a source of trouble within the Taliban as well, constantly violating the Taliban's rules of engagement and supporting hardline positions within the organization.[70] IS-K members dismiss the importance of the distinction between Afghans and Pakistanis, as 'we are all Pashtuns',[71] but elders saw things differently:

When they are talking with the villagers, they are shouting at villagers, not talking, and never ask for advice from the elders as the Taliban are doing.[72]

It would seem that IS-K's leaders felt that 'hearts and minds' policies were only needed for the very early stages of deployment to new areas of operations, or that after fighting started its commanders on the ground rapidly lost their nerve. After the initial honeymoon period, IS-K relied increasingly on terror tactics, and they were certainly effective in a way:

> They became very aggressive and really scared the villagers when they bombed a few of our villagers and villagers from other districts, then published their video. After that video Daesh in Shinwar districts became very famous and really the villagers were scared of them and also villagers and elders understood that this group is very aggressive and they came here only for killing Muslims.[73]

One elder in Kajaki commented that

> I think that Daesh is a group for fighting and this group is not made in Afghanistan to seize control of government in the future, but Taliban is fighting to establish an Islamic government one day. We can at least say that Taliban can be a political group but not Daesh.[74]

By the time the executions started, there was little space left for a soft approach. In one small cluster of villages in Nangarhar, at least six executions occurred in the 8 months between May 2015 and January 2016.[75]

Similar patterns of IS-K initially being welcomed by villagers, which then changed once it started implementing its strict policies, were found to apply to Kunar province as well.[76]

Enter Abu Yasir Al-Afghani

The growing trouble IS-K found itself in during the summer of 2015 forced IS-Central to send a new Special Envoy with full powers to make the necessary changes and sort the situation out. Al-Baghdadi chose Abu Yasir Al-Afghani (see Chapter 4 for a biography).

IS-K sources insist that Al-Afghani resolved the conflict between Muslim Dost and Wahidi, although the two leaders still kept their groups separated.[77] In late 2015, Muslim Dost and Hafiz Saeed each sent a representative to Mosul to meet al-Baghdadi to resolve their differences, but even that did not work, in part because al-Baghdadi was busy elsewhere and could not meet them. Another meeting was called for February 2016.[78] After these efforts by IS-Central to deal with the crisis failed, Abu Yasir Al-Afghani was tasked to deal with the issue along with two other envoys from ISIS, Abu Mustafa Anbari and Abu Azeem Al Khorasani. He would end up spending a substantial amount of time and energy trying to fix the problem.[79] Reportedly, the Afghans and Pakistanis eventually had to mend fences after Al-Afghani and IS-K's donors threatened to cut their funding.[80] Al-Baghdadi was reportedly very angry with them.[81] A source opposed to IS-K also confirmed that an agreement was reached.[82]

The TKP commanders continued occupying Mohmand Valley, on condition that they would only occupy or destroy properties belonging to the enemies of IS-K (Taliban and Afghan government people):

> We told them 'you must not capture the houses of civilians, you must seize the houses of Taliban and police or those local people who stand against IS'. They also agreed with us. Two or three days ago we burned the houses of local people who stood against us. They were not common people; they were people who were against us. In these activities there were no Pakistanis with us, we all were Afghans. Now there are not any kinds of problems, all the problems are finished.[83]

In reality, despite assertions that Abu Yasir Al-Afghani had resolved the issue, atrocities continued, albeit on a smaller scale, and were still going on in the summer of 2016.[84]

> Still Daesh is killing people but before they were killing everyone without any evidence but now they are not killing everyone. Before they were also saying different things, like that those women whose husbands died, they should get another husband, those girls who are single, they must marry, people should place flag on their roof to signal there is a girl or a woman whose husband died. Daesh said, if these kinds of women and girls are not getting husbands, then we will get them married, but nowadays these things have changed, from Daesh side but the pressure decreases a little.[85]

The stories about IS-K forcing unmarried women to marry IS-K fighters without dowry did not turn into reality, but it did force women off the farming fields to stay segregated at home.[86]

The persistence of Hafiz Saeed and TKP in indulging in abusive behaviour in the face of criticism from within IS-K and even from Al-Afghani is in part explained by the fact that Hafiz Saeed controlled IS-K's logistics in Nangarhar and had the whole TKP to back him up, compared to an Afghan IS-K presence which was much more dispersed. It was not a negotiation between parties of equal standing.[87] Hafiz Saeed's Afghan critics were left congratulating themselves for having contained TKP behaviour:

> The people of Hafiz Saeed did a lot of cruel and brutal activities against common people in Nangarhar province. If Muslim Dost did not show criticism about Hafiz Saeed, maybe Hafiz Saeed's people increase these cruel and brutal activities against the common people of Afghanistan in Nangarhar Province.[88]

At one point, Bakhtiar, one of IS-K's main figures in Nangarhar, was even detained by the TKP for a few months over his criticism of their behaviour.

The detention caused another major upset, and one of his combat groups (thirty men in total) even surrendered to the NDS in protest in October 2015.[89] After Bakhtiar's release by Al-Afghani, he returned to his job of Chief of Intelligence for Nangarhar.[90]

Special Envoy Al-Afghani also imposed a new line of mending fences with the Taliban and other jihadist groups; he was most successful in northern Afghanistan and perhaps with the TTP to some extent (see Chapter 8). In most other places, he could only achieve temporary truces, as the Taliban had by then been made aware that IS-K's ultimate aim was to replace them.[91]

Al-Afghani was also credited with replacing several cadres in the military and financial fields, and with increasing discipline. He interviewed many commanders and, based on his findings, replaced a number of them.[92] In Kunar, for example, 40 per cent were replaced.[93]

Al-Afghani was less successful with the task of looking into the issue of unified leadership and particularly of finding a suitable appointee for leader of the TKK. As explained in Chapter 2, IS-K was structured from the beginning as a diarchy, with the governor of Wilayat Khorasan and the head of the TKK being placed at the same level in terms of authority. However, consensus on the name of the TKK head could never be found. Al-Afghani toured the different areas of activity of IS-K for consultation, but he could not resolve this issue.[94] When he was posted to Khorasan in November 2015, he was also nominated as acting head of the TKK; he immediately proceeded to overhaul the leadership structure of the TKK and appoint new people.[95] Significantly, however, as of November 2016 al-Baghdadi had not yet chosen the leader of the TKK, despite repeated promises from April 2015 onwards that he would address the issue 'very soon'. The names of several candidates had been circulating for some time: Farooq Safi, Hafiz Saeed Khan, Abu Yasir Al-Afghani and Qari Wahidullah Alizai.[96] As discussed above, Muslim Dost put himself forward as a candidate, but was not popular among all IS-K leaders—or, perhaps, with IS-Central—and he was ruled out as a serious contender.[97]

Al-Afghani was also busy purging IS-K of corrupt practices, which had proliferated before his arrival. He found widespread corruption in the Finance Commission and had to completely overhaul it, replacing most of the senior cadres and punishing some, inserting IS advisers and moving all offices.[98] There were also accusations that the Commission was hiring people based on nepotistic practices.[99] The head of the Finance Commission, Mawlavi Noor Ahmad Zadran, was accused of having misappropriated $10 million and was detained. Three other senior members of the Commission were fired (out of a total of five). The representatives of the Commission in the provinces were also replaced. Mawlavi Abdul Ahad Wasall was appointed as the new head.[100] Zadran was later executed in Achin on 16 May 2016, as was the representative of the Finance Commission in Nangarhar, Mawlavi Mohammad Zubir. Another fourteen members of the commission were tried, but their fate is unknown.[101]

While corruption issues were being investigated, for 2 months IS-K operated without any contractors in logistics, before new contracts were issued. Most if not all of the private companies contracted to do logistics were replaced as well, as it was also found that some companies were bribing the cadres in charge of logistics in order to overcharge IS-K, or were colluding with them to produce fake contracts, or again were delivering goods of interior quality.[102]

In order to prevent future corruption, Al-Afghani established a new rule which prevented the Finance Commission from issuing any new contract over 1 million Afs without the approval of the Special Envoy. He also imposed a rule that records of all activities should be kept.[103] Contractors started being monitored, and some members of IS-K were tasked to keep an eye on bazaar prices, in order to make sure the contractors were not overcharging.[104] Whether or not the reformed system was better at preventing corruption is not possible to say based on the available information.

Mosul's fall

By early 2017, there were signs that the leadership of IS-Central was preparing IS-K to brace for the impact of the fall of Mosul—and possibly the complete loss of Raqqa as well—and for the increased responsibilities it would have to assume in that event. According to IS-K sources, the head of the Military Commission in Mosul (by then effectively relocated near the Syrian border), Gulmorad Halimov, visited Khorasan in March 2017 for a couple of weeks, visiting various locations to boost morale, inspect the preparation of the forces and boost negotiations with various Central Asian groups to implement plans for merging them into IS-K.[105] Then a few weeks later Abu Yasir Al-Afghani also returned to Afghanistan, possibly also to inspect and boost morale, but was caught in the bombing of an IS-K tunnel complex in Achin in April and killed.[106] These two visits seemed to suggest that IS-Central wants Khorasan to be ready to host leaders, should they seek refuge in the region, and to upgrade operations, ultimately taking over the flag of top IS battlefront. They also suggest IS-Central's worries about the potential impact of military defeat in Iraq and Syria.

The possible impact of the fall of Mosul on IS-K's morale is not mere speculation. Hundreds of IMU members defected back to AQ in Afghanistan and Uzbekistan during the latter part of 2016 and early 2017, depriving IS-K of most of its already limited foothold in Uzbekistan; a few (about thirty-five) even left Syria for Afghanistan to escape IS-Central.[107]

At the same time, it was also clear that IS-K had not yet completely resolved its internal issues. A council planned for March 2017 to select a permanent governor of Wilayat Khorasan, in place of interim appointment Hasibullah Logari, was cancelled because of the 'difficulties IS was going through' at that time. It is likely that the real reason was to avoid a choice that would be divisive at a time when IS-K was under military and psychological pressure.[108]

As of August 2017, 2 months after the fall of Mosul, there was no obvious sign of IS-K evaporating or disintegrating, but the leadership crisis described at the end of *Leadership rifts* above, which slightly preceded the actual fall of IS in Mosul, was clearly linked to the military difficulties of IS in Iraq and Syria. In October, the battle for Raqqa was also over. The killing of Halimov in September in Deir Ezzor had a particularly strong impact in Central Asia, especially Tajikistan. Gulmorad was the main lobbyist for Central Asian and in particular Tajik interests within the central leadership of the Islamic State. Following his death, Central Asia fell considerably as a priority for the Islamic State, within the context of shrinking resources. Many members of IS-aligned groups in Tajikistan simply went home, and a few crossed into Afghanistan. Inside Afghanistan, some 200 IMU members and some 85 Jamaat Ansarullah members defected back to pro-AQ groups.[109] By October 2017, signs were emerging that the loss of Mosul and Raqqa were impacting negatively on IS-K's image, affecting recruitment and cracking its reputation for invincibility.[110]

Pragmatism and resilience under Faruqi

Still, despite this long list of issues, IS-K proved resilient throughout 2017. The tribal shuras of Nangarhar assessed that the degree of control exercised by IS-K (Faruqi faction) in their province was growing, despite the strong military pressure applied on it. In mid- to late 2017, IS-K was expanding in the west of the province, establishing large pockets of control in districts such as Hissarak and Khogyani, and expanding the small pocket it had in Sherzad. It is also still expanding in some of the southern districts, such as Rodat, while contracting in others.[111]

In northern and north-eastern Afghanistan, IS-K (Moawiya) was fighting its own war against Taliban groups linked to Iran and Russia, particularly in the north-west (Jowzjan), where it was establishing its second main concentration of forces after Badakhshan.[112]

IS-K had also by 2017 emerged as a serious competitor of the Taliban as far as terrorist attacks in Kabul were concerned. It claimed several attacks against Shi'a targets and the devastating 31 May 2017 truck bomb in central Kabul. By 'making the headlines' with its Kabul attacks, IS-K could maintain its jihadist profile while reducing the need for engaging Afghan and US forces on the ground.

Faruqi showed greater pragmatism than his predecessors and softened some IS-K policies, in particular lifting the ban on the drug trade in the south-west (see Chapter 7). There have also been attempts to make deals with tribal leaderships, exploiting disenchantment with both the Taliban and Afghan state, particularly in remote parts of Afghanistan. Results on this front have been limited, with some tactical success with the Kakar and Zazai tribes (Zabul and Paktia), but little else. Generally speaking, tribal shuras seem to still be seeing IS-K as an utterly violent force with little base in the country, even if during 2017 IS-K had been deploying its governance structures (courts in particular) more widely, at least in the southern parts of Nangarhar.[113]

Faruqi also dusted off the old idea of negotiating with the Taliban. Prospects of co-operation between IS-K and some Taliban groups were back in vogue between the end of 2016 and early 2017, some months before Faruqi was chosen. From late 2016 onwards, Serajuddin Haqqani was forced to once again adopt a soft approach towards IS-K. Serajuddin had approached his donors (often the same as IS-K's) to complain about IS-K's prevarication after the Zazai district incident, only to be told that he was expected to start working towards an alliance with IS-K. The first example of the new trend was a co-operation agreement signed in April 2017 between the Haqqani network representative in Zabul, Mawlavi Raz Mohammad Zadran, and IS-K commander Mullah Mustafa. Then in May the two groups co-operated in a local offensive against Afghan government forces. The 31 May truck bomb attack in Kabul was also reported by IS-K sources as having been carried out in co-operation with the Haqqani network.[114] A source within the Haqqanis confirmed in December 2018 that the group had signed local collaboration agreements and was reportedly negotiating a wider protocol with IS in Afghanistan.[115]

Even the Quetta Shura resumed attempts to negotiate with IS-K, which resulted in the first top-level ceasefire, agreed on 18 October 2017. There were major issues to be sorted out: foremost among them was the partition of territorial control and sources of revenue, as well as IS-K's recruitment of Taliban commanders and fighters. IS-K (Faruqi) did not intend to roll back any of its territorial conquests, and even demanded that the Taliban withdraw from more territory.[116] The question was whether IS-K (Faruqi) could carve a niche for itself alongside the Taliban. On the one hand, its demonstrated resilience advised caution to those Taliban who would prefer to crush it as a dangerous competitor. On the other, finding a *modus vivendi* with the Taliban was never going to be easy. Indeed, the October 2017 ceasefire lasted only 3 weeks.

Eventually, in March 2018 Faruqi even managed to get his governorship recognized by IS-Central. His rival Moawiya bowed to him, under pressure from the leaders, and renounced the position of deputy governor.[117] Internationally, however, the confirmation of Aslam Faruqi as governor was only acknowledged in April 2019.[118]

10

CRISIS AND ... RELAUNCH?

2018–21

Defeat in Derzab

Rising pressure from the Taliban—whose leadership was increasingly set on taking decisive action against IS-K's relentless expansion—compounded IS-K's internal problems. For the Taliban, decisive action against IS-K was a complex matter, logistically as well as politically. IS-K's bases were in remote areas, difficult to reach and away from usual Taliban targets such as government-held cities. Concentrating forces against IS-K was not easily compatible while a large-scale campaign against the Afghan government was going on. In the north, the Taliban's Shura of the North rarely co-operated with the Quetta Shura, and according to a source inside the Shura of the North, contacted in March 2018, by early 2018 it had been accused by Quetta and Taliban donors such as Iran and Russia of being in cahoots with IS-K.[1] The Quetta Shura was more active in the west, especially Farah, where it has carried out repeated raids in co-operation with Iranian forces, and in the south, especially the northern districts of Zabul, where it has tried twice (in 2015 and 2016) to crush IS-K.

IS-K established itself in Jowzjan in late 2016 after a former Taliban commander, Qari Hekmatullah, joined with his men. Derzab is a very remote area, hard to reach and isolated. It makes a perfect hideout, although hardly a suitable point of departure for a typical Islamic State blitzkrieg operation. The

Kosh Tepa base was therefore not as overtly important as some other IS-K bases in the east, north-east or south. It was more of a seed, whose fruits IS-K hoped to harvest in the relatively distant future. Taliban sources, contacted in February 2018, reported constant pressure from Russia to wipe out IS-K's presence in Derzab. The Russians, according to Taliban sources, went as far as sending supplies by helicopter to the remote region and offering to fund a Taliban offensive against the Kosh Tepa base. Still, it took several months to get the offensive going.[2]

Although estimating the strength of the Kosh Tepa IS-K force is hard to do with any precision, even the Taliban commanders who defeated it (and who have a vested interest in overstating its size now) did not put it at more than 400. An IS-K commander, who by contrast had a vested interest in minimizing the defeat and maximizing the unfavourable odds, put it at around half that number. Moreover, the quality of IS-K's forces there was poor, as they had been mostly recruited from 2016 onwards from other organizations, such as the Taliban, Jamiat and Junbesh, without much vetting.[3]

This force of 200–400 men survived the killing of its leader Qari Hekmatullah in April and then still put up a brave fight in August. IS-K sources claimed that the Taliban received support from US forces, a small IRGC contingent and local militias, but none of this could be confirmed.[4]

IS-K denied that it had been completely eradicated from Derzab, despite the loss of most of its local fighters. However, despite his obvious attempt to understate the scale of the defeat, the source when pressed admitted that the loss of the Kosh Tepa base in Derzab was one of the most serious blows to the 'prestige' of IS-K, and that it impacted negatively on recruitment and even on the morale of existing members in northern Afghanistan. Abdul Aziz Yuldash, at that time commander of IS-K for all of northern Afghanistan, was reportedly very upset by the defeat and surrender of tens of IS-K men, and so was the leadership council of IS-K.[5]

Derzab was not a decisive defeat for IS-K. Despite the difficulties, there was no sense in IS-K as of August 2018 that a retrenchment might be necessary. A source said that 'We are ready to defend all our bases and positions'. Focusing solely on eastern Afghanistan, which is where IS-K is on more solid ground and the Taliban are weakest, was still not an acceptable compromise for the leadership of the Islamic State.[6]

Still, there were other signs that IS-K was on a downward trend. By the beginning of the summer of 2018, recruitment was also slowing, and an IS-K source admitted that the numerical strength of IS-K was in decline. In fact that trend might have been more negative than mere numbers would seem to suggest; as pointed out above, in the north-west and south, IS-K was drawing recruits among clearly opportunistic elements, which had no ideological affinity with the group. IS-K enjoyed little success in these regions in recruiting genuinely committed elements, and had to stiffen its ranks with large injections of Central Asians and other foreign fighters.[7] Another sign of its decline was the fact that during 2018 there were, for example, a number of IS cadres roaming around Wilayat Khorasan, claiming the status of special representatives of al-Baghdadi, and for some months the leadership of IS-K was unable to confirm their status with the central leadership.[8] This suggests that the leadership's control was fraying, possibly due to the internal divisions discussed above, and that communication with the Caliphate's leadership was getting more difficult.

Defeat in Nangarhar

After August 2018, the malaise of IS-K intensified. Initially, IS-K made an attempt to go back on the offensive, especially in Kunar where in late March 2019 IS-K took five districts from the Taliban, according to Taliban sources. The Taliban were taken aback, as after Derzab they had assumed they had definitely gained an edge over IS-K. The Taliban's losses in Kunar occurred at the time that they stepped up operations against the Afghan security forces, as customary each spring.

Another aspect of IS-K's rebound in early 2019 appears to have been the seemingly successful Taliban–US talks in Doha. A number of jihadist actors got seriously worried about the trend, and by the willingness of the Taliban leadership to question long-standing alliances with jihadist organizations. That not only upset many hardline Taliban, but scared Al-Qaida and allied jihadists—like IMU, TTP and others—who suddenly started viewing their being deprived of any safe haven in Afghanistan as a real possibility. In the following months, a new wave of defections from the Taliban and other jihadist organizations such as TTP and IMU took place in eastern Afghanistan, strengthening the ranks of IS-K.[9]

The IS-K leadership tried to leverage this momentum and invited Serajuddin Haqqani to join IS-K with his men. Serajuddin's opposition to the peace process in Afghanistan and to the Taliban breaking up with the jihadists was well known, and IS-K seemed to think that there was a chance of co-opting him. An IS-K source, contacted in May 2019, said that they were negotiating with some other relatively high-profile Taliban, including at least one shadow provincial governor, who were known to be disgruntled with the Quetta Shura.[10]

IS-K envisaged establishing a jihadist safe haven in eastern Afghanistan. The Taliban were relatively weak there in the first half of 2019, making IS-K's gains there seem not impossible to achieve.

Perhaps more importantly, among those worried about the Taliban leadership's new attitudes were narcotics traders, who feared a peace agreement would be damaging for their business. IS-K agreed to allow the passage of drugs aimed for Central Asia through its territory (see Chapter 7 above).

Despite the rebound, even the first part of 2019 was not all good news for IS-K. The rivalries between the Afghans and the Pakistanis, and between the Pakistanis and the Central Asians, were never completely healed. Even the Central Asians split into two separate groups, known as the Samarqandi Group and the Bukhari Usmani Group, and developed divergences with Shamali Khilafat, the group that gathered the Afghan Tajiks and Uzbeks of IS-K. The two Central Asian groups reportedly merged in the late summer of 2019, but the friction with Shamali Khilafat remained. Deputy governor Abdul Aziz Yuldash defected back to the pro-AQ faction of the IMU, a significant blow to the influence of IS-K among Central Asians.[11]

This and other fissures had been latent for over a year, but were revived by the catastrophic event of the killing of al-Baghdadi in Syria on 27 October 2019. An IS-K cadre, contacted in the days when the Taliban were approaching the Mohmand Valley headquarter, admitted that 'certainly, IS-K and the holy fighters have been impacted by the loss of caliphate. The impact was much greater than what was expected'. The loss of the supreme leader removed one source of discipline that was preventing internal rivalries from resurfacing. According to the same source, 'our senior leaders are trying their best to maintain unity among the ranks'. Al-Baghdadi's then Special Representative to Khorasan, Abu Mohammad Zafar Safi, who was second only to the governor in terms of power, became powerless, as many members of IS-K started contesting his authority with al-Baghdadi dead. Although all operations and major attacks were still supposed to be authorized by the top leadership, as an IS-K source admitted, 'after the loss of the caliphate, our connection and contacts with the Central Council and the new leaders are not so strong'.[12]

Perhaps the extent of the crisis in IS-K is best exemplified by Aslam Faruqi's decision to fake his own death in order to escape US airstrikes. He even went as far as having a figurehead appointed as governor, after several months in which all members except the top leaders of IS-K believed Khorasan had no governor. The fifteen-member leadership shura appointed Abu Omer, a Safi Pashtun from Nurgul district of Kunar province, as this figurehead. He had already served some time as deputy of Hafiz Saeed, the first governor of Khorasan.[13]

The turning point in IS-K's fortunes was really the Taliban offensive in the east towards the end of 2019. According to a Taliban commander in Achin who participated in the fighting, the decision was taken in mid-October by the Taliban leadership to mount the largest offensive against IS-K, with the intent of rooting it out of Nangarhar once and for all. With the fighting season approaching its winter slowdown, the Taliban calculated that they would be able to concentrate a large portion of their mobile forces against IS-K.[14] And so they did. For the leader of the Taliban, Haibatullah, the offensive offered the opportunity to ease the controversy within Taliban ranks over his refusal to authorize major strikes against Afghan government forces throughout 2019, and would consolidate his leadership with a much-needed battlefield victory.

The Taliban first struck in the west of the province, taking from IS-K a pocket of sixteen villages in Shirzad district. Then the Taliban moved into neighbouring Khogyani, taking another thirty-four villages from Khorasan. Next was Pachir wa Agam district, where an IS-K pocket of thirteen villages was rapidly eliminated, and then two small pockets of five villages taken in Haska Mina and Kot. Finally, the Taliban took six villages controlled by IS-K in Achin. By that point, the supply lines into Mohmand Valley had already been cut, and the position of the main base of IS-K inside Afghanistan was fast becoming untenable. The Taliban immediately entered Mohmand Valley, while they were also advancing on Spinghar, where IS-K was holding another six villages. By the end of the third week of November, it was over.[15]

IS-K pulled leaders and cadres out of Mohmand Valley as the Taliban advanced, while fighters withdrew into the mountains. The Taliban claim, according to this commander, to have killed 190 members of IS-K during the offensive. Perhaps 200–300 more surrendered to the authorities. IS-K also left behind plenty of equipment, including heavy weapons, horses and vehicles.[16] The final humiliation was the surrender of over 600 fighters and family members in Achin over the second and third weeks of November, which was widely reported in the media. Although IS-K's fighters and family members surrendered to the Afghan authorities, which then proceeded to claim responsibility for the victory, it was in fact the Taliban who had defeated IS-K. The role of the Afghan security forces was rather marginal. Perhaps the Afghan security forces saw that the Taliban were gaining the upper hand and decided to score some easy tactical victories as well.[17]

An IS-K cadre interviewed in November 2019 admitted the gravity of the defeat. He reckoned that 700 or so members fled to Pakistan, their whereabouts unknown. The IS-K leadership was so shocked that it started considering the possibility of concentrating its residual resources in north-eastern Afghanistan—where it had some strong presence, mainly in Badakhshan—and at the same time resuming its efforts to infiltrate western Afghanistan.[18]

The Taliban went on to attack IS-K positions in Kunar in March 2020. This time too, IS-K forces put up a less-than-spirited defence, with significant numbers surrendering. IS-K forces were wiped out of Manogai, Watapor, Asad Abad, Naraang, Noorgul and Chawki districts, all in about 2 weeks. Taliban sources say that more IS-K fighters surrendered than were killed. The damage was lasting. By April 2020, according to an IS-K source, IS-K had 400 men in Nangarhar and 300 in Kunar, hanging on in the mountains, but with very little offensive capabilities due to the loss of the old headquarters in Achin.[19]

Then, in April the governor of Wilayat Khorasan, Aslam Faruqi, was caught by Afghan intelligence in a hideout in Kandahar, together with other senior IS-K figures. Although Wilayat Khorasan had lost many governors before, this was the first time one was captured. Even worse for IS-K, under interrogation Faruqi disclosed information about the whereabouts of the figurehead who was signing decrees on his behalf (while Faruqi was in hiding, pretending to be dead): Omer Khorasani was caught by Afghan security forces in May in his hideout in north Kabul, again in the company of other senior figures. With him were detained IS-K's head of intelligence and the head of public relations.[20] The damage was even worse because Faruqi had been declared dead already (see above), and discovering that he had been alive and in hiding the whole time did not make a good impression on the rank and file of IS-K. By April 2020, about 2,000 members of IS-K had either surrendered or deserted.[21]

IS-K's relationship with the Haqqani network also weakened after the Nangarhar defeat, as the Haqqanis were beginning to doubt of the viability of IS-K.[22] There were signs of impending disintegration. The Haqqani component of IS-K ('defectors' from the Haqqani network, who actually maintained links to their mother organization) was acting more and more independently of the leadership, a big affront to an organization that prided itself in its strict discipline. The Haqqanis were exploiting the broken chain of command to essentially hijack parts of IS-K for their own purposes.[23] IS-K then received very concerning intelligence that the Haqqanis were linking up to the IRGC. IS-K urged the Haqqanis to desist, as this might create major issues between the two organizations.[24]

By April 2020, according to an internal source, losses and desertions had cut IS-K numbers in Afghanistan to 4,000, compared to 10,000 a year earlier. Another 1,500–2,000 were usually based in three main camps in Pakistan (Tirah, Mohmand Jang). Then, in April the desertion back to Al-Qaida of Haji Furqan—IS-K's amir for Badakhshan province—with perhaps 300 Central Asian fighters struck a huge blow for IS-K.[25]

The overall impact on the morale of IS-K members was devastating. As Osman reported,

> From 2015 through 2018, ISKP's propaganda and ISKP members (in conversations with the author both in Kabul and in the east of the country) were convinced that ISKP would dislodge the Taliban from the position of the primary insurgent actor in almost half of Afghanistan; the ISKP, they confidently assumed, would expand its control of territory to all of the eastern and northern provinces. By late 2019, this optimism had all but disappeared, chiefly it seems because of ISKP's loss of territory and leaders, as well as the routing of Islamic State forces in Syria and Iraq.[26]

The competition of Wilayat Pakistan

When the leadership of the Islamic State decided to form Wilayat Pakistan and the new IS branch of IS-Pakistan (IS-P) in May 2019, the members of IS-K dismissed it as a sideshow and claimed that there would be no substantial transfer of members from IS-K to IS-P. Those Pakistanis being sent to Wilayat Pakistan were merely 'on loan', they claimed. But things turned out differently. The leadership of the Islamic State established Wilayat Pakistan on 14 May 2019 for the purpose of stimulating recruitment in Pakistan, a country seen as very promising due to the plethora of jihadist groups of all tendencies based there. It was hoped that Wilayat Pakistan could act as a catalyst for these groups and start a process of consolidation under the leadership of the Islamic State.[27]

In practice, and perhaps naturally, the new Wilayat started competing with Khorasan for recruits and funds. According to the cadre contacted in November 2019, some 900 Pakistani members of IS-K moved to IS-P in 6 months. That corresponded to about 8–10 per cent of the total strength claimed by IS-K in mid-2019. It was a significant loss that affected Nangarhar province in a particular way, as many of IS-K's Pakistani members were operating there. During the Taliban offensive of October/November, hundreds more Pakistani IS-K members crossed into Pakistan for safety, and a number of them appear to have joined IS-P.[28]

It was essentially Pakistani Pashtuns and Punjabis who left IS-K. IS-P also tried to attract Baluchis, Central Asians, Uyghurs and other foreigners serving within the ranks of IS-K, but apparently with little success. One source admitted that the real reason why these groups stayed loyal to IS-K is that they expected little mercy from the Pakistani authorities, and still saw Afghanistan as the safer option, despite everything. The source describes there being serious friction between the two branches of IS due to competition for recruits. In addition, the budget allocated to IS-P came at least partially at the expense of IS-K, weakening it financially. The source might have been trying to find a scapegoat for the defeat in Nangarhar, but he used unusually strong words and, a first in tens and tens of interviews that the author organized with IS-K members over the years, implicitly criticized the leadership of the Islamic State: 'The creation of Wilayah Pakistan and the immediate move of experienced Pakistani members and fighters were a total disaster for Khorasan.'[29]

An attempt was made to ease tension in 2020 through the creation of an office called Diwan of Co-ordination, based in Pakistan. This office was tasked to co-ordinate between Wilayat Khorasan, Wilayat Pakistan and Wilayat Hind. Each Wilayat had its own representatives in the Diwan. Wilayat Pakistan was also ordered to actively support and help IS-K with funding, supplies and other different types of material support such as weapons and ammunition, housing, medical support and others.[30]

A takeover?

After a very bad start of 2020 in terms of recruitment, from May 2020 onwards hundreds of recruits started flocking to IS-K. That would normally be considered good news, and did push IS-K's membership back up by perhaps 1,000. But a source noted that the recruits were all from the Haqqani network and Lashkar-e Taiba, two groups closely linked to the Pakistani ISI. Aside from these two flows, very few volunteers were approaching IS-K. Within IS-K, the suspicion started spreading that the ISI might be using these two groups to take over IS-K. One IS-K source estimated in June 2020 that 25 per cent of the membership of IS-K—probably exaggerating (see Table 12)—was by then made of pro-Haqqani elements, organized in component groups called Defenders of Haqqania (the successor to the Azizullah Haqqani Group). A Haqqani source put the number of Haqqani network loyalists within IS-K at 600 (=7.5%) at about the same time, although Defenders of Haqqania could well have incorporated others as well.[31] By March 2021, an IS-K source again estimated 1,500–1,700 (=19–22%) former Haqqani members in IS-K, and their numbers were still growing.[32]

The suspicions just discussed emerged against a backdrop of rising tension between IS-K and ISI, after the capture of Faruqi. IS-K sources, contacted in April and June 2020, believed that the Taliban offensives of November 2019 and March 2020 would not have happened without the endorsement of the ISI. Several IS-K sources indicated that the ISI wanted to recruit IS-K, or at least as many of its men as possible, for a renewed campaign in Kashmir. The thinking was that with Lashkar-e Taiba discredited as an Islamabad proxy, Pakistan might need new blood in Kashmir in order to keep India under pressure while retaining plausible deniability. Islamabad also reportedly wanted to further 'internationalize' the Kashmir conflict, by getting not just Pakistanis but also larger numbers of Afghans and other foreign fighters involved.[33]

Lashkar-e Taiba was also sending more members, but there was some opposition to their arrival within IS-K. There were considerable objections and fears that Haqqanis and Lashkar-e Taiba were instruments of an ISI gradual takeover of the group, to which the leadership responded by subjecting the new arrivals to a brainwashing course of 3 months. IS-K is also very cautious before appointing any of them to positions of responsibility.[34]

Under new management

Initially, the successor to al-Baghdadi, Caliph Abu Ibrahim, did not pay much attention to IS-K. An IS-K source indicated in April 2020 that the Caliph was planning to send a group of representatives to evaluate IS-K and make recommendations for changes. Abu Ibrahim let the leaders of IS-K know that he was considering major changes for IS-K, including in the composition of the central shura. He promised additional funding and support for going on the offensive with 'guerrilla operations'. The Caliph also let it be known that he wanted IS-K to concentrate more forces in Badakhshan and promised he would send new Central Asian members from the Middle East with extra funding. IS-K duly complied, more than doubling the size of its deployment in Badakhshan.[35]

In fact, IS-K was in the process of transferring its HQ to Badakhshan, at least temporarily. For that, a separate IS-K structure was established in

Badakhshan, under the direct control of the governor, alongside that of Amir of Khorasan.[36] It proved hard to supply the Badakhshan bases due to the isolation of the area. IS-K, however, negotiated agreements with local people, Jamiati militia commanders and leaders and with Taliban commanders. IS-K supplies were allowed to reach Badakhshan through Nuristan, Kunar and Panjshir, and in exchange IS-K acknowledged their right to exploit mines and smuggle heroin towards Central Asia.[37] A that point, the plan was to have a single main base in Khastaq and to keep only small bases in the east, with an entirely underground presence in the rest of the country.[38]

Pressure for strengthening the presence of IS-K in Badakhshan likely derived from donors, who were ready to fund IS-K as long as it was in a position to have access to the borders of Tajikistan and China. Indeed, an IS-K source indicated that after Caliph Ibrahim imposed the strengthening of Badakhshan, infiltration into Tajikistan resumed. IS-K had at that point the ability to send twenty to thirty men per month across the border, thanks to the help of Afghan smuggling gangs.[39]

While in deep crisis, the easiest and cheapest way for IS-K to reassert its relevance, at least media-wise, was to carry out high-profile attacks in Kabul. However, it had little control over its Kabul unit at the moment, as it was dependent on logistical support from the Haqqani network. The unit itself was actually mostly composed of 'defectors' (or 'infiltrators', as one IS-K source contacted in June described them) from the Haqqani network itself, who were often co-operating with the Haqqanis without reporting through the IS-K chain of command. Three IS-K sources, for example, claimed in June that the May 2020 attack on a maternity hospital in Kabul, run by MSF, was carried out by an IS-K unit under Haqqani command. This, of course, could be a means of scapegoating the Haqqanis for a ferocious attack, in which pregnant women were executed point blank in their beds. In any case, IS-K sources claimed that the organization was seeking to strengthen its Kabul unit as a matter of priority, and thus recover its ability to operate independently. The budget for the Kabul unit was increased for this purpose, despite big budget constraints.[40]

After Faruqi's detention in early April, the head of the central shura of IS-K, Mawlavi Attaullah Al Khorasani, was in charge as acting governor. There were different views within the central shura of IS-K with regard to whether to wait for IS-Central to send the name of a new governor or choose him straight away. Bilal Swati, a Pakistani commander, was initially rumoured to be the favourite for the governor job. Then the Pakistanis proposed Abdul Shakur Orakzai as their candidate. The Afghans within the IS-K leadership proposed Sheikh Bakhtiyar. The Central Asians protested against a Pakistani being appointed, as they saw it as a reaffirmation of Pakistani ISI influence, which they strongly rejected.[41] Moawiya was in control of the IS-K base in Khastaq (Badakhshan), and his group was again operating de facto independently. Already towards the end of Faruqi's tenure, infighting between Faruqi and the Central Asians had resurfaced, and he often clashed with them in the central shura.[42]

Eventually, IS-Central decided to impose its own choice in the first half of June, Dr. Shehab Al-Muhajir (a.k.a. Abu Hesham Al-Muhajir).[43] Born in Zelah Mardan District of Khayber Pakhtunkhwa province of Pakistan in 1967, he earned degrees in religious law. Al-Mujahir had a long background of activism in Islamic groups, starting with Jamiat-e Ulama-e Islam and ending with the Haqqani network, before joining the would-be IS in 2014 while in Iraq. He served in various positions in Islamic State, first in Iraq and then in Syria.[44]

The central leadership of IS refused to discuss the matter with IS-K leaders. As a result, the new appointment left Afghan and Pakistan IS-K leaders unhappy. Initially, they knew little about the new governor aside from his nom de guerre. Only the Central Asian members of the IS-K leadership were happy, presumably because they thought he was going to be an Arab and therefore neither an Afghan nor a Pakistani. Their satisfaction would not last long.[45]

Shehab Al-Muhajir was said to be reporting on a regular basis to Abu Basher Khatab, who was in charge of supervising Wilayat Khorasan within IS-Central. One source claimed that Shehab Al-Muhajir was speaking to the leadership of the Caliphate 'every weekend', reporting developments to them, receiving new orders, discussing plans, receiving advice.[46] Another source differed somewhat and stated that the frequency of direct communications between the Khorasan governor and the IS leaders increased after Al-Muhajir was appointed and it was now one to three times per month.[47] IS-Central maintained control over decision-making in the case of major military operations, while minor decisions could be decided autonomously by the leaders of IS-K.[48]

The other elements of the strategy dictated by the Caliphate were:

- focusing on intensifying recruitment;
- opening or establishing influence over more madrasas in Afghanistan and Pakistan;
- establishing 'make a more cordial relationship with the people' in order to attract them to IS-K;
- making deals with the South Asian and Central Asian Jihadist groups and with Al-Qaida;
- trying to get closer to Iran's borders.[49]

The IS-K leadership decided that in order to achieve these aims, it had to avoid confrontations with the Taliban while it was still recovering strength.[50] Whereas in the past the Taliban were IS-K's primary target, now the Taliban and the Afghan government ranked at the same level as enemies.[51]

The transition from Faruqi was made even harder by the IS-Central's delay in assigning a budget to IS-K for 2020 and making transfers of cash (see Chapter 7). By April 2020, IS-K's cash reserves were down to $20 million, according to an internal source.[52] Recruitment was at a very low level and Caliph Ibrahim's promises of reinforcements from the Middle East did not materialize, in part due to the COVID-19 pandemic hindering travel. Some eighty ex-IS members, who had returned to Central Asia, were all that reportedly crossed the border to join IS-K in Afghanistan in spring 2020, presumably feeling at risk in their home countries. A significant source of recruits emerged in Hizb ut-Tahrir, which had quite a large following in Badakhshan.[53]

Once the new governor reached Afghanistan, he finally decided to concentrate forces in Badakhshan and in the east, and he set out to re-organize the group. Demoralized members of IS-K, who had fled to Pakistan, started getting pushed back into Nangarhar in order to lay the conditions for going on the offensive. The 2–3 August 2020 attack against Jalalabad prison was aimed at advertising the fact that IS-K was alive and kicking in Nangarhar; by fighting for twenty hours in the provincial capital, IS-K highlighted its determination to keep fighting. Nangarhar returned to being a focus of IS-K activity, with total IS-K presence there doubling and reaching close to 1,000 by the summer of 2020. Fighting resumed in Nangarhar during the summer, although IS-K was unable to make substantial territorial gains and accused the Taliban of receiving help from the Americans in the shape of air strikes.[54]

Under Al-Muhajir, Pakistani dominance of IS-K continued. In Nangarhar in July 2020, more than half of 1,000 or so members were Pakistanis, with Afghans accounting for just over a third. The rest were South Asians and Arabs, while Central Asians accounted for less than 2 per cent, showing how, despite the formal healing of the dispute between Faruqi and Moawiya, IS-K continued to look very different in the east as it did in the north-east, where Central Asians were concentrated.[55] As of mid-2021, the leadership council of IS-K included governor and chair of the council Al-Muhajir, his deputy governor Abu Jawad and the second deputy of the chair of the council Umran, all Pakistani Pashtuns from Bajaur.

The top Afghan was Zia ul-Haq Arabi, from Kunar, first deputy of the council's chair, despite the fact that by 2020 Wilayat Khorasan was in practice essentially reduced to Afghanistan (the Iran and Central Asian branches operate autonomously, and Pakistan is under Wilayat Pakistan). The remaining members of the council were six Pakistanis, of which at least five were Pashtuns, and three Afghans, two of whom were from Kunar and one from Nangarhar. One notes the absence of the Central Asians, even if it should be considered that four of them were provincial amirs for Badakhshan, Kunduz, Saripul and Faryab.[56] Al-Mujahir at least tried to pacify the Afghans, whom Aslam Faruqi had antagonized, by reinstating Zia ul-Haq and another member, Sheikh Salim Dost, whom Faruqi had sacked from the council.[57] Still, even Al-Muhajir did not get close to meeting the demands of the non-Pakistanis. The Afghans had asked to get at least the first deputy. The Central Asians also asked to get one of the deputies. The leadership was considering increasing the number of deputies to four in the future, with one deputy each for Pakistanis, Afghans, Central Asians and other South Asians.[58]

Under Al-Muhajir, IS-K restarted negotiating with AQ and TTP in earnest, from July 2020 onwards. AQ was soon allowed to enter areas under IS-K's control, on condition that they avoid maintaining relations with Taliban and collaborate instead with IS-K. AQ reciprocated by allowing IS-K members to enter AQ areas. Al-Muhajir viewed an alliance as strategic because AQ still had access to considerable funding, and several jihadist groups followed its advice.[59]

There were, however, divisions over the alliance with Al-Qaida.[60] Among those opposed to the alliance with AQ were senior figures such as Sheikh Assadullah Orakzai, Qari Abdullah, Mawlavi Abdul Jalal Safi and Mawlavi Fada Muhammad Ibrahim Khil, as well as some Arabs. They argued that AQ had fought against IS in Syria, still had relations with the Taliban and most importantly had relations with Iran. However, the majority of the IS-K leadership was favourable, because they assessed that the alliance would boost IS-K's chances in opposition to the Taliban and Afghan government.[61] IS-K started building a joint AQ–IS-K base in Nuristan. It was clear, in any case, that IS–AQ co-operation would remain limited to Afghanistan and would not be advertised.[62]

Under Al-Muhajir, there were also big debates about the utility of extreme violence to IS-K. Many in the leadership council of IS-K argued that violence 'brings cruelties and isolation'. Afghans especially were concerned, whereas Pakistani were less interested. With plans to extend taxation of NGOs and businesses, extreme violence was starting to seem counter-productive. The effort to improve relations with local people had already started, with a policy implemented in 2019 of improving relations with NGOs providing health care, education and construction work, subject to them accepting to undergo security checks. The policy was controversial within IS-K when it was introduced; military leaders in particular opposed it, claiming that NGOs were often used to spy on IS-K activities. The leadership insisted on rolling out a system where NGOs could register and pay taxes and would then be allowed to operate in IS-K held areas. Then, because of the loss of most IS-K territory between late 2019 and early 2020, the policy lost relevance and was implemented only to a very modest degree (see also Chapter 7).[63]

Relaunch 2021–?

As of August 2021, just before the fall of Kabul, IS-K's strength was down 20 per cent compared to its peak of June 2016. In reality, the decline was greater than it appeared, because IS-K was expanding its part-time militias, essentially villagers who are only mobilized when fighting reaches close to their villages (see Chapter 4, *Military organization*). The number of these part-timers is not known, but their presence implies that the decline since 2016 in the number of full-time IS-K members is higher than 20 per cent.[64]

IS-K still viewed attracting Taliban to its ranks as difficult. At that time, not a single Taliban commander was negotiating to join IS-K. IS-K alleged that the Americans were still supporting the Taliban with air strikes. Taliban members, explained a source, were also reluctant to join IS-K because they usually do not share IS-K's Salafist ideology. Most of the Taliban who joined IS-K were killed in battle, mostly in 2019–20.[65] As a result, there were not that many known former Taliban figures in IS-K who could act as a bridge to attract their disaffected comrades.

The picture changed significantly after 15 August. Intra-Taliban diatribes, especially between southern and eastern Taliban; disappointment among many poorly educated Taliban that they had not been appointed to positions of prestige in the new government; and funds and logistical shortages affecting the Taliban, at least in Kunar, raised the prospects of Taliban defections. According to several contacts with Taliban and IS-K members in Kunar and Nangarhar, a commander with 70 men defected to IS-K in Kunar at the end of August, while two other commanders—one with 100 men and the other with 150 men—between Nangarhar and Kunar were negotiating their defection. One of the two commanders negotiating was quite a well-known figure, and his defection would not go unnoticed.[66]

IS-K was hoping to draw new strength from the members of IS-K who had been released from prison, including many new converts recruited in prison. Overall, sources claim as many as 4,000 new members were added to IS-K strength after the fall of Kabul. However, at the same time there have been defections from IS-K ranks, with some hundreds of Pakistanis leaving the organization. One source, considering that probably not all the released prisoners will join IS-K (some might just want to go home or join other branches of IS, such as IS-P), estimated that the membership of IS-K as of September 2021 was around 10,000 members. According to him, most of these escapees joined IS-K in Kunar, boosting its strength there to as many as 3,500 men, although this does not look entirely credible.[67]

A source in the intelligence of the Taliban's Emirate estimated the number going back to IS-K at 1,500.[68] Indiscriminate repression, targeting Salafis suspected of being inclined towards IS-K, might also have fuelled recruitment into IS-K.[69] IS-K might well have deliberately invited Taliban retaliation against Salafi clerics with attacks against pro-Taliban Hanafi clerics from 2016 onwards.[70] Some Central Asians and other foreigners have also been leaving in recent times, a few for their home countries and a large number for Turkey. There were also some new arrivals from Syria through Turkey, from where they head for Uzbekistan and Tajikistan, where new fake documents are prepared for Pakistan. The overall impact of these movements on numbers has however been almost negligible.[71]

Nonetheless, the capability of IS-K to absorb large numbers of Taliban defectors was at that time limited by the lack of funding. Unable to raise significant amounts of money locally through taxes, and with the central leadership of IS-K only able to send a relatively limited amount, as of August IS-K was still suffering from lack of funding.[72] Even integrating the prison escapees into the organization represented a considerable financial challenge.

Indeed, even the once-powerful logistical system of IS-K had decayed to some extent. Although in some areas the logistical commission still provided food, in other areas IS-K fighters depended on the villagers, as the Taliban used to do. The villagers would sometimes provide it willingly, and sometimes the fighters would take it by force. There were also agreements with private companies for providing food supplies as in the past, but on the whole IS-K was not as well supported logistically as it used to be.[73]

The new situation created by the Taliban victory against the Islamic Republic offered IS-K opportunities, but it also involved risks. A threat, because the Emirate appeared likely to press on and try to destroy IS-K; even the Pakistani authorities seemed to intend to help the Emirate in doing this, and they encouraged LeT—once close to IS-K—to collaborate with the Taliban as well. If the Emirate could enlist help from America, Russia and other countries with significant military assets, IS-K's position would be even harder. Combined land and air attacks would make the conquest of the valleys held by IS-K easier. Its leadership believed that the Taliban's strategy would be to attack IS-K in Badakhshan, where its forces were more limited, with Russian support. IS-K therefore started considering withdrawing from Badakhshan to Kunar and Nuristan in order to consolidate forces.[74]

Most of the international jihadist groups operating in Afghanistan started thinking that with the Taliban and Washington on poor terms, the chance of a Taliban crackdown on the jihadists became more remote.[75] Al-Qaida, for example, edged closer to the Taliban again. The agreement signed by IS-K and Al-Qaida in 2020, according to which they would both co-operate against Taliban, was pushed aside. Still, both organizations were keen to avoid friction and to maintain relations.[76] This was likely to continue, at least so far as the Taliban did not take a decisive turn against the foreign jihadists. Even the Jamiati militias of Badakhshan, which had made pragmatic deals with IS-K, IS-K started seeing as enemies and accused them of collaborating with the Taliban and the Russians. There were reportedly cases of Jamiati militiamen guiding the Taliban towards IS-K posts and bases.[77]

Therefore, at the root of IS-K's growing isolation was not just the renewed plausibility of the Afghan Taliban as an ally, but also the deterioration of relations with the Pakistani ISI. IS-P attacks in Pakistan had complicated IS-K's relationship with the ISI, and had in fact led to open hostilities. The fear of TTP and IS-K coming closer to each other might have also worried the ISI. The ISI moved to shut down IS-K bases IS-K in Pakistan, as well as its logistics.[78]

This new situation also represented an opportunity, because if IS-K was able to resist long enough, the internal difficulties of the Emirate could start producing significant benefits for it. The power struggle within the Taliban, especially between southern Taliban and the Haqqani network, could be turned to an advantage for IS-K, depending on its evolution. The main problem for IS-K was to secure additional sources of funding.

In line with the Caliph's orders, IS-K shifted tactics towards guerrilla operations, often assassinations. The decision was taken and communicated down the ranks by the spring of 2020.[79] IS-K also started to disperse forces in order to deny easy targets to US air strikes.[80] Most of the assassinations carried out until 15 August in Kabul and Jalalabad targeted Islamic Republic officials, but several Taliban and clerics sympathizing with the Taliban were also assassinated in Afghanistan and Pakistan. The assassinations were cleared by the 'Qaza' Commission.[81] The Qaza (Judicial) Commission is composed of ten highly educated (in Islamic Law) members (five Afghans, three Pakistanis, two Arabs). It appears to work as a kind of supreme court, but it also vets the lists of people to be targeted.[82]

After August 2021, IS-K suspended operations while it proceeded to rapidly re-deploy cells to a number of Afghan cities, where it have never been active before, such as Charikar, Kandahar and Kunduz.[83] Taliban sources contacted in late August, however, believe that IS-K has strengthened its position in Kabul, exploiting the security vacuum created by the collapse of the Islamic Republic. They estimated that IS-K moved 200–300 fighters into Kabul, for the first time gaining a significant autonomous capability to strike, independent of any support from the Haqqani network, which had helped them in the past.[84]

While Kunar province in eastern Afghanistan became the main centre of IS-K (see Map 10), the organization also started forming underground units in the districts of Nangarhar and in the city, enabling a campaign of targeted assassinations in Jalalabad. In Nangarhar, IS-K no longer held any area after 15 August, but had camps in the mountains and wooded areas. In Kunar, it had several small bases in the upper valleys. An IS-K source in Kunar acknowledged that in Kunar the population supported the Taliban as of September 2021. The Pakistani militias of Lashkar-e Taiba were also collaborating with the Taliban against IS-K. Taliban pressure forced IS-K to abandon Dara e Pech in early September, re-deploying its forces to Chapadara. Before mid-September, IS-K decided to abandon Ghaziabad as well, again in order to re-deploy to Chapadara. IS-K chose Chapadara for its main base in Kunar because of its strategic location, between Nuristan, the Alingar district of Laghman and Nurgal district of Kunar. As of September, an IS source claimed that there were 1,500 IS-K men there.[85]

IS-K also continued its efforts to re-establish cells in Farah along the border with Iran, presumably with the intent to help infiltrations into Iran.[86]

Table 12: Factional composition of IS-K, circa June 2020, according to an IS-K source (see text for comments)[87]

	%
Defenders of Haqqania (Modafe'yin Haqqania)	25
Muslim Dost, Khilafat Afghan, TKK, other Afghan Pashtuns	13
Shamal Khilafat	4
Pakistanis with no previous affiliation to other groups.	37
Ex-TTP	5
Lashkar-e Khilafat (ex-Lashkar-e Taiba)	3
Ex-SSP	3
Mujahidin of Central Asia, led by Sheikh Akbar Samarqandi	4
Uyghurs	1
Others, incl. Arabs, Indians, Bangladeshi ...	5

Map 10: Concentration of IS-K forces, August 2021, by province. Only concentrations of fifty men or over are shown[88]

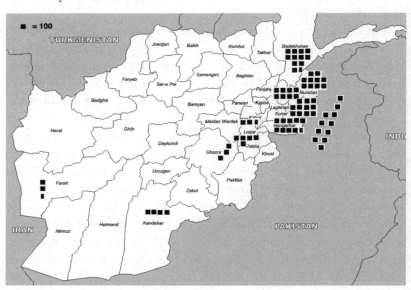

CONCLUSION

More than spin

IS-K was not a mere media operation, nor an opportunistic exploitation of a successful brand of jihadism. It was a genuine attempt by the leadership of IS-Central to expand into what they considered a promising environment. To them, 'promising' did not mean that there was a chance of setting deep roots in the countries of the region (an issue that might have been alien even to their mindset), but rather that turmoil among the existing jihadist groups and dissatisfaction with their performance among their donors seemed to offer opportunities for a new entrant in the arena. If IS could attract a substantial number of fighters and commanders away from the existing jihadist organizations and secure sufficient funding, it could establish a beachhead in 'Khorasan' and from there deploy its renowned military and organizational skills to great effect.

In this sense, IS-K like IS-Central itself is a product of decades of conflict in the region. These wars have created a 'military class' of professional insurgents so large that from within its ranks have emerged movements and organizations that aim to appeal primarily if not exclusively to that very military class, oblivious to the wider social context of the region. Although IS is not the only organization catering to this 'military class', it positioned itself as particularly competitive by offering better employment conditions, claiming to understand and respect insurgent 'professionalism' and most importantly promising never-ending conflict (implicit in its ambitious aims). This is what gives IS its chance in 'Khorasan': what the Middle East and Khorasan have in common is the existence of this military class of professional insurgents, if not much else. The ideological and cultural equivalent of this military class has been what Osman called the 'jihadi-celebrating literature' generated from the 1980s jihad onwards:

> This literature has created a culture in which dying in the fight against incumbent authority for an Islamic cause is the heroic sacrifice of a martyr. Violence becomes particularly compelling if undertaken against a foreign, non-Muslim entity that is perceived as challenging Afghan sovereignty or pride. This decades-long romanticizing of aggressive jihad has been inspiring all of the various strands of jihadists in Afghanistan and the region.[1]

The plan was in line with IS's self-perception and philosophy, but it appeared far-fetched (to say the least) to everybody else. Many observers believed it was simply a 'mission impossible'. Almost nobody initially believed IS could grow any roots in the region, and the near consensus was that the extent of what IS-K would achieve would be recruiting a few opportunists and making some noise for a while. Still, IS-K turned out to be more than the flare-up of a single summer in Afghanistan. From the perspective of the author, writing in autumn 2021, it still looks premature to write IS-K off as having failed its mission.

The fighting and the territorial gains of the summer of 2015, while dramatic, were never part of the original plan, and as such were not affected by being rolled back during 2016. IS-K was not looking to seize territory for good, but rather to undermine Taliban governance and uproot it from its turf. All IS-K needed to hold onto were its main base in Afghanistan, in Mohmand Valley of Achin district, and a few smaller bases sprinkled around Nangarhar. These bases allowed IS-K to maintain its command and control system, its logistics and its administration, as well as to 'garrison' its men when the fighting was not going on. IS-K did not initially have the same policy as the Taliban of quartering its men in the villages. The IS-K leadership assumed that the Taliban, busy fighting the US-supported Islamic Republic, would not be able to commit sufficient forces to crush IS-K. This strategy, however, entailed two risks: a dragged-on confrontation with the Taliban, at the expense of IS-K's other objectives, could alienate donors who played an essential role in funding IS-K, while if the Taliban entered peace talks with the Americans that could allow them to concentrate their forces against IS-K.

All about money?

Clearly, the financial resources made available by IS-Central and Arab Gulf donors were instrumental in making such an ambitious operation as IS-K happen.

Does this mean that the support IS-K gathered was essentially mercenary in nature? If the people who joined IS-K had been mercenaries, they could well have joined the Afghan security forces or the Pakistani Frontier Corps, or any of the many militias roaming around the region (especially Afghanistan). They would have enjoyed an easier life, better prospects to stay alive, lower salaries but greater opportunities for making money on the side, and they would not have been bothered by Salafi trainers and advisers trying to instil alien ideas in their minds.

It seems more appropriate to speak of 'professional jihadis' who saw in IS-K a better vehicle than the Taliban or TTP for them to keep pursuing their jihadist aims. The funds made it possible for this mix of professional insurgents and believers in global jihad to quit the local insurgent organizations where they were 'trapped' and join a new organization more in line with their ambitions.

The IS template

To what extent is IS-K a clone of IS-Central? The harsh and rigid implementation of an extremist Salafist interpretation of Shari'a appears to have been almost universal in IS-K territory, at least as long as Hafiz Saeed was governor. The only concession, at least until opposition arose to IS-K control, was the temporary sidelining of *takfir*. Initially, IS-K also offered a polite approach to the village elders and the (selective) waiving of local taxes. The experience of IS-Central in Iraq and Syria suggests that the latter two would have been temporary concessions in any case.

IS-K has also adopted practices such as an exaggerated show of force to intimidate its adversaries and spread panic. This seems to have worked, even if it should be taken into account that IS-K mostly confronted local Taliban militias rather than their better-trained and equipped mobile forces. If IS-K seemed better in general than the Taliban at concentrating forces rapidly to achieve tactical superiority, it was also because crack Taliban units were mostly focused against the Taliban's main objectives, such as Kunduz, Lashkargah and a few other cities. This same ability and tendency to concentrate forces has, however, also exposed IS-K and its command centres to US air strikes, which took a heavy toll. After the deaths of Logari and a group of other senior figures in Kunar in August 2017, IS-K lowered its profile and focused more on small groups tactics, which allowed it to operate under the (American) radar.

Given the absence of such assets as the former Ba'athist officers and specialists, who form the backbone of IS-Central's army, we should expect that sophisticated military skills might prove hard to transfer to IS-K. The advisers and trainers sent in relatively large numbers from the summer of 2015 would take years to shape a new IS-K 'officer corps'. IS-K faced a conventional offensive against its stronghold in Nangarhar (Mohmand Valley) for the first time in spring 2017, where it showed resilience against superior forces. More in general, it remained able to operate despite the loss of several senior figures, which suggests the existence of a strong cadre structure. However, their ability to inflict casualties on the mix of Afghan and US forces that engaged them in that and other occasions is not clear. When faced with an offensive by a hybrid Taliban force in late 2019, IS-K forces collapsed. They were already demoralized before the Taliban offensive began, but the hybridity of the attacking forces clearly represents a bigger challenge for IS-K than the clumsy and slow joint Islamic Republic–US offensive of 2017.

The IS-K interviewees certainly displayed a strengthened, if not altogether new, pride of belonging to a genuinely global jihadist movement. Hostility towards Shi'as was not quite as universal as might be expected, but several interviewees admitted that their views of Shi'as had hardened considerably after joining IS-K. Should we take this as evidence that IS-Central has been able, through its advisers and by keeping IS-K members in Syria and Iraq for shifts of 6 months or more, to inculcate its ideological views? Interestingly, IS-K interviewees all deny being members of a Salafist organization, but virtually all the village and tribal elders interviewed (in Kajaki and Nangarhar) viewed them as Salafis or, even worse, 'Wahabis', a term of abuse in Afghanistan.[2] It would appear that, whether or not out of genuine belief, IS-K has been putting into practice the ideology that it has imported from IS-Central. This is important because Salafism has especially weak roots in Afghanistan; even in Pakistan it was mostly Panjpiris who joined IS-K, as opposed to Deobandis. Even the Salafis found in growing numbers in eastern Afghanistan (Nuristan, Kunar, parts of Nangarhar) are usually not as rigid as the Middle Eastern ones.

If IS-K had wanted to make quick gains in Khorasan for solely pragmatic reasons, applying such strict enforcement of Salafi Shari'a would have made little sense. However, it is true that IS-K abstained from using *takfir* against its enemies. Perhaps as IS-K leaders such as Hafiz Saeed and his successors perceived it, they were already going quite a long way in accommodating local conditions.

In the few areas that it brought under its control for any length of time, IS-K appears to have adopted the same type of top-down governance IS relied on in

Syria and Iraq, with subject communities allowed very little say over the rigid rules imposed on them. In fact, the Taliban and TTP have also engaged with local elders only to a very limited extent on governance issues, so in this case the attitude displayed by IS-K might not necessarily derive from IS-Central.

Busy establishing a foothold in the region, it took until the summer of 2016 for IS-K to launch its campaign against Shi'as on a significant scale. Were the attacks against Shi'as merely efforts to please donors in the Arab Gulf, or were they the beginning of an attempt to create chaos, provoke indiscriminate retaliation by Shi'as against Sunni Muslims and then position IS-K as the defender of Sunnism in Khorasan? While IS-K sources indicate that the main terrorist attacks against Shi'as in Kabul were the direct result of donor pressure, a longer-term plan to unleash a spiral of sectarian violence is not incompatible. For sure, IS-K has been focusing on 'near enemies', and, despite its anti-American and anti-Western rhetoric, it hardly paid any attention to Western targets in Kabul or elsewhere.

The jury is still out over the actual degree of centralization of IS-K. While the links to IS-Central are clear, within Khorasan the local leadership has clearly struggled to assert its authority. This has led some authors to conclude, like Mielke and Miszak, that IS-K lacked 'a central and Khorasan-wide co-ordination of Daesh's activities'.[3] As discussed in the book, IS implicitly accepted over time that running a centralized effort throughout Khorasan was not possible: IS-K/Bukhara and IS-K/Iran soon became de facto completely autonomous, and in 2019 Wilayat Pakistan and Wilayat Hind emerged. By then, the leadership of IS-K was only controlling the Afghan theatre of operations. Not only were these regions far-off and hard to communicate with, but in none of them did IS have sufficient forces to make a centralized effort worthwhile: its presence there was limited to tens or at most a few hundred cells operating underground and planning terror attacks.

However, in Afghanistan IS-K insisted on concentrating ethnically and nationally mixed forces and moving them between distant locations until 2019–20, something very hard to do without some kind of relatively capable central leadership. At one point, the various component groups of IS-K and their individual leaders were even banned from raising any revenue of their own. The loosening of the ban seems to reflect more that the leadership had accepted the impossibility of implementing it, rather than a real need for more revenue overall.

IS-K initially struggled to forge the disparate groups that merged into it into a coherent whole, but by 2019 that seemed to have been largely achieved.

However, some sub-groupings survived (the Haqqania, Khilafat Shamal, Central Asians), and ethnic fault lines consolidated (the Pakistanis, the Afghan Pashtuns). Despite this negative assessment, IS-Central's efforts to export its organizational skills to Khorasan were partially successful. IS-K members all raved about how their new home organization excelled at meritocracy:

> In the Taliban it works like this, those who are selected, they are selected based on friendship, based on tribe, those who have a lot of men and recommendations even if they are not intelligent. They cannot do a great job and cannot control their men and cannot advance the cause of Taliban in their areas. On the other hand, Daesh is not selecting such people even if they have a lot of followers, they are selecting those people who are intelligent, have military skills and spent a lot of time fighting.[4]

While IS-K members might not be reliable sources, as discussed in the text above they are not the only ones who viewed it as having superior organization and skills; perhaps the only exception was an officer of the Revolutionary Guards (Iran), who was dismissive of the fighting skills of IS-K.

Tampering with the template

External donors' dissatisfaction with IS-K's obsession with the Taliban obsession soon became obvious. By the spring of 2016, IS-K's leadership was trying to steer the organization in a different direction, but getting rid of the conflict with the Taliban proved difficult. IS-K members talked openly about their intention to compete with the Taliban and eventually to replace them. This made appeasement quite unappealing for the Taliban, even if in some cases factions within it had specific, short-term reasons for establishing a *modus vivendi* with IS-K.

Appeasement with the Taliban was probably meant to buy some IS-K some time while it sorted out some internal issues. By autumn 2016, IS-K was in any case ready to go on the offensive again. This time, IS-K even risked compromising its relationship with the Haqqani network in south-eastern Afghanistan, as it could not resist the temptation of exploiting and manipulating tribal rivalries in the region. In Zabul, IS-K spent the second half of 2016 fighting the Taliban. The death of 'governor' Hafiz Saeed allowed a more pragmatic approach to emerge, with local IS-K members being asked to co-opt their own communities, along the lines of what was done in Iraq and Syria during the advance of IS-Central. The lifting of the ban on the narcotics trade in south-western Afghanistan was a major example of this new-found pragmatism.

CONCLUSION

Implications of IS-K's arrival

IS-K did not need to take over much of Khorasan to deeply affect the political and military landscape of the region. Indeed, it was already having a major impact during 2015, as some regional powers (Iran first and foremost, but increasingly also Russia, China and Pakistan) started tweaking their regional diplomacy in order to confront what they perceived as a threat. Afghanistan's politics were affected as the emergence of IS-K entrenched Iran's opposition to a Kabul–Taliban reconciliation, as the Iranians feared a massive flow of disgruntled Taliban hardliners towards IS-K. At the same time, the Iranians stopped pushing their Taliban allies towards intensified military operations against Afghan and NATO forces, and instead started asking them to re-orient efforts towards IS-K.

By the second half of 2016, seemingly stung by IS-K's attacks on Pakistan territory, the Pakistani authorities were also reconsidering their earlier flirtation with IS-K and edging closer to the Russians and Iranians in an effort to contain it. As IS-K increasingly turned into a jihadist hub inside Pakistan, either incorporating jihadist groups or establishing alliances with them, the Islamabad authorities seem to have started becoming worried about where it could lead. Still, even after 2016 they continued wavering between confrontation and co-optation.

The jihadist organizations of Khorasan, already among the protagonists of the political life of at least Afghanistan and Pakistan, were of course affected by the arrival of IS-K more than any other actor. Appendix 4 tries to represent the impact graphically. Comparing Appendix 3 and Appendix 4 shows clearly how the jihadist landscape changed between 2011 and 2017. At one stage or another, almost all organizations and factions engaged with IS-K, and most of them established a clientele relationship with it. A new stream of funding became available, allowing several of these organizations to break free of their previous allegiances. The debates kickstarted by IS-K's arrival eventually split the jihadist galaxy, which had previously been loosely organized around AQ, between two camps: pro-IS and pro-AQ. Initially, the various jihadist groups tried to ride two horses, but this study suggests that such an option was available only for a limited time. The example of the Central Asian jihadists is particularly illustrative: during 2015 and 2016 the attraction of two opposite poles (IS and AQ) ended up splitting them into two rival alliances.

What this 'deep dive' into IS-K tells us

The period of IS-K's existence covered in this study represents the inception phase of the group in the 'Khorasan' region. When measured against the huge ambitions stated by IS-Central, IS-K appears a failure. In reality, in its first 2 years or so of existence IS-K did start playing a significant role, at least in the Afghan political and military environment; it also had an impact on the worlds of Central Asian and Baluchi—and, to a lesser extent, Pakistani—jihadists. Although in the case of the Central Asians the process owed a lot to developments taking place in the Middle East (where a large portion of the members of the Central Asian jihadist organizations had been in 2013–16), these achievements are not exactly modest ones for an insurgent organization to achieve in its first 2 years of existence. Historically, most successful insurgent organizations barely achieve name recognition in their inception phase, which is why few if any insurgencies have ever had their initial stages of development studied in detail.

The picture emerging from our deep dive on the immature IS-K of 2014–16 shows a messy picture of blunders and mistakes, arguments and internecine conflict, personal rivalries and lengthy negotiations with potential future stakeholders. The initial instinct of IS-Central as well as many local IS-K members was to replicate as much as possible the original IS template: a militarist-centralized approach, where strong Salafi indoctrination would provide the glue keeping the organization together and equip it with an esprit de corps unmatched by any rival organization.

The original template, unsurprisingly, did not work. As evidence of this failure started emerging, many observers were tempted to write IS-K off as a shipwreck. IS-K, however, with input from IS-Central, demonstrated an ability to act pragmatically and flexibly, and to learn from its mistakes. IS-Central managed to steer IS-K in a different direction by appointing more politically minded leaders, first Abu Yasir Al-Afghani and then Hasibullah Logari. The process was bumpy and slow, as even IS-Central would not dare remove the controversial 'governor' of Wilayat Khorasan, Hafiz Saeed, lest the largest component group within IS-K, the TKP, disintegrate. Hafiz Saeed's death in August 2016 eventually made leadership change possible.

Luckily for IS-K, its weaknesses in the inception phase were not exploited by any of its enemies. As IS-K approached maturity and consolidated organizationally and ideologically, defeating it became much harder. One would be tempted to infer (in line with recent literature on counter-insurgency) that the early stages of an insurgency's development should thus warrant more attention at the policy-making level, as opposed to dismissing the existence of the problem until it gets out of hand.

What does the experience of IS-K up to early 2017 tell us about IS as such? Although there was clearly a strong ideological thrust in the emergence of IS, the 'Caliphate' was clearly not so blinded by Salafi principles that it was unable to make pragmatic decisions, at least at its highest level. It is also clear that IS's strategy goes far beyond the Middle East, and that IS-K was never meant to be a sideshow. While the Caliphate might not be about building a real Caliphate (at least not in the short and medium term), it seems to genuinely be about establishing hegemony first and asserting undisputed leadership over the global jihad started by AQ years back. IS-Central poured considerable resources into IS-K in 2014–15 and continued to do so at a time when it was more and more embattled in Iraq and Syria, in 2016 and early 2017.

The jury is still out with regard to IS-Central's ability to export its specific 'know-how' as a jihadist organization. This study has shown that IS-Central has been struggling so far in implementing its template, and that it has had to accept modifications in a number of ways. IS-Central's insistence on aiming towards a monolithic organization, with a single chain of command, had to be compromised in Afghanistan in order to keep the disparate groups that came to form IS-K together. In 2017–21, the process of adaptation continued, but IS-Central seems to have ultimately have lost patience with the never-ending power struggles affecting IS-K and imposed a new governor of its own choice in 2020.

Potential for further expansion

The first condition that will have to be in place for IS-K to keep growing is of course continued large-scale funding. The average cost of keeping an IS-K fighter on the ground was significantly higher that the Taliban's, who were themselves dependent on external funding even if their internal revenue collection was much higher than IS-K's. Therefore, even if IS-K were to greatly improve local revenue collection, its dependency on external funding would continue, especially if the organization were to expand its ranks. Perhaps the only alternative option for IS-K would be to attract substantial funding from drug-smuggling gangs. As of October 2021, there was no obvious reason why the gangs would want to boost IS-K with substantial funding, although that could change if for whatever reason the Taliban were to curb drug smuggling.

The likelihood of IS-K being able to draw large amounts of funding has depended on its positioning along the axes of the regional rivalries opposing Pakistan and India, Iran and Saudi Arabia and, to a lesser extent, Saudi Arabia and Russia. IS-K had to deliver 'goods' in exchange for this funding, and its failure to do so in many cases accounts for the fluctuation in its funding. Still, the rivalries were still there in 2021. While Afghanistan was turning into a regional proxy battlefield, Pakistan was different: it was clear that Arab Gulf donors were not interested in seeing it destabilized, even if they might not mind attacks targeted at Pakistan's Shi'a minority. It is noteworthy that IS-K appears to have defied the views and desires of many of its donors by continually trying to kickstart operations in Pakistan. Perhaps the underlying idea was to force the hand of the pro-jihadist circles in the Gulf and start a sectarian conflict in Pakistan, then position itself as the only real defender of Sunni Muslims against Shi'a retaliatory attacks.

Indeed, IS-K has long been courting LeJ and Jundullah, as well as anti-Shi'a elements in TTP, but as late as October 2021 it had not yet been able to absorb them, possibly because its position in Pakistan was not that well established. Another possible reason, however, is low support among real and potential donors for IS-K operations in Pakistan. Donors might have to accept the *fait accompli* if IS-K manages to get a sectarian jihad going in Pakistan, but the initial hurdle to clear for IS-K has always been a steep one. There have been signs of Shi'a activism in response to sectarian violence against them being on the rise. Hence, IS-K's calculus of investing its (limited) capabilities in Pakistan to push further in the direction of a sectarian civil war does not appear too far-fetched. In addition, such a strategy would have the additional benefit of putting to 'good use' the growing number of Punjabi recruits.

The drawbacks are also obvious: the Pakistani authorities would not tolerate attacks inside Pakistan beyond a low threshold. As mentioned above, the Pakistani authorities reached out quite early on to both Russia and Iran to co-ordinate against IS-K, and to Iran to defuse sectarian tensions in Pakistan. During 2016, violence against Shi'as recorded a big drop on the previous year, probably indicating a crackdown by the Pakistani authorities on sectarian groups.[5] They seemed to be taking another turn against IS-K after the fall of Kabul to the Taliban.

Assuming funding is available, IS-K might have the chance of exploiting various new opportunities for growth inside Afghanistan. The difficulties of the Taliban after they took Kabul on 15 August 2021 left many of their members feeling disgruntled and unrewarded for their sacrifices. IS-K is known to have tried to attract such elements; as of the end of October 2021, it was enjoying some tactical successes. There was also clear potential for IS-K to absorb some of the professional military of the Islamic Republic, who had been left jobless, dejected and full of hatred for the Taliban following the fall of their government. Again, as of October 2021, there were indications that IS-K was enjoying some initial success in this regard too. The same would apply to the TTP if they were ever to accede to reconciliation with Islamabad, which seemed a remote possibility at the time of writing.

In the past too IS-K proved capable of being tactically shrewd and dynamic, capable of exploiting any fissure within the ranks of its enemies and competitors. With Hafiz Saeed gone, IS-K appears to have become more pragmatic, and more willing to push Salafism to the side, for the time being at least. Tribal elders were offered a lot of autonomy in exchange for allowing IS-K into their areas, and the opium ban was lifted. However, the heavy-handed approach of the early years, whose impact was renewed by repeated gruesome terrorist attacks in the cities, prevented any breakthrough in expanding IS-K's appeal.

Signs of youth radicalization were already there years before the fall of Kabul in 2021. The Taliban's power grab looked particularly frustrating to university students, who mostly had little faith in the ability of the Emirate to provide job and career opportunities for them. This seemed to be offering opportunities for IS-K, which had already established a modest presence in the campuses before.

Overpopulation in the rural areas of Afghanistan and the tribal areas of north-west Pakistan generates growing numbers of increasingly loose youth, who might not be aligned with IS-K ideologically but could conceivably be attracted and socialized into the organization. For now, IS-K has stayed mostly away from recruiting ideologically spurious elements, but the situation might change once it is in a position to recruit and deploy large numbers of fighters.

In sum, for IS-K Afghanistan remained by far the most promising ground in Khorasan in 2021, with Pakistan as the distant runner-up. Conversely, any chance of IS-K being able to kickstart jihads in Central Asia and China appeared to have evaporated.

Vulnerabilities of IS-K

IS-K's most obvious vulnerability is its extreme dependency on external funding. While the debate on IS-Central finances and funding is still going on, it is clear that IS-K has not just been dependent on funding from IS-Central, but that it has also needed additional external funding from third-party donors in order to establish itself and expand. While regional rivals' proxy wars might seem destined to last forever, so did the Cold War. Like the Cold War insurgencies, sponsored by either the Soviets or the Americans, IS-K might suddenly cease to be useful to its patrons, and indeed the level of third-party funding has been declining for years.

Were funding from IS-Central to dry up entirely, IS-K would suffer from the final collapse of IS-Central structures, in particular of the latter's ability to send money to its branches. Such a collapse could be in part mitigated by the re-direction of donor funding (previously accruing to IS-Central) towards IS-K.

If the Taliban's regime were able to consolidate, it would be well positioned to crush IS-K, which is unpopular among locals:

> One thing in which IS-K is better than Taliban is that it is not collecting *Ushr* from the villagers. But villagers are ready to pay every time tax to Taliban in order to avoid Daesh operating in their area, because villagers became tired of Daesh brutality. Before Daesh appeared in our district, villagers always tried to somehow support the Afghan government to push back the Taliban from their villages, but now the villagers are trying to somehow support the Taliban to push back Daesh from their villages.[6]

> When there were only Taliban groups in our area before Daesh appeared in our district, we prayed for the Afghan government to take the control of our area but from the time when Daesh appeared and started their operations, now we are praying that Taliban come to our area, now we prefer Taliban to Daesh. We lost our hope from the Afghan government to come and take control of our area.[7]

Although in late 2021 IS-K was trying to exploit heavy-handed Taliban repression, which often targeted Salafis as suspected members of IS-K, it remains to be seen whether this will be enough to create some kind of mass base for IS in eastern Afghanistan.

The diplomatic crisis between Qatar and Saudi Arabia, which burst into the public domain in June 2017, had the potential to seriously disrupt IS-K funding. Qatari and Saudi sources of funding, always competing for influence, are likely to step up their competition and impose on IS-K increasingly incompatible aims.

A fugitive IS-Central leadership would face even greater difficulties in managing IS-K than the one based in Mosul and Raqqa, although some of its members could relocate to Afghanistan itself, as IS-K sources suggest. Deprived of external guidance, the latter's internal rivalries could resurface and conceivably paralyze the organization again, and possibly split it altogether. The prospect of IS-K resembling AQ more and more in the way it is organized (as discussed in the Introduction) appears increasingly likely.

The web of fundraising that IS-K (with IS-Central support) weaved has also trapped it in a conundrum, where whichever course of action it takes is bound to upset one or the other donor. IS-K promised to kickstart or revamp all kinds of 'jihads' everywhere, in Khorasan and beyond, when its reputation of invincibility seemed to be still holding. It ended up being a prisoner of its own promises: to start jihad in Pakistan, and at the same time not to destabilize Pakistan; to start jihads in Iran and Central Asia within 1–2 years, without having capabilities even remotely approaching those needed; to start a sectarian war in Afghanistan, while needing to establish a firm foothold first (which brought it into conflict with the Taliban).

It is worth mentioning that among IS-K vulnerabilities was the risk of being caught in a renewed US air-strike campaign, in retaliation for the 26 August attack at Kabul airport, that killed thirteen US servicemen. The IS-K leadership appears to have kept itself safer after April 2020, probably hanging around in the wooded areas of Kunar. In the future, the United States will have limited intelligence assets of its own, meaning its drones will find fewer targets to hit, unless it establishes forms of co-operation with the Taliban.

APPENDIX 1

THE NEW *LAYHA* OF TEHRIK-E-KHALIFAT

1: Tehrik-e-Khalifat of Pakistan must invite those Pakistani Taliban who are working for TTP to join the Tehrik-e-Khalifat (Abubakar Bughdadi). For this purpose, to make our group bigger, and perform operations against Pakistan Government and Afghan Government.

2: Those who joined Tehrik-e-Khalifat of Pakistan but were working with the TTP must return to the TTP the weapons which were given to them by TTP leaders. New types of weapons and money will be given to them by Tehrik-e-Khalifat of Pakistan.

3: When someone joined with Tehrik-e-Khalifat and then breaks his oath, he will not be forgiven. If someone wants to recommend him for a second time, he needs to talk with the higher authority of Tehrik-e-Khalifat.

4: If a fighter from Pakistani Taliban or the Afghan Taliban joins Tehrik-e-Khalifat, the leaders and commanders of Tehrik-e-Khalifat will promise him that he will be safe. In case this new recruit is killed or harmed by Pakistan Taliban or Afghan Taliban, then Tehrik-e-Khalifat will enquire and protest.

5: Tehrik-e-Khalifat must maintain good relations with all the tribal communities and the Taliban, so that they are always welcome and are able to get help from the local people and the Taliban.

6: The higher authority can always consult with their subordinates regarding Jihadi equipment and money. These must be given to them from Tehrik-e-Khalifat.

7: The higher authority and the commanders do not have the right to collect donations such as *zakat* and *ushr* from local people.

8: The uniform of Tehrik-e-Khalifat must be different from that of the Taliban, so that they can be recognized to their leaders. It means they must have mask and black dresses.

9: Tehrik-e-Khalifat must work under the Black Flag, which is representing Abu Bakr al-Baghdadi.

APPENDIX 2

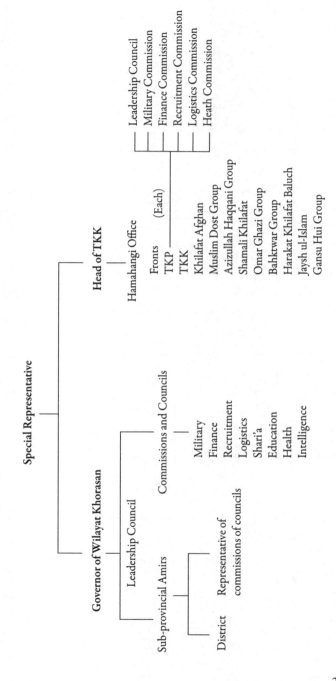

Special Representative

Head of TKK

Hamahangi Office

(Each)

Fronts
TKP
TKK
Khilafat Afghan
Muslim Dost Group
Azizullah Haqqani Group
Shamali Khilafat
Omar Ghazi Group
Bahktwar Group
Harakat Khilafat Baluch
Jaysh ul-Islam
Gansu Hui Group

Leadership Council
Military Commission
Finance Commission
Recruitment Commission
Logistics Commission
Heath Commission

Governor of Wilayat Khorasan

Leadership Council

Commissions and Councils

Military
Finance
Recruitment
Logistics
Shari'a
Education
Health
Intelligence

Sub-provincial Amirs

Representative of
commissions of councils

District

Sources: Notebook of senior cadre; interviews with cadres and leaders of IS-K.

255

APPENDIX 3

The Jihadist network of Khorasan in 2011, according to interviewees. Only the main groups and organizations are mentioned.

Relations with AQ are shown with thick lines when the connection is strong, and with thin lines when it is weak or limited to elements within the organization. The graph is only for illustrative purposes and is a greatly simplified representation. It should be kept in mind that the complexities and nuances of the relationship between AQ and other organizations cannot be represented in such a way.

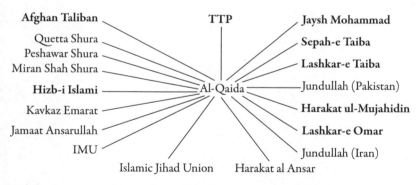

Sources: Interviews with members of jihadist organizations, 2013–17.

APPENDIX 4

The Jihadist network of Khorasan in 2017, according to interviewees. Only the main groups and organizations are mentioned.

Relations with AQ or IS are shown with thick lines when the connection was strong, and with thin lines when it was weak or limited to elements within the organization. The graph is only for illustrative purposes and is a greatly simplified representation. It should be kept in mind that the complexities and nuances of the relationship between AQ, IS and other organizations cannot be represented in such a way.

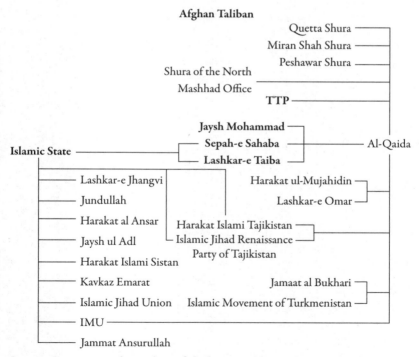

Sources: Interviews with members of jihadist organizations, 2013–17.

NOTES

INTRODUCTION

1. Haleem, 'Will IS turn guns towards Afghanistan?', *Xinhua*, 20 September 2014.
2. Interview with IS-K 1, Khorasan-level leader, June 2015; interview with IS-K 2, leader, October 2015.
3. Amir Mir, 'IS makes inroads into Pakistan', *Asia Times*, 27 June 2016.
4. Borhan Osman, 'The shadows of "Islamic State" in Afghanistan: what threat does it hold?', AAN, 12 February 2015, https://www.afghanistan-analysts.org/wp-admin/post.php, downloaded: 19 February 2015.
5. Franz J. Marty, 'The looming specter of Daesh in Afghanistan', *Foreign Policy*, 9 February 2015. See also Saleha Sadat, 'Militants posing as ISIS are Taliban: Nazari', *TOLOnews.com*, 19 January 2015.
6. 'Taliban militants raise Daesh Flags in Jowzjan: Officials', *TOLOnews.com*, 11 February 2015.
7. Carlo Munoz and Jon Harper, 'Intelligence gaps may help Islamic State gain foothold in Afghanistan', *Stripes*, 20 April 2015.
8. Qadir Habib and Michael Scollon, 'Afghanistan wakes up to Islamic State threat', *Rferl*, 15 February 2015.
9. Interview with Elder 1, Kajaki, Helmand, December 2015.
10. See, for example, Akhilesh Pillalamarri, 'Taliban vs. ISIS: the Islamic State is doomed in Afghanistan', *The National Interest*, 11 June 2015; Barnett R. Rubin, 'ISIS cannot succeed in Afghanistan. No Afghans will give up their national identity. Not like Arab world or Pakistan', Twitter post, 30 December 2014. (https://twitter.com/brrubin/status/549937898108510208, checked 5 February 2017).
11. Rivka Azoulay, 'Islamic State franchising tribes, transnational jihadi networks and generational shifts', CRU report, April 2015, p. 41.
12. Jack Covarrubias, Tom Lansford, *The New Islamic State: Ideology, Religion and Violent Extremism in the 21st Century*, London: Routledge, 2016; Cole Bunzel, 'From paper state to Caliphate: the ideology of the Islamic State', Brookings,

Analysis Paper No. 19, March 2015; Dominique Thomas, *Générations djihadistes: Al-Qaïda—Etat islamique: histoire d'une lutte fratricide*, Paris: Michalon, 2016.

13. Brian H. Fishman, *The Master Plan*, New Haven, CT: Yale University Press, 2016, p. 137.

14. Lina Khatib, 'The Islamic State's strategy: lasting and expanding', Carnegie Middle East Center, 29 June 2015.

15. Fishman, op. cit., p. 93, quoting Abu Bakr Naji's *The Management of Savagery*.

16. Charles Lister, 'Profiling the Islamic State', Brookings Doha Center Analysis Paper, No. 13, December 2014, p. 7.

17. Fawaz A. Gerges, *ISIS: A History*, Princeton, NJ: Princeton University Press, 2016, locations 444–52.

18. Gerges, op. cit., location 3854.

19. Malcolm Nance, *Defeating ISIS: Who They Are, How They Fight, What They Believe*, New York: Skyhorse Publishing, 2016, location 5089ff; Michael Weiss and Hassan Hassan, *ISIS: Inside the Army of Terror*, New York: Regan Arts, 2015, location 3343; Gerges, op. cit., location 797.

20. Moubayed, op. cit., location 2704; Gerges, op. cit., location 749.

21. Gerges, op. cit., location 4373.

22. Laurentina Cizza and Karim Mezran, 'Libia: la sfida dello Stato Islamico', in ISPI, *L'Italia e la minaccia jihadista. Quale politica estera?*, ed. by Stefano M. Torelli and Arturo Varvelli, May 2015.

23. Gerges, op. cit., location 3408.

24. Gerges, op. cit., location 4838.

25. Gerges, op. cit., location 4418.

26. Scott Atran, *L'état Islamique est une revolution*, Paris: LLL, 2016, p. 76, quoting Abu Bakr Naji.

27. Audrey Kurth Cronin, 'ISIS is not a terrorist group', *Foreign Affairs*, March/April 2015.

28. Lister, 2014, op. cit., p. 21.

29. Gabi Siboni, 'The military power of the Islamic State', http://www.inss.org.il/, 29 January 2015, pp. 68–9.

30. Moubayed, op. cit., location 1870–979; Nance, op. cit., location 5659.

31. Moubayed, op. cit., location 1946.

32. Moubayed, op. cit., location 1002. Note that not every analyst agrees on Abu Musaab al-Suri's key role in shaping AQ's strategy.

33. Brian H. Fishman, *The Master Plan*, pp. 268–9, 275.

34. Baczko et al., *Syrie: anatomie d'une guerre civile*, Paris: CNRS, 2016, p. 245 ff.

35. Gerges, op. cit., location 3413.

36. Brian H. Fishman, op. cit., pp. 188–9.

37. Brian H. Fishman, op. cit., p. 185.

38. Brian H. Fishman, op. cit., p. 232, quoting Uthman bin Abd al-Rahman al-Tamimi,

Informing the People About the Islamic State of Iraq, Islamic State of Iraq Ministry of Shariah, 2006.

39. Aymenn Jawad Al-Tamimi, 'How the Islamic State governs', *The Journal of International Security Affairs*, winter 2016, No. 30.

40. Brian H. Fishman, op. cit., p. 522.

41. Deveed Gartenstein-Ross et al., 'Islamic state vs. al-Qaeda: strategic dimensions of a patricidal conflict', New America Foundation, 2015.

42. Gerges, op. cit., location 4100.

43. Moubayed, op. cit.; Lister, 2014, op. cit.

44. Weiss and Hassan, op. cit.; Sami Moubayed, *Under the Black Flag: At the Frontier of the New Jihad*, London: IB Tauris, 2015; Charles Lister, 'Profiling the Islamic State', Brookings Doha Center Analysis Paper, No. 13, December 2014; Jack Covarrubias and Tom Lansford, op. cit.; Moubayed, op. cit., locations 1979–2074.

45. Baczko et al., *Syrie: anatomie d'une guerre civile*, p. 245 ff.

46. William McCants, *The ISIS Apocalypse: The History, Strategy, and Doomsday Vision of the Islamic State*, New York: St. Martin's Press, 2015, locations 2374, 2649; Weiss and Hassan, op. cit., locations 3011–12, 3028, 3269; Frederic Wehrey and Ala' Alrababah'h, 'An elusive courtship: the struggle for Iraq's Sunni Arab tribes', New York: Carnegie, 7 November 2014; Koumay al-Mulhem, 'Le tribù di Ninive: la base dello «Stato islamico»', in Massimiliano Trentin (ed.), *L'ultimo califfato: L'Organizzazione dello Stato islamico in Medio Oriente*, Bologna, Italy: Il Mulino, 2017.

47. Barbara de Poli, 'Il Califfato di al-Baghdadi: l'ideologia dello Stato Islamico', in Massimiliano Trentin (ed.), *L'ultimo califfato: L'Organizzazione dello Stato islamico in Medio Oriente*, Bologna, Italy: Il Mulino, 2017.

48. Matthieu Rey, 'Dall'Iraq al Medio Oriente', in Massimiliano Trentin (ed.), *L'ultimo califfato: L'Organizzazione dello Stato islamico in Medio Oriente*, Bologna, Italy: Il Mulino, 2017.

49. Interview with External Observer/Participant 6, Taliban military cadre, Helmand, January 2016; 'Al-Zawahiri denounces US, argues for reign of Islamic law and Caliphate, jihad against crusaders and Jews', FBIS Report-GMP20050131000021, 31 January 2005; Hamid Mir, 'Pakistan interviews Usama Bin Ladin', FBIS, 18 March 1997; Ayman Al-Zawahiri, *Knights Under the Prophet's Banner*, Manzel al Tawhid al Jihad, n.d. (2001); Edwin Bakker and Leen Boer, 'The evolution of Al-Qaedaism', The Hague, Netherlands: Clingendael, December 2007; Murad Batal al-Shishani, 'Al Qaeda grows as its leaders focus on the "near enemy"', *The National*, 30 August 2013; Murad Batal al-Shishani, 'Understanding strategic change in al-Qaeda's central leadership after Bin Laden', *Terrorism Monitor*, Vol. 9, Iss. 23, 9 June 2011; Sajjan M. Gohel, 'Deciphering Ayman Al-Zawahiri and

Al-Qaeda's strategic and ideological imperatives', *Perspectives on Terrorism*, Vol. 11, No. 1 (2017).

50. Thomas F. Lynch III, 'The Islamic State as Icarus', Washington, DC: Woodrow Wilson Center, 2015.

51. Baczko et al., op. cit., p. 271; Graeme Wood, *The Way of the Strangers: Encounters With the Islamic State*, New York: Random House, 2016, locations 2094ff, 4468ff.

52. Fishman, op. cit., p. 232.

53. Bunzel, op. cit.; Fishman, op. cit.

54. Azoulay, op. cit., p. 41.

55. Daveed Gartenstein-Ross, op. cit.

56. Thomas F. Lynch III, The Impact of ISIS on Global Salafism and South Asian Jihad, Hudson Institute, August 2015.

57. Charles Lister, 'Jihadi rivalry: the Islamic State challenges al-Qaida', Brookings Doha Center Analysis Paper, No. 16, January 2016; Paul Rogers, 'Irregular war: ISIS and the new threat from the margins', London: IB Tauris, location 1891; Dominique Thomas, *Générations djihadistes: Al-Qaïda—Etat islamique: histoire d'une lutte fratricide*, Paris: Michalon, 2016.

58. Ari Heistein, 'ISIS's fight with Al Qaeda is making both stronger', *The National Interest*, 7 January 2016.

59. Moubayed, op. cit., location 1985.

60. Joby Warrick, *Black Flags: The Rise of ISIS*, New York: Anchor, 2016, location 4542.

61. Moubayed, op. cit., Location 2453ff.

62. Nance, op. cit., location 4541ff.

63. Moubayed, op. cit., location 2504; Nance, op. cit., location 4306ff and 5272ff.

64. Azoulay, op. cit., p. 41.

65. See 'The Rafidah', *Rabi al Akhir*, No. 13, 1437 (January/February 2016), for the position of IS towards Shi'ism.

66. Omar Ashour, 'Enigma of "Baqiya wa Tatamadad": the Islamic State organization's military survival', Al Jazeera Centre for Studies, 19 April 2016.

67. Seth G. Jones et al., *Rolling Back the Islamic State*, Santa Monica, CA: Rand, 2017, p. 329.

68. Seth G. Jones et al., op. cit., p. 330.

69. Thomas F. Lynch III, 'The Islamic State as Icarus', op. cit.

70. Abū Jarīr ash-Shamālī, 'Al-Qa'idah of Waziristan: a testimony from within', *Dabiq* 6, Rabi' al-Awwal 1436.

71. Anne Speckhard and Ahmet S. Yayla, *ISIS Defectors: Inside Stories of the Terrorist Caliphate*, McLean, VA: Advances Press, 2016.

72. Gerges, op. cit., location 1348.

73. Mohamed Eljarh, 'Islamic State in Libya', in Katherine Bauer (ed.), *Beyond Syria*

and Iraq, Washington Institute for Near East Policy, 2016; Geoff D. Porter, 'How Realistic Is Libya as an Islamic State "Fallback"?', *CTC Sentinel*, March 2016.

74. Mokhtar Awad, 'IS in the Sinai', in Katherine Bauer (ed.), *Beyond Syria And Iraq*, Washington Institute for Near East Policy, 2016; Jantzen W. Garnett, 'An Islamic State in the Sinai', *Journal of International Security Affairs*, Spring/Summer 2015, No. 28; Garnett, op. cit.; Zack Gold, 'Violence in Egypt's North Sinai', ICCT Research Paper, April 2016; Michael Shkolnik and Uri Marantz, 'Jihad in the Jazeera: explaining the Islamic State's growing insurgent threat in Egypt', TSAS Working Paper Series No. 16–11, July 2016.

75. Katherine Zimmerman, 'Islamic State in the Sinai', in Katherine Bauer (ed.), op. cit.

76. Yasir Yosef Kuoti, 'Islamic State in Yemen', *Terrorism Monitor*, 15 December 2016.

77. Lina Khatib, 'The Islamic State's strategy: lasting and expanding', Carnegie Middle East Center, 29 June 2015.

1. HOW IT ALL BEGAN

1. For more details on dynamics internal to the Taliban, see A. Giustozzi, *The Taliban at War*, forthcoming.

2. On the flow of foreign volunteers to Syria, see Thomas Hegghammer, 'Syria's foreign fighters', *Foreign Policy*, 9 December 2013; Charles R. Lister, *The Syrian Jihad*, London: Hurst, 2015.

3. According to Amir Khan Muttaqi, senior member of the Quetta Shura. See C. Franco, 'The Tehrik-e Taliban Pakistan', in A. Giustozzi (ed.), *Decoding the New Taliban*, London: Hurst, p. 283.

4. 'Siriiskie povstantsi vydvinuli ul'timatum Asadu', *BBC Russian Service*, 31 May 2012; 'Inostrannye naemniki v Sirii', Moscow: FSSB, 29 April 2013.

5. 'Siriiskie povstantsi vydvinuli ul'timatum Asadu', *BBC Russian Service*, 31 May 2012.

6. Interview with IS-K 1, Khorasan-level leader, June 2015.

7. 'Pakistan Taliban set up camps in Syria, join anti-Assad war', *Reuters*, 14 July 2013; Zia Ur Rehman, 'Pakistani Fighters Joining the War in Syria', *CTC Sentinel*, 24 September 2013; Abdul Basit, 'IS penetration in Afghanistan–Pakistan assessment, impact and implications', *Perspectives on Terrorism*, Vol. 11, No. 3 (June 2017), pp. 19–39.

8. Interview with ISIL cadre in Syria, June 2014.

9. 'Islamic State influence is growing in Pakistan and Afghanistan', *The Australian*, 2 November 2014; AMIR MIR, 'IS makes inroads into Pakistan', *Asia Times Online*, 27 June 2016; 'Hundreds of Pakistanis joining Daesh: IB', *The Nation*, 11 February 2016.

10. Interview with IS-K 1, Khorasan-level leader, June 2015.

11. Interview with IS-K 3, senior cadre, February 2015; interview with IS-K 11, senior cadre, ex-Haqqani network, January 2016.

12. Interview with IS-K 4, cadre, February 2016.

13. On the dynamics leading to massive financial support for anti-regime groups in Syria, see C. Phillips, *The Battle for Syria*, New Haven, CT and London: Yale University Press, 2016.

14. Interview with IS-K 1, Khorasan-level leader, June 2015.

15. Interview with IS-K 1, Khorasan-level leader, June 2015. The ten commanders were Saad Emarati, Khaled Mansouri, Sheikh Mohsen, Sheikh Mofti Hossan, Qari Shah Wali Zadran, Mullah Obidullah Alizai, Sheikh Habibullah Safi, Qari Jawad, Mullah Nasrullah Mangal and Qari Mir Ahmad.

16. Interview with IS-K 4, cadre, February 2016.

17. Interview with IS-K 5, senior cadre, December 2014; interview with IS-K 51, commander in transit to Syria, Turkey, June 2016.

18. Interview with IS-K 1, Khorasan-level leader, June 2015.

19. Abdul Basit, 'IS penetration in Afghanistan–Pakistan assessment, impact and implications', *Perspectives on Terrorism*, Vol. 11, No. 3 (June 2017), pp. 19–39, 27.

20. Interview with IS-K 1, Khorasan-level leader, June 2015.

21. Interview with IS-K 1, Khorasan-level leader, June 2015; 'Islamic State influence is growing in Pakistan and Afghanistan', *The Australian*, 2 November 2014.

22. Interview with IS-K 1, Khorasan-level leader, June 2015.

23. Interview with IS-K 1, Khorasan-level leader, June 2015.

24. Interview with IS-K 1, Khorasan-level leader, June 2015.

25. Interview with IS-K 49, finance cadre of Azizullah Haqqani, April 2015; interview with IS-K 3, senior cadre, February 2015.

26. Interview with IS-K 5, senior cadre, December 2014.

27. Dawood Azami, 'The Islamic State in South and Central Asia', *Survival*, 19 July 2016 (http://dx.doi.org/10.1080/00396338.2016.1207955).

28. Rebecca Kheel, 'Top US general: ISIS in Afghanistan connected to core group', *The Hill*, 27 July 2016; David Loyn, 'Afghanistan fighters "linked to Islamic State in Syria"', *BBC News*, 30 June 2015.

29. Azami, op. cit.; 'Islamic State influence is growing in Pakistan and Afghanistan', *The Australian*, 2 November 2014; Zahir Shah Sherazi, 'Islamic State footprints surface in parts of Bannu—Pakistan', *DAWN.COM*, 9 April 2016 (http://www.dawn.com/news/1144256/islamic-state-footprints-surface-in-parts-of-bannu/print 1/5); 'Spillover effect: ISIS makes inroads into Pakistan', *The Express Tribune*, 3 September 2014.

30. Marty, 'The Looming ...', op. cit.; 'Islamic State influence is growing in Pakistan and Afghanistan', *The Australian*, 2 November 2014.

31. Qadir Habib and Michael Scollon, op. cit.

32. 'Da'ish's official propaganda reaches Kabul', *Weesa*, 25 March 2015.

33. Interview with IS-K 1, Khorasan-level leader, June 2015.

34. Interview with IS-K 1, Khorasan-level leader, June 2015.

35. Interview with IS-K 1, Khorasan-level leader, June 2015; interview with IS-K 6, cadre, April 2015.
36. Osman, 2015, op. cit.
37. Interview with IS-K 1, Khorasan-level leader, June 2015.
38. Interview with IS-K 1, Khorasan-level leader, June 2015.
39. Interview with IS-K 10, senior cadre, October 2015.
40. Interview with IS-K 1, Khorasan-level leader, June 2015.
41. Interview with IS-K 6, cadre, April 2015; interview with IS-K 2, leader, October 2015.
42. Interview with IS-K 1, Khorasan-level leader, June 2015; Casey Garret Johnson, 'The rise and stall of the Islamic State in Afghanistan', *USIP*, November 2016; interview with IS-K 9, senior cadre, October 2015; interviews with IS-K 1, Khorasan-level leader, June 2015.
43. Interview with IS-K 3, senior cadre, February 2015; interview with IS-K 11, senior cadre, January 2016.
44. Interview with IS-K 11, senior cadre, January 2016.
45. Interview with IS-K 11, senior cadre, January 2016.
46. Interview with IS-K 12, cadre Zazai, November 2016.
47. Interview with IS-K 1, Khorasan-level leader, June 2015.
48. Borhan Osman, 'The Islamic State in 'Khorasan': how it began and where it stands now in Nangarhar', *AAN*, 27 July 2016 (https://www.afghanistan-analysts.org/wp-admin/post.php).
49. Mufti Hassan Swati, quoted in Mushtaq Yusufzai, 'ISIS in Pakistan and Afghanistan: Taliban fighters sign up, commanders say', NBC News.com, 3 February 2015 (http://www.nbcnews.com/news/world/isis-pakistan-afghanistan-taliban-fighters-sign-commanders-say-n296707); interview with External Observer/Participant 24, TTP commander in Bajaur, January 2016.
50. Don Rassler, 'Situating the emergence of the Islamic State of Khorasan', *CTC Sentinel*, March 2015. Vol. 8, Iss. 3.
51. Interview with External Observer/Participant 2, ISI officer, Pakistan, January 2016; interview with IS-K 5, senior cadre, December 2014; Zoha Waseem, 'Daesh in Pakistan: an evolving militant landscape—Part I', *Strife*, 6 February 2016.
52. Mufti Hassan Swati, quoted in Yusufzai, op. cit.
53. Interview with External Observer/Participant 2, ISI officer, Pakistan, January 2016.
54. Interview with Elder 2, Achin, Nangarhar, January 2016; interview with IS-K 53, commander, Achin, Nangarhar, August 2016.
55. Interview with IS-K 5, senior cadre, December 2014.
56. *Jihadology*, 26 January 2015.
57. Interview with Elder 8, Alizai tribe, Kajaki district; interview with Elder 10, Kajaki, Helmand, December 2015; interview with Elder 4, Achin, Nangarhar, March

2016; interview with Elder 2, Achin, Nangarhar, January 2016; interview with Elder 3, Kot, Nangarhar, March 2016; interview with IS-K 47, commander, Kajaki, Helmand, December 2015; interview with IS-K 40, fighter, Kot, Nangarhar, April 2016; interview with IS-K 41, cadre, Nangarhar, March 2016; interview with Elder 13, Achin, Nangarhar, March 2016; interview with Elder 7, Kot, Nangarhar, February 2016; interview with Elder 5, Kot, Nangarhar, February 2016; interview with IS-K 48, fighter, Kajaki, Helmand, December 2015; interview with Elder 1, Kajaki, Helmand, December 2015.

58. Interview with IS-K 37, commander, Achin, Nangarhar, April 2016.

59. See, for example, Borhan Osman, 'Descent into chaos: why did Nangarhar turn into an IS hub?', Berlin: *AAN*, 27 September 2016; Daud Khattak, 'Is there an Islamic State of AfPak?', *Foreign Policy*, 10 February 2015; Gen. Nicholson of RS in Rebecca Kheel, 'Top US general: ISIS in Afghanistan connected to core group', *The Hill*, 27 July 2016.

60. Mehwish Rani, 'The marketplace of terrorist ideas: is ISIS beating the competition in Pakistan?', *Foreign Affairs Snapshot*, 31 August 2016.

61. Interview with IS-K 1, Khorasan-level leader, June 2015.

62. Interview with IS-K 20, cadre, July 2016.

63. Katja Mielke and Nick Miszak, 'Making sense of Daesh in Afghanistan: a social movement perspective', Bonn, Germany: BICC, Working Paper 6, 2017, pp. 37–8.

64. Interview with IS-K 15, cadre, Pakistan, January 2016; interview with Ally 6, commander, IMT, northern Afghanistan, May 2016; interview with IS-K 14, cadre, Kunduz, October 2015; interview with IS-K 47, commander, Kajaki, Helmand, December 2015; interview with IS-K 41, commander, Achin, Nangarhar, March 2016; Katja Mielke and Nick Miszak, 'Making sense of Daesh in Afghanistan: a social movement perspective', Bonn, Germany: BICC, Working Paper 6, 2017.

65. Interview with IS-K 47, commander, Kajaki, Helmand, December 2015.

66. David Ignatius, 'What did Pakistan know about bin Laden?', *Washington Post*, 17 February 2012.

67. Interview with IS-K 3, senior cadre, February 2015; interview with IS-K 50, adviser from IS, December 2015.

68. Adam Baczko and Gilles Dorronsoro, 'Logiques transfrontalières et Salafisme globalisé', *Critique Internationale*, 2017/1 No. 74, pp. 137–52.

69. Interview with IS-K 16, cadre, Pakistan, December 2015.

70. Interview with IS-K 5, senior cadre, December 2014.

71. Interview with IS-K 48, fighter, Kajaki, Helmand, December 2015; interview with IS-K 41, commander, Achin, Nangarhar, March 2016.

72. Interview with IS-K 39, commander, Kajaki, Helmand, January 2016.

73. Interview with IS-K 41, commander, Achin, Nangarhar, March 2016. See next footnote for Mielke and Miszak's work.

74. Katja Mielke and Nick Miszak, 'Making sense of Daesh in Afghanistan: a social movement perspective', Bonn, Germany: BICC, Working Paper 6, 2017, p. 45.
75. Borhan Osman, 'Bourgeois jihad: why young, middle-class Afghans join the Islamic State', Washington, DC: USIP, June 2020.
76. Borhan Osman, 2020, op. cit.
77. Interview with IS-K 11, senior cadre, January 2016.
78. Interview with IS-K 17, cadre, Nangarhar, June 2016.
79. Katja Mielke and Nick Miszak, 'Making sense of Daesh in Afghanistan: a social movement perspective', Bonn, Germany: BICC, Working Paper 6, 2017, p. 52.
80. Interview with External Observer/Participant 7, Nangarhar, January 2016.
81. Interview with IS-K 36, deserter, Nangarhar, January 2016.
82. Interview with IS-K 57, provincial cadre, March 2017; interview with IS-K 60, financial cadre, April 2017.
83. Interview with IS-K 11, senior cadre, January 2016.
84. Interview with IS-K 29, cadre, Kunar, February 2016.
85. Osman, 12 February 2015, op. cit.
86. Interview with Elder 12, Kajaki, Helmand, December 2015.
87. Interview with Elder 8, Kajaki, Helmand, December 2015.
88. Interview with IS-K 21, commander, Ghazni, April 2016.
89. Interview with IS-K 34, interpreter, November 2015; interview with IS-K 37, commander, Achin, Nangarhar, April 2016.
90. Interview with IS-K 47, commander, Kajaki, Helmand, December 2015.
91. On this point see also Katja Mielke and Nick Miszak, 'Making sense of Daesh in Afghanistan: a social movement perspective', Bonn, Germany: BICC, Working Paper 6, 2017, p. 22.
92. Abdul Sayed, 'Islamic State Khorasan province's Peshawar seminary attack and war against Afghan Taliban Hanafis', *Terrorism Monitor*, Vol. 18, Iss. 21, 20 November 2020; Borhan Osman, 2020, op. cit.; Zia Ur Rehman, '"Terror ties" of Panjpiri madrassas being probed', *The News*, 25 July 2015; Muhammad Feyyaz, 'Facets of religious violence in Pakistan', *Counter Terrorist Trends and Analysis*, Vol. 5, Iss. 2, 2013.
93. Interview with IS-K 10, senior cadre, October 2015.
94. Interview with IS-K 51, commander, Turkey, June 2016. For a recent report on Iran's relations with the Taliban, see Carlotta Gall, 'Iran gains ground in Afghanistan as U.S. presence wanes', *New York Times*, 5 August 2017.
95. See, for example, Alireza Nader et al., *Iran's Influence in Afghanistan: Implications for the U.S. Drawdown*, Santa Monica, CA: Rand, 2014, p. 16.
96. David Gardner, 'The toxic rivalry of Saudi Arabia and ISIS', *Financial Times*, 16 July 2015.
97. Patrick Cockburn, 'We finally know what Hillary Clinton knew all along—US allies Saudi Arabia and Qatar are funding ISIS', *The Independent*, 14 October 2016;

'Joe Biden slips up and admits Saudi Arabia, Qatar and Turkey finance ISIS, al Nusra front', published on 26 October 2016 (https://www.youtube.com/watch?v=k2mMkmAa-Z4).

98. See Thomas Small and Jonathan Hacker, *Path of Blood: The Story of Al Qaeda's War on Saudi Arabia*, London: Simon & Schuster, 2014; Bruce Riedel and Bilal Y. Saab, 'Al Qaeda's Third Front: Saudi Arabia', *Washington Quarterly*, Vol. 31, No. 2, pp. 33–46, Spring 2008; Kim Sengupta, 'Turkey and Saudi Arabia alarm the West by backing Islamist extremists the Americans had bombed in Syria', *The Independent*, 12 May 2015; Daveed Gartenstein-Ross and Luke Lischin, 'Doha's dangerous dalliance', *International Security Affairs*, Fall/Winter 2014, No. 27; David Andrew Weinberg, 'Qatar and terror finance. Part I: negligence', Washington, DC: FDD Press, December 2014; 'Congrats!', email From:john.podesta@gmail.com To: hrod17@clintonemail.com, Date: 2014-09-27 15:15, published on wikileaks.com; Zalmay Khalilzad, 'We misled you': how the Saudis are coming clean on funding terrorism', *politico.com*, 14 September 2016; Al Manar, 'Terrorist financing: Washington admits that Saudi Arabia and Gulf States are funding Al Qaeda', Global Research, 11 June 2016; Gareth Porter, 'Obama's failure on Saudi–Qatari aid to al-Qaeda affiliate', *Middle East Eye*, 23 May 2015.

99. However, see also Katja Mielke and Nick Miszak, 'Making sense of Daesh in Afghanistan: a social movement perspective', Bonn, Germany: BICC, Working Paper 6, 2017, p. 53.

100. Interview with External Observer/Participant 11, Saudi intelligence officer, Pakistan, December 2014.

101. Interview with External Observer/Participant 11, Saudi intelligence officer, Pakistan, December 2014.

102. Interview with IS-K 49, finance officer, Waziristan, April 2015.

103. Interview with IS-K 58, financial commission cadre, March 2017.

104. Interview with External Observer/Participant 5, Qatar intelligence, April 2015.

105. Interview with External Observer/Participant 5, Qatar intelligence, April 2015; interview with IS-K 42, cadre, Finance Commission, Arab Gulf country, April 2015.

106. Interview with IS-K 3, senior cadre, February 2015; interview with External Observer/Participant 21, adviser of Serajuddin Haqqani, January 2015; interview with External Observer/Participant 22, close collaborator of Serajuddin Haqqani, January 2015; Taliban cadre operating within Quetta Shura, December 2014.

107. Interview with IS-K 42, cadre, Finance Commission, Arab Gulf country, April 2015.

2. THE ORIGINAL AIMS AND STRATEGY, 2014–17

1. Interview with Ally 1, IMU cadre, Faryab, May 2016.
2. Interview with IS-K 13, cadre, Jowzjan, May 2016.
3. Interview with IS-K 27, commander, northern Afghanistan, July 2016.
4. Interview with IS-K 18, cadre of Gansu Hui Group, Nangarhar, July 2016; interview with IS-K 45, commander, Gansu Hui Group, northern Afghanistan, May 2016. AQ and former AQ sources admit that IS-Central and IS-K were successful in attracting substantial numbers of Chinese Muslims from AQ itself in 2014–16 (interview with External Observer/Participant 19, Uyghur Fatah as-Sham commander in Syria, February 2017; interview with External Observer/Participant 14, Hui TTP commander, Pakistan, November 2016; interview with Ally 12, TIP Uyghur commander in northern Afghanistan, May 2016).
5. Interview with IS-K 31, cadre, Herat, December 2015.
6. Interview with IS-K 21, commander, Ghazni, April 2016.
7. Interview with IS-K 22, Finance Commission, March 2015; interview with IS-K 7, senior commander of Omar Ghazi Group, April 2015; interview with IS-K 50, adviser from IS, December 2015; interview with IS-K 9, leader of front, October 2015; interview with IS-K 20, Finance Commission, July 2016; interview with IS-K 28, senior cadre, Kunar province, July 2016; interview with IS-K 1, Khorasan-level leader, June 2015.
8. Interview with IS-K 28, cadre, Kunar, July 2016.
9. Interview with elders from Nangarhar, November 2016.
10. Interview with IS-K 5, senior cadre, December 2014.
11. Interview with IS-K 5, senior cadre, December 2014.
12. Interview with External Observer/Participant 1, Revolutionary Guard (Iran) officer, Afghanistan, January 2016.
13. Interview with IS-K 17, cadre, Nangarhar, June 2016.
14. Interview with IS-K 28, cadre, Kunar, July 2016.
15. Interview with IS-K 14, cadre, Kunduz, October 2015; interview with IS-K 9, senior cadre, October 2015.
16. 'Secret ISIS document found in Pakistan attempts to unite Pak-Afghan Taliban and al-Qaeda', *Khaama Press*, 17 August 2015.
17. Interview with IS-K 50, adviser, December 2015.
18. Interview with IS-K 2, leader, October 2015.
19. Interview with External Observer/Participant 2, ISI officer, Pakistan, January 2016.
20. Interview with IS-K 7, cadre, April 2015.
21. United Nations Security Council, 19 July 2016, op. cit.
22. Interview with IS-K 17, cadre, Nangarhar, June 2016; interview with IS-K 41, commander, Achin, Nangarhar, March 2016.

23. Interview with External Observer/Participant 7, Nangarhar, January 2016.

24. Interview with IS-K 17, cadre, Nangarhar, June 2016.

25. Interview with IS-K 17, cadre, Nangarhar, June 2016; interview with IS-K 41, commander, Achin, Nangarhar, March 2016.

26. Interview with IS-K 17, cadre, Nangarhar, June 2016.

27. Interview with IS-K 2, leader, October 2015.

28. Interview with IS-K 13, cadre, Jowzjan, May 2016.

29. Interview with IS-K 3, senior cadre, February 2015; interview with IS-K 28, cadre, Kunar, July 2016.

30. Interview with IS-K 9, senior cadre, October 2015; interview with IS-K 21, commander, Ghazni, April 2016.

31. Interview with IS-K 50, adviser, December 2015.

32. Interview with Elder 14, Sherzad, Nangarhar, January 2016.

33. Interview with IS-K 17, cadre, Nangarhar, June 2016; interview with IS-K 21, commander, Ghazni, April 2016.

34. Interview with IS-K 2, leader, October 2015; interview with IS-K 54, senior commander, Pakistan, January 2017; Jawad Sukhanyar and Rod Nordland, 'ISIS, aided by ex-Taliban groups, makes inroads in northern Afghanistan', *New York Times*, 28 June 2017.

35. Michael R. Gordon, 'ISIS building 'little nests' in Afghanistan, U.S. Defense Secretary warns', *New York Times*, 18 December 2015.

36. 'IS has presence in Afghan Zabol province as well as Helmand—report', *Noor TV*, Kabul, in Dari 13.00 GMT 11 January 2015.

37. 'IS supporters abduct 30 people in Afghan Zabol Province—report', *Afghan Islamic Press News Agency*, Peshawar, in Pashto 17.52 GMT 23 February 2015.

38. Ghafoor Saboory, 'ANA overtakes Daesh recruitment center in Zabul', *TOLOnews*, 10 May 2015.

39. Tamim Hamid, 'Khak-e-Afghan district a Daesh stronghold: security sources', *TOLOnews*, 12 November 2015.

40. Nathaniel Barr, 'Wilayat Khorasan stumbles in Afghanistan', *Terrorism Monitor*, Vol. 14, Iss. 5, 3 March 2016.

41. Ayaz Gul, 'Officials: no evidence of IS presence in southern Afghanistan', *VOA News*, 15 August 2016; Mirwais Khan and Lynne O'Donnell, 'ISIS in Afghanistan grows presence near Pakistan border', *Associated Press*, 14 August 2016.

42. Interview with External Observer/Participant 3, NDS officer, Kabul, January 2016.

43. Interview with IS-K 62, cadre in Zabul, November 2016.

44. Interview with IS-K 62, cadre in Zabul, November 2016.

45. Interview with IS-K 62, cadre in Zabul, November 2016; elder 16, Kakar from Zabul, January 2017; External Observer 27, Taliban cadre in Quetta Shura, contacted January 2017.

46. Interview with External Observer/Participant 3, NDS officer, Kabul, January 2016.
47. Interview with IS-K 59, commander, Achin, April 2017.
48. Interview with IS-K 5, senior cadre, December 2014.
49. Interview with IS-K 25, cadre, Pakistan, October 2015.
50. Interview with IS-K 25, cadre, Pakistan, October 2015.
51. Interview with IS-K 1, Khorasan-level leader, June 2015.
52. Interview with Elder 7, Kot, Nangarhar, February 2016; Johnson, op. cit.
53. Interview with Elder 5, Kot, Nangarhar, February 2016.
54. Interview with IS-K 5, senior cadre, December 2014.
55. Interview with IS-K 5, senior cadre, December 2014.
56. Interview with Elder 9, Kajaki, Helmand, November 2015.
57. Ziar Yad, 'Parts of Nangarhar fall to Daesh once again: residents', *TOLOnews*, 16 September 2016.
58. Osman, 27 July 2016, op. cit.
59. Joseph Goldstein, 'U.S. steps up airstrikes in Afghanistan', *New York Times*, 15 July 2015; Harleen Gambhir, 'ISIS in Afghanistan', Institute for the Study of War, 3 December 2015.
60. 'US airstrikes target Islamic State in Afghanistan', *Associated Press*, 11 February 2016.
61. 'Laghman residents concerned over Daesh activities', *TOLOnews*, 26 December 2015.
62. Interview with IS-K 31, cadre, Herat, December 2015.
63. Interview with IS-K 31, cadre, Herat, December 2015.
64. Arif Musawi, 'Daesh surfaces in Balkh: Atta Noor', *TOLOnews*, 13 March 2016.
65. Interview with Elder 11, Kajaki, Helmand, December 2015.
66. Interview with External Observer/Participant 6, Taliban military cadre, Helmand, January 2016.
67. Communication with Quetta Shura source, January 2017.
68. Interview with Elder 12, Kajaki, Helmand, December 2015; interview with Elder 9, Kajaki, Helmand, November 2015; interview with Elder 8, Kajaki, Helmand, December 2015; interview with Elder 11, Kajaki, Helmand, December 2015; interview with Elder 1, Kajaki, Helmand, December 2015; interview with IS-K 47, commander, Kajaki, Helmand, December 2015; interview with Elder 10, Kajaki, Helmand, December 2015.
69. 'Islamic State fighters in Afghanistan flee to Kunar province', *Reuters*, 24 March 2016.
70. Interview with IS-K 28, cadre, Kunar, July 2016.
71. Ghafoor Saboory, 'Daesh militants recruiting in Kunar', *TOLOnews*, 3 September 2016.
72. Personal communication with Taliban source in Quetta, contacted December 2016.

73. Interview with IS-K 28, cadre, Kunar, July 2016.

74. Interview with IS-K 59, commander, Achin, April 2017.

75. Interview with IS-K 28, cadre, Kunar, July 2016.

76. Jessica Donati and Habib Khan Totakhil, 'Taliban, Islamic State forge informal alliance in eastern Afghanistan', *Wall Street Journal*, 7 August 2016.

77. See also Katja Mielke and Nick Miszak, 'Making sense of Daesh in Afghanistan: a social movement perspective', Bonn, Germany: BICC, Working Paper 6, 2017, p. 22.

78. Interview with IS-K 28, cadre, Kunar, July 2016.

79. Interview with IS-K 25, cadre, Pakistan, October 2015; interview with IS-K 7, cadre, April 2015; interview with IS-K 5, senior cadre, December 2014.

80. Interview with IS-K 28, cadre, Kunar, July 2016.

81. Interview with IS-K 25, cadre, Pakistan, October 2015.

82. Interview with IS-K 24, commander, February 2016.

83. Interview with IS-K 16, cadre, Pakistan, December 2015.

84. MIR, op. cit.

85. Rafiq Sherzad, 'Islamic State claims suicide attack on Pakistani consulate in Afghan city', *Reuters*, 13 January 2016.

86. Chishti, op. cit.

87. Interview with External Observer/Participant 2, ISI officer, Pakistan, January 2016.

88. Interview with IS-K 43, cadre, former Hizb-i Islami member, Pakistan, January 2016.

89. Interview with IS-K 22, cadre, March 2015.

90. Interview with IS-K 24, commander, Jaysh ul-Islam, February 2016.

91. Borhan Osman, 'Another ISKP leader "dead": where is the group headed after losing so many amirs?', Berlin: *AAN*, 23 July 2017.

92. For an alternative view, which claims IS-K simply failed to establish a significant capability in Pakistan, see Justin V. Hastings and Farah Naz, 'The trials and travails of the Islamic State in Pakistan', *Australian Journal of International Affairs*, Vol. 71, No. 3, 335–53.

93. Ziar Yad, 'Former Daesh fighters claim Pakistan funded them', *TOLOnews*, 24 February 2016.

94. Interview with External Observer/Participant 6, Taliban military cadre, Helmand, January 2016.

95. Interview with External Observer/Participant 12, donor, Pakistan, January 2016.

96. Interview with External Observer/Participant 2, ISI officer, Pakistan, January 2016; Zoha Waseem, 'Daesh in Pakistan: an evolving militant landscape—Part I', *Strife*, 6 February 2016.

97. Interview with External Observer/Participant 2, ISI officer, Pakistan, January 2016.

98. Interview with External Observer/Participant 2, ISI officer, Pakistan, January 2016.

99. Interview with External Observer/Participant 2, ISI officer, Pakistan, January 2016.

100. Interview with External Observer/Participant 1, Revolutionary Guards (Iran) officer, Afghanistan, January 2016.

101. 'What happened to ISIS's Afghanistan–Pakistan province?', *The Diplomat*, 19 February 2016.

102. Interview with External Observer/Participant 2, ISI officer, Pakistan, January 2016.

103. 'Daesh group in competition for recruits in Pakistan', *Associated Press*, 2 March 2016.

104. Interview with IS-K 28, cadre, Kunar, July 2016.

105. Interview with IS-K 26, cadre, Pakistan, July 2016.

106. Interview with External Observer/Participant 25, Haqqani commander in Zabul, May 2017; interview with Observer/Participant 26, senior member of Haqqani network, May 2017.

107. The Quetta Police Academy attack was initially attributed to Lashkar-e Jhangvi by the police; the Quetta hospital attack, according to IS-K, was carried out in collaboration with Jamaat ul-Ahrar ('Daesh claims attack on Pakistani police college', *Gulf News*, 24 December 2016).

108. 'Ghani condemns Daesh bombing in Quetta', *TOLOnews*, 9 August 2016.

109. Interview with IS-K 54, senior commander, Pakistan, January 2017.

110. Fatima Bhojani, 'ISIS is on the decline in the Middle East, but its influence in Pakistan is rising', *Washington Post*, 5 May 2017.

111. Interview with IS-K 52, cadre, Nangarhar, December 2016.

112. Interview with External Observer 28, Revolutionary Guards (Iran) official in Iran, November 2017.

113. Interview with IS-K commander in Jowzjan, August 2018.

114. Amira Jadoon, Andrew Mines, 'Taking aim: Islamic State Khorasan's leadership losses', *CTC Sentinel*, September 2019, Vol. 12, 8.

115. Interview with External Observer/Participant 2, ISI officer, Pakistan, January 2016.

116. Interview with IS-K commander in Nangarhar, June 2020; interview with IS-K 63, commander from Pakistan in Kunar, May 2020.

117. Interview with IS-K 64, cadre from Pakistan in Khogyani, March 2021.

118. Interview with member of IS-K 65, military commission for Kabul, March 2021.

119. Interview with IS-K 64, cadre from Pakistan in Khogyani, March 2021.

120. Interview with IS-K 66, cadre, January 2021.

121. Interview with IS-K 66, cadre, January 2021; interview with IS-K 64, cadre from Pakistan in Khogyani, March 2021; interview with IS-K 66, cadre, January 2021.

122. Interview with member of IS-K 65, military commission for Kabul, March 2021.

123. Interview with IS-K 64, cadre from Pakistan in Khogyani, March 2021.

124. Interview with External Observer/Participant 1, Revolutionary Guards (Iran) officer, Afghanistan, January 2016.

125. Frud Bezhan, op. cit.

126. Borhan Osman, 'With an active cell in Kabul, ISKP tries to bring sectarianism to the Afghan War', *AAN*, 19 October 2016.

127. Interview with IS-K 16, cadre, Pakistan, December 2015.

128. Bezhan, op. cit.

129. Interview with IS-K 21, commander, Ghazni, April 2016.

130. Interview with IS-K 25, cadre, Pakistan, October 2015; interview with IS-K 5, senior cadre, December 2014.

131. Interview with IS-K 53, commander, Achin, Nangarhar, August 2016.

132. 'Islamic State claims deadly bus attack on Karachi Shias—first in Pakistan', *AFP*, 13 May 2015.

133. On the Baluchi insurgents of Iran, see A. Giustozzi and S. Mangal, 'Iranian insurgent groups maintain Baluch threat', *IHS Jane's Intelligence Review*, 2 January 2015; Zia Ur Rehman, 'The Baluch insurgency: linking Iran to Pakistan', Oslo, Norway: NOREF, 2014; Daniele Grassi, 'Iran's Baloch insurgency and the IS', *Asia Times Online*, 20 October 2014; Abubakar Siddique, 'Iran's Sunni Baloch extremists operating from bases in Pakistan', *Terrorism Monitor*, Vol. 12, Iss. 6, 20 March 2014; Chris Zambelis, 'Iran confronts intensifying insurgent offensive in Sistan-Balochistan province', *Terrorism Monitor*, Vol. 13, Iss. 8, 17 April 2015.

134. Interview with IS-K 1, Khorasan-level leader, June 2015; interview with IS-K 30, district amir, Farah, December 2015; interview with IS-K 33, Harakat Khilafat Baluch commander, January 2016.

135. Interview with External Observer 5, Qatari intelligence, April 2015.

136. Interview with IS-K 1, Khorasan-level leader, June 2015.

137. Interview with IS-K 7, cadre, April 2015.

138. Interview with Fatah as-Sham commander, Syria, February 2017.

139. Interview with Ally 10, ETIM member, October 2016; Olga Dzyubenko, 'Kyrgyzstan says Uighur militant groups behind attack on China's embassy', *Reuters*, 7 September 2016; 'MIA of the RT: in attack on Chinese Embassy in Bishkek were used passports of Tajiks ISIL fighters', *Asia-Plus*, 8 September 2016 [https://news.tj/en/news/tajikistan/security/20160908/230649].

140. Interview with IS-K 44, cadre, Kyrghizstan, September 2016.

141. Interview with IS-K 44, cadre, Kyrghizstan, September 2016.

142. Interview with IS-K 44, cadre, Kyrghizstan, September 2016.

143. Interview with IS-K 18, cadre of Gansu Hui Group, Nangarhar, July 2016; interview with IS-K 19, member of Gansu Hui Group, Pakistan, July 2016.

144. Interview with IS-K 18, cadre of Gansu Hui Group, Nangarhar, July 2016; inter-

view with IS-K 19, member of Gansu Hui Group, Pakistan, July 2016; interview with IS-K 27, commander, northern Afghanistan, July 2016.

145. Interview with IS-K 44, cadre, Kyrghizstan, September 2016.
146. Interview with IS-K 44, cadre, Kyrghizstan, September 2016.
147. Interview with IS-K 52, cadre, Nangarhar, December 2016.

3. EFFORTS TO 'SYNCHRONIZE' IS-K WITH IS-CENTRAL

1. Interview with IS-K 6, senior finance cadre, April 2015.
2. Interview with IS-K 50, adviser, December 2015.
3. MIR, op. cit.; Zahid Gishkori, 'Some foreign militants recruiting for Daesh in Pakistan', *The News*, 5 June 2016.
4. Interview with IS-K 50, adviser, December 2015.
5. Interview with IS-K 54, senior commander, Pakistan, January 2017.
6. Interview with IS-K 16, cadre, Pakistan, December 2015.
7. Interview with IS-K 34, interpreter, November 2015.
8. Interview with IS-K 32, cadre, Finance Commission, November 2015.
9. Interview with IS-K 14, cadre, Kunduz, October 2015; interview with IS-K 31, cadre, Herat, December 2015; interview with IS-K 10, senior cadre, October 2015; interview with IS-K 9, senior cadre, October 2015; interview with IS-K 30, cadre, Farah, December 2015; interview with IS-K 15, cadre, Pakistan, January 2016; interview with IS-K 8, senior cadre, January 2016; interview with IS-K 29, cadre, Kunar, February 2016; interview with IS-K 24, commander, Jaysh ul-Islam, February 2016; interview with IS-K 26, cadre, Pakistan, July 2016; interview with IS-K 28, cadre, Kunar, July 2016; interview with IS-K 33, commander, Pakistan, January 2016; interview with IS-K 11, senior cadre, January 2016; interview with IS-K 17, cadre, Nangarhar, June 2016.
10. Interview with IS-K 1, Khorasan-level leader, June 2015.
11. Interview with IS-K 50, adviser, December 2015.
12. Interview with IS-K 50, adviser, December 2015; interview with IS-K 34, interpreter, November 2015.
13. Interview with IS-K 50, adviser, December 2015; interview with IS-K 33, commander, Pakistan, January 2016; interview with IS-K 24, commander, Jaysh ul-Islam, February 2016; interview with IS-K 29, cadre, Kunar, February 2016; interview with IS-K 8, senior cadre, January 2016; interview with IS-K 15, cadre, Pakistan, January 2016.
14. Interview with IS-K 11, senior cadre, January 2016.
15. Interview with IS-K 33, commander, Pakistan, January 2016.
16. Interview with IS-K 50, adviser, December 2015.
17. Interview with IS-K 50, adviser, December 2015.
18. Interview with IS-K 53, commander, Achin, Nangarhar, August 2016.

19. Interview with IS-K 47, commander, Kajaki, Helmand, December 2015; interview with IS-K 48, fighter, Kajaki, Helmand, December 2015; interview with IS-K 41, commander, Achin, Nangarhar, March 2016; interview with IS-K 39, commander, Kajaki, Helmand, January 2016; interview with Elder 9, Kajaki, Helmand, November 2015.
20. Interview with IS-K 34, interpreter, November 2015.
21. Interview with IS-K 34, interpreter, November 2015.
22. Interview with IS-K 11, senior cadre, January 2016; interview with IS-K 33, commander, Pakistan, January 2016; interview with IS-K 24, commander, Jaysh ul-Islam, February 2016; interview with IS-K 29, cadre, Kunar, February 2016; interview with IS-K 15, cadre, Pakistan, January 2016.
23. Interview with IS-K 50, adviser, December 2015.
24. Interview with Ally 3, commander, October 2015; interview with Ally 6, commander, IMT, Northern Afghanistan, May 2016; interview with IS-K 14, cadre, Kunduz, October 2015.
25. Interview with IS-K 15, cadre, Pakistan, January 2016.
26. Interview with IS-K 50, adviser, December 2015.
27. Interview with IS-K 11, senior cadre, January 2016; interview with IS-K 50, adviser, December 2015; interview with IS-K 33, commander, Pakistan, January 2016; interview with IS-K 24, commander, Jaysh ul-Islam, February 2016; interview with IS-K 29, cadre, Kunar, February 2016; interview with IS-K 8, senior cadre, January 2016; interview with IS-K 15, cadre, Pakistan, January 2016; interview with IS-K 9, senior cadre, October 2015; interview with IS-K 16, cadre, Pakistan, December 2015; interview with IS-K 14, cadre, Kunduz, October 2015.
28. Interview with IS-K 26, cadre, Pakistan, July 2016; interview with IS-K 24, commander, Jaysh ul-Islam, February 2016.
29. Interview with IS-K 34, interpreter, November 2015.
30. Jim Kouri, 'ISIS spreads its bloody jihad into Afghanistan', *The Examiner*, 18 April 2015.
31. Interview with IS-K 15, cadre, Pakistan, January 2016.
32. Interview with IS-K 33, commander, Pakistan, January 2016.
33. Interview with IS-K 32, cadre, Finance Commission, November 2015.
34. Interview with IS-K 43, cadre, former Hizb-i Islami member, Pakistan, January 2016. See also Malcolm Nance, *Defeating ISIS: Who They Are, How They Fight, What They Believe*, location 2830.
35. Katja Mielke and Nick Miszak, 'Making sense of Daesh in Afghanistan: a social movement perspective', Bonn, Germany: BICC, Working Paper 6, 2017, p. 24.
36. Interview with IS-K 48, fighter, Kajaki, Helmand, December 2015.
37. Interview with IS-K 39, commander, Kajaki, Helmand, January 2016.
38. Interview with IS-K 37, commander, Achin, Nangarhar, April 2016.
39. Interview with IS-K 47, commander, Kajaki, Helmand, December 2015.

40. Interview with IS-K 40, fighter, Kot, Nangarhar, April 2016.
41. Interview with IS-K 11, senior cadre, January 2016; interview with IS-K 50, adviser, December 2015; interview with IS-K 33, commander, Pakistan, January 2016; interview with IS-K 8, senior cadre, January 2016; interview with IS-K 15, cadre, Pakistan, January 2016.
42. Interview with IS-K 34, interpreter, November 2015.
43. Interview with IS-K 24, commander, Jaysh ul-Islam, February 2016.
44. Interview with IS-K 33, commander, Pakistan, January 2016.
45. Interview with IS-K 50, adviser, December 2015.
46. Interview with IS-K 11, senior cadre, January 2016.
47. Interview with IS-K 34, interpreter, November 2015.
48. Interview with IS-K 34, interpreter, November 2015.
49. Interview with IS-K 50, adviser, December 2015.
50. Interview with IS-K 50, adviser, December 2015.
51. Interview with IS-K 33, commander, Pakistan, January 2016.
52. Interview with IS-K 1, Khorasan-level leader, June 2015.
53. Interview with IS-K 34, interpreter, November 2015.
54. Interview with IS-K 1, Khorasan-level leader, June 2015.
55. The quote is from interview with IS-K 11, senior cadre, January 2016.
56. Interview with IS-K 24, commander, Jaysh ul-Islam, February 2016; interview with IS-K 29, cadre, Kunar, February 2016.
57. Interview with IS-K 15, cadre, Pakistan, January 2016.
58. Interview with IS-K 33, commander, Pakistan, January 2016; interview with IS-K 36, deserter, Nangarhar, January 2016; interview with IS-K 15, cadre, Pakistan, January 2016; interview with IS-K 34, interpreter, November 2015; interview with IS-K 9, senior cadre, October 2015; interview with IS-K 16, cadre, Pakistan, December 2015; interview with IS-K 21, commander, Ghazni, April 2016; interview with IS-K 14, cadre, Kunduz, October 2015; interview with IS-K 39, commander, Kajaki, Helmand, January 2016; interview with IS-K 11, senior cadre, January 2016.
59. Interview with IS-K 24, commander, Jaysh ul-Islam, February 2016.
60. Interview with External Observer/Participant 6, Taliban military cadre, Helmand, January 2016.
61. Interview with IS-K 8, senior cadre, January 2016.
62. Interview with IS-K 47, commander, Kajaki, Helmand, December 2015.
63. Interview with IS-K 48, fighter, Kajaki, Helmand, December 2015.
64. Interview with IS-K 47, commander, Kajaki, Helmand, December 2015.
65. Interview with Ally 3, commander, October 2015.
66. Interview with Ally 6, commander, IMT, northern Afghanistan, May 2016.
67. Interview with Ally 3, commander, October 2015.
68. Interview with IS-K 43, cadre, former Hizb-i Islami member, Pakistan, January

2016; interview with IS-K 33, commander, Pakistan, January 2016; interview with IS-K 8, senior cadre, January 2016; interview with External Observer/Participant 6, Taliban military cadre, Helmand, January 2016; interview with IS-K 15, cadre, Pakistan, January 2016; interview with IS-K 34, interpreter, November 2015; interview with IS-K 32, cadre, Finance Commission, November 2015.

69. Interview with IS-K 24, commander, Jaysh ul-Islam, February 2016.

70. Interview with IS-K 11, senior cadre, January 2016.

71. Interview with IS-K 37, commander, Achin, Nangarhar, April 2016.

72. Interview with IS-K 24, commander, Jaysh ul-Islam, February 2016.

73. Interview with IS-K 33, commander, Pakistan, January 2016.

74. Interview with IS-K 29, cadre, Kunar, February 2016.

75. Interview with IS-K 8, senior cadre, January 2016.

76. Interview with IS-K 15, cadre, Pakistan, January 2016.

77. Interview with IS-K 10, senior cadre, October 2015; interview with IS-K 16, cadre, Pakistan, December 2015; interview with IS-K 14, cadre, Kunduz, October 2015.

78. Interview with IS-K 32, cadre, Finance Commission, November 2015.

79. Interview with IS-K 33, commander, Pakistan, January 2016; interview with IS-K 15, cadre, Pakistan, January 2016; interview with IS-K 50, adviser, December 2015; interview with IS-K 29, cadre, Kunar, February 2016.

80. Interview with IS-K 11, senior cadre, January 2016.

81. Interview with IS-K 33, commander, Pakistan, January 2016.

82. Interview with IS-K 8, senior cadre, January 2016.

83. Interview with IS-K 34, interpreter, November 2015.

84. Interview with External Observer/Participant 4, NDS officer, Jalalabad, January 2016.

85. Interview with External Observer/Participant 3, NDS officer, Kabul, January 2016.

86. Interview with External Observer/Participant 1, Revolutionary Guards (Iran) officer, Afghanistan, January 2016.

87. Interview with External Observer/Participant 7, Nangarhar, January 2016.

88. Interview with External Observer/Participant 2, ISI officer, Pakistan, January 2016.

89. Interview with External Observer/Participant 6, Taliban military cadre, Helmand, January 2016.

90. Interview with IS-K 52, cadre, Nangarhar, December 2016.

91. Interview with IS-K 14, cadre, Kunduz, October 2015.

92. Interview with IS-K 24, commander, Jaysh ul-Islam, February 2016; interview with Ally 3, commander, October 2015; interview with IS-K 16, cadre, Pakistan, December 2015; interview with IS-K 37, commander, Achin, Nangarhar, April 2016; interview with IS-K 47, commander, Kajaki, Helmand, December 2015; interview with IS-K 41, commander, Achin, Nangarhar, March 2016; interview with IS-K 48, fighter, Kajaki, Helmand, December 2015.

93. 'Daesh expands Afghan footprint with terror campaign', Associated Press, 19 December 2015. Pictures from the video are found at http://heavy.com/news/2015/08/new-isis-islamic-state-khorasan-video-killing-the-apostates-in-revenge-for-the-monotheists-1-2-full-uncensored-youtube-video-screen-shots-screengrabs-stills/2/.

94. Interview with External Observer/Participant 6, Taliban military cadre, Helmand, January 2016.

95. Interview with Ally 3, commander, October 2015.

96. Interview with IS-K 15, cadre, Pakistan, January 2016.

97. Interview with IS-K 34, interpreter, November 2015.

98. Interview with IS-K 10, senior cadre, October 2015.

99. Interview with Elder 7, Kot, Nangarhar, February 2016; interview with Elder 5, Kot, Nangarhar, February 2016.

100. Interview with Elder 13, Achin, Nangarhar, March 2016.

101. Interview with IS-K 34, interpreter, November 2015.

102. Interview with IS-K 33, commander, Pakistan, January 2016.

103. Interview with Elder 15, Zazai tribe, Paktia, January 2017; interview with Elder 16, Kakar tribe, Zabul, January 2017. See also Katja Mielke and Nick Miszak, 'Making sense of Daesh in Afghanistan: a social movement perspective', Bonn, Germany: BICC, Working Paper 6, 2017, p. 42.

104. Interview with IS-K 11, senior cadre, January 2016.

105. Interview with IS-K 47, commander, Kajaki, Helmand, December 2015.

106. Brian Dodwell et al., 'The Caliphate's global workforce', West Point, NY: CTC, 2016.

107. Interview with IS-K 51, commander of group en route through Turkey to Syria, June 2016.

108. 'Afghani terrorists netted in Ramadi', AIN, 7 April 2014; '19 Afghan ISIS elements killed while booby-trapping vehicles east of Mosul', AIN, 6 January 2016; 'Iraqi warplanes kill 5 Afghan ISIS fighters near Fallujah', AIN, 12 June 2016; '29 ISIS elements killed in missile strike southern Anbar', AIN, 22 January 2015.

109. CNN News, 27 October 2016, 'ISIS fighters streaming into Mosul', Aired 4.00–4.30 ET.

110. 'Kazakhstanets v novov video ot boevikov Afganistana peredal privet brat'yam v Sirii', InformBuro.Kz, 11 January 2017; Alice Speri, 'Afghan refugees and jihadis are reportedly fighting on opposite sides of Syria's war', Vice News, 31 May 2014; 'Pakistani Taliban claim joining Syria war', YouTube, https://www.youtube.com/watch?v=QP2AH6zTMZw; 'Taliban Pakistan is sending hundreds of its fighters to Syria', https://www.youtube.com/watch?v=IBNjtLu7aYY.

111. Griff Witte et al., 'Flow of foreign fighters plummets as Islamic State loses its edge', Washington Post, 9 September 2016.

112. Interview with IS-K 51, commander of group en route through Turkey to Syria, June 2016.
113. Interview with IS-K 54, senior commander, Pakistan, January 2017.
114. Interview with IS-K 59, commander, Achin, April 2017.
115. Interview with IS-K 1, Khorasan-level leader, June 2015.
116. 'Foreign fighters: an updated assessment of the flow of foreign fighters into Syria and Iraq', Soufan Group, December 2015.
117. Interview with IS-K 51, commander, Turkey, June 2016. Abu Yasir Al-Afghani was replaced by Abu Sayed Sadat Al Afghani in Syria.
118. Interview with IS-K 26, cadre, Pakistan, July 2016; interview with IS-K 24, commander, Jaysh ul Islam, February 2016.
119. Interview with IS-K 2, leader, October 2015.
120. Interview with IS 61, logistics cadre in Syria, April 2017.
121. Interview with IS-K 29, cadre, Kunar, February 2016; interview with IS-K 8, senior cadre, January 2016; interview with IS-K 15, cadre, Pakistan, January 2016.
122. Interview with IS-K 51, commander, Turkey, June 2016; interview with IS-K 2, leader, October 2015.
123. Interview with IS-K 15, cadre, Pakistan, January 2016; interview with Ally 3, commander, October 2015; interview with IS-K 34, interpreter, November 2015.
124. Notebook of IS-K leader, obtained July 2015, July 2015.
125. Interview with IS-K 51, commander, Turkey, June 2016.
126. Interview with IS-K 51, commander, Turkey, June 2016.
127. Interview with IS-K 51, commander, Turkey, June 2016; interview with IS-K 2, leader, October 2015.
128. Interview with IS-K 51, commander, Turkey, June 2016.
129. Interview with IS-K 51, commander, Turkey, June 2016.
130. Interview with IS-K 51, commander, Turkey, June 2016.
131. Interview with IS-K 51, commander, Turkey, June 2016.
132. Interview with IS-K 11, senior cadre, January 2016; interview with IS-K 29, cadre, Kunar, February 2016; interview with IS-K 8, senior cadre, January 2016; interview with IS-K 13, cadre, Jowzjan, May 2016; interviews with IS-K 1, Khorasan-level leader, June 2015; interview with IS-K 14, cadre, Kunduz, October 2015; interview with IS-K 31, cadre, Herat, December 2015; interview with IS-K 25, cadre, Pakistan, October 2015; interview with IS-K 16, cadre, Pakistan, December 2015; interview with IS-K 9, senior cadre, October 2015; interview with IS-K 30, cadre, Farah, December 2015; interview with IS-K 6, cadre, April 2015; interview with IS-K 13, cadre, Jowzjan, May 2016; interview with IS-K 7, cadre, April 2015; interviews with IS-K 1, Khorasan-level leader, June 2015; interview with IS-K 14, cadre, Kunduz, October 2015; interview with IS-K 14, cadre, Kunduz, October 2015.
133. Interview with IS-K 2, leader, October 2015; interview with IS 61, logistics cadre

in Syria, April 2017; interview with IS-K 1, Khorasan-level leader, June 2015; interview with IS-K 51, commander of group en route through Turkey to Syria, June 2016; interview with IS-K 54, senior commander, Pakistan, January 2017.

4. HYBRID: IS-K STRUCTURE BETWEEN CENTRALIZATION AND CENTRIFUGAL TENDENCIES

1. Interview with IS-K 2, leader, October 2015.
2. Interview with IS-K 2, leader, October 2015.
3. Interview with External Observer/Participant 2, ISI officer, Pakistan, January 2016.
4. Johnson, op. cit., citing Afghan security officials.
5. Interview with IS-K 1, Khorasan-level leader, June 2015.
6. Interview with IS-K 1, Khorasan-level leader, June 2015; interview with IS-K 58, Financial Commission cadre, March 2017; interview with IS-K 20, cadre, July 2016; IS-K 22, cadre, March 2015.
7. Interview with IS-K 4, cadre, Kunar, February 2016.
8. Interview with IS-K 26, cadre, Pakistan, July 2016.
9. Interview with IS-K 2, leader, October 2015.
10. Source in IS, contacted in January 2016.
11. Interview with IS-K 54, senior commander of TKP, Nangarhar, January 2017.
12. Interview with IS-K 24, commander, Jaysh ul-Islam, February 2016; interview with IS-K 29, cadre, Kunar, February 2016.
13. Interview with IS-K 3, senior cadre, February 2015; interview with IS-K 7, cadre, April 2015; interviews with IS-K 1, Khorasan-level leader, June 2015.
14. Interview with IS-K 7, cadre, April 2015.
15. Interview with IS-K 1, Khorasan-level leader, June 2015.
16. Interview with IS-K 2, leader, October 2015.
17. Interview with IS-K 32, cadre, Finance Commission, November 2015.
18. Interview with IS-K 32, cadre, Finance Commission, November 2015.
19. Interview with IS-K 21, commander, Ghazni, April 2016.
20. Interview with IS-K 1, Khorasan-level leader, June 2015; interview with IS-K 60, financial cadre, April 2017.
21. Interview with IS-K 1, Khorasan-level leader, June 2015.
22. Interview with IS-K 2, leader, October 2015.
23. Interview with External Observer/Participant 7, Nangarhar, January 2016; Franz J. Martin, 'On the trail of the Islamic State in Afghanistan', The Foreign Policy, April 05, 2016.
24. Chris Sands and Fazelminallah Qazizai, 'ISIL emerges in Afghanistan "stronger than the Taliban"', The National, 29 October 2015.
25. Interview with IS-K 1, Khorasan-level leader, June 2015.

26. Interview with IS-K 1, Khorasan-level leader, June 2015.

27. Interview with IS-K 33, commander, Pakistan, January 2016; interview with IS-K 29, cadre, Kunar, February 2016.

28. Interview with IS-K 20, financial cadre, July 2016; interview with IS-K 22, financial cadre, March 2015; interview with IS-K 58, Financial Commission cadre, March 2017; interviews with IS-K 60, financial cadre, April 2017.

29. Interview with IS-K 57, provincial cadre, March 2017; interview with IS-K 58, Financial Commission cadre, March 2017; interview with IS-K 59, commander in Achin, April 2017; interviews with IS-K 60, financial cadre, April 2017. On the role of NGOs see also Katja Mielke and Nick Miszak, 'Making sense of Daesh in Afghanistan: a social movement perspective', Bonn, Germany: BICC, Working Paper 6, 2017, p. 41.

30. Interview with IS-K 67, Financial Commission member, March 2021.

31. Interview with IS-K 67, Financial Commission member, March 2021.

32. Interview with IS-K 67, Financial Commission member, March 2021

33. Interview with IS-K 67, Financial Commission member, March 2021.

34. Interview with IS-K 67, Financial Commission member, March 2021.

35. Interview with IS-K 20, cadre, July 2016.

36. Interview with IS-K 20, cadre, July 2016.

37. Interview with IS-K 20, cadre, July 2016.

38. Interview with IS-K 15, cadre, Pakistan, January 2016.

39. Patrick B. Johnston et al., 'Foundations of the Islamic State: management, money, and terror in Iraq, 2005–2010', Santa Monica, CA: Rand, 2016.

40. Interview with IS-K 20, cadre, July 2016.

41. Interview with IS-K 3, senior cadre, February 2015.

42. Interview with IS-K 18, cadre of Gansu Hui Group, Nangarhar, July 2016; interview with IS-K 19, member of Gansu Hui Group, Pakistan, July 2016.

43. Interview with IS-K 20, cadre, July 2016.

44. Interview with IS-K 59, commander in Achin, April 2017.

45. Interview with IS-K 1, Khorasan-level leader, June 2015.

46. Interview with IS-K 21, commander, Ghazni, April 2016; interview with IS-K 4, cadre, February 2016; interview with IS-K 7, cadre, April 2015.

47. Interview with IS-K 20, cadre, July 2016.

48. Interview with IS-K 20, cadre, July 2016.

49. Interview with IS-K 22, cadre, March 2015.

50. Interview with IS-K 28, cadre, Kunar, July 2016; interview with IS-K 29, cadre, Kunar, February 2016.

51. Interview with IS-K 20, cadre, July 2016.

52. Interview with IS-K 30, cadre, Farah, December 2015.

53. Interview with IS-K 31, cadre, Herat, December 2015.

54. Interview with IS-K 6, cadre, April 2015; interview with External Observer/

Participant 5, Qatar intelligence, April 2015; interview with IS-K 21, commander, Ghazni, April 2016.

55. Interview with IS-K 22, cadre, March 2015.
56. Interview with IS-K 29, cadre, Kunar, February 2016.
57. Interview with IS-K 30, cadre, Farah, December 2015.
58. Interview with IS-K 30, cadre, Farah, December 2015.
59. Interview with IS-K 7, cadre, April 2015.
60. Interview with IS-K 22, cadre, March 2015.
61. Interview with IS-K 60, financial cadre, April 2017.
62. Interview with External Observer/Participant 2, ISI officer, Pakistan, January 2016.
63. Interview with External Observer/Participant 4, NDS officer, Jalalabad, January 2016.
64. Interview with IS-K 23, cadre, June 2016.
65. Interview with IS-K 23, cadre, June 2016.
66. Interview with IS-K 26, cadre, Pakistan, July 2016.
67. Interview with IS-K 21, commander, Ghazni, April 2016.
68. Interview with IS-K 26, cadre, Pakistan, July 2016.
69. Interview with IS-K 32, cadre, Finance Commission, November 2015.
70. Interview with IS-K 32, cadre, Finance Commission, November 2015.
71. Interview with IS-K 32, cadre, Finance Commission, November 2015.
72. Interview with IS-K 21, commander, Ghazni, April 2016.
73. Interview with IS-K 11, senior cadre, January 2016; interview with IS-K 24, commander, February 2016; interview with IS-K 34, interpreter, November 2015.
74. Interview with IS-K 16, cadre, Pakistan, December 2015.
75. Interview with IS-K 37, commander, Achin, Nangarhar, April 2016.
76. Meetings with Elder 6, focus group, December 2015, and interview with Elder 14, January 2016; interview with IS-K 15, cadre, Pakistan, January 2016; interview with IS-K 30, cadre, Farah, December 2015.
77. Interview with Elder 6, focus group, Nangarhar, December 2015; meeting with Western diplomats in Kabul, November 2015.
78. Interview with External Observer/Participant 6, Taliban military cadre, Helmand, January 2016.
79. Interview with IS-K 32, cadre, Finance Commission, November 2015.
80. Interview with IS-K 32, cadre, Finance Commission, November 2015.
81. Interview with IS-K 26, cadre, Pakistan, July 2016.
82. Interview with IS-K 33, commander, Pakistan, January 2016.
83. Interview with IS-K 32, cadre, Finance Commission, November 2015.
84. Interview with IS-K 32, cadre, Finance Commission, November 2015.
85. Interview with IS-K 32, cadre, Finance Commission, November 2015; interview with IS-K 1, Khorasan-level leader, June 2015.

86. Interview with IS-K 33, commander, Pakistan, January 2016; interview with IS-K 29, cadre, Kunar, February 2016; interview with IS-K 32, cadre, Finance Commission, November 2015; interview with IS-K 10, senior cadre, October 2015.

87. Interview with IS-K 24, commander, Jaysh ul-Islam, February 2016.

88. Interview with IS-K 30, cadre, Farah, December 2015.

89. Interview with IS-K 32, cadre, Finance Commission, November 2015; interview with IS-K 31, cadre, Herat, December 2015; interview with IS-K 34, interpreter, November 2015; interview with IS-K 32, cadre, Finance Commission, November 2015.

90. Interview with IS-K 34, interpreter, November 2015.

91. Interview with IS-K 32, cadre, Finance Commission, November 2015.

92. Interview with External Observer/Participant 3, NDS officer, Kabul, January 2016.

93. Interview with IS-K 35, private contractor, January 2016.

94. Interview with IS-K 35, private contractor, January 2016.

95. Interview with IS-K 35, private contractor, January 2016.

96. Interview with IS-K 35, private contractor, January 2016.

97. Interview with IS-K 32, cadre, Finance Commission, November 2015.

98. Interview with IS-K 32, cadre, Finance Commission, November 2015; interview with External Observer/Participant 6, Taliban military cadre, Helmand, January 2016; interview with External Observer/Participant 3, NDS officer, Kabul, January 2016.

99. Interview with IS-K 25, cadre, Pakistan, October 2015.

100. Notebook of IS-K leader, obtained July 2015, July 2015.

101. Interview with Elder 7, Kot, Nangarhar, February 2016; interview with Elder 5, Kot, Nangarhar, February 2016.

102. Interview with External Observer/Participant 7, Nangarhar, January 2016; interview with IS-K 36, deserter, Nangarhar, January 2016.

103. Katja Mielke and Nick Miszak, 'Making sense of Daesh in Afghanistan: a social movement perspective', Bonn, Germany: BICC, Working Paper 6, 2017, p. 46.

104. Interview with IS-K 1, Khorasan-level leader, June 2015.

105. Interview with IS-K 1, Khorasan-level leader, June 2015.

106. Interview with IS-K 1, Khorasan-level leader, June 2015.

107. Interview with IS-K 38, cadre, Kot, Nangarhar, June 2016.

108. Interview with Elder 5, Kot, Nangarhar, February 2016.

109. Interview with IS-K 17, cadre, Nangarhar, June 2016.

110. Interview with IS-K 36, deserter, Nangarhar, January 2016.

111. Interview with IS-K 1, Khorasan-level leader, June 2015.

112. Interview with IS-K 68, cadre in Badakhshan, July 2020.

113. Interview with IS-K 39, commander, Kajaki, Helmand, January 2016.

114. Interview with IS-K 36, deserter, Nangarhar, January 2016.
115. Interview with IS-K 11, senior cadre, January 2016.
116. Interview with IS-K 41, cadre, Nangarhar, March 2016.
117. Interview with IS-K 21, commander, Ghazni, April 2016; interview with IS-K 37, commander, Achin, Nangarhar, April 2016; interview with IS-K 40, fighter, Kot, Nangarhar, April 2016; interview with IS-K 41, commander, Achin, Nangarhar, March 2016.
118. Interview with IS-K 59, commander in Achin, April 2017.
119. Interview with IS-K 14, cadre, Kunduz, October 2015.
120. Interview with IS-K 10, senior cadre, October 2015.
121. Interview with IS-K 9, senior cadre, October 2015; interview with IS-K 16, cadre, Pakistan, December 2015; interview with IS-K 14, cadre, Kunduz, October 2015
122. Interview with IS-K 15, cadre, Pakistan, January 2016.
123. For the Taliban see T. Farrell and A. Giustozzi, 'The Taliban at war', *International Affairs*, July 2013.
124. Johnson, op. cit.
125. Interview with IS-K 53, commander, Achin, Nangarhar, August 2016.
126. Interview with External Observer/Participant 4, NDS officer, Jalalabad, January 2016; Masjal, op. cit.
127. Interview with IS-K 1, Khorasan-level leader, June 2015.
128. Interview with Elder 8, Kajaki, Helmand, December 2015.
129. Interview with External Observer/Participant 7, Nangarhar, January 2016.
130. Interview with IS-K 1, Khorasan-level leader, June 2015.
131. Interview with IS-K 1, Khorasan-level leader, June 2015.
132. Interview with IS-K 1, Khorasan-level leader, June 2015.
133. United Nations Security Council, 'Letter dated 19 July 2016 from the Chair of the Security Council Committee pursuant to resolutions 1267 (1999), 1989 (2011) and 2253 (2015) concerning Islamic State in Iraq and the Levant (Da'esh), Al-Qaida and associated individuals, groups, undertakings and entities addressed to the President of the Security Council', S/2016/629, 16-11359 (E) 100816, 19 July 2016.
134. 'Daesh group in competition for recruits in Pakistan', Associated Press, 2 March,2016.
135. Interview with IS-K 56, cadre in the propaganda department, March 2017.
136. Interview with IS-K 56, cadre in the propaganda department, March 2017.
137. Borhan Osman, 'ISKP's battle for minds: what are its main messages and who do they attract?', Berlin: Afghanistan Analyst Network, 12 December 2016.
138. Interview with IS-K 56, cadre in the propaganda department, March 2017.
139. Interview with Elder 6, focus group, Nangarhar, December 2015.
140. Thomas Joscelyn, '"Voice of the Caliphate" radio broadcasts anti-Taliban propaganda in Afghanistan', *Long War Journal*, 31 December 2015.

141. Katja Mielke and Nick Miszak, 'Making sense of Daesh in Afghanistan: a social movement perspective', Bonn, Germany: BICC, Working Paper 6, 2017, pp. 43, 46, 51.

142. Katja Mielke and Nick Miszak, 'Making sense of Daesh in Afghanistan: a social movement perspective', Bonn, Germany: BICC, Working Paper 6, 2017, p. 46.

143. Interview with External Observer/Participant 3, NDS officer, Kabul, January 2016; interview with External Observer/Participant 4, NDS officer, Jalalabad, January 2016.

144. Katja Mielke and Nick Miszak, 'Making sense of Daesh in Afghanistan: a social movement perspective', Bonn, Germany: BICC, Working Paper 6, 2017, pp. 43–4.

145. MIR, op. cit.

146. Interview with Elder 11, Kajaki, Helmand, December 2015; interview with Elder 8, Kajaki, Helmand, December 2015.

147. Interview with IS-K 56, cadre in the propaganda department, March 2017.

148. Interview with IS-K 56, cadre in the propaganda department, March 2017.

149. Interview with IS-K 56, cadre in the propaganda department, March 2017.

150. Interview with Elder 9, Kajaki, Helmand, November 2015.

151. Interview with Elder 8, Kajaki, Helmand, December 2015; interview with Elder 11, Kajaki, Helmand, December 2015; interview with Elder 10, Kajaki, Helmand, December 2015; interview with Elder 2, Achin, Nangarhar, January 2016; interview with Elder 7, Kot, Nangarhar, February 2016; interview with Elder 5, Kot, Nangarhar, February 2016; interview with Elder 1, Kajaki, Helmand, December 2015; interview with Elder 12, Kajaki, Helmand, December 2015; interview with Elder 4, Achin, Nangarhar, March 2016; interview with Elder 13, Achin, Nangarhar, March 2016.

152. Interview with Elder 3, Kot, Nangarhar, March 2016.

153. Interview with Elder 4, Achin, Nangarhar, March 2016; interview with Elder 5, Kot, Nangarhar, February 2016.

154. Interview with IS-K 52, cadre, Nangarhar, December 2016.

155. Interviews with members of the Haqqani network, 2014–15.

156. Interview with IS-K 52, cadre, Nangarhar, December 2016.

157. Osman, 19 October 2016, op. cit.

158. Osman, 19 October 2016, op. cit.

159. Interview with External Observer/Participant 13, Haqqani network cadre, December 2016.

160. Interview with IS-K 52, cadre, Nangarhar, December 2016.

161. Interview with IS-K 52, cadre, Nangarhar, December 2016.

162. Interview with IS-K 7, cadre, April 2015.

163. Interview with IS-K 34, interpreter, November 2015.

164. Interview with IS-K 8, senior cadre, January 2016; interview with IS-K 9, senior

cadre, October 2015; interview with IS-K 10, senior cadre, October 2015; interview with IS-K 2, leader, October 2015; interviews with IS-K 1, Khorasan-level leader, June 2015.

165. Interview with IS-K 1, Khorasan-level leader, June 2015; see on bayat 'Uzbek group in Afghanistan pledge allegiance to Islamic State', *RFE/RL's Uzbek Service*, 30 March 2015; Don Rassler, 'Situating the emergence of the Islamic State of Khorasan', *CTC Sentinel*, March 2015. Vol. 8, Iss. 3.

166. Interview with IS-K 26, cadre, Pakistan, July 2016.

167. Interview with IS-K 10, senior cadre, October 2015; interview with IS-K 9, senior cadre, October 2015; interview with IS-K 7, cadre, April 2015; interview with IS-K 26, cadre, Pakistan, July 2016; interview with IS-K 3, senior cadre, February 2015.

168. Interview with IS-K 21, commander, Ghazni, April 2016; interview with IS-K 2, leader, October 2015.

169. Interview with IS-K 1, Khorasan-level leader, June 2015.

170. Interview with IS-K 29, cadre, Kunar, February 2016.

171. Interview with IS-K 36, deserter, Nangarhar, January 2016.

172. Interview with IS-K 30, cadre, Farah, December 2015.

173. Interview with IS-K 37, commander, Achin, Nangarhar, April 2016.

174. Interview with IS-K 1, Khorasan-level leader, June 2015.

175. Interview with IS-K 1, Khorasan-level leader, June 2015; interview with IS-K 11, senior cadre, January 2016.

176. Interview with IS-K 1, Khorasan-level leader, June 2015.

177. Interview with IS-K 23, cadre, June 2016.

178. Interview with IS-K 9, senior cadre, October 2015; interview with IS-K 1, Khorasan-level leader, June 2015; interview with IS-K 15, cadre, Pakistan, January 2016; interview with IS-K 5, senior cadre, December 2014; interview with IS-K 16, cadre, Pakistan, December 2015; interview with IS-K 25, cadre, Pakistan, October 2015; interview with IS-K 33, commander, Pakistan, January 2016.

179. Interview with IS-K 49, finance officer, Waziristan, April 2015.

180. See sources for Table 5.

181. Interview with IS-K 22, cadre, March 2015; interview with IS-K 23, cadre, June 2016; interview with IS-K 24, commander, Jaysh ul-Islam, February 2016; interview with IS-K 15, cadre, Pakistan, January 2016; interview with IS-K 5, senior cadre, December 2014; interview with IS-K 16, cadre, Pakistan, December 2015; interview with IS-K 25, cadre, Pakistan, October 2015; interview with IS-K 10, senior cadre, October 2015; interview with IS-K 1, Khorasan-level leader, June 2015; interview with IS-K 14, cadre, Kunduz, October 2015; interview with IS-K 9, senior cadre, October 2015; interview with IS-K 26, cadre, Pakistan, July 2016.

182. Interview with IS-K 11, senior cadre, January 2016; interview with IS-K 15,

cadre, Pakistan, January 2016; interviews with IS-K 1, Khorasan-level leader, June 2015; interview with IS-K 8, senior cadre, January 2016.

183. Interview with IS-K 26, cadre, Pakistan, July 2016.

184. Interview with IS-K 26, cadre, Pakistan, July 2016.

185. Interview with IS-K 36, deserter, Nangarhar, January 2016.

186. Interview with IS-K 37, commander, Achin, Nangarhar, April 2016.

187. Interview with IS-K 1, Khorasan-level leader, June 2015.

188. Interview with IS-K 59, commander in Achin, April 2017; interviews with IS-K 60, financial cadre, April 2017.

189. Interview with IS-K 28, cadre, Kunar, July 2016.

190. Interview with IS-K 10, senior cadre, October 2015.

191. Interview with IS-K 10, senior cadre, October 2015; interview with IS-K 31, cadre, Herat, December 2015; interview with IS-K 9, senior cadre, October 2015.

192. Interview with IS-K 14, cadre, Kunduz, October 2015.

193. Interview with IS-K 26, cadre, Pakistan, July 2016.

194. Interview with IS-K 1, Khorasan-level leader, June 2015.

195. Chris Sands and Fazelminallah Qazizai, 'ISIL emerges in Afghanistan "stronger than the Taliban"', *The National*, 29 October 2015. Pictures of IS-K men on horses appeared on the web: https://twitter.com/saladinaldronni/status/858 022521433731073; http://www.longwarjournal.org/assets_c/2015/02/Islamic-State-Khorasan-province-march-5738.php.

196. Hamid Shalizi, 'Exclusive: in turf war with Afghan Taliban, Islamic State loyalists gain ground', *Reuters*, 29 June 2015.

197. Interview with IS-K 10, senior cadre, October 2015.

198. Adam Baczko et Gilles Dorronsoro, 'Logiques transfrontalières et Salafisme globalisé', *Critique Internationale*, No. 74, 2017, pp. 137–52.

199. Interview with Elder 8, Kajaki, Helmand, December 2015; Katja Mielke and Nick Miszak, 'Making sense of Daesh in Afghanistan: a social movement perspective', Bonn, Germany: BICC, Working Paper 6, 2017, p. 52; interview with Elder 9, Kajaki, Helmand, November 2015.

200. Personal observation, February 2017. The Facebook pages of IS-K change all the time, so it is not possible to provide an address.

201. Interview with Elder 9, Kajaki, Helmand, November 2015.

202. Interview with Elder 10, Kajaki, Helmand, December 2015.

203. Interview with IS-K 56, cadre in the propaganda department, March 2017.

5. DRIVERS OF SUPPORT FOR IS-K

1. Interview with IS-K 17, cadre, Nangarhar, June 2016; Taliban source in Peshawar, contacted in September 2016; Taliban source in Peshawar, contacted in December 2016.

2. Interview with IS-K 17, cadre, Nangarhar, June 2016.

3. Interview with IS-K 2, leader, October 2015.

4. Interview with External Observer/Participant 1, Revolutionary Guards (Iran) officer, Afghanistan, January 2016; interview with External Observer/Participant 6, Taliban military cadre, Helmand, January 2016; interview with IS-K 8, senior cadre, January 2016; interview with IS-K 40, fighter, Kot, Nangarhar, April 2016; interview with IS-K 41, commander, Achin, Nangarhar, March 2016; interview with IS-K 48, fighter, Kajaki, Helmand, December 2015; interview with IS-K 31, cadre, Herat, December 2015.

5. Interview with External Observer/Participant 7, Nangarhar, January 2016; interview with External Observer/Participant 4, NDS officer, Jalalabad, January 2016; interview with IS-K 1, Khorasan-level leader, June 2015; Borhan Osman, 'Descent into chaos: why did Nangarhar turn into an IS', AAN, 27 September 2016.

6. Katja Mielke and Nick Miszak, 'Making sense of Daesh in Afghanistan: a social movement perspective', Bonn, Germany: BICC, Working Paper 6, 2017, p. 43.

7. Johnson, op. cit.

8. Interview with External Observer/Participant 3, NDS officer, Kabul, January 2016.

9. Communication with External Observer/Participant 29, development organization security official, 12 January 2016.

10. Interview with External Observer/Participant 6, Taliban military cadre, Helmand, January 2016; interview with IS-K 40, fighter, Kot, Nangarhar, April 2016; interview with IS-K 41, commander, Achin, Nangarhar, March 2016.

11. See Antonio Giustozzi, *The Taliban at War* (2nd edition), London: Hurst, 2022.

12. Interview with IS-K 51, commander, Turkey, June 2016; interview with IS-K 1, Khorasan-level leader, June 2015.

13. Interview with IS-K 51, commander, Turkey, June 2016.

14. Interview with IS-K 29, cadre, Kunar, February 2016.

15. See Giustozzi, *Taliban at War*, op. cit..

16. Interview with IS-K 39, commander, Kajaki, Helmand, January 2016.

17. Interview with IS-K 8, senior cadre, January 2016.

18. Interview with Ally 6, commander, IMT, northern Afghanistan, May 2016.

19. Interview with IS-K 3, senior cadre, February 2015.

20. Interview with External Observer/Participant 6, Taliban military cadre, Helmand, January 2016; interview with External Observer/Participant 3, NDS officer, Kabul, January 2016.

21. Interview with Elder 8, Kajaki, Helmand, December 2015.

22. Interview with Elder 12, Kajaki, Helmand, December 2015.

23. Interview with Elder 6, focus group, Nangarhar, December 2015.

24. Interview with IS-K 20, cadre, July 2016.

25. Interview with IS-K 2, leader, October 2015.

26. Interview with IS-K 21, commander, Ghazni, April 2016; interview with IS-K 3, senior cadre, February 2015; interview with Elder 11, Kajaki, Helmand, December 2015; interview with Elder 4, Achin, Nangarhar, March 2016.

27. Interview with IS-K 40, fighter, Kot, Nangarhar, April 2016.

28. Interview with External Observer/Participant 6, Taliban military cadre, Helmand, January 2016.

29. Interview with IS-K 3, senior cadre, February 2015.

30. Interview with External Observer/Participant 6, Taliban military cadre, Helmand, January 2016.

31. Interview with External Observer/Participant 4, NDS officer, Jalalabad, January 2016.

32. Interview with External Observer/Participant 3, NDS officer, Kabul, January 2016.

33. Interview with External Observer/Participant 7, Nangarhar, January 2016.

34. Sarah Ladbury, 'Radicalisation in Pakistan and Afghanistan: taking a joined up perspective', Independent Report for the Department for International Development, London: DFID and United Kingdom, Foreign and Commonwealth Office, 2009; Antonio Giustozzi, 'Thirty years of conflict', Kabul: AREU, 2012.

35. Interview with Elder 14, Sherzad, Nangarhar, January 2016.

36. Interview with IS-K 51, commander, Turkey, June 2016.

37. Interview with External Observer/Participant 6, Taliban military cadre, Helmand, January 2016.

38. Interview with IS-K 1, Khorasan-level leader, June 2015.

39. Johnson, op. cit.

40. Interview with IS-K 2, leader, October 2015.

41. Obaid Ali and Khalid Gharanai, 'War and peace: hit from many sides (2): the demise of ISKP in Kunar', Berlin: AAN, 3 March 2021.

42. Interview with External Observer/Participant 2, ISI officer, Pakistan, January 2016.

43. Interview with IS-K 16, cadre, December 2015; Notebook of IS-K leader, obtained July 2015, July 2015.

44. Notebook of IS-K leader, obtained July 2015; interview with External Observer/Participant 4, NDS officer, Jalalabad, January 2016; interview with IS-K 29, cadre, Kunar, February 2016; interview with IS-K 13, cadre, Jowzjan, May 2016; interview with External Observer/Participant 6, Taliban military cadre, Helmand, January 2016; interview with IS-K 10, senior cadre, October 2015; interview with IS-K 16, cadre, Pakistan, December 2015; interview with IS-K 49, finance officer, Waziristan, April 2015; interview with IS-K 21, commander, Ghazni, April 2016.

45. Interview with IS-K 48, fighter, Kajaki, Helmand, December 2015; interview with IS-K 51, commander, Turkey, June 2016.

46. Interview with IS-K 11, senior cadre, January 2016; interview with IS-K 29, cadre,

Kunar, February 2016; interview with IS-K 8, senior cadre, January 2016; interview with IS-K 13, cadre, Jowzjan, May 2016; interviews with IS-K 1, Khorasan-level leader, June 2015; interview with IS-K 14, cadre, Kunduz, October 2015; interview with IS-K 31, cadre, Herat, December 2015; interview with IS-K 25, cadre, Pakistan, October 2015; interview with IS-K 16, cadre, Pakistan, December 2015; interview with IS-K 9, senior cadre, October 2015; interview with IS-K 30, cadre, Farah, December 2015.

47. Interview with IS-K 5, senior cadre, December 2014.
48. Interview with IS-K 39, commander, Kajaki, Helmand, January 2016.
49. Interview with Elder 2, Achin, Nangarhar, January 2016.
50. Interview with Elder 10, Kajaki, Helmand, December 2015.
51. Interview with IS-K 41, commander, Achin, Nangarhar, March 2016.
52. Interview with IS-K 37, commander, Achin, Nangarhar, April 2016.
53. Interview with IS-K 48, fighter, Kajaki, Helmand, December 2015.
54. Interview with IS-K 47, commander, Kajaki, Helmand, December 2015.
55. Interview with IS-K 21, commander, Ghazni, April 2016.
56. Interview with Ally 6, IMT commander, northern Afghanistan, October 2015.
57. Interview with IS-K 7, cadre, April 2015.
58. Interview with IS-K 18, cadre of Gansu Hui Group, Nangarhar, July 2016; interview with IS-K 19, member of Gansu Hui Group, Pakistan, July 2016; interview with External Observer/Participant 14, Hui commander, TTP, November 2016.
59. Interview with IS-K 45, commander, Gansu Hui Group, Northern Afghanistan, May 2016.
60. Interview with IS-K 37, commander, Achin, Nangarhar, April 2016; interview with IS-K 47, commander, Kajaki, Helmand, December 2015; interview with IS-K 41, commander, Achin, Nangarhar, March 2016; interview with IS-K 39, commander, Kajaki, Helmand, January 2016; interview with IS-K 47, commander, Kajaki, Helmand, December 2015; interview with IS-K 40, fighter, Kot, Nangarhar, April 2016; Franz J. Marty, 'Speaking to an Afghan disciple of the Caliphate', *The Diplomat*, 28 July 2016.
61. Interview with IS-K 39, commander, Kajaki, Helmand, January 2016.
62. Interview with External Observer/Participant 1, Revolutionary Guards (Iran) officer, Afghanistan, January 2016.
63. Interview with IS-K 30, cadre, Farah, December 2015; interview with IS-K 31, cadre, Herat, December 2015.
64. Interview with Elder 8, Kajaki, Helmand, December 2015.
65. Interview with Elder 8, Kajaki, Helmand, December 2015.
66. Interview with IS-K 29, cadre, Kunar, February 2016; interview with IS-K 19, member of Gansu Hui Group, Pakistan, July 2016; interview with IS-K 27, commander, northern Afghanistan, July 2016; interview with IS-K 13, cadre, Jowzjan, May 2016; interview with IS-K 30, cadre, Farah, December 2015; interview with

IS-K 31, cadre, Herat, December 2015; interviews with IS-K 1, Khorasan-level leader, June 2015; interview with IS-K 2, leader, October 2015; interview with IS-K 69, commander in Jowzjan, August 2018; interview with Tajikistani IS-K 70, commander in Badakhshan, April 2020; interview with IS-K 71, commander in Nangarhar, June 2020.

67. Katja Mielke and Nick Miszak, 'Making sense of Daesh in Afghanistan: a social movement perspective', Bonn, Germany: BICC, Working Paper 6, 2017, p. 51.

68. Interview with IS-K 1, Khorasan-level leader, June 2015.

69. Interview with IS-K 47, commander, Kajaki, Helmand, December 2015.

70. Interview with Elder 12, Kajaki, Helmand, December 2015; interview with Elder 9, Kajaki, Helmand, November 2015; interview with Elder 8, Kajaki, Helmand, December 2015; interview with Elder 11, Kajaki, Helmand, December 2015; interview with Elder 10, Kajaki, Helmand, December 2015; interview with IS-K 48, fighter, Kajaki, Helmand, December 2015.

71. Osman, 12 February 2015, op. cit.

72. Interview with Elder 10, Kajaki, Helmand, December 2015.

73. Interview with IS-K 9, senior cadre, October 2015.

74. Interview with IS-K 10, senior cadre, October 2015.

75. Interview with IS-K 21, commander, Ghazni, April 2016.

76. Interview with Elder 2, Achin, Nangarhar, January 2016; interview with Elder 13, Achin, Nangarhar, March 2016.

77. Interview with Elder 3, Kot, Nangarhar, March 2016; interview with Elder 7, Kot, Nangarhar, February 2016; interview with Elder 5, Kot, Nangarhar, February 2016.

78. Interview with IS-K 14, cadre, Kunduz, October 2015.

79. Interview with IS-K 37, commander, Achin, Nangarhar, April 2016; interview with IS-K 40, fighter, Kot, Nangarhar, April 2016; interview with IS-K 41, commander, Achin, Nangarhar, March 2016; interview with IS-K 39, commander, Kajaki, Helmand, January 2016; interview with IS-K 48, fighter, Kajaki, Helmand, December 2015.

80. Interview with Elder 2, Achin, Nangarhar, January 2016; interview with Elder 3, Kot, Nangarhar, March 2016; interview with Elder 13, Achin, Nangarhar, March 2016; interview with Elder 7, Kot, Nangarhar, February 2016; interview with Elder 5, Kot, Nangarhar, February 2016; interview with Elder 1, Kajaki, Helmand, December 2015; interview with Elder 8, Kajaki, Helmand, December 2015.

81. Interview with Elder 11, Kajaki, Helmand, December 2015.

82. Interview with Elder 3, Kot, Nangarhar, March 2016.

83. Interview with Elder 10, Kajaki, Helmand, December 2015.

84. Interview with External Observer/Participant 3, NDS officer, Kabul, January 2016.

85. Interview with IS-K 54, senior commander in Zazai, November 2016; interview with Elder 15, Zazai, January 2017.

86. Interview with Elder 15, Zabul, January 2017.

87. Adam Baczko et Gilles Dorronsoro, 'Logiques transfrontalières et Salafisme globalisé', *Critique Internationale*, 2017/1, No. 74, pp. 137–52.

88. Fazul Rahim and Alexander Smith, 'ISIS-linked fighters tighten grip in Afghanistan, outmatch Taliban brutality, NBC News, 1 May 2015.

89. Interview with IS-K 16, cadre, Pakistan, December 2015.

90. Interview with IS-K 1, Khorasan-level leader, June 2015; interview with IS-K 21, commander, Ghazni, April 2016.

91. Interview with External Observer/Participant 3, NDS officer, Kabul, January 2016.

92. On Salafi networks linked to the Gulf and to Daesh, see Katja Mielke and Nick Miszak, 'Making sense of Daesh in Afghanistan: a social movement perspective', Bonn, Germany: BICC, Working Paper 6, 2017, p. 39.

93. Adam Baczko et Gilles Dorronsoro, 'Logiques transfrontalières et Salafisme globalisé', *Critique Internationale*, 2017/1, No. 74, pp. 137–52.

94. Interview with Elder 9, Kajaki, Helmand, November 2015; interview with Elder 11, Kajaki, Helmand, December 2015; interview with Elder 2, Achin, Nangarhar, January 2016; interview with Elder 3, Kot, Nangarhar, March 2016; interview with Elder 1, Kajaki, Helmand, December 2015.

95. Interview with Elder 5, Kot, Nangarhar, February 2016; interview with Elder 14, Sherzad, Nangarhar, January 2016.

96. Interview with External Observer/Participant 4, NDS officer, Jalalabad, January 2016.

97. Interview with IS-K 3, senior cadre, February 2015.

98. Interview with External Observer 30, NGO source in Pakistan, January 2017.

99. Interview with Elder 10, Kajaki, Helmand, December 2015; interview with Elder 4, Achin, Nangarhar, March 2016; interview with Elder 7, Kot, Nangarhar, February 2016.

100. 'ISIS loyalists kill Mullah Imam in Nangarhar province', *Khaama Press*, 11 September 2015; Ashiqullah Rahhimzoy and Ibrahim Nasar, 'Islamic State running prisons inside Afghanistan', *VOA News*, 9 September 2015.

101. Johnson, op. cit.

102. Johnson, op. cit.

103. Interview with Elder 12, Kajaki, Helmand, December 2015.

104. Chishti, op. cit.

105. Interview with External Observer/Participant 2, ISI officer, Pakistan, January 2016.

106. Interview with IS-K 5, senior cadre, December 2014.

107. Interview with IS-K 1, Khorasan-level leader, June 2015.

108. Interview with IS-K 16, cadre, Pakistan, December 2015.

109. NGO source in Pakistan, interviewed in January 2017.

110. Borhan Osman, 'With an active cell in Kabul, ISKP tries to bring sectarianism to the Afghan War', *Afghanistan Analysts Network*, 19 October 2016.

111. Interview with IS-K 20, cadre, July 2016.

112. Samira Shackle, 'Karachi's brightest young minds swear allegiance to Isis', *The Times*, 21 June 2016; Zoha Waseem, 'Daesh in Pakistan: an evolving militant landscape—Part I', *Strife*, 6 February 2016; 'Daesh group in competition for recruits in Pakistan', Associated Press, 2 March 2016; Fatima Bhojani, 'ISIS is on the decline in the Middle East, but its influence in Pakistan is rising', *Washington Post*, 5 May 2017.

113. Azami, op. cit.

114. Chishti, op. cit.

115. Interview with IS-K 70, Tajikistani commander in Badakhshan, April 2020.

116. Animesh Roul, 'Islamic State gains ground in Afghanistan as its Caliphate crumbles elsewhere', *Terrorism Monitor*, Vol. 16, Iss. 2, 26 January 2018.

117. Interview with IS-K 17, cadre, Nangarhar, June 2016.

118. Tariq Majidi, 'Nangarhar University students raise Taliban, Daesh flags', *TOLOnews*, 9 November 2015.

119. Interview with External Observer/Participant 3, NDS officer, Kabul, January 2016.

120. Interview with External Observer/Participant 4, NDS officer, Jalalabad, January 2016.

121. Mir Abed Joenda, '27 Nangarhar Students arrested for raising Taliban, Daesh flags', *TOLOnews*, 17 November 2015.

122. Interview with External Observer/Participant 3, NDS officer, Kabul, January 2016; interview with IS-K 36, deserter, Nangarhar, January 2016.

123. Interview with IS-K 17, cadre, Nangarhar, June 2016.

124. Ezzatullah Mehrdad, 'How Islamic State infiltrated Kabul University', *The Diplomat*, 12 August 2019.

125. Emran Feroz, 'In Afghanistan, the Islamic State threatens long-term peace', *Foreign Policy*, 4 June 2020.

6. THE EXPANSION OF IS-K, 2015–17

1. Azami, op. cit.

2. 'US airstrikes target Islamic State in Afghanistan', Associated Press, 11 February 2016.

3. United Nations Security Council, 19 July 2016, op. cit.

4. http://www.rs.nato.int/article/transcripts/brig.-gen.-charles-cleveland-speaks-with-tv1-dec.-17.html.

5. Communications with Taliban cadres in the Quetta Shura and the Mashhad Office, taking place repeatedly over the course of 2015 and 2016.

6. Ibid. and personal communication with official of the Afghan National Security Council, October 2016; Edwin Mora, 'Afghanistan: Russia openly aligns with Taliban, says U.S. presence 'disturbing', *Breitbart*, 16 February 2017; Samuel Ramani, 'Russia and the Taliban: a closer look', *The Diplomat*, 29 December 2016; Ankit Panda, 'How Russia may approach the Taliban and Afghanistan in 2017', *The Diplomat*, 4 January 2017.

7. Zahid Gishkori, 'Some foreign militants recruiting for Daesh in Pakistan', *The News*, 5 June 2016.

8. Personal communication with Indian diplomat, February 2017.

9. Interview with External Observer/Participant 1, Revolutionary Guards (Iran) officer, Afghanistan, January 2016.

10. Interview with External Observer/Participant 2, ISI officer, Pakistan, January 2016.

11. Interview with External Observer/Participant 3, NDS officer, Kabul, January 2016.

12. Hekmatullah Azamy, 'Challenges and prospects for Daesh in Afghanistan and its relations with the Taliban', *Panorama—Insights into Asian and European Affairs*, October 2016.

13. Interview with External Observer/Participant 24, TTP commander in Bajaur, January 2016; External Observer 27, Taliban cadre in Quetta, contacted in June 2017.

14. Interview with External Observer/Participant 3, NDS officer, Kabul, January 2016; interview with External Observer/Participant 4, NDS officer, Jalalabad, January 2016.

15. Interview with IS-K 54, senior commander, Pakistan, January 2017.

16. Interview with IS-K 10, senior cadre, October 2015; interview with IS-K 9, senior cadre, October 2015; interviews with IS-K 1, Khorasan-level leader, June 2015; interview with IS-K 6, cadre, April 2015; interview with IS-K 13, cadre, Jowzjan, May 2016; interview with IS-K 7, cadre, April 2015; interview with IS-K 14, cadre, Kunduz, October 2015; 'Uzbek militants pledge allegiance to Daesh', *TOLOnews. com*, 1 April 2015; 'Uzbek group in Afghanistan pledge allegiance to Islamic State', RFE/RL Uzbek Service, 30 March 2015; Damon Mehl, 'The Islamic movement of Uzbekistan opens a door to the Islamic State', *CTC Sentinel*, 29 June 2015; interview with Ally 1, IMU cadre, Faryab, May 2016; interview with Ally 2, IMU commander, Kunduz, October 2015; interview with IS-K 15, cadre, Pakistan, January 2016; interview with IS-K 16, cadre, Pakistan, December 2015; interview with IS-K 6, cadre, April 2015; interview with IS-K 2, leader, October 2015; interview with External Observer/Participant 1, Revolutionary Guards (Iran) officer, Afghanistan, January 2016; interview with External Observer/Participant 3, NDS

officer, Kabul, January 2016; interview with IS-K 17, cadre, Nangarhar, June 2016; interview with IS-K 54, senior commander, in Nangarhar, January 2017; interview with IS-K 72, cadre in Badakhshan, April 2020; interview with IS-K 71, commander in Nangarhar, June 2020; Gul, Ayaz, 'Russia says about 10,000 IS militants now in Afghanistan', *Voice of America*, 23 December 2017; Abdul Sayed, 'ISIS-K is ready to fight the Taliban. Here's how the group became a major threat in Afghanistan', *Washington Post*, 29 August 2021; United Nations Security Council, Letter dated 10 June 2019 from the Chair of the Security Council Committee established pursuant to resolution 1988 (2011) addressed to the President of the Security Council S/2019/481, 13 June 2019; Jeff Seldin, 'Islamic State in Afghanistan growing bigger, more dangerous', *Voice of America*, 21 May 2019; Hekmatullah Azamy, 'Challenges and prospects for Daesh in Afghanistan and its relations with the Taliban', Kabul: Konrad Adenauer Foundation, October 2016.

17. Interview with IS-K 2, leader, October 2015.

18. Interview with External Observer/Participant 3, NDS officer, Kabul, January 2016.

19. 'Iran smashes terrorist cell, reports direct link to ISIS', *Teheran Times*, 14 October 2016; 'Iran defuses Daesh bombing plot, confiscates 2 tonnes of explosives', *Press TV*, 15 November 2016; 'Iran disbands two terror cells, Intelligence Ministry says', *Press TV*, 21 November 2015; Ali Hashem, 'Iran's new challenge: the Islamic State in Persia?', *Al Monitor*, 24 October 2016; 'ISIS has support networks in Iran and smuggled in explosives: army chief', *Rudaw*, 24 November 2015.

20. Interview with IS-K 62, commander in Iran, June 2017.

21. 'The Asian Age', Delhi, 21 April 17; Vinod Janardhanan, 'How Islamic State is spreading wings in Indian states, slowly but surely', *Hindustan Times*, 3 May 2017.

22. Interview with IS-K 59, commander in Achin, April 2017.

23. 'Net chats between Kashmir and Syria, Iraq on security radar', *The Deccan Herald*, 8 May 2017.

24. Interview with Ally 13, commander of Jamaat Ansarullah, Badakhshan, January 2017; interview with IS-K 44, cadre, Kyrghizstan, September 2016.

25. Interview with IS-K 44, cadre, Kyrghizstan, September 2016.

26. Interview with IS-K 44, cadre, Kyrghizstan, September 2016. On Kazakhs fighting with the Islamic State, see Zhulduz Baizakova, '"Our people in an alien war": Kazakhstanis fighting for the Islamic State', *Eurasia Daily Monitor*, Vol. 11, Iss. 206, 18 November 2014.

27. Igor Rotar, 'Political Islam in Tajikistan after the formation of the IS', CERIA Briefs No. 5.

28. Interview with IS-K 1, Khorasan-level leader, June 2015; personal communication with security officer of development organization, June 2015.

29. Notebook of IS-K leader, obtained July 2015.

30. Notebook of IS-K leader, obtained July 2015.

31. Interview with IS-K 7, cadre, April 2015; interviews with IS-K 1, Khorasan-level leader, June 2015; 'Uzbek militants pledge allegiance to Daesh', *TOLOnews.com*, 1 April 2015; 'Uzbek Group in Afghanistan pledge allegiance to Islamic State', RFE/RL Uzbek Service, 30 March 2015; Damon Mehl, op. cit.

32. Interview with Ally 2, IMU commander, Kunduz, October 2015.

33. Interview with Ally 1, IMU cadre, Faryab, May 2016. It should be noted that the IMU has long adopted a sub-branding strategy in order to neutralize internal tensions: the Islamic Jihad Union, for example, first split from the IMU and then rejoined, but maintained a separate identity.

34. Katja Mielke and Nick Miszak, 'Making sense of Daesh in Afghanistan: a social movement perspective', Bonn, Germany: BICC, Working Paper 6, 2017, pp. 24–5, 41.

35. Interview with IS-K 1, Khorasan-level leader, June 2015.

36. Interview with IS-K 6, cadre, April 2015; interview with IS-K 13, cadre, Jowzjan, May 2016; interview with IS-K 7, cadre, April 2015; interviews with IS-K 1, Khorasan-level leader, June 2015; interview with IS-K 14, cadre, Kunduz, October 2015; interview with IS-K 14, cadre, Kunduz, October 2015.

37. Interview with IS-K 1, Khorasan-level leader, June 2015.

38. Interview with IS-K 7, cadre, April 2015; interviews with IS-K 1, Khorasan-level leader, June 2015.

39. Interview with IS-K 18, cadre, Gansu Hui Group, July 2016; interview with IS-K 19, member of Gansu Hui group, Pakistan, July 2016.

40. Interview with IS-K 18, cadre of Gansu Hui Group, Nangarhar, July 2016; interview with IS-K 19, member of Gansu Hui Group, Pakistan, July 2016.

41. Interview with IS-K 71, commander in Nangarhar, June 2020.

42. Interview with External Observer/Participant 8, donor, Arab Gulf country, January 2016.

43. Interview with IS-K 33, commander, Pakistan, January 2016.

44. Interview with IS-K 33, commander, Pakistan, January 2016.

45. Interview with IS-K 42, cadre, Finance Commission, Arab Gulf country, April 2015.

46. Interview with IS-K 33, commander, Pakistan, January 2016.

47. Interview with IS-K 33, commander, Pakistan, January 2016.

48. Interview with IS-K 33, commander, Pakistan, January 2016.

49. Interview with IS-K 24, commander, Jaysh ul-islam, February 2016.

50. Interview with IS-K 24, commander, Jaysh ul-islam, February 2016.

51. Interview with IS-K 26, cadre, Pakistan, July 2016.

52. Interview with IS-K 26, cadre, Pakistan, July 2016.

53. Interview with IS-K 26, cadre, Pakistan, July 2016.

54. Interview with IS-K 54, senior commander, Pakistan, January 2017.

55. Interview with IS-K 43, cadre, former Hizb-i Islami member, Pakistan, January

2016. The inhabitants of Shamsatoo are supposed to have relocated to Afghanistan following the peace agreement between Hizb-i Islami and the Kabul authorities, signed in September.

56. Interview with IS-K 43, cadre, former Hizb-i Islami member, Pakistan, January 2016.

57. Interview with IS-K 43, cadre, former Hizb-i Islami member, Pakistan, January 2016.

58. Interview with IS-K 43, cadre, former Hizb-i Islami member, Pakistan, January 2016; interview with External Observer/Participant 7, Nangarhar, January 2016; interview with IS-K 11, cadre, Khost, January 2016; interview with IS-K 14, cadre, Kunduz, October 2015.

59. Neil MacFarquhar, 'A nation challenged: warlords; Tehran shuts offices of Afghan hard-liner as calls to expel him increase', *New York Times*, 11 February 2002; 'Iran expels Hekmatyar', *UPI*, 26 February 2002.

60. Interviews with Hizb-i Islami cadres, September 2016 and May 2017.

61. Interview with IS-K 43, cadre, former Hizb-i Islami member, Pakistan, January 2016.

62. Interview with IS-K 7, cadre, April 2015; interview with IS-K 11, senior cadre, January 2016; interview with IS-K 26, cadre, Pakistan, July 2016; interview with IS-K 8, senior cadre, January 2016; interview with IS-K 13, cadre, Jowzjan, May 2016; interview with IS-K 9, senior cadre, October 2015; interview with IS-K 10, senior cadre, October 2015; interview with IS-K 25, cadre, Pakistan, October 2015; interview with IS-K 14, cadre, Kunduz, October 2015; interview with IS-K 3, senior cadre, February 2015; interview with IS-K 5, senior cadre, December 2014; interviews with IS-K 1, Khorasan-level leader, June 2015.

63. For a sceptical view, see Ed Lemon, 'Tajikistan really Jihad's next frontier?', Exeter Central Asian Studies Network, 13 June 2015, and Ed Lemon, 'Myth or reality? Tajik fighters in Syria', Exeter Central Asian Studies Network, 6 May 2014; Edward J. Lemon 'Daesh and Tajikistan: the regime's (in)security policy', *The RUSI Journal*, Vol. 160, No. 5, 2015, 68–76; 'Interview: Noah Tucker, "The 'growing threat' from Afghanistan is vastly overstated"', *The Diplomat*, 29 January 2016; Bayram Balci and Didier Chaudet, 'Jihadism in Central Asia: a credible threat after the Western withdrawal from Afghanistan?', Carnegie Endowment for International Peace, 13 August 2014. For the alarmist position, see 'Syria calling: radicalisation in Central Asia', Crisis Group Europe and Central Asia Briefing, No. 72, 20 January 2015.

64. Interview with IS Ally 11, Jamaat Ansarullah, February 2017.

65. Interview with IS-K ally 3, IJRPT commander, October 2015; interview with IJRPT commander, March 2015.

66. Interview with Ally 3, commander, October 2015; interview with IS-K 7, cadre, April 2015.

67. Interview with Ally 3, commander, October 2015.
68. Mehl, op. cit.
69. Merhat Sharipzhan, 'IMU declares it is now part of the Islamic State', *RFL*, 6 August 2015; Nathaniel Barr, 'Wilayat Khorasan stumbles in Afghanistan', *Terrorism Monitor*, Vol. 14, Iss. 5, 3 March 2016.
70. Interview with Ally 2, IMU commander, Kunduz, October 2015.
71. Interview with IS-K 7, cadre, April 2015.
72. Interview with External Observer 16, IMU commander, February 2017; interview with External Observer 20, Jamaat Al Bukhari commander, March 2017.
73. Interview with External Observer/Participant 1, Revolutionary Guards (Iran) officer, January 2016; Osman, op. cit.
74. Bill Roggio, 'Former IMU cleric latest to denounce Islamic State', *Long War Journal*, 30 August 2016; interview with Ally 2, IMU commander, Kunduz, October 2015; interview with Ally 1, IMU cadre, May 2016; interview with IS-K 7, cadre, April 2015; interview with Ally 4, IMU commander, June 2016.
75. Interview with IS-K 7, cadre, April 2015.
76. Interview with IS-K 27, commander, Gansu Hui Group, northern Afghanistan, July 2016; interview with IS-K 45, commander, Gansu Hui Group, northern Afghanistan, May 2016; interview with Ally 5, cadre, ETIM, northern Afghanistan, May 2016; interview with IS-K 13, cadre, Jowzjan, May 2016; interview with External Participant/Observer 23, TIP commander in Syria, May 2017.
77. Interview with IS-K 70, Tajikistani commander in Badakhshan, April 2020.
78. Interview with Ally 6, commander, IMT, northern Afghanistan, May 2016.
79. Interview with IS-K 7, cadre, April 2015.
80. Interview with Ally 6, commander, IMT, northern Afghanistan, May 2016.
81. External Observer 16, IMU, February 2017.
82. For a background on Jamaat Ansarullah, see Erlan Karin, *The Soldiers of the Caliphate: The Anatomy of a Terrorist Group*, Astana, Kazakhstan: The Kazakhstan Institute for Strategic Studies, 2016, pp. 143ff.
83. Interview with Ally 7, commander, Jamaat Ansarullah, northern Afghanistan, October 2015.
84. Interview with Ally 7, commander, Jamaat Ansarullah, northern Afghanistan, October 2015.
85. External Observer 16, IMU, February 2017; interview with IS Ally 11, Jamaat Ansarullah, February 2017.
86. Interview with IS-K 70, Tajikistani commander in Badakhshan, April 2020.
87. Interview with Ally 3, commander, October 2015; 'Interview with the "deceased" Takhir Yuldashev. Objectives and tasks of the IMU in Afghanistan, Pakistan and Central Asia', www.furgon.com (translated in http://easttime.info/analytics/tajikistan/interview-deceased-takhir-yuldashev-objectives-and-tasks-imu-afghanistan-pakist), 29 July 2010.

88. Interview with IS-K 7, cadre, April 2015.

89. Interview with External Observer/Participant 3, NDS officer, Kabul, January 2016; interview with External Observer/Participant 4, NDS officer, Jalalabad, January 2016.

90. Tahir Khan, 'Enemy of enemy: Hekmatyar support for IS stuns observers', *Express Tribune*, 7 July 2015.

91. Interview with Ally 8, cadre, Hizb-i Islami, Kunar, November 2016.

92. Interview with Ally 8, cadre, Hizb-i Islami, Kunar, November 2016.

93. Interview with Ally 14, Ex-HiG member, IIA commander, December 2020.

94. Interview with IS-K 5, senior cadre, December 2014; United Nations Security Council, 19 July 2016, op. cit.; interview with IS-K 24, commander, Jaysh ul-Islam, February 2016; interview with IS-K 25, cadre, Pakistan, October 2015; interview with IS-K 1, Khorasan-level leader, June 2015.

95. Interview with IS-K 54, senior commander, Pakistan, January 2017.

96. Interview with member of IS-K 65, military commission for Kabul, March 2021.

97. Interview with Qari Salim, IS-K 73, commander in Dara e Pech, Kunar, August 2021.

98. Interview with IS-K 5, senior cadre, December 2014.

99. Osman, 2016, op. cit.; interview with IS-K 54, senior commander, Pakistan, January 2017.

100. 'New release from Iḥsān Allah Iḥsān: "The story of the rise and fall of ISIS in Khurāsān"', (https://jihadology.net/2020/07/26/new-release-fromi%e1%b8%a5san-allah-i%e1%b8%a5san-the-story-of-therise-and-fall-of-isis-in-khurasan/), 26 July 2020.

101. 'New release from Iḥsān Allah Iḥsān: "The story of the rise and fall of ISIS in Khurāsān"', (https://jihadology.net/2020/07/26/new-release-fromi%e1%b8%a5san-allah-i%e1%b8%a5san-the-story-of-therise-and-fall-of-isis-in-khurasan/), 26 July 2020.

102. Mir, op. cit.; Rassler, op. cit.

103. 'TTP faction denies links to Islamic State after Quetta terrorist attack', *Express Tribune*, 16 August 2016.

104. Interview with IS-K 46, cadre, Pakistan, November 2016.

105. Interview with Ally 15, Jamaat ul-Ahrar cadre, April 2020.

106. Interview with IS-K 71, commander in Nangarhar, June 2020.

107. Interview with IS-K 5, senior cadre, December 2014.

108. Interview with IS-K 25, cadre, Pakistan, October 2015; IS-K 24, cadre, Pakistan, February 2016; interview with IS-K 1, Khorasan-level leader, June 2015; notebook of IS-K leader, obtained July 2015.

109. Interview with IS-K 16, cadre, Pakistan, December 2015.

110. Interview with Ally 9, commander, LeT, Pakistan, October 2016.

111. Abdul Basit, 'IS penetration in Afghanistan–Pakistan assessment, impact and implications', *Perspectives on Terrorism*, Vol. 11, No. 3, June 2017, pp. 19–39, 22.

112. Interview with IS-K 25, cadre, Pakistan, October 2015.

113. Interview with IS-K 74, district amir, Nangarhar, June 2020; interview with IS-K 76, cadre, Nangarhar, June 2020.

114. Interview with IS-K 75, commander in Kunar, September 2021.

115. Interview with IS-K 33, commander, Pakistan, January 2016; interview with IS-K 54, senior commander, Pakistan, January 2017.

116. Interview with IS-K 57, provincial cadre, March 2017.

117. Interview with Ally 16, Jundullah commander (Iran), December 2014; interview with Ally 17, Jundullah commander (Pakistan), January 2017.

118. Zoha Waseem, 'Daesh in Pakistan: an evolving militant landscape—Part I', *Strife*, 6 February 2016; Rassler, op. cit.; Animesh Roul, 'Growing Islamic State influence in Pakistan fuels sectarian violence', *Terrorism Monitor*, Vol. XIII, Iss. 13, 26 June 2015; 'Jundullah vows allegiance to Islamic State', *Reuters*, 18 November 2014.

119. Interview with IS-K 55, Harakat Khilafat Baluch commander, January 2017.

120. Interview with IS-K 71, commander in Nangarhar, June 2020.

7. THE FUNDING OF IS-K

1. Interview with External Observer/Participant 1, Revolutionary Guards (Iran) officer, Afghanistan, January 2016.

2. Interview with IS-K 11, senior cadre, January 2016; interview with IS-K 33, commander, Pakistan, January 2016; interview with IS-K 29, cadre, Kunar, February 2016; interview with IS-K 15, cadre, Pakistan, January 2016; interview with IS-K 9, senior cadre, October 2015; interview with IS-K 10, senior cadre, October 2015; interview with IS-K 14, cadre, Kunduz, October 2015; interview with Elder 12, Kajaki, Helmand, December 2015; interview with Elder 11, Kajaki, Helmand, December 2015; interview with IS-K 8, senior cadre, January 2016; interview with IS-K 41, commander, Achin, Nangarhar, March 2016.

3. Interview with IS-K 31, cadre, Herat, December 2015.

4. Katja Mielke and Nick Miszak, 'Making sense of Daesh in Afghanistan: a social movement perspective', Bonn, Germany: BICC, Working Paper 6, 2017, p. 42.

5. Interview with External Observer/Participant 7, Nangarhar, January 2016.

6. Interview with IS-K 10, senior cadre, October 2015; interview with IS-K 14, cadre, Kunduz, October 2015.

7. Interview with IS-K 30, cadre, Farah, December 2015.

8. Interview with IS-K 4, cadre, Kunar, February 2016; Katja Mielke and Nick Miszak, 'Making sense of Daesh in Afghanistan: a social movement perspective', Bonn, Germany: BICC, Working Paper 6, 2017, p. 52.

9. Interview with IS-K 57, provincial cadre, March 2017.

10. Interview with IS-K 72, cadre in Badakhshan, April 2020.

11. Interview with IS-K 74, district-level amir in Nangarhar June 2020.

12. Interview with IS-K 72, cadre in Badakhshan, April 2020; interview with IS-K 74, district-level amir in Nangarhar, June 2020.

13. Interview with Elder 6, focus group, Nangarhar, December 2015.

14. 'Islamic State smuggling timber in Afghanistan', *Voice of America*, 10 February 2016.

15. Rebecca Kheel, 'Top US general: ISIS in Afghanistan connected to core group', *The Hill*, 27 July 2016.

16. Interview with IS-K 1, Khorasan-level leader, June 2015.

17. Interview with IS-K 20, cadre, July 2016.

18. Interview with IS-K 2, leader, October 2015.

19. Interview with IS-K 57, provincial cadre, March 2017; interview with External Participant 18, mining businessman, March 2017; interview with IS-K 60, financial cadre, April 2017; Katja Mielke and Nick Miszak, 'Making sense of Daesh in Afghanistan: a social movement perspective', Bonn, Germany: BICC, Working Paper 6, 2017, p. 42.

20. Interview with IS-K 33, commander, Pakistan, January 2016.

21. Interview with IS-K 9, senior cadre, October 2015.

22. Interview with IS-K 24, commander, Jaysh ul-Islam, February 2016.

23. Interview with IS-K 16, cadre, Pakistan, December 2015.

24. Interview with IS-K 33, commander, Pakistan, January 2016; interview with External Observer/Participant 12, donor, Pakistan, January 2016.

25. Interview with Elder 12, Kajaki, Helmand, December 2015; interview with Elder 9, Kajaki, Helmand, November 2015; interview with Elder 8, Kajaki, Helmand, December 2015; interview with Elder 11, Kajaki, Helmand, December 2015; interview with Elder 10, Kajaki, Helmand, December 2015; interview with Elder 4, Achin, Nangarhar, March 2016; interview with Elder 2, Achin, Nangarhar, January 2016; interview with IS-K 47, commander, Kajaki, Helmand, December 2015; interview with Elder 3, Kot, Nangarhar, March 2016; interview with IS-K 40, fighter, Kot, Nangarhar, April 2016; interview with IS-K 41, commander, Achin, Nangarhar, March 2016; interview with Elder 13, Achin, Nangarhar, March 2016; interview with Elder 5, Kot, Nangarhar, February 2016; interview with IS-K 39, commander, Kajaki, Helmand, January 2016; interview with Elder 1, Kajaki, Helmand, December 2015; interview with IS-K 48, fighter, Kajaki, Helmand, December 2015.

26. Interview with Elder 7, Kot, Nangarhar, February 2016.

27. Interview with IS-K 39, commander, Kajaki, Helmand, January 2016.

28. Interview with Elder 10, Kajaki, Helmand, December 2015.

29. Interview with Elder 8, Kajaki, Helmand, December 2015.

30. Interview with IS-K 10, senior cadre, October 2015; interview with IS-K 15, cadre, Pakistan, January 2016.

31. Interview with IS-K 77, district-level military leader, July 2020.

32. Interview with IS-K 78, NGO department cadre, Nangarhar, June 2020.

33. Interview with IS-K 29, cadre, Kunar, February 2016; interview with IS-K 17, cadre, Nangarhar, June 2016; interview with IS-K 28, cadre, Kunar, July 2016; interview with IS-K 30, cadre, Farah, December 2015; interview with IS-K 31, cadre, Herat, December 2015; interview with IS-K 14, cadre, Kunduz, October 2015; interview with IS-K 57, provincial cadre, March 2017.

34. Hekmatullah Azamy, 'Challenges and prospects for Daesh in Afghanistan and its relations with the Taliban', Kabul: Konrad Adenauer Foundation, October 2016.

35. Interview with IS-K 64, cadre from Pakistan in Khogyani, March 2021.

36. Interview with IS-K 67, financial commission member, March 2021.

37. On the declining financial fortunes of IS-Central, see Seth G. Jones, 'Rolling back the Islamic State', Santa Monica, CA: RAND, 2017; S. Heißner et al., 'Caliphate in decline: an estimate of Islamic State's financial fortunes', London: ICSR, 2017.

38. Interview with IS-K 22, cadre, March 2015.

39. Interview with IS-K 72, cadre in Badakhshan, April 2020.

40. Hekmatullah Azamy, 'Challenges and prospects for Daesh in Afghanistan and its relations with the Taliban', Kabul: Konrad Adenauer Foundation, October 2016.

41. Interview with IS-K 22, cadre, March 2015.

42. Interview with External Observer/Participant 3, NDS officer, Kabul, January 2016.

43. Interview with External Observer/Participant 4, NDS officer, Jalalabad, January 2016.

44. Interview with External Observer/Participant 12, donor, Pakistan, January 2016.

45. Interview with IS-K 23, cadre, Finance Commission, June 2016.

46. Interview with External Observer/Participant 12, donor, Pakistan, January 2016.

47. Interview with IS-K 22, cadre, March 2015; interview with IS-K 23, cadre, June 2016.

48. Interview with IS-K 6, cadre, April 2015.

49. Interview with External Observer/Participant 8, donor, Arab Gulf country, January 2016; interview with IS-K 22, cadre, March 2015; interview with IS-K 25, cadre, Pakistan, October 2015; interview with IS-K 5, senior cadre, December 2014.

50. Interview with IS-K 6, cadre, April 2015.

51. Interview with IS-K 42, cadre, Finance Commission, Arab Gulf country, April 2015.

52. Interview with External Observer/Participant 2, ISI officer, Pakistan, January 2016.

53. Interview with IS-K 22, cadre, March 2015.

54. Interview with IS-K 60, financial cadre, April 2017.

55. Interview with IS-K 1, Khorasan-level leader, June 2015; interview with IS-K 58, financial cadre, March 2017; interview with IS-K 60, financial cadre, April 2017; Interview with IS-K 72, cadre in Badakhshan, April 2020; Interview with IS-K 79, commander, the Faruqi faction, October 2017; interview with IS-K 80, commander, Moawiya faction, October 2017.

56. Interview with IS-K 23, cadre, June 2016.

57. Interview with External Observer/Participant 8, donor, Arab Gulf country, January 2016; interview with IS-K 22, cadre, March 2015.

58. Interview with IS-K 6, cadre, April 2015; interview with IS-K 22, cadre, March 2015.

59. Interview with External Observer/Participant 8, donor, Arab Gulf country, January 2016; interview with External Observer/Participant 12, donor, Pakistan, January 2016.

60. Interview with External Observer/Participant 8, donor, Arab Gulf country, January 2016.

61. Interview with External Observer/Participant 12, donor, Pakistan, January 2016.

62. Interview with External Observer/Participant 12, donor, Pakistan, January 2016.

63. Interview with External Observer/Participant 8, donor, Arab Gulf country, January 2016; interview with IS-K 3, senior cadre, February 2015.

64. Interview with External Observer/Participant 8, donor, Arab Gulf country, January 2016.

65. Interview with IS-K 23, cadre, June 2016.

66. Interview with IS-K 44, cadre, Kyrghizstan, September 2016.

67. Interview with External Observer/Participant 8, donor, Arab Gulf country, January 2016.

68. Interview with IS-K 22, cadre, March 2015; interview with External Observer/Participant 12, donor, Pakistan, January 2016.

69. Interview with IS-K 22, cadre, March 2015.

70. Interview with External Observer/Participant 8, donor, Arab Gulf country, January 2016; interview with IS-K 20, cadre, July 2016; interview with External Observer/Participant 2, ISI officer, Pakistan, January 2016.

71. Interview with IS-K 20, cadre, July 2016.

72. Interview with External Observer/Participant 12, donor, Pakistan, January 2016.

73. Interview with External Observer/Participant 8, donor, Arab Gulf country, January 2016.

74. Interview with External Observer/Participant 8, donor, Arab Gulf country, January 2016.

75. Interview with External Observer/Participant 12, donor, Pakistan, January 2016.

76. Interview with External Observer/Participant 8, donor, Arab Gulf country, January 2016.

77. Interview with External Observer/Participant 12, donor, Pakistan, January 2016.

78. Interview with IS-K 6, cadre, April 2015.

79. Interview with External Observer/Participant 8, donor, Arab Gulf country, January 2016.

80. Interview with External Observer/Participant 5, Qatar intelligence, April 2015.

81. Interview with IS-K 22, cadre, March 2015.

82. A. Giustozzi, *The Taliban at War*, op. cit.

83. Interview with IS-K 54, senior commander, Pakistan, January 2017.

84. Interview with External Observer/Participant 3, NDS officer, Kabul, January 2016.

85. Interview with IS-K 69, commander in Jowzjan, August 2018.

86. Interview with IS-K 67, Finance Commission member, March 2021.

87. Interview with IS-K 67, Finance Commission member, March 2021.

88. Interview with IS-K 22, cadre, Finance Commission, March 2015; interview with IS-K 23, cadre, Finance Commission, June 2016; interview with IS-K 20, cadre, Finance Commission, July 2016; interview with IS-K 67, Finance Commission member, March 2021.

89. Interview with External Observer/Participant 8, donor, Arab Gulf country, January 2016; interview with IS-K 6, cadre, April 2015; interview with External Observer/Participant 12, donor, Pakistan, January 2016.

90. Interview with External Observer/Participant 8, donor, Arab Gulf country, January 2016.

91. Katja Mielke and Nick Miszak, 'Making sense of Daesh in Afghanistan: a social movement perspective', Bonn, Germany: BICC, Working Paper 6, 2017, p. 53.

92. Interview with IS-K 53, commander, Achin, Nangarhar, August 2016.

93. Interview with External Observer/Participant 12, donor, Pakistan, January 2016.

94. Interview with IS-K 20, cadre, July 2016.

95. Interview with IS-K 20, cadre, July 2016.

96. Interview with IS-K 20, cadre, July 2016.

97. Interview with External Observer/Participant 8, donor, Arab Gulf country, January 2016.

98. Interview with External Observer/Participant 12, donor, Pakistan, January 2016.

99. Interview with External Observer/Participant 12, donor, Pakistan, January 2016.

100. Interview with IS-K 1, Khorasan-level leader, June 2015; interview with IS-K 50, adviser, December 2015.

101. Interview with IS-K 1, Khorasan-level leader, June 2015.

102. Interview with IS-K 80, commander, Moawiya faction, October 2017; External Observer 31, Taliban cadre in the Shura of the North, September 2017.

103. Interview with IS-K 79, commander, the Faruqi faction, October 2017; interview with External Observer 28, Revolutionary Guards (Iran), November 2017.

8. SHAKING UP THE WORLD OF KHORASAN'S JIHADISM, 2014–16

1. Mohammad Hoseyn Ja'farian, 'What is the mission of Da'ish in Afghanistan?' Qods website, Mashhad, in Persian, 10 February 2015.

2. Brian H. Fishman, *The Master Plan*, New Haven, CT: Yale University Press, 2016, p. 178.

3. Shahid Zuī, 'Dāish Kā Peshraft Aur Irāq Kā Mustaqbal' [ISIS's advance and Iraq's future]. *Sharī'at*, Vol. 31, 2014 (September); Hasan Momand, 'Daulat-e Islāmīya Kē Khilāf Nayā Faujī Ittihād Aur Is Jang Kā Anjām' [The new military alliance against the Islamic State and the conclusion of this war], *Sharī'at*, Vol. 33, 7–8, 2014, both cit. in Neil Krishan Aggarwal, 'Exploiting the Islamic State–Taliban rivalry for counterterrorism messaging', *Journal of Policing, Intelligence and Counter Terrorism*, Vol. 12, No. 1, 1–15, 2017.

4. Abū Jarīr ash-Shamālī, 'Al-Qa'idah of Waziristan: a testimony from within', *Dabiq* 6, Rabi' al-Awwal 1436; Abū Maysarah ash-Shāmī, 'The Qa'idah of adh-Dhawahiri, al-Harari, and an-Nadhari, and the absent Yemeni wisdom', *Dabiq* 6, Rabi' al-Awwal 1436 (December 2014–January 2015).

5. 'Interview with: the Wali of Khurasan', *Dabiq 13*, Rabi al Akhir 1437 (January/ February 2016); Abū Jarīr ash-Shamālī, 'Al-Qa'idah of Waziristan: a testimony from within', *Dabiq 6*, Rabi' al-Awwal 1436.

6. Interview with IS-K 5, senior cadre, December 2014.

7. Borhan Osman, op. cit. 27 July 2016.

8. Interview with IS-K 25, cadre, Pakistan, October 2015.

9. Interview with IS-K 5, senior cadre, December 2014.

10. 'Taliban leader: allegiance to ISIS "haram"', *RUDAW*, 13 April 2015.

11. 'Taliban leader: allegiance to ISIS "haram"', *RUDAW*, 13 April 2015.

12. Azami, op. cit.; Osman, 27 July 2016, op. cit.. The letter was also published in July in the Taliban's media: 'Muhtaram Abu Bakr Al-Baghdādī Kē Nām Par Imārat-e Islāmīya-e Afghānistān Kē Rahbarī Shūra Kā Khatt', *Shariat*, Vol. 41, pp. 3–6, July 2015.

13. Interview with IS-K 1, Khorasan-level leader, June 2015.

14. 'A fatwā for Khurāsān', *Dabiq 10*, Ramadan 1436 (June–July 2015).

15. 'Taliban condemns 'brutal' Isis video of Afghan prisoners being murdered', *Reuters*, 11 August 2015.

16. 'Foreword', *Dabiq 11*, Dhul-Qadah 1436 (July–August 2015). See also Borhan Osman, 'ISKP's battle for minds: what are its main messages and who do they attract?', Berlin: Afghanistan Analyst Network, 12 December 2016.

17. Afghan Arzu TV report on 25 February 2015; Joseph Goldstein, 'In ISIS, the Taliban face an insurgent threat of their own', *New York Times*, 4 June 2015.

18. Interview with IS-K 30, cadre, Farah, December 2015.

19. Text of report by private Pakistan-based Afghan Islamic Press news agency, Kabul, 17 January 2015.

20. Frud Bezhan, 'Mass abduction of Hazaras in Afghanistan raises fears of Islamic State', *Tolo TV*, 22 February 2015, in Dari 13.30 GMT 22 February 2015; 'Da'ish burns shrine in eastern Afghanistan—Report', *Tolo News*, Kabul, in Dari 06.30 GMT 22 February 15.

21. Ziar Yad, 'Parts of Nangarhar fall to Daesh once again: residents', *TOLOnews*, 16 September 2016.

22. Interview with Elder 10, Kajaki, Helmand, December 2015; interview with IS-K 48, fighter, Kajaki, Helmand, December 2015; interview with Elder 9, Kajaki, Helmand, November 2015.

23. Interview with IS-K 47, commander, Kajaki, Helmand, December 2015.

24. Interview with IS-K 48, fighter, Kajaki, Helmand, December 2015.

25. Zakir was brought back into his old position at the end of 2014, but then sacked again in 2015. He allied with the Iranian Revolutionary Guards for a period, turning into a foe of IS-K. He then left Iran in disgrace in spring 2016 and has since been in Pakistan trying to get appointed back to some senior position in Quetta Shura.

26. Johnson, op. cit.

27. Interview with IS-K 3, senior cadre, February 2015.

28. Interview with External Observer/Participant 9, Taliban cadre, Quetta Shura, May 2016.

29. Interview with IS-K 19, member of Gansu Hui Group, Pakistan, July 2016; interview with IS-K 49, finance officer, Waziristan, April 2015; interview with External Observer/Participant 13, senior Haqqani cadre, December 2016.

30. Interview with Elder 14, Sherzad, Nangarhar, January 2016.

31. Interview with IS-K 1, Khorasan-level leader, June 2015.

32. Interview with IS-K 7, cadre, April 2015.

33. Osman, 27 July 2016, op. cit.

34. Interview with Elder 3, Kot, Nangarhar, March 2016.

35. Osman, 27 July 2016, op. cit.

36. Chris Sands and Fazelminallah Qazizai, 'ISIL emerges in Afghanistan "stronger than the Taliban"', *The National*, 29 October 2015.

37. Goldstein, op. cit.

38. Interview with IS-K 1, Khorasan-level leader, June 2015.

39. Osman, 27 July 2016, op. cit.

40. Mujib Mashal, 'Afghan ISIS branch makes inroads in battle against Taliban', *New York Times*, 13 October 2015.

41. Hamid Shalizi, 'Exclusive: in turf war with Afghan Taliban, Islamic State loyalists gain ground', *Daily Mail*, 29 June 2015.

42. Osman, 27 July 2016, op. cit.

43. Osman, 27 July 2016, op. cit.

44. Osman, 27 July 2016, op. cit.

45. Interview with IS-K 36, deserter, Nangarhar, January 2016.
46. Interview with External Observer/Participant 7, Nangarhar, January 2016; interview with External Observer/Participant 4, NDS officer, Jalalabad, January 2016; interview with External Observer/Participant 3, NDS officer, Kabul, January 2016.
47. Interview with Elder 4, Achin, Nangarhar, March 2016; interview with Elder 2, Achin, Nangarhar, January 2016; interview with Elder 13, Achin, Nangarhar, March 2016.
48. Interview with Elder 3, Kot, Nangarhar, March 2016; interview with Elder 7, Kot, Nangarhar, February 2016; interview with Elder 5, Kot, Nangarhar, February 2016; interview with Elder 5, Kot, Nangarhar, February 2016.
49. Interview with Elder 4, Achin, Nangarhar, March 2016; interview with Elder 2, Achin, Nangarhar, January 2016; interview with Elder 13, Achin, Nangarhar, March 2016.
50. Interview with Elder 4, Achin, Nangarhar, March 2016.
51. Interview with External Observer/Participant 7, Nangarhar, January 2016; interview with External Observer/Participant 4, NDS officer, Jalalabad, January 2016; Mashal, op. cit.
52. Jamshed Baghwan, 'Bloody battle: Afghan Taliban capture Da'ish stronghold in Nangarhar province', *Pakistan Tribune*, 5 January 2016; Osman, 27 July 2016, op. cit.; Taliban sources in Peshawar and Quetta, contacted in January 2016.
53. United Nations Security Council, 19 July 2016, op. cit.
54. Osman, 27 July 2016, op. cit.
55. Azami, op. cit.
56. Thomas Joscelyn, 'Islamic State's 'Khorasan province' threatens Taliban in latest video', *Long War Journal*, 4 June 2015; Mirwais Harooni and Kay Johnson, 'Taliban urge Islamic State to stop "interference" in Afghanistan', *Reuters*, 16 June 2015; 'Interview du cheikh Ḥâfiẓ Sa'îd Khân, gouverneur de la wilâyah du Khurâsân, *Dar al Islami*, No 8, 1437.
57. Borhan Osman, 'Bourgeois jihad: why young, middle-class Afghans join the Islamic State', Washington, DC: USIP, June 2020, 15–6.
58. Interview with IS-K 7, cadre, April 2015.
59. Gilad Shiloach, 'ISIS bolsters war of words against the Afghan Taliban', *Reuters*, 26 January 2016.
60. Interview with IS-K 47, commander, Kajaki, Helmand, December 2015; interview with IS-K 41, commander, Achin, Nangarhar, March 2016.
61. Interview with IS-K 17, cadre, Nangarhar, June 2016.
62. Interview with IS-K 1, Khorasan-level leader, June 2015.
63. Interview with IS-K 1, Khorasan-level leader, June 2015.
64. Interview with IS-K 21, commander, Ghazni, April 2016.
65. Interview with Elder 9, Kajaki, Helmand, November 2015; interview with Elder 11, Kajaki, Helmand, December 2015; interview with Elder 10, Kajaki, Helmand,

December 2015; interview with Elder 7, Kot, Nangarhar, February 2016; interview with Elder 1, Kajaki, Helmand, December 2015.

66. Interview with IS-K 11, senior cadre, January 2016. Mullah Naeem is one of the Revolutionary Guards (Iran)'s oldest clients among the Taliban and is currently one of the leading figures among the Taliban operating from Sistan.

67. Interview with External Observer/Participant 6, Taliban military cadre, Helmand, January 2016; interview with IS-K 30, cadre, Farah, December 2015; interview with IS-K 9, senior cadre, October 2015; interview with IS-K 21, commander, Ghazni, April 2016; interview with IS-K 31, cadre, Herat, December 2015; interview with IS-K 1, Khorasan-level leader, June 2015; interview with IS-K 21, commander, Ghazni, April 2016.

68. Interview with IS-K 2, leader, October 2015.

69. Interview with IS-K 17, cadre, Nangarhar, June 2016.

70. Interview with Elder 11, Kajaki, Helmand, December 2015; interview with Elder 1, Kajaki, Helmand, December 2015.

71. Interview with IS-K 3, senior cadre, February 2015.

72. Interview with IS-K 1, Khorasan-level leader, June 2015.

73. Interview with IS-K 37, commander, Achin, Nangarhar, April 2016.

74. Interview with Elder 13, Achin, Nangarhar, March 2016.

75. Interview with IS-K 1, Khorasan-level leader, June 2015.

76. Interview with External Observer/Participant 6, Taliban military cadre, Helmand, January 2016.

77. Interview with IS-K 1, Khorasan-level leader, June 2015.

78. Interview with IS-K 1, Khorasan-level leader, June 2015.

79. Communication with External Observer 32, Quetta Shura source, January 2016.

80. Interview with IS-K 1, Khorasan-level leader, June 2015.

81. Interview with External Observer/Participant 1, Revolutionary Guards (Iran) officer, Afghanistan, January 2016.

82. Interview with IS-K 30, cadre, Farah, December 2015; interview with IS-K 10, senior cadre, October 2015.

83. Interview with IS-K 10, senior cadre, October 2015.

84. Interview with IS-K 10, senior cadre, October 2015.

85. Interview with IS-K 1, Khorasan-level leader, June 2015.

86. Interview with IS-K 28, cadre, Kunar, July 2016; Taliban sources in Peshawar, December 2016; The Shura of the North was essentially a splinter of the Peshawar Shura, but by summer 2016 overshadowed it and was expanding beyond the north, towards eastern Afghanistan.

87. Interview with IS-K 14, cadre, Kunduz, October 2015.

88. Interview with IS-K 13, cadre, Jowzjan, May 2016.

89. Interview with IS-K 9, senior cadre, October 2015; interview with IS-K 1, Khorasan-level leader, June 2015; Reza Hashimi, 'Daesh, Taliban united behind

attack on ANA in Badakhshan', *TOLOnews.com*, 13 April 2015; interview with IS-K 14, cadre, Kunduz, October 2015.

90. Interview with IS-K 14, cadre, Kunduz, October 2015.

91. Interview with IS-K 54, senior commander, Pakistan, January 2017.

92. Interview with IS-K 45, commander, Gansu Hui Group, northern Afghanistan, May 2016; interview with IS-K 13, cadre, Jowzjan, May 2016.

93. Interview with IS-K 13, cadre, Jowzjan, May 2016.

94. Mullah Salam, one of the most prestigious Taliban commanders, was the only one to ever cumulate the positions of military leader and governor at the provincial level.

95. Interview with External Observer/Participant 15, senior Taliban cadre, Kunduz, February 2017. The Taliban media office attributed the death of Salam to a US airstrike in order to hide the Taliban's internal divisions.

96. Interview with IS-K 28, cadre, Kunar, July 2016; interview with IS-K 29, cadre, Kunar, February 2016; interview with IS-K 59, commander, Achin, April 2017.

97. Interview with IS-K 28, cadre, Kunar, July 2016.

98. Interview with IS-K 14, cadre, Kunduz, October 2015.

99. Interview with IS-K 11, senior cadre, January 2016; interview with IS-K 3, senior cadre, February 2015.

100. Interview with IS-K 3, senior cadre, February 2015; interview with IS-K 49, finance officer, Waziristan, April 2015.

101. Interview with IS-K 28, cadre, Kunar, July 2016.

102. Jessica Donati and Habib Khan Totakhil, 'Taliban, Islamic State forge informal alliance in eastern Afghanistan', *Wall Street Journal*, 7 August 2016; interview with IS-K 53, commander, Achin, Nangarhar, August 2016.

103. Notebook of IS-K leader, obtained July 2015.

104. Interview with IS-K 2, leader, October 2015.

105. 'Taliban leader Mullah Mansoor Dadullah joined ISIS, the terror group claims', *Khaama Press*, 8 September 2015.

106. Painda Hikmat, 'Taliban breakaway leader calls Daesh "fitna"', 4 July 2016.

107. Interview with Ally 18, district governor of Rasool Shura, December 2016.

108. Interview with IS-K 57, provincial cadre, March 2017; interview with External Observer/Participant 6, Taliban military cadre, Helmand, January 2016; interview with IS-K 60, financial cadre, April 2017.

109. Farhan Zahid and Muhammad Ismail Khan, 'Prospects of the Islamic State in Pakistan', Hudson Institute, 2016.

110. Interview with IS-K 25, cadre, Pakistan, October 2015.

111. Ali K Chishti, 'ISIS is the talk of the town', *TFT*, 12 September 2014.

112. Interview with IS-K 16, cadre, Pakistan, December 2015.

113. 'Interview du cheikh Ḥâfiẓ Saʿîd Khân, gouverneur de la wilâyah du Khurâsân', *Dar al Islam*, No. 8, 1437.

114. Interview with IS-K 28, cadre, Kunar, July 2016.
115. Interview with IS-K 46, cadre, Pakistan, November 2016.
116. Interview with IS-K 16, cadre, Pakistan, December 2015.
117. Interview with IS-K 5, senior cadre, December 2014.
118. Interview with IS-K 25, cadre, Pakistan, October 2015.
119. Interview with IS-K 25, cadre, Pakistan, October 2015.
120. Interview with IS-K 1, Khorasan-level leader, June 2015.
121. Interview with IS-K 1, Khorasan-level leader, June 2015.
122. Interview with External Observer/Participant 10, AQ cadre, September 2016.
123. Interview with IS-K 14, cadre, Kunduz, October 2015.
124. Interview with IS-K 28, cadre, Kunar, July 2016.
125. Interview with External Observer/Participant 10, AQ cadre, September 2016.
126. Interview with IS-K 54, senior commander, Pakistan, January 2017; External Observer 17, AQ cadre, February 2017.
127. External Observer 33, AQ cadre, January 2018.
128. Interview with External Observer 34, AQIS commander in Kashmir, September 2019.
129. Bunzel, op. cit.
130. Bunzel, op. cit.
131. McCants, op. cit., location 2248.
132. Bunzel, op. cit.
133. Thomas Joscelyn, 'Mullah Omar's death is a big blow to al Qaeda—and a win for ISIS', *The Daily Beast*, 30 July 2015; Barak Mendelsohn, 'Al Qaeda after Omar', *Foreign Affairs Snapshot*, 9 August 2015; Rosa Brooks, 'Mullah Omar, we hardly knew ye', *Foreign Policy*, 4 August 2015.
134. Interview with External Observer 35, AQ cadre in Afghanistan, August 2016.

9. THE DEAD END OF SALAFISM AND IS-K ADAPTATION

1. Borhan Osman, 'Another ISKP leader "dead": where is the group headed after losing so many amirs?', Berlin: AAN, 23 July 2017; Amira Jadoon, Andrew Mines, 'Taking aim: Islamic State Khorasan's leadership losses', *CTC Sentinel*, September 2019, Vol. 12, 8.
2. Johnson, op. cit. 6.
3. Interview with IS-K 1, Khorasan-level leader, June 2015.
4. Interview with IS-K 1, Khorasan-level leader, June 2015.
5. Interview with IS-K 26, cadre, Pakistan, July 2016.
6. Interview with External Observer/Participant 1, Revolutionary Guards (Iran) officer, Afghanistan, January 2016.
7. Interview with IS-K 8, senior cadre, January 2016.
8. Mashal, op. cit.; see also Katja Mielke and Nick Miszak, 'Making sense of Daesh in

Afghanistan: a social movement perspective', Bonn, Germany: BICC, Working Paper 6, 2017, p. 21.

9. Katja Mielke and Nick Miszak, 'Making sense of Daesh in Afghanistan: a social movement perspective', Bonn, Germany: BICC, Working Paper 6, 2017, p. 42.

10. Franz J. Martin, 'On the trail of the Islamic State in Afghanistan', *Foreign Policy*, 5 April 2016.

11. Katja Mielke and Nick Miszak, 'Making sense of Daesh in Afghanistan: a social movement perspective', Bonn: BICC, Working Paper 6, 2017, p. 21.

12. Interview with Elder 13, Achin, Nangarhar, March 2016; interview with Elder 7, Kot, Nangarhar, February 2016; interview with Elder 5, Kot, Nangarhar, February 2016; interview with Elder 2, Achin, Nangarhar, January 2016; interview with Elder 4, Achin, Nangarhar, March 2016; interview with Elder 14, Sherzad, Nangarhar, January 2016.

13. Interview with IS-K 36, deserter, Nangarhar, January 2016.

14. Interview with External Observer/Participant 3, NDS officer, Kabul, January 2016; interview with External Observer/Participant 4, NDS officer, Jalalabad, January 2016; interview with IS-K 53, commander, Achin, Nangarhar, August 2016.

15. Interview with IS-K 9, senior cadre, October 2015.

16. Interview with Elder 9, Kajaki, Helmand, November 2015; interview with Elder 1, Kajaki, Helmand, December 2015.

17. Interview with IS-K 47, commander, Kajaki, Helmand, December 2015.

18. Mir Abed Joenda, 'Daesh commander in Afghanistan cuts ties with group', *TOLOnews*, 20 October 2015; Abdulrahim Muslim Dost, 'Hafiz Saeed Khan ne dabarait a'lan', http://rohi.af/fullstory.php?id=41196, 17 October 2015.

19. Interview with IS-K 15, cadre, Pakistan, January 2016.

20. Interview with IS-K 47, commander, Kajaki, Helmand, December 2015; interview with IS-K 41, commander, Achin, Nangarhar, March 2016; interview with IS-K 39, commander, Kajaki, Helmand, January 2016; interview with IS-K 48, fighter, Kajaki, Helmand, December 2015; interview with IS-K 8, senior cadre, January 2016; interview with IS-K 40, fighter, Kot, Nangarhar, April 2016.

21. Interview with IS-K 15, cadre, Pakistan, January 2016.

22. Interview with IS-K 37, commander, Achin, Nangarhar, April 2016.

23. Interview with IS-K 9, senior cadre, October 2015; interview with IS-K 10, senior cadre, October 2015.

24. Interview with IS-K 9, senior cadre, October 2015.

25. Interview with External Observer/Participant 2, ISI officer, Pakistan, January 2016.

26. Interview with IS-K 53, commander, Achin, Nangarhar, August 2016.

27. Interview with IS-K 37, commander, Achin, Nangarhar, April 2016; interview

with IS-K 34, interpreter, November 2015; interview with IS-K 28, cadre, Kunar, July 2016.

28. Interview with IS-K 53, commander, Achin, Nangarhar, August 2016.
29. Interview with IS-K 50, adviser, December 2015; interview with IS-K 8, senior cadre, January 2016.
30. Interview with IS-K 17, cadre, Nangarhar, June 2016; interview with IS-K 50, adviser, December 2015.
31. Bill Roggio, 'Afghan military again claims it killed emir of Islamic State's Khorasan province', *Long War Journal*, 9 August 2016.
32. Interview with IS-K 53, commander, Achin, Nangarhar, August 2016; interview with IS-K 54, senior commander, Pakistan, January 2017.
33. Mujib Mashal, 'Leader of ISIS branch in Afghanistan killed in special forces raid', *New York Times*, 7 May 2017; contact with IS-K source in Nangarhar, June 2017; contact with TKP source, June 2017; Hugh Tomlinson and Haroon Janjua, 'Jihadist factions vie for control of Afghan Isis', *The Times*, 18 July 2017.
34. Mujib Mashal, 'Leader of ISIS branch in Afghanistan killed in special forces raid', *New York Times*, 7 May 2017; contact with IS-K source in Nangarhar, June 2017; contact with TKP source, June 2017; Hugh Tomlinson and Haroon Janjua, 'Jihadist factions vie for control of Afghan Isis', *The Times*, 18 July 2017. See also Borhan Osman, 'Another ISKP leader "dead": where is the group headed after losing so many amirs?', Berlin: AAN, 23 July 2017.
35. Interview with IS-K 79, commander, the Faruqi faction, October 2017; interview with IS-K 80, commander, Moawiya faction, October 2017.
36. 'Letter dated 15 July 2019 from the Chair of the Security Council Committee pursuant to resolutions 1267 (1999), 1989 (2011) and 2253 (2015) concerning Islamic State in Iraq and the Levant (Da'esh), Al-Qaida and associated individuals, groups, undertakings and entities addressed to the President of the Security Council', United Nations Security Council, 15 July 2019, S/2019/570.
37. Interview with IS-K 80, commander, Moawiya faction, October 2017.
38. Interview with IS-K 80, commander, Moawiya faction, October 2017; External Observer 31, Taliban source in the Shura of the North, September 2017.
39. Interview with Elder 13, Achin, Nangarhar, March 2016.
40. Interview with IS-K 21, commander, Ghazni, April 2016; interview with Elder 12, Kajaki, Helmand, December 2015; interview with Elder 10, Kajaki, Helmand, December 2015; interview with Elder 9, Kajaki, Helmand, November 2015; interview with IS-K 39, commander, Kajaki, Helmand, January 2016; interview with Elder 12, Kajaki, Helmand, December 2015.
41. Interview with Elder 8, Kajaki, Helmand, December 2015.
42. Johnson, op. cit.
43. Interview with Elder 4, Achin, Nangarhar, March 2016; interview with Elder 2, Achin, Nangarhar, January 2016; interview with Elder 13, Achin, Nangarhar,

March 2016; interview with Elder 7, Kot, Nangarhar, February 2016; interview with Elder 5, Kot, Nangarhar, February 2016.

44. Interview with Elder 7, Kot, Nangarhar, February 2016.
45. Interview with Elder 11, Kajaki, Helmand, December 2015.
46. Interview with Elder 12, Kajaki, Helmand, December 2015.
47. Interview with Elder 12, Kajaki, Helmand, December 2015; interview with Elder 8, Kajaki, Helmand, December 2015; interview with Elder 11, Kajaki, Helmand, December 2015.
48. Interview with Elder 9, Kajaki, Helmand, November 2015.
49. Interview with IS-K 29, cadre, Kunar, February 2016; interview with IS-K 30, cadre, Farah, December 2015; interview with IS-K 31, cadre, Herat, December 2015; interview with Elder 11, Kajaki, Helmand, December 2015; interview with Elder 10, Kajaki, Helmand, December 2015; interview with Elder 2, Achin, Nangarhar, January 2016; interview with Elder 13, Achin, Nangarhar, March 2016; interview with Elder 7, Kot, Nangarhar, February 2016; interview with Elder 5, Kot, Nangarhar, February 2016; Chris Sands and Fazelminallah Qazizai, 'ISIL emerges in Afghanistan "stronger than the Taliban"', *The National*, 29 October 2015; interview with Elder 6, focus group, Nangarhar, December 2015. See also Adam Baczko and Gilles Dorronsoro, 'Logiques transfrontalières et Salafisme globalisé', *Critique Internationale*, 2017/1, No. 74, pp. 137–52.
50. Interview with Elder 12, Kajaki, Helmand, December 2015; interview with Elder 8, Kajaki, Helmand, December 2015.
51. Interview with Elder 12, Kajaki, Helmand, December 2015.
52. Interview with Elder 9, Kajaki, Helmand, November 2015.
53. Interview with Elder 9, Kajaki, Helmand, November 2015.
54. Shalizi, op. cit.
55. Interview with IS-K 8, senior cadre, January 2016.
56. Interview with External Observer/Participant 7, Nangarhar, January 2016; interview with External Observer/Participant 4, NDS officer, Jalalabad, January 2016.
57. Interview with Elder 8, Kajaki, Helmand, December 2015; interview with Elder 11, Kajaki, Helmand, December 2015; interview with Elder 10, Kajaki, Helmand, December 2015; interview with Elder 4, Achin, Nangarhar, March 2016; interview with Elder 3, Kot, Nangarhar, March 2016; interview with Elder 1, Kajaki, Helmand, December 2015; interview with Elder 1, Kajaki, Helmand, December 2015; Johnson, op. cit.
58. Interview with Elder 10, Kajaki, Helmand, December 2015.
59. Interview with Elder 9, Kajaki, Helmand, November 2015.
60. Interview with Elder 9, Kajaki, Helmand, November 2015.
61. Interview with Elder 12, Kajaki, Helmand, December 2015.
62. Interview with Elder 12, Kajaki, Helmand, December 2015.

63. Interview with Elder 8, Kajaki, Helmand, December 2015; interview with Elder 11, Kajaki, Helmand, December 2015.
64. Interview with Elder 12, Kajaki, Helmand, December 2015.
65. Interview with Elder 4, Achin, Nangarhar, March 2016.
66. Interview with Elder 11, Kajaki, Helmand, December 2015; interview with Elder 1, Kajaki, Helmand, December 2015; interview with Elder 12, Kajaki, Helmand, December 2015.
67. Interview with Elder 8, Kajaki, Helmand, December 2015.
68. Interview with Elder 9, Kajaki, Helmand, November 2015.
69. Interview with Elder 4, Achin, Nangarhar, March 2016.
70. Interview with IS-K 36, deserter, Nangarhar, January 2016.
71. Interview with IS-K 40, fighter, Kot, Nangarhar, April 2016.
72. Interview with Elder 4, Achin, Nangarhar, March 2016.
73. Interview with Elder 3, Kot, Nangarhar, March 2016.
74. Interview with Elder 11, Kajaki, Helmand, December 2015.
75. Interview with Elder 14, Sherzad, Nangarhar, January 2016.
76. Obaid Ali and Khalid Gharanai, 'War and peace: hit from many sides (2): the demise of ISKP in Kunar', Berlin: AAN, 3 March 2021.
77. Interview with IS-K 11, senior cadre, January 2016; interview with IS-K 8, senior cadre, January 2016.
78. Interview with IS-K 50, adviser, December 2015.
79. Interview with IS-K 17, cadre, Nangarhar, June 2016; interview with IS-K 50, adviser, December 2015; interview with IS-K 8, senior cadre, January 2016.
80. Interview with IS-K 17, cadre, Nangarhar, June 2016.
81. Interview with IS-K 50, adviser, December 2015.
82. Interview with External Observer/Participant 7, Nangarhar, January 2016.
83. Interview with IS-K 17, cadre, Nangarhar, June 2016.
84. Interview with Elder 2, Achin, Nangarhar, January 2016.
85. Interview with External Observer/Participant 7, Nangarhar, January 2016.
86. Franz J. Martin, 'On the trail ...', op. cit.; Johnson, op. cit.
87. Interview with External Observer/Participant 7, Nangarhar, January 2016.
88. Interview with IS-K 43, cadre, former Hizb-i Islami member, Pakistan, January 2016.
89. Interview with External Observer/Participant 4, NDS officer, Jalalabad, January 2016.
90. Interview with IS-K 17, cadre, Nangarhar, June 2016.
91. Interview with IS-K 13, cadre, Jowzjan, May 2016.
92. Interview with IS-K 17, cadre, Nangarhar, June 2016.
93. Interview with IS-K 28, cadre, Kunar, July 2016.
94. Interview with IS-K 8, senior cadre, January 2016.
95. Interview with IS-K 8, senior cadre, January 2016.

96. Interview with IS-K 50, adviser, December 2015.
97. Interview with IS-K 50, adviser, December 2015.
98. Interview with IS-K 17, cadre, Nangarhar, June 2016; interview with IS-K 23, cadre, June 2016.
99. Interview with IS-K 20, cadre, July 2016.
100. Interview with IS-K 20, cadre, July 2016.
101. Interview with IS-K 20, cadre, July 2016; interview with IS-K 32, cadre, Finance Commission, November 2015.
102. Interview with IS-K 17, cadre, Nangarhar, June 2016; interview with IS-K 28, cadre, Kunar, July 2016; interview with IS-K 28, cadre, Kunar, July 2016; interview with IS-K 20, cadre, July 2016.
103. Interview with IS-K 20, cadre, July 2016.
104. Interview with IS-K 20, cadre, July 2016.
105. Interview with IS-K 60, financial cadre, April 2017; interview with IS-K 59, commander in Achin, April 2017.
106. Interview with IS-K 59, commander in Achin, April 2017.
107. Interview with IS-K 59, commander in Achin, April 2017.
108. Interview with IS-K 59, commander, Achin, April 2017.
109. Interview with IS-K 81, commander, Kunduz, February 2018.
110. Interview with IS-K 79, commander, Faruqi faction, October 2017; interview with IS-K 80, commander, Moawiya faction, October 2017.
111. Interviews with Elders 17–20, members of Nangarhar tribal shuras, November 2017.
112. Interview with IS-K 80, commander, Moawiya faction, October 2017; Taliban sources contacted in various provinces throughout 2017.
113. Interviews with tribal elders and IS-K commanders, taking place in several locations between autumn 2016 and autumn 2017.
114. Interview with External Observer/Participant 25, Haqqani commander in Zabul, May 2017; interview with Observer/Participant 26, member of Haqqani network central council, May 2017.
115. Interview with Ally 19, Haqqani network cadre, December 2018.
116. External Observer 36, Taliban source in the Quetta Shura, contacted in November 2017. See also Farhan Zahid, 'Attacks in Kabul highlight Taliban–Islamic State', *Militant Leadership Monitor*, Vol. 9, Iss. 1, 7 February 2018.
117. Interview with IS-K 69, commander in Jowzjan, August 2018.
118. John Foulkes, 'Aslam Farooqi: head of Islamic State-Khorasan arrested', *Militant Leadership Monitor*, Vol. 11, Iss. 4, 5 May 2020.

10. CRISIS AND ... RELAUNCH?: 2018–21

1. External Observer 37, Taliban Shura of the North cadre, March 2018.

2. External Observer 38, Taliban Quetta Shura, February 2018.
3. Interview with IS-K 69, commander in Jowzjan, August 2018.
4. Interview with IS-K 69, commander in Jowzjan, August 2018.
5. Interview with IS-K 69, commander in Jowzjan, August 2018.
6. Interview with IS-K 69, commander in Jowzjan, August 2018.
7. Interview with IS-K 69, commander in Jowzjan, August 2018.
8. Interview with IS-K 69, commander in Jowzjan, August 2018.
9. Communications with Taliban cadres, March–June 2019.
10. IS-K 82, Cadre, May 2019.
11. Interview with IS-K 83, Finance Commission cadre, November 2019.
12. Interview with IS-K 68, cadre in Badakhshan, July 2020.
13. Interview with IS-K 68, cadre in Badakhshan, July 2020.
14. Interview with IS-K 78, NGO department cadre, Nangarhar, June 2020.
15. Interview with External Observer 39, Taliban commander in Achin, November 2019.
16. Interview with External Observer 39, Taliban commander in Achin, November 2019.
17. See also Obaid Ali, 'Hit from many sides 1: unpicking the recent victory against the ISKP in Nangrahar', Berlin: *Afghanistan Analyst Network*, 1 March 2020.
18. Interview with IS-K 83, Finance Commission cadre, November 2019.
19. Interview with IS-K 72, cadre in Badakhshan, April 2020; Obaid Ali and Khalid Gharanai, 'War and peace: hit from many sides (2): the demise of ISKP in Kunar', Berlin: *AAN*, 3 March 2021.
20. 'IS regional leader Sheikh Khorasani "arrested in Afghanistan"', *BBC News*, 11 May 2020.
21. Interview with IS-K 72, cadre in Badakhshan, April 2020.
22. Interview with Pakistani IS-K 85, commander in Kunar, April 2020.
23. Interview with IS-K 72, cadre in Badakhshan, April 2020.
24. Interview with IS-K 84, military commission cadre, June 2020; interview with IS-K 74, district amir in Nangarhar, June 2020.
25. Interview with IS-K 72, cadre in Badakhshan, April 2020.
26. Borhan Osman, 'Bourgeois jihad: why young, middle-class Afghans join the Islamic State', Washington, DC: USIP, June 2020, 16–17.
27. Interview with Ally 20, IS-P Commander Pakistan, August 2020; interview with Ally 21, IS-P member, Baluchistan, July 2020; interview with Ally 22, IS-P Commander, Baluchistan, July 2020.
28. Interview with IS-K 83, Finance Commission cadre, November 2019.
29. Interview with Ally 20, IS-P Commander Pakistan, August 2020; interview with Ally 21, IS-P member, Baluchistan, July 2020; interview with Ally 22, IS-P Commander, Baluchistan, July 2020.
30. Interview with IS-K 76, commander in Nangarhar, June 2020.

31. Interview with Ally 23, senior adviser to Serajuddin Haqqani, August 2020.

32. Interview with member of IS-K 64, military commission for Kabul, March 2021.

33. Interview with IS-K 76, cadre, Nangarhar, June 2020, and IS-K 72, cadre, Badakhshan, April 2020.

34. Interview with member of IS-K 64, military commission for Kabul, March 2021.

35. Interview with IS-K 72, cadre in Badakhshan, April 2020.

36. Interview with IS-K 68, cadre in Badakhshan, July 2020.

37. Interview with IS-K 76 commander in Nangarhar, June 2020.

38. Interview with IS-K 64, cadre from Pakistan in Khogyani, March 2021.

39. Interview with IS-K 68, cadre, Badakhshan, July 2020.

40. Interview with IS-K 86, Kabul military commission cadre, June 2020.

41. Interview with IS-K 72, cadre in Badakhshan, April 2020; contact with IS-K 87, cadre, August 2020.

42. Interview with IS-K 70, Tajikistani commander in Badakhshan, April 2020.

43. Contact with IS-K 87, cadre, August 2020.

44. Contact with IS-K 87, cadre, August 2020.

45. Contact with IS-K 87, cadre, August 2020.

46. Interview with IS-K 64, cadre from Pakistan in Khogyani, March 2021.

47. Interview with member of IS-K 65, military commission (Kabul), March 2021.

48. Interview with member of IS-K 65, military commission (Kabul), March 2021.

49. Interview with member of IS-K 65, military commission (Kabul), March 2021; interview with IS-K cadre from Pakistan in Khogyani, March 2021.

50. Interview with member of IS-K 65, military commission (Kabul), March 2021.

51. Interview with member of IS-K 65, military commission (Kabul), March 2021.

52. Interview with IS-K 72, cadre in Badakhshan, April 2020.

53. Interview with IS-K 70, Tajikistani commander in Badakhshan, April 2020; interview with IS-K 72, cadre in Badakhshan, April 2020.

54. Interview with IS-K 77, district-level military leader, July 2020; interview with IS-K 74, district amir, Nangarhar, June 2020.

55. Interview with IS-K 77, district-level military leader, July 2020; interview with IS-K 74, district amir, Nangarhar, June 2020.

56. Communication with IS-K 91, cadre in Nangarhar, June 2021.

57. Communication with IS-K 91, cadre in Nangarhar, June 2021.

58. Interview with member of IS-K 65, military commission (Kabul), March 2021.

59. Interview with IS-K 77, district-level military leader, July 2020; interview with IS-K 74, district amir, Nangarhar, June 2020; interview with IS-K 68, cadre in Badakhshan, July 2020.

60. Interview with IS-K 64, cadre from Pakistan in Khogyani, March 2021.

61. Interview with member of IS-K 65, military commission (Kabul), March 2021.

62. Interview with IS-K 64, cadre from Pakistan in Khogyani, March 2021; interview

with member of IS-K 65, military commission (Kabul), March 2021; interview with IS-K 66, cadre in the IIA, January 2021.

63. Interview with member of IS-K 65, military commission (Kabul), March 2021.
64. Interview with IS-K 73, commander in Kunar, August 2021.
65. Interview with IS-K 73, commander in Kunar, August 2021.
66. Contact with IS-K 90, commander in Nangarhar, September 2021.
67. Interview with IS-K 88, commander in Kunar, September 2021; interview with IS-K 89, commander in Kunar, August 2021.
68. Interview with External Observer 21, cadre of Emirate intelligence in Kabul, November 2021.
69. Saeed Shah and Yaroslav Trofimov, 'Islamic State attacks in eastern Afghanistan challenge Taliban rule', *Wall Street Journal*, 22 September 2021.
70. Abdul Sayed, 'Islamic State Khorasan province's Peshawar seminary attack and war against Afghan Taliban Hanafis', *Terrorism Monitor*, Vol. 18, Iss. 21, 20 November 2020.
71. Interview with IS-K 88, commander in Kunar, September 2021.
72. Interview with IS-K 89, commander in Kunar, August 2021.
73. Interview with IS-K 89, commander in Kunar, August 2021.
74. Interview with IS-K 88, commander in Kunar, September 2021.
75. Interview with IS-K 88, commander in Kunar, September 2021.
76. Interview with IS-K 89, commander in Kunar, August 2021; interview with IS-K 88, commander in Kunar, September 2021.
77. Interview with IS-K 89, commander in Kunar, August 2021.
78. Interview with IS-K 89, commander in Kunar, August 2021.
79. J.P. Lawrence, 'A bloodied ISIS still a threat in Afghanistan as it looks to recruit disgruntled Taliban', *Stars and Stripes*, 31 July 2020.
80. Interview with IS-K 89, commander in Kunar, August 2021.
81. Interview with IS-K 64, cadre from Pakistan in Khogyani, March 2021.
82. Interview with member of IS-K 65, military commission (Kabul), March 2021.
83. 'Afghanistan: surge in Islamic State attacks on Shia', *Human Rights Watch*, 25 October 2021; 'Daesh hideout raided in Charikar, say Taliban', *Pajhwok News*, 2 October 2021.
84. Contact with External Observer 40, Taliban commander, Kabul, August 2021.
85. Interview with IS-K 88, commander in Kunar, September 2021.
86. Interview with IS-K 89, commander in Kunar, August 2021
87. Interview with IS-K 76, commander in Nangarhar, June 2020.
88. Interview with IS-K 89, commander in Kunar, August 2021.

CONCLUSION

1. Borhan Osman, 'Bourgeois jihad: why young, middle-class Afghans join the Islamic State', Washington, DC: USIP, June 2020, 20.

2. Wahabism is a particular (radical) type of Salafism and is the official doctrine of the Saudi monarchy.

3. Katja Mielke and Nick Miszak, 'Making sense of Daesh in Afghanistan: a social movement perspective', Bonn, Germany: BICC, Working Paper 6, 2017, p. 53.

4. Interview with IS-K 8, senior cadre, January 2016.

5. www.satp.org/satporgtp/countries/pakistan/database/shias_killed_pakistan.htm

6. Interview with Elder 3, Kot, Nangarhar, March 2016.

7. Interview with Elder 13, Achin, Nangarhar, March 2016.

INDEX

INDEX

INDEX

INDEX